THE HAND-BOOK OF INDIA

THE HAND-BOOK OF INDIA

A

GUIDE TO THE STRANGER

AND

THE TRAVELLER

AND A

COMPANION TO THE RESIDENT

J. H. STOCQUELER

GYAN

Published by

GYAN

Gyan Publishing House
5, Ansari Road
Daryaganj, New Delhi-110002
Phone: 011-47034999, 9811692060
E-mail: books@gyanbooks.com

Distribution Network
gyanbooks.com
India, USA, Canada, UK, Australia

ISBN: 978-93-7097-274-2 (PB)
First Published, 1844

2nd Impression 2025

Printed at: Gyan Press, Delhi.

THE HAND-BOOK OF INDIA
Arthur J. H. STOCQUELER

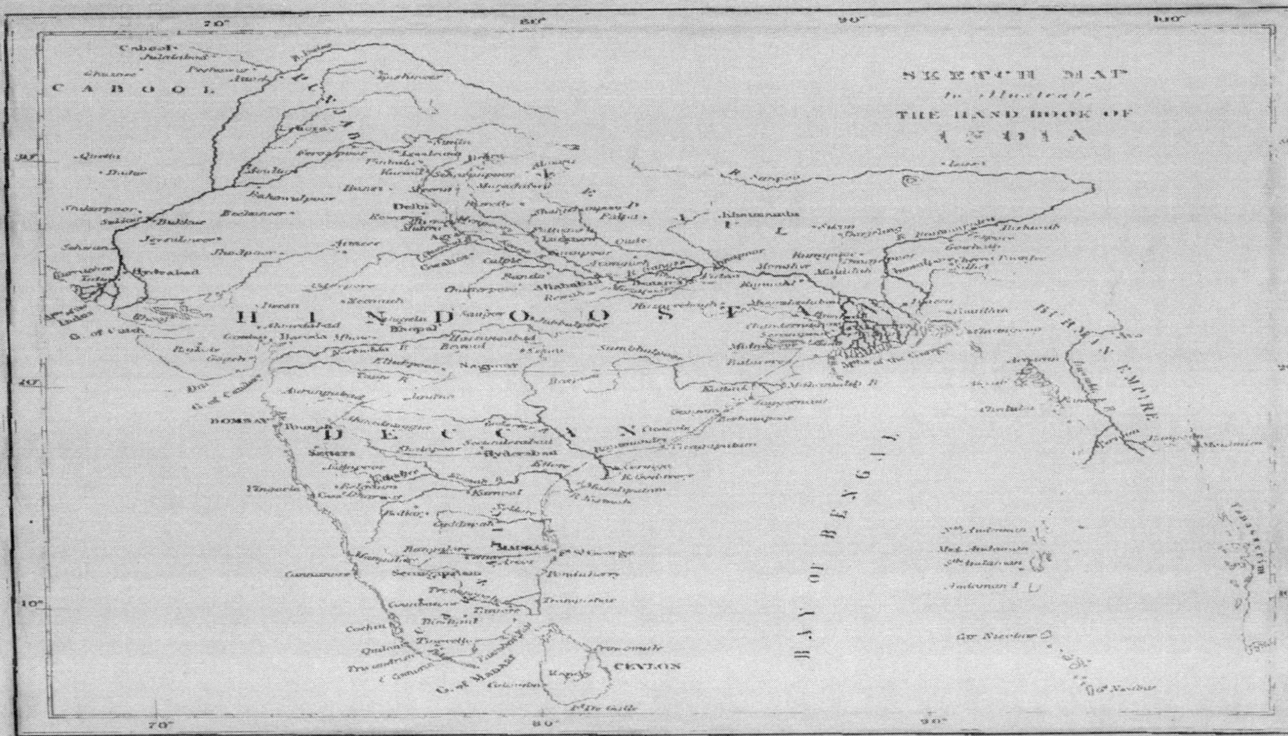
SKETCH MAP
to illustrate
THE HAND BOOK OF
INDIA
CABOOL
HINDOOSTAN
DECCAN
BURMAN EMPIRE
BAY OF BENGAL
CEYLON
BOMBAY
MADRAS
Delhi
Hydrabad
Nagpoor
Bhopal
Allahabad
Jubbulpoor
Hyderabad
Sattara
Trincomalie
Kandy
Columbo
Pt. De Galle
G. of Cutch
G. of Manaar
Mouths of the Indus
Mouths of the Ganges
Balasore
Juggernaut
Masulipatam
Pondicherry
Tranquebar
Cochin
Quilon
Cannanore
Andaman I.
Gt. Nicobar
Tenasserim
R. Sanpoo
Lassa
70°
80°
90°
100°
10°
20°
30°

THE

HAND-BOOK OF INDIA,

A

GUIDE TO THE STRANGER

AND

THE TRAVELLER,

AND A

COMPANION TO THE RESIDENT.

BY

J. H. STOCQUELER,

LATE EDITOR OF THE "CALCUTTA ENGLISHMAN;" AUTHOR OF "FIFTEEN MONTHS' PILGRIMAGE THROUGH KHUZISTAN, PERSIA, TURKEY, NEW RUSSIA, GERMANY, ETC.;" "MEMORIALS OF AFFGHANISTAN," ETC.

LONDON:
Wm. H. ALLEN & CO.

1844.

TO

DWARKANATH TAGORE,

WHOSE NOBLE QUALITIES

HAVE RENDERED THE COUNTRY WHICH HE HAS SERVED,

BY HIS LIBERALITY AND HIS EXAMPLE,

AN OBJECT OF INTEREST TO ALL CLASSES OF ENGLISHMEN,

These Pages

ARE RESPECTFULLY DEDICATED,

BY ONE WHO ADMIRES HIS VIRTUE AND PUBLIC SPIRIT,

AND CHERISHES A GRATEFUL RECOLLECTION OF

HIS MANY PAST KINDNESSES.

J. H. S.

PREFACE.

THE object of the present work is to combine, within the smallest possible space, all the information respecting British India, which an individual proceeding to any one of the presidencies might desire, at first, to possess. Innumerable excellent publications are before the world, some of which treat of the history of India, the form of government, the topography, productions, and commerce of the country, while many are confined to sketches of habits, customs, and religions; the revenue and monetary systems; the manner of European life, laws, and institutions, &c. But there is not one single volume extant which presents, at one view, an outline of *every thing* relating to the country. To supply the desideratum has been the purpose of the author, or compiler, of the present Hand-Book.

Although a long residence in India has afforded the writer many opportunities of collecting information respecting several important sections of the country, and more especially the metropolis of British India, the magnificent city of Calcutta, he has necessarily consulted and quoted from the works of others who have traversed portions of the empire which it never was his fortune to visit. Among these authors, the late Miss Emma Roberts, Mrs. Postans, and Colonel Davidson stand in the foreground. Much has also been derived from the *Bengal and Agra Guide and Gazetteer*, published in India, the *Asiatic Journal* (the articles from which were originally contributed by the author of the "Hand-Book" himself), *Milburn's Oriental Commerce, Galloway's Law and Constitution, Thornton's History, the East-India United Service Journal*, and some others.

The proportion of the following pages relating to Calcutta was originally intended to form part of a separate publication, in a work illustrative of the present position of that capital, of which so little appears to be really known in England; but it has been thought preferable to include the sketch in the present volume. The occupation of so much space, however, with one subject, has necessarily induced much brevity in the treatment of the other presidencies; but as these are, in a great degree, reduced copies of the megapolis of British India, the omissions, in respect to them, may easily be supplied by a diligent study of all that is said of the latter, due allowance being made for the difference in the dimensions of the three cities.

ERRATA.

Page 1, line 15.—*For* " procession," *read* " precession."
" 16 " 3.—*For* " England, who," *read* " England, which."
" 33 " 12.—After " nature's hand " put a full stop, and commence paragraph " From the eagle, &c." And at the 16th line, *dele* full stop after " south " and place a comma, continuing, " the ornithological, &c."
" 37 " 3.—*For* " people in the world who are so little distinguished," *dele* " who are."
" — " 31.—*For* " in whom is supposed to rest," *read* " in whom are."
" 46 " 8.—*For* " some of which, " *read* " some of whom."
" 76 " last.—*For* " changeable," *read* " chargeable."
" 80 " 5.—*For* " £10,000," *read* " £14,000."
" 148 " 5.—*For* " prosperty," *read* " prosperity."
" 161 " 2.—*For* " bunghy-bearers," *read* " baughy bearers."
" 166 " 7.—*For* " there are pleasant," *read* " these are pleasant."
" 167 " 12.—" If bound to Calcutta," *add* " or Madras."
" 172 " 13.—*For* " transfixed " *read* " transferred."

THE

HAND-BOOK OF INDIA,

&c.

INDIAN CHRONOLOGY.

THE natives of India use a great variety of epochs, some of which are but little understood, even by themselves, and almost all are deficient in universality and uniformity, so that the same epoch nominally will be found to vary many days, or even a year, in different provinces.

The solar, or more properly, the sidereal year, is that which is most in use for public business, particularly since the introduction of European power into India. This year is calculated by the Indian astronomers at 365 days, 7 hours, 12 minutes, 30 seconds, or, according to others, 36 seconds. Therefore in sixty Indian years there will be a day more than in sixty Gregorian years. The difference arises from not taking into consideration the procession of the equinoxes, being equal in reality to something more than 20 minutes, though by them calculated at 23 minutes.

The luni-solar computation is not at present so common as it formerly was, although still much used in some parts of India, and common everywhere in the regulation of festivals, and in domestic arrangements. But the solar and luni-solar forms may be used with most of the Indian eras, though some more particularly affect one form and some the other.

The luni-solar mode varies in different provinces, some beginning the month at full moon, others at new moon: we shall describe that beginning by the full moon, which is used in Bengal; the other method will be easily understood when this is known. Each year begins on the day of full moon preceding the beginning of the solar year of the same date. The months are divided into halves, the first of which is entitled *badi,* or dark, being from the full moon to the new, and the last, *sudi,* or bright, from new to full moon. These divisions are sometimes of 14 and sometimes of 15 days, and are numbered generally from 1 to 15, though the last day of the badi half is called 15, and that of a sudi is called 30. By a complicated arrangement, a day is sometimes omitted, and again a day is intercalated, so that, instead of going on regularly in numerical order, these days may be reckoned 1, 1, 2, 3, 4, 5, 6, 7, 8, 10. The subject is enveloped in some obscurity, and it will be perhaps sufficient to observe, the time of a lunation is divided into 30 parts, called *tiths,* and when two tiths occur in the same solar day, that day is omitted in the lunar reckoning, and restored, by intercalation, at some other period. When two full moons occur in one solar month, the month also is named twice, making a year of 13 months. In the case also of a short solar month, in which there would be no full moon, the month would be altogether omitted. All these circumstances render the luni-solar computation a matter of much difficulty; and to reduce it exactly to our era would require a perfect knowledge of Hindoo astronomy. But as the solar reckoning is by far the most general, we shall only observe that the lunar month precedes the solar month by a lunation at *most*, and consequently a lunar date may be nearly known from the solar time, which is of easy calculation.

We shall begin by the eras which are generally known, and follow with those of more limited use.

The Caliyug.—This era is the most ancient of India, and dated from a period 3101 years before Christ. It begins with the entrance of the sun into the Hindoo sign Aswin, which is now on the 11th April, N.S. In the year 1600 the year began on the 7th April, N.S., from which it has now advanced four days, and from the procession of the equinoxes, is still advancing at the rate of a day in sixty years; the number produced by subtracting 3102 from any given year of the Caliyug will be the Christian year in which the given year begins.

The era of Saliwahana may be joined here to that of the Caliyug, being identical with it as to names of months, divisions, and commencement, and differing only in the date of the year, which is 3179 years more recent than that, and therefore seventy-seven years since our era. It is much used in the southern and western provinces of India, and papers are frequently dated in both eras. The years of this era are called Saca. The number 77 must be added to find the equivalent year of the Christian era. Both these eras are most commonly used with solar time.

The era of Vicramadety, which has its name from a sovereign of Malwa, may also be placed here, as it uses the same months as the two above mentioned, but it is more generally used with lunar time; this era is much employed in the north of India, and its years are called Samvat. It began fifty-seven years before Christ, and that number must be deducted, to bring it to our era.

In Guzerat this era is used, but it begins there about the autumnal equinox.

The following are the names of the months of the Hindustani year :—

Bysakh,	Bhadon,	Poos,
Jeth,	Koonar, or Asin,	Magh,
Asar,	Katick,	Fagoon,
Sawan,	Aghan,	Chyt.

These months all begin on the days of the entrance of the sun into a sign of the Hindoo zodiac, and they vary from twenty to thirty-two days in length, though making up 365 days in the total, in common years, and 366 in leap years. The intercalation is made when and where it is required, not according to any arbitrary rule, but by continuing the length of each month, until the sun has completely passed each sign. This will bring about twenty-six leap years in every century. It would require long and complicated calculations to find exactly the commencement and duration of each month, but we shall not err more than a day or two by considering them to be of thirty and thirty-one days alternately.

The Bengalee year appears to have been once identical with the Hegira; but the solar computation having subsequently been adopted, of which the years exceed those of the Hegira by eleven days, it has lost nearly eleven days every year, and is now about nine years later, the year 1245 of the Hegira beginning in July, 1829, and the Bengalee year 1236 beginning 13th April of the same year.

The number 593 must be added to bring this to the Christian era. The Bengalee months are similar to those of the Hindustani, given before, differing only in dialect. They are as follow, according to the orthography of the English resident there.

Baysakha,	Sravona,	Kartic,	Maugh,
Joishta,	Bhadra,	Ugrohoyna,	Falgoon,
Assan,	Aussin,	Pouse,	Chotira.

The first of Baysakha is now on the 13th April, and in our leap years, on the 12th April. There is, however, a difference of one day in about sixty years, as observed before, in speaking of the eras of Caliyug, &c.

The Fuslee year is pretty generally known in India, and is supposed to be derived from the Hegira. One or two eras are used in India by this name, being chiefly used in revenue accounts; its commencement alone is much attended to, the subdivisions being neglected.

The Fuslee year, as used in Bengal, begins with Aussin, in September. The year is lunar, and the full moon preceding the autumnal equinox is the first day. The date also differs from the common Fuslee, being now 1247.

It may be observed that, notwithstanding this variety of dates, the months agree pretty nearly.

Thus, Poos in all the eras begins somewhat before the winter solstice, and is followed by Maugh, &c.

The era of Parasurama is used in Malayala, in the south of India. This era began in the year 1176 B.C., and is divided into cycles of 1000 years, and at the end of a hundred years, instead of 1001, the next year was called 1. The first cycle ended 176 B.C., the second 825 A.D., and the third should have finished in 1825, in which case the present year would have been 15. But, whether from inattention or otherwise, the end of the third cycle was not noticed, and they call 1005, the year which began on the 15th September, 1829. The year 177 of the second cycle began August 17th, A.D. 1, but the year, like the other years of India, advancing one day in about sixty years, now begins as above stated. In our leap years, the 14th of September will agree with its commencement.

A cycle of ninety years, called Grahaparivrithi, is used in the southern provinces of India. The year 1840 corresponds with the 64th year of the 21st cycle. The first cycle began twenty-four years before our era.

To reduce it to the Christian year, multiply the elapsed cycles by 90 and the odd years, then deduct 24 from the sum, and the remainder will be the year required.

The days of the week, as used by the Hindoos, are as follow:—

Rubbeebar,	Sunday	Brihuspotcebar,	Thursday
Soambar,	Monday	Shukrobar,	Friday
Mongolbar,	Tuesday	Sunneebar,	Saturday
Boodbar,	Wednesday		

THE MAHOMETAN ERA OF HEGIRA

dates from the flight of Mahomet to Medina, which event took place in the night of Thursday, the 15th July, A.D. 622. The era commences on the following day, viz. the 16th July. Many chronologists have computed this era from the 15th of July, but Cantemir has given examples, proving that, in most ancient times, the 16th was the first day of the era; and now there can be no question that such is the practice of Mahometans. The year is purely lunar, consisting of twelve months, each month commencing with the appearance of the new moon, without any intercalation to bring the commencement of the year to the same season. It is obvious that, by such an arrangement, every year will begin much earlier in the season than the preceding, being now in summer, and, in the course of sixteen years, in winter. Such a mode of reckoning, so much at variance with the order of nature, could scarcely have been in use beyond the pastoral and semi-barbarous nation by whom it was adopted, without the powerful aid of fanaticism, and even that has not been able to prevent the use of other methods by learned men in their computations, and by governments in the collection of revenue. It will also be remarked that, as the Mahometans begin each month with the appearance of the new moon, a few cloudy days might retard the commencement of a month, making the preceding month longer than usual. This, in fact, is the case, and two parts of the same country will sometimes differ a day in consequence; although the clear skies of those countries where Islamism prevails rarely occasion much inconvenience on this head.

But in chronology and history, as well as in all documents, they use months of thirty and twenty-nine days alternately, making the year thus to consist of 354 days. Eleven times in thirty years, one day is added to the last month, making 355 days in that year. Consequently, the average length of a year is taken 354, 11-30th days, the twelfth of which is 29, 191-360ths, differing from the true lunation very little more than three seconds, which will not amount to a day in less than 2260 years, a degree of exactness which could not have been attained without long-continued observations.

The intercalary year of 355 days occurs on the second, fifth, seventh, tenth, thirteenth, fifteenth, eighteenth, twenty-first, twenty-fourth, twenty-sixth, and twenty-ninth years of every thirty years. Any year being given, to know whether it be intercalary or not, divide by 30, and if either of the above numbers remain, the year will be one of 355 days.

The names of the months, as used by the Turks, with the length of each, are as follow :—

Moharem	30	Shaban	29
Saphar	29	Ramadan	30
Rabiu I.	30	Shawall	29
Rabiu II.	29	Dhu'l kadah	30
Jomadhi I.	30	Dhu'l hajjah	29
Jomadhi II.	29	and in intercal. 30 days.	
Regeb	30		

They have weeks of seven days, named as follow :—

	TURKS.	PERSIANS.	INDIANS.	ANC. ARABIC.	MOD. ARABIC.
Su.	Pazar gun,	Yekshambe,	Etwar,	Bawal,	Yom abad.
M.	Pazar ertesi,	Doshambe,	Peeror Somwar,	Bahun,	Yom thena.
Tu.	Sale,	Sishambe,	Mangul,	Jebar,	Yom tulta.
W.	Charshambe,	Charshambe,	Boodh,	Dabar,	Yom arba.
Th.	Pershambe,	Panjshambe,	Jumerat,	Femunes,	Yom hamsa.
F.	Juma,	Juma or Adina,	Juma,	Aruba,	Juma.
Sa.	Juma ertesi,	Shambe or Hafta,	Suneecher,	Chiyar,	Sabt.

DIVISIONS OF THE DAY.—MAHOMETAN.

The division of the day among Mahometans is chiefly subservient to the stated times of performing their devotions, and is not generally very accurate. They begin their account at sunset, reckoning twelve hours from thence to sunrise, whether the night be long or short; from sunrise to sunset they also reckon twelve hours, and consequently a night hour is longer in the winter than an hour of the day, and in summer the hours of the day are longer than those of the night. At the equinoxes alone, all the hours are of equal length, and then they coincide with those adopted by us, in commencement and duration, differing, of course, six hours in enumeration, so that our six o'clock is their twelve, our seven is their one, &c. At other periods of the year, also, their six o'clock coincides with our twelve, but every other hour differs more or less from ours. The time of sunrise, and consequently the length of the day, being known, the length of each hour will be easily found by division, and the period of any given hour determined. Thus, if the sun rise at seven o'clock, the length of the day will be ten hours (of sixty minutes each), and that of each hour fifty minutes. One o'clock, Mahometan reckoning, will then be at fifty minutes after seven, two o'clock forty minutes after eight, and three o'clock will be half-past nine, and so on of the others. When the sun rises at five o'clock, the three first hours of the day will be completed severally at ten minutes after six, twenty minutes after seven, and half-past eight. In every case six o'clock arrives exactly at mid-day.

Hindoo.

The Hindoos divide the day into four watches, and the night into the same number; the day being considered to extend from sunrise to sunset. The watches are again divided into *ghurees,* which are twenty-four minutes each in length. As in summer the days are longer than the nights, each day-watch will then be longer than any watch of the night, though, from the necessity of each watch comprising an exact number of ghurees, there will generally be the difference of one ghuree between two watches of the same day. There is much variation in this respect, and although, in the latitude of India, the difference is not so great as it would be in a country more towards the north, it is still so inconvenient that the natives of India rarely understand their own method of dividing the day, and readily adopt the English mode when they are in the neighbourhood of one of our factories.

In order to explain the mode of subdividing the watches, we shall detail the correspondence of ghurees with our hours in March and September, when the days and nights are equal, and when, in consequence, more regularity may be expected than at other seasons. It must be remembered that a ghuree contains twenty-four minutes, and that sixty ghurees make up the twenty-four hours; thirty ghurees, therefore, make up the time between sunrise and sunset at this season; if these thirty ghurees were equally divided between the four watches, giving seven ghurees and a half to each watch, their correspondence with our hours would be easily made.

OUTLINE

OF THE

HISTORY OF BRITISH INDIA.

THE attempt to comprise within a few pages any thing approaching to an accurate sketch of the main incidents which have distinguished the history of the British empire on the continent of Asia, would prove so perfectly futile, that the following rough outline is offered rather as an apology than a substitute for the record which should be preliminary to a picture of India as it is. By no process of condensation could the contents of the pyramids of volumes which have been written to portray the progress of our power, from the hour when the first factory was established in India, to that which placed Sinde at our feet, be reduced within the compass of a reasonable library, much less comprised in a brief chapter of a single volume. Our excuse must therefore be, in venturing upon even a very slight abstract, that we wished to form, for the benefit of the stranger who may never have bestowed any attention upon India, a connecting link between the history of the country and its remarkable position at the present moment.

The early history of the vast continent of India is veiled in obscurity. The wonderful subterranean remains of architecture which exist to this moment in the western parts of the country demonstrate that they must have been inhabited by a people not inferior to the Babylonians and the Cushites in antiquity, and a knowledge of the arts of peace; but we obtain no other information respecting the inhabitants, although the historians of ancient Egypt have endeavoured to connect them with the victories of Sesostris. All that we know for certain is, that the Tyrians carried on a trade with India by means of the Red Sea, and that the Greeks, beginning with Alexander and ending with Antiochus, penetrated as far as the upper part of the Ganges,* taking possession of large tracts of country upon either side of the Indus; that the dominion of the Greeks was succeeded by that of the Scythian nomades, who invaded Bactria, and that these, in their turn, were driven out by the Tartars. Next came the Mahometans, under Mahmoud of Ghuzni, who, about the year 1000, carried into effect his father's project for the conquest of India, and, after a series of aggressive expeditions, established Mussulman authority from the west of the Ganges to the province of Guzerat. From this time until the middle of the eighteenth century, the power of these invaders augmented, and the whole continent gradually fell under their yoke; the government of the various provinces being vested in Nawaubs, who exercised sovereign control, with a reservation of obedience or fealty to the supreme power of the Great Mogul, who reigned in absolute despotism at Delhi. But in all these conquests and political aggrandisements, no European power took the slightest share. The intercourse with India,

* Embassy of Megasthenes.

from the time of the expulsion of the Greeks, was confined entirely to commercial operations. The Egyptians and the Romans followed the Tyrians, sending their argosies down the Red Sea to the coast of Malabar, and receiving, in exchange for their commodities, the rich stuffs, drugs, dyes, gold, silver, ivory, &c., which formed the staples of Western India. The conquest of Egypt by the Saracens threw the whole trade into the hands of the latter, who made great efforts to extend it by carrying their enterprise beyond the extreme point of the peninsula of India to the islands of the Eastern Archipelago, thence to Siam, and ultimately to China. But the Saracens held no intercourse with Europe. Closing the port of Alexandria against the Christian trader, they preferred transmitting their return cargoes to Constantinople, through Asiatic Turkey and the Black Sea. The city of the Sultan, consequently, soon became the great mart for East-India and China produce, and to it the eyes of the Venetian and Italian states were directed. For a long time, however, the antipathy which the Christians and Mahometans bore to each other formed a bar to commercial intercourse of any kind; at length, the cupidity of the Califs overcame their religious hatred, and a traffic commenced which, while it gratified the anxiety of the Europeans to possess the products and manufactures of the East, conferred wealth upon the mercantile followers of the prophet. In this state the trade with India continued until the Crusades gave territorial possession and influence to the southern European powers, and converted the expeditions, which were originally of a holy character, into commercial and secular enterprises. Partly by means of conquest, and partly through negotiation, the whole of the East-India trade at last passed from the Saracens into the hands of the Italians, and the port of Alexandria, until then closed by Mahometan hatred, was reopened to the ships of the Mediterranean. Florence, Genoa, and Venice were the first to reap the fruits of the great monopoly; but the latter, by deputing an ambassador to India, to open a communication with ports until then not known even by name to the Europeans, obtained exclusive supplies and benefits, which soon gave them an immense preponderance over their neighbours. To these advantages were shortly to be added the diminution of the Genoese trade by the destruction of Constantinople, where they had established themselves to the entire exclusion of the Greeks. Thus, at the close of the fifteenth century, Venice supplied nearly all Europe with the products of the East, and soon raised herself, by her wealth, to an eminence that excited the jealousy and hostility of surrounding nations. Great efforts were made by several states—the Dutch, the Germans, and the Spaniards—to obtain a share in this vastly lucrative commerce; but neither intrigue nor the most tempting offers made to the rulers of Egypt and of Syria could shake the stability of Venetian power. Events, however, occurred, perfectly independent of commercial rivalry, which struck at the root of the great monopoly, and almost entirely diverted Oriental commerce into new channels. Christopher Columbus had discovered America, and the Portuguese had found a way to India round the Cape of Good Hope. In 1497, the King of Portugal deputed Vasco de Gama to India, to ascertain whence the riches of the Venetians were drawn, and to endeavour to open a trade with the same sources by the route available to the ships of Portugal. The mission was successful; the key to vast wealth was now obtained, and the Portuguese lost no time in improving their opportunities. Fleet after fleet was fitted out; every port in India was visited; possession was forcibly taken of several places upon the Malabar coast, the islands lying between Madagascar and the Moluccas, and the island of Ormus, in the Persian Gulf; and a papal grant was obtained, confirming the prior discovery of the Portuguese, and thereby checking for a time the rivalry of other Catholic nations. Prodigious efforts were made by the Venetians, supported by the Mameluke government of Egypt, and subsequently by the Sultan, to counteract the advantages obtained by the Portuguese, but all was in vain. While, on the one hand, the latter defended with great skill and bravery their acquisitions in India and the Gulf of Persia from their enemies in the Red Sea and the coasts, they, on the other, continued to pour into Europe the products of the Oriental world in quantities and at a price against which the Venetians could not possibly contend. For more than a century the trade remained in the hands of the Portuguese. But the high road which they had discovered was open to all the world beside, and it was not to be supposed that they would retain exclusive right of way longer than it might suit the convenience of other nations to yield them the privilege. Accordingly, we find that as the maritime power of Holland increased, and her domestic cares diminished, the Dutch found it worth their while to turn their eyes to India. The example of Holland was speedily followed by England, who, under the reign of Elizabeth, obtained leisure from foreign quarrels and religious discord, for commercial schemes of magnitude. From the hour of the arrival of these Protestant powers, the Portuguese date the downfal of their influence in India. Through the combined efforts of religious zeal and the conscious possession of superior physical force, they had been guilty of great oppression wherever they had planted the national flag, and had, consequently, raised up enemies amongst the natives, who were only too glad to afford support to any other Europeans whose interest came in collision with those of the Portuguese. Contests soon ensued between the new visitors and the old settlers, and the result was the expulsion of the latter from nearly all their positions, and the perfect annihilation of their commercial relations with the East.

The English, obtaining from their own sovereign a charter permitting them to trade to the East Indies, and securing to them a monopoly of the advantages of such commerce, directed their attention in India to the establishment of factories, under the protection, and with the consent, of the different potentates then ruling over her shores. On the Coromandel and Malabar coasts, and on the banks of the Hooghly, they planted their feet as humble traders. Bombay, which had been acquired by the Portuguese, was soon after ceded to the English, as part of the dowry of the Infanta, who became the consort of our Charles II.; and very shortly afterwards the chartered merchants commenced a trade with China, whose tea was acquiring a certain degree of popularity in Great Britain. The success of one company of merchants suggested the formation of another, to whom the British government, in its distress for money, likewise granted a charter; but as this led to disputes abroad, and materially affected the interests of the new trade, a union of the two contending companies was effected in 1702.

The prosperity of Holland and of England, naturally exciting the jealousy of France, an East-India company was formed by the French, who sent out ships and soon obtained permission to establish agencies in Pondicherry and Chandernagore. These three nations, with the Danes and the Spaniards, who had also acquired small possessions, now constituted the European trading community in India, and through their enterprise and rivalry, the whole of the Western world was supplied with every thing that the rich soil of the East, and the ingenuity and industry of her inhabitants, could produce. Some little molestation to their trade was occasionally offered by the barbarous and covetous princes in whose territories they were located, and small bodies of soldiers were therefore allowed to be maintained by the home government to protect the factories, around which defences were erected. But it was not until the year 1745 that the corner stone was laid of those occurrences which converted the humble traders, content to defend their property from outrage, and to follow their commercial pursuits in peace and security, into warriors and politicians, and finally rendered them masters of the entire empire of

India. In the year 1746, the Nabob of Arcot having died, the succession of his son was disputed by a cousin named Moozafur Sing. This pretender, mistrusting his own strength, applied to Dupleix, who commanded the French troops in India, for assistance, which was promptly afforded, under the hope and expectation of reaping certain advantages from the connection, should the aid solicited prove effective. The legitimate heir to the musnud, on the other hand, sought the support of Major Laurence, who was in command of the British soldiery in the Carnatic, and Major Laurence did not turn a deaf ear to the appeal. Hence arose a collision, which, with only occasional intervals of peace, has continued for nearly a century, until power after power has succumbed to the British arms, and what was gained by defensive warfare has been maintained by treaty, and consolidated by good government. Every victory obtained from the French and the Mahometan sovereigns, in whose behalf they fought, brought with it an extension of British privileges and the cession of additional territory. The government at home, to aid the merchants in their contest, sent out reinforcements of troops and ships. The French authorities in a similar manner recruited their forces abroad, and it was not until ten years had elapsed, from the date of the first outbreak, that the latter sustained a complete and decisive defeat. But new and permanent enemies had arisen in the meanwhile. The great chieftains who divided the sovereignty of the Deccan, the Carnatic, in short, the whole peninsula of India not occupied by the British, beheld with dismay the growth of the new

European power, and formed alliances for its destruction. Hyder Ali, a political adventurer and soldier of fortune, undertook the lead in these measures, and proved a formidable antagonist. He wrested several of their possessions from the English, wasted much of their territory with fire and sword, threatened Madras, and, compelling a large British force to lay down its arms, massacred nearly every man. For thirteen years were the whole resources of the British applied to resist this warrior, who, aided by the French, between whom and the British a war had arisen in Europe, vigorously prosecuted his operations, now gaining certain advantages, and anon suffering severe defeats. Hyder Ali died in 1782, but his son, Tippoo Saib, continued to wage war with the English, and they likewise found abundant employment in a contest which had arisen with the Mahrattas, on whom, for certain considerations, it was deemed expedient to attempt to force a rajah that they had expelled. It would be vain to attempt to follow the course of history through the multitudinous wars which were dovetailed into each other from the hour when Lord Cornwallis, in 1792, deprived Tippoo Saib of half his territory. Scarcely was the sword sheathed in one quarter, than it was drawn from the scabbard to chastise a new enemy in another direction. Sir John Shore (afterwards Lord Teignmouth), who succeeded Lord Cornwallis as Governor-General of India, was engaged in a war with the Rohillas. The Marquis of Wellesley, in 1798, found Tippoo Saib actively employed in new intrigues against the British, while the confederated Mahratta chiefs directed their hostility to our power in the west and north of India. Aided by his brother, the present Duke of Wellington, and General Lord Lake, the marquis applied his energies and the resources at his command to the destruction of these formidable opponents, and although their operations were guided and directed by French officers, engineers, and artillerists, he entirely destroyed the power of Tippoo, annexed his dominions to those of the East-India Company, broke the Mahratta confederacy, and added 33,000 square miles to the British possessions.

The Marquis of Wellesley was succeeded in his government by Sir George Barlow and Lord Minto, whose rule was more distinguished by domestic dissensions, intrigues, and the settlement of the provinces acquired, than by campaigns against external foes. The Marquis of Hastings assumed the reins of government in 1813, and during his administration found it necessary to take the field against the Pindarries, the kingdom of Nepaul, and a host of Mahratta chieftains, whose restless spirit had induced them to violate the engagements they had entered into, and endeavour to re-establish themselves in independent authority. After a long campaign, the Pindarries were exterminated, an advantageous peace was made with the Nepaulese, and many states, hitherto independent, were compelled to become tributary to the Company. The effect of the policy of Lord Hastings was to spread peace throughout India, and the attention of the government was now turned to the means of consolidating the vast empire which had been won by the sword. The army which had proved strong enough for conquest in detail was not of sufficient extent to preserve the territory intact and suppress fresh attempts at insurrection. It was, therefore, largely augmented (in 1824), and as the close of the long war which had devastated Europe for a quarter of a century now placed many experienced soldiers at the disposal of the government for employment in the colonies and elsewhere, advantage was taken of the circumstance to put the troops in India under the command of some of those generals who had most distinguished themselves in the field against Napoleon and his generals. The result of this arrangement was soon obvious in the conversion of a somewhat irregular, but brave and devoted force, into a large, well-organized, and admirably disciplined army, capable of bearing a comparison with the most effective troops on the continent of Europe. Scarcely, however, had the country rested from the turbulence of war, and the troops been dispersed over the empire to occupy posts which best protected the people in their peaceful pursuits, and held in check the quarrelsome disposition of neighbours, when the trumpet again sounded the alarm. In 1820 an expedition was despatched to the Persian Gulf, under Sir W. Keir Grant, to put down the pirates who infested its shores. In 1821, another force, under Sir Lionel Smith, proceeded thither to avenge the treachery under which a garrison belonging to the first had been put to the sword. In 1824, the Burmese obliged the government of Lord Amherst to despatch an armament against them, to punish their invasion of British territory; whence ensued a contest which lasted for two years, terminating in the surrender by the Burmese of 50,000 square miles of territory, and their agreement to pay ten crores of rupees towards the expenses of the campaign. In 1826, Lord Combermere, then commander-in-chief in India, reduced the fortress of Bhurtpore, and took prisoner its intriguing possessor, whose machinations threatened to disturb the peace of Upper India. From this time, and for twelve years subsequently, the operations of the military were confined to petty warfare in the country of the Coles (Bengal), in the rajahship of Coorg, in Rajpootana, and the unsettled districts in the south of India; but in 1838, events arose which gave employment to nearly every soldier in the service, and led to a campaign attended with disasters to which a British army had hitherto been strangers. The designs of Russia upon the English possessions in India had for a long time been a subject of suspicion and of discussion. Excepting, however, in the instance of her advances upon the Persian frontier, nothing had occurred to awaken particular alarm, or render any measures, beyond those of the commonest precaution, at all necessary. But in 1837 it became apparent that her emissaries and agents were at work in Affghanistan, to foment and keep alive disputes between the Ameer ruling in Cabul and the government of the Punjab, with which we were on terms of amity; and there was good reason to suppose that if we did not interfere to check the progress of the quarrel, the Affghans would approach, by force of conquest, near enough to India to precipitate a dangerous collision between the British and the power that was suspected of instigating them to aggression. Overtures of friendship were consequently made to the Ameer of Cabul, Dost Mahomed; but, failing of effect, it was resolved to send an army to dethrone him, and to place on the musnud, in his room, an exiled sovereign, who would be more favourable to our views, and in whose kingdom we might be permitted to retain a force that should at once protect him in his seat and oppose a barrier to advances from the north. Accordingly, an army of 15,000 men, under Sir John Keane, was despatched, during the government of Lord Auckland, to place Shah Soojah upon the throne, and to enter into alliance or friendly arrangements with the people occupying the large tracts of country lying between India and Affghanistan. Sir John Keane went, saw, and conquered, and returned to England to enjoy the reward of his easy victory. Shah Soojah maintained his sovereignty for three years, with the continual help of British bayonets; but at the end of that time, the chieftains, whose power had terminated with his restoration, combined to dethrone him and expel his allies, a measure which they were enabled to effect, partly through the division of councils in the British camp, and partly through the extreme severity of the season. Our troops were driven to capitulate, and, marching out of Affghanistan in the depth of winter, destitute of supplies and ammunition, were assailed in the mountains and massacred almost to a man. This sad blow to our arms was avenged a year afterwards by a fresh body of troops under Generals Pollock and Nott, acting under the directions of Lord Ellenborough, who had now become Governor-General of India; but the original purposes of the first expedition having been frustrated, and further interference in the affairs of Affghanistan offering no compensation, either in present or prospective security, for the great expense of occupation, the country was desolated and then abandoned.

While these events were taking place to the north-west of India, occupation was found for a considerable proportion of the army in China. The Chinese government had insulted a British envoy, imprisoned British subjects, and sequestrated and destroyed British property. To chastise these outrages, obtain indemnification for the pecuniary injury, and security for future commercial dealings, expeditions were fitted out, and after a contest of two or three years' duration, a peace was obtained, under circumstances as honourable to the arms of Great Britain as it promises to be fruitful of advantage to her trade.

Here, it was supposed, strife and bloodshed had reached a termination, and in the confidence of this belief the governor-general proclaimed perpetual peace in Asia, declaring his purpose of abstaining from all intervention in foreign affairs. Hardly, however, had the pacific declaration been published in every corner of the empire, when it was found necessary to punish the Scindians for alleged treacherous conspiracies against a part of the force retiring from Southern Affghanistan, and for certain overt acts of hostility subsequent to our evacuation of that country. The Ameers of Scinde refused the satisfaction demanded at their hands, took arms, attacked the British residency at Hydrabad while negotiations were yet on foot, gave battle to the small army under Sir Charles Napier, which had been employed to sustain the demand for reparation, were defeated, and their territory became a part of the British empire!

Here the military history of India, as sketched in these pages, may fitly close, for the revolts in Bundlecund and Central India, which have recently engaged attention, are of too trifling a character to merit special mention. From the Himalayan chain in the north, to Cape Comorin in the south,—from the Assamese frontier in the east, to the mouths of the Indus in the west,—the British are omnipotent; and it requires no extensive powers of vaticination to prophesy that, ere long, the Punjab will likewise become part and parcel of the wondrous empire.

In the foregoing sketch, we have confined ourselves entirely to a rough and hasty narrative of the progress of conquest. The outline of history, rude as it is, would, however, be still more imperfect were all mention to be omitted of the various measures which had gradually been introduced to render the tenure of the country firm, and to confer upon the people a better description of civil government than that which had been displaced.

In 1784, a bill was passed by the parliament of Great Britain, placing the government of India under a board of control, composed of the king's ministers. This measure, while it in some degree affected the patronage of the Company, afforded a guarantee of protection to the people, and strengthened the hands of the local authorities in their quarrels with the French and the native powers.

Between 1760 and 1773, charters were granted, establishing commissions for the trial of pirates at all the presidencies; and in 1774, a supreme court of judicature was established in Bengal, with powers co-extensive with the courts in England. Courts of justice were likewise erected at Bombay and Madras, and by 1837, each presidency, and the settlement of Penang, had its supreme court. In 1813, the trade to India was partially opened to the public under certain restrictions; and in 1833, the trading monopoly of the East-India Company was entirely abolished; the country thrown open to European adventurers of all classes; places of trust made accessible to the natives and people of all denominations; the ecclesiastical establishment augmented, and the number of members of the Supreme Council increased. The press in India has since then been freed; education is spreading its effects over the country; the vast products of the soil are, under the influence of useful societies and active officers, evolving and improving; and the formation of a regular steam communication between England and India by the old channel of the Red Sea, is promoting the cause of good government and general improvement, by bringing the empire nearer to its rulers, and to the people from whose intelligence and sense of justice she has derived strength and virtue, knowledge and civilization.

CLIMATE.—PRODUCTIONS.

Over so extensive a tract of country as that comprised within the limits of Hindostan, it is not to be supposed that the climate is uniform in its temperature, or that the seasons change everywhere at the same period. The prevalence of particular winds, the existence of chains of mountains, the alternations of forests and tracts of land where vegetation is comparatively scanty, exercise material influence in India, as elsewhere; while the difference of latitude is not, of course, without its ordinary effects in yielding various degrees of heat and cold. The sun burns with equal intensity in the north and the south, but the soil and the wind determine the quality of its action. The north of Hindostan is cold, mountainous, sandy, and barren; the south is hot, level, moist, and fertile. Nevertheless, the extreme points of the country have their varieties of season—periods when the bracing hyperborean atmosphere tempers the meridional regions, and the Himalayas change their coating of snow for a rich and verdant garment. In Bengal, for example, during the months of November, December, January, and February, the thermometer ranges from 50° to 75°; the days are clear and fine; the air pure and elastic; the north wind bracing; the nights are foggy, but not a drop of rain, excepting, perhaps, a partial shower at Christmas, falls during the four months. At such a season, the European constitution, harassed and broken by a long continuance of moist and oppressive weather, becomes invigorated; the appetite and strength, which had previously failed, return, and the whole frame becomes light and springy. Vegetable nature partakes of the generally salubrious effects of the season, and garden plants now shoot up with freshness and vigour. In March, the weather begins to grow warm; the sun is powerful, but is prevented from being oppressive by strong and steady southerly winds and occasional storms, known by the name of *north-westers.* April resembles March, excepting towards the close of the month, when the wind gets warmer, and the thermometer ranges between 75° and 90°. May brings with it burning winds, alternated by close, still, and oppressive weather, trying alike to vegetable and animal nature. With June commence the periodical rains, which begin to fall about the middle of the second week, and continue without intermission until the end of September. At first, the relief from excessive heat and aridity is agreeable and beneficial, but after a few weeks' rain, the excessive humidity of the atmosphere, accompanied by a cold easterly wind, or undisturbed by any zephyrs, is most unpleasant, and productive of disease. In the west of India, the climate resembles that which is here described as common to Bengal, with this difference, that the cold is less bracing and the heat less oppressive. Gentle sea-breezes blow for the greater part of the year from the south and west, rendering salubrious the Malabar coast, while the level country above the Ghauts, or western chain of mountains, derives advantage from the purity of atmosphere consequent upon its elevation. In the south of India, upon the Coromandel coast, the heavy rains fall somewhat later than in Bengal and to the westward, but in all other respects the climate approximates closely to those districts. As we proceed northerly, the climate becomes more temperate. Agra, Delhi, Meerut, and Kurnaul are all more moderate than the southern provinces, though the hot winds which blow during the months of April and May are extremely oppressive and pernicious. In Central India, those parching winds are felt in only a moderate degree; and during the rains, the range of the thermometer is very small, seldom falling below 70° at night, or rising above 75° in the day time. In the cold season (December), it has been known as low as 28°!

The diseases most common to India are fever, dysentery, liver complaints, and cholera morbus. These annually sweep away their tens of thousands, the latter disease baffling the skill of the most eminent physicians, and leaving even the theory of its causes enveloped in doubt and uncertainty. But there are a multitude of other diseases peculiar to the country, though less fatal in their general results. Elephantiasis, or the swelling of the leg, is common to the natives in every province. In the hilly districts, goître is very prevalent, and ophthalmia afflicts myriads in the upper provinces, where the soil is sandy and the people careless of their persons. Leprosy is often seen in the most hideous form; and rheumatism counts its victims amongst the thinly-clad and exposed poor during the rainy season. Biles, ulcers, inflammations, and a peculiar eruption, popularly called prickly heat, are extremely prevalent, more particularly amongst Europeans, whose habits of life are less regulated by climate than consists with a proper regard for health and longevity. Influenza and diseases of the lungs sometimes make demands upon the leech's skill, but they do not present themselves in the formidable guise which distinguishes their appearance in more northerly regions; neither do hooping-cough, the measles, or other complaints, afflict infants so severely as the same maladies in England. Still, the mortality amongst the newly born is considerable, arising in some measure from convulsions, teething, fever, &c., but more commonly from the ignorance of midwives, and the carelessness, if nothing worse, of native nurses. Small-pox was a terrible scourge to the population of Hindostan; but its ravages are now diminishing, thanks to the philanthropic exertions of the medical officers in the East-India Company's service, who have zealously laboured to introduce vaccination.

It is the custom to speak of India as a country of great wealth in respect to its natural produce. There is no doubt that the soil is susceptible of vast powers of production, if properly fertilized and cultivated, but it is perfectly preposterous to call that country rich which is only partially visited by the hand of the husbandman, and which is so capricious in its fruitfulness, even where the labour of tillage has been bestowed upon it, that scarcely a year elapses in which a part of the land is not desolated by famine. Deduct the immense tracts overrun with noxious jungle, or occupied by swamps, or composed entirely of sandy and sterile land, or unavoidably left waste, and the residue scarcely suffices to support the assertion that India is moderately wealthy, much less that she is generous and abundant. The great staple of the lower and southerly parts of India is rice, which constitutes the food of a vast majority of the population. In the upper country, wheat is the principal article of produce to the same useful end. Barley, gram, and other pulses are likewise grown in large quantities, and are consumed indifferently by man and the beasts of the field. Following these in importance are the cotton and the mulberry tree; the indigo and tobacco plants; the sugar-cane and the cocoa-tree; for their produce is convertible to purposes of commerce, and composes the true riches of the country. The poppy is largely cultivated in the province of Behar, and in Central India, whence is manufactured the opium of which the East-India Company preserves a monopoly, as they do also of the immense quantities of salt manufactured for common consumption. Of the fruits and vegetables grown in India, the principal are the mango, the pine-apple, the plantain, pomegranates, lemons, oranges, pumplenosas, grapes, tamarinds, plums, figs, almonds, guavas, leechees, citrons, melons, potatoes, cabbages, cucumbers, yams, brinjalls; a great variety of vegetables, compounded of the cucumber and the melon tribes; and where climate assists the labours of the agricultural and horticultural societies, all the produce of the kitchen-gardens of Europe. The *Flora* of India is gay but scentless; the flowers, opening at dawn of day, are robbed by the sun of their fragrance at the moment that he drinks the dew-drops which bespangle them. In the forests we find the teak-tree, the mighty banian, whose branches spread over acres, yielding a grateful shade to the traveller and a rendezvous for the wild denizens of the woods; the bamboo, the saul, the palm, and a vast affluence of timber, convertible to building purposes, fuel, and the construction of boats, all connected, covered, choked, by masses of vegetation, in the form of high grasses, gigantic shrubs, and luxuriant creepers. These, and a countless variety of roots, herbs, and small trees, bearing spices and drugs, constitute the sum of the Indian vegetable kingdom.

The animal creation partakes of the exuberance of the sister world. Of tame and domestic beasts, India possesses the elephant, the camel, the horse, the ox, the ass, the mule, the dog, the cat, the goat, the sheep, the hog, the buffalo, the ichneumon, the rabbit—all, however inferior in size to the animals of Europe, consecrated to the service of man. Of wild beasts, the jungles produce an immense number, and of different species. The principal are the tiger, lion, leopard, panther, rhinoceros, boar, bison, deer, wolves, jackals, bears, foxes, wild cats, hyenas, &c. Reptiles are likewise extremely numerous, from the enormous boa-constrictor, which makes a single meal of a heifer, to the scorpion and the centipede, which infest alike the houses of the rich and poor, in populous town or in wretched hamlet. The rivers of India, and the seas which wash her shores, abound with fish, which afford cheap and nutritive food to her millions. The delicious pomphret, the delicate bummelow, the seer and rock fish, the prawn and the sole, are found upon the coasts; the hilsa, the bekhtee, the mullet, the whiting, the delicate mango-fish, the oyster, the lobster, craw-fish, and shoals of the most minute members of the piscatorial creation, swarm in the great rivers. But they are not without other enemies than man. The alligator and the porpoise assist the gull and the stork to destroy countless myriads; the former animal, which often grows to the length of fifteen feet, occasionally visiting the banks of rivers likewise, to bear off a stray cow, a human being, incautiously bathing near his haunts, or any smaller living object that offers meat for his capacious maw. The feathered part of the creation is of corresponding magnitude, in point of numbers and diversity, with the rest of the wonderful offspring of nature's hand; from the eagle, exercising sovereign sway in the mountains of the north, to the solemn and stately hargillah (adjutant), which aids the vulture to perform the useful office of scavenger in the south. The ornithological inhabitants of Hindostan comprise almost every known variety; to name them all would be an impossibility, within the prescribed limits of this section, comprehending, as they do, the domestic fowls of Europe, the birds of prey common to all climates, a prodigious quantity of game-birds, and innumerable tenants of the grove, whose plumage is as unrivalled for its splendour as their song is unparalleled by the sweetest notes of the warblers of the West.

For a supplemental notice of the products of the East, the reader is referred to the section descriptive of the commerce of that part of the world. To proceed further with the subject in this division of the Hand-Book would involve needless repetition.

POPULATION—MANNERS AND CUSTOMS.

THE estimated population of India is one hundred millions. This, however, is a very rough computation, for no census has ever been taken of the inhabitants, nor, if a judgment may be formed from the extreme difficulty of ascertaining the number of residents in towns which have for the longest period formed part of the British possessions, could a fair census by any possibility be prepared. The estimate is probably offered as the aggregate of returns from the local officers of the different districts, who have hazarded a guess founded upon the rough calculations of their native subordinates.

The natives of India may be divided into two classes—the Hindoos and the Mussulmans; the former of whom are the pure and legitimate descendants of the aborigines, and the latter the offspring of the successive generations of Mahometan conquerors. In addition to these great classes, of which the Hindoos are in the proportion of four to one of the Mussulmans, there are many tribes who have established themselves in India originally as traders, or who have found shelter from foreign persecution, and are now become part and parcel of the gross population. Such are the Parsees, descendants of the ancient Guebres, or fire-worshippers; the Armenians, formerly refugees from Persian persecution; the Arabs, Jews, Persians, chiefly traders from the Red Sea and Persian Gulf; the Portuguese, coloured descendants of the early conquerors; the Eurasians, or East-Indians, offspring of English, Dutch, French, and

Danish connection with Hindoo, Mussulman, or Portuguese females; the Chinese, settlers from the Celestial empire; Burmese, chiefly employed in menial pursuits; Seikhs and Affghans, merchants from the neighbouring states; the English, soldiers, civil officers, merchants, agriculturists, lawyers, seamen, ecclesiastics, &c.; French, merchants and agriculturists; a few Americans, and others from the Western world.

The Hindoos are separated into four great castes, or religious divisions—Brahmins, Katries, or Rajpoots, Bhyses, and Soudras. Of these, the former occupy the highest place in the esteem of their countrymen. To them are intrusted the performance of religious ceremonies and the instruction of the people, and they alone are permitted to read the Vedas, or sacred books. Extraordinary privileges are accorded to them, and when they are detected in crime, a milder punishment is inflicted than would fall to the lot of any other caste. The *Kutries* are of royal and military descent. *Bhyses*, or *Banians*, are the trading class, and the *Soudras* comprehend the labourers and artificers. These four castes are subdivided into an infinite number of smaller tribes or sects, differing in some degree from the highest and most orthodox in matters of religion and in domestic usage; while a fifth great class, called Pariahs, or Chandalas, comprehends all who have violated some leading principle in the religion of the other four, and have been banished the society of the faithful; and all who follow the lowest professions in the scale of Indian society. The religion of the Hindoos, which indicates these distinctions and regulates the actions of their lives, is contained in certain books, called the Vedas, or Shasters, written in the Sanscrit language. It is pretended that these volumes are the work of an inferior deity, named Brimha, descended from Bramha, the supreme god. They inculcate certain moral precepts, but are more precise in describing the forms and ceremonies, the charities and regimen, of the Hindoo, and constitute, in fact, the foundation of a system of idolatry and superstition, transcending in extravagance the worship of the ancient Greeks, Romans, and Egyptians.

The Mussulmans, who are for the most part traders, soldiers, police-officers, menial servants, seamen, &c., profess the religion of Mahomet, and observe the ceremonies of the Ramazan, the Buckra Eed, the Mohurrim, &c., but the great masses are neither as fierce nor as fanatical as the Persians, from whom they derive their descent, nor will all the articles of their faith or the strictness of their lives bear the test of a close comparison with the precepts of the Koran.

All the other races in India adhere to the religion of their ancestors; and, as the most perfect toleration is extended by the government to every persuasion, the Roman Catholic church will be found in juxta-position with the Augiaree of the Parsee, and the mosque of the Arab *vis-à-vis* the cathedral of the Protestant or the chapel of the Baptist.

It is a problem to this moment, whether the character of a people is formed by the government or the government influenced by the character of the people. If the former proposition were admitted, the English would have slight cause for self-gratulation; for, considered in the gross, there is not perhaps a people in the world who are so little distinguished by the virtues which adorn the human race as the inhabitants of Hindostan. They are not insensible to the natural affections, nor are the examples they present of patience and resignation under calamity, and charity in the bestowal of alms, by any means rare; but the *per contra* exhibits a selfishness, a sensuality, a cowardice, a degree of avarice, cunning, falsehood, malevolence, prejudice, inertness, and a host of minor vices, with which it is needless to swell our catalogue; still, there are brilliant instances of exceptions to the ordinary rule. The charge of supineness does not lie at the door of the Parsee—he is industrious and energetic, and generous in the use he makes of his accumulated wealth. Cowardice is not the characteristic of the Rajpoot, nor can the educated classes be accused of an indifference to truth or the indulgence of strong prejudice.

The manner of life of the native of India is regulated partly by his religion, partly by the climate, and partly by his circumstances. The temperance and frugality suggested by inclination are counterbalanced by inordinate extravagance in the performance of ceremonials. The accumulation of years is often dissipated in a single week, to swell the pomp of a marriage procession, to honour the memory of a parent, or to propitiate some one of the imaginary deities in whom is supposed to rest the means of vengeance or the power of absolution. The ordinary food of the Hindoo is of the simplest character—

pulse, vegetables, fruit, fish, constituting the chief solids upon his table; water, milk, or clarified butter reduced to a liquid, the fluids with which he regales. Some sects go the length of eating fowl or mutton, and there are not a few who will so far forget their religious obligations as to indulge in fermented and intoxicating liquors; but these, with the exception of the Pariahs, to whom no description of food is unpalatable or unwelcome, are the exceptions to the *habit* of the race. The Mussulman is less scrupulous than the Hindoo; he objects to no viands that are not cut from the unclean beast, nor is he very rigid in his abstinence from the beverage proscribed by the prophet.

The usages of the mass of the people, where they are not regulated by religion, are tolerably uniform. Rising early, they apply themselves to copious ablutions,—the Hindoo bathing in the waters of the Ganges when accessible; thence they betake themselves to their temples, or address themselves to their household gods, in the form prescribed by their teachers. The extemporaneous prayer, springing from the religion of the heart, is almost unknown. The morning meal, taken in nearly a state of nudity, follows the ceremony of prayer; then the toilette is made, and the business of the day commences. The merchant, the clerk, the government functionary, all, in short, of the superior orders, whose duty calls them from their homes, preserve their muslin costume, turban, and slippers* throughout the day;

* In entering the house of a superior or an equal, the slippers, or shoes, are removed, and left in the vestibule or at the foot of the stairs. The same ceremony is observed in public offices, private establishments, &c.

the artisan, the shopkeeper (except where European customers are numerous), the venders of goods in public market, the labourer, the fisherman, &c., divest themselves of all their upper clothing and a great proportion of the lower, as soon as they commence their diurnal toils. Returning to their homes at the close of day, the ceremony of prayer and ablution is repeated, preparatory to the evening meal, and the hours, until bedtime, are passed in the zenana, or, in other words, in the pleasure of domestic intercourse; for though the laws of polygamy obtain among the Mussulmans and a proportion of the Brahmins, and concubinage is tolerated by all classes of Hindoos, the great majority are satisfied with the affections of one wife and the caresses of a family of children. In truth, there are few people in the world over whom the paternal affections exercise more potent sway than the inhabitants of British India. The young men pass much of their leisure in the interchange of visits, gambling, and the society of the fair. There are few public entertainments amongst the natives. They do not worship Terpsichore; they do not sing, but regale themselves with the performances of a certain class of dancing, or nautch girls, who go through a series of pantomimic evolutions to the accompaniment of their own songs and a trio of *sitars,* or rude violins, played by bearded auxiliaries. A more monotonous exhibition can scarcely be imagined; but it suits the drowsy and inactive genius of the Hindoo, and is therefore much patronized, especially upon the occasion of great religious festivals, marriage ceremonies, &c. These *bayadères,* with the jugglers, who are wonderfully expert; snake-charmers, wrestlers, tumblers, fireworks, kite-flying, illuminations, puppet-shows, and occasional dramas, of which mythological subjects, or the ridicule of the English, constitute the *matériel*, form the whole of the out-of-door amusements of the natives, excepting at the presidencies, where the educated people share in the entertainments peculiar to Europeans.

The dwellings of the better order of the natives are spacious, but, excepting in the infrequent instances of a partiality for the European style of decoration, their furniture is simple. The mat, the carpet, and the cushion cover the floors; mirrors, a few framed prints, and some wall-shades, decorate the walls. Their beds consist of a simple mat, or mattress, spread upon the floor, or upon a raised pallet, termed a charpoy, over which gauze curtains are sometimes hung, to protect the sleeper from the musquitoes. Their domestic utensils are chiefly of copper or of silver. In vessels of such material, or in earthen pots, the meals are prepared, and served up on circular flat dishes, placed upon the ground, over a cloth of the commonest texture. The cook (where the food is not dressed by the females of the house) is a person of the same caste as the master, and the greatest care is used, that, while the culinary operations are going on, no person of an inferior sect touches, or even approaches, the utensils. Water is drunk from small copper vessels, but the lips are not permitted to touch the edge of the cup, which is accordingly held an inch or two above the mouth, while the liquid is poured, as it were, into the throat. After each refection, the hookah is brought, and smoked with the gusto which distinguishes the Turkish use of the chibouque, or the European indulgence in the cigar. Nor is it merely at meal-times that smoking is resorted to by the native. He will quit his business to enjoy an occasional whiff, and seldom repairs to his couch until the fumes of tobacco have made the tour of the chambers of his brain.

If patriotism is not a principle with the Hindoo—and when was patriotism ever co-existent with foreign government?—he is at all events sufficiently attached to his home to be averse to locomotion on a grand scale. Curiosity seldom leads him beyond the district in which the accident of birth or the nature of his vocation has established him. He has no passion for travel, and rarely even allows the most pressing suggestions of self-interest to carry him beyond seas, for such peregrinations would involve, by throwing him amongst the impure, the possible forfeiture of caste.* In the fulfilment of a sacred vow, or in the hope of propitiating the Deity, pilgrimages will occasionally be performed to places remarkable for their sanctity; and in prosecution of these enterprises, neither fatigue, privation, nor expense is regarded for a single moment. Nay, where a powerful religious fervour operates, the Hindoo will set aside every worldly consideration, and either become an ascetic, or, covering his person with ashes,

* Moor, in his Pantheon, records an instance of the re-admission among the faithful of certain Hindoos who had paid a visit to England, but the indulgence was purchased at a heavy pecuniary sacrifice, and by a degrading process figurative of regeneration. More recently, the voyage of the enlightened Dwarkanath Tagore has been visited by the penalty of expulsion from his family circle.

and suffering his hair and nails to grow, wander over the vast continent, depending for a scanty subsistence upon the alms vouchsafed to him by the pious and superstitious.

Whatever may once have been the state of the arts and sciences amongst the natives of India, they are now confessedly at a very low ebb. Their architecture is tame, monotonous, mixed, and irregular, though the carving of the ornamental parts may be exquisitely beautiful; their carts, carriages, boats, and agricultural machinery are all rude, cumbrous, and rickety; their drawing and painting set at defiance form, perspective, light, shade, and harmony; their astronomy is a puzzle; their notions of geography crude and limited, and their medicine a quackery. On the other hand, they are ingenious as workers in gold, silver, and ivory; and their achievements in ship-building, under the guidance and tutorage of the intelligent Parsee, have elicited the admiration of the European shipwright. For his skill in embroidery, and the fabrication of the finest muslins, the native of India has likewise obtained a name, but his reputation in this respect, and as a fabricator of rattan and osier basket-work, is more than counterbalanced by the worthlessness of his attempts at the manufacture of every description of hardware, leather, glass, the implements of trade, crockery, and common cloths.

And if in the cultivation of the arts of peace the native of Hindostan has failed to occupy high ground, still more limited is his knowledge of the art of war. With the lance, the matchlock, the sword, the bow and arrow, for his weapons, he has never been capable, unaided by Europeans, of organizing a system of tactics, or of introducing into his armies a controlling discipline, at once the source of strength in the peaceful garrison, and formidableness in the field of battle. Trusting to the crushing effect of the fierce onslaught of numbers, he has disregarded alike the importance of a series of complicated manœuvres and the virtue of calm and steady resistance, and as a natural consequence, he has, in all his wars, been overcome by small and compact bodies, who relied upon union, moral courage, and the lights of science. That he is deficient in personal courage it were a scandal to pronounce, for while the history of the conflicts during the past century, which have followed the first dissensions between the European and the native in the south, records innumerable instances of personal intrepidity upon the part of the hordes opposed to the British, our own experience of the sepoys, through whom we have won the country, supplies us with hundreds of thousands of reasons for testifying to their valour, constancy, and fidelity.

The condition of the women of India is deplorable, if judged by European views of the right of the sex to at least a moral equality with the lords of the creation. Debarred the advantages of even the most elementary branches of education, the upper classes are held captive in the harem, passing their hours in personal adornment, idle chat, or (if mothers) in performing the duties of nurses; while on the lower classes are imposed menial offices, household drudgery, and labour in the fields and markets. In no grade of society are the women permitted to eat with their husbands, or to enjoy the society of other males, or to marry again, if left widows. Until recently, and even now, where British rule does not extend, conjugal slavery went beyond the grave, or rather the funeral pile (for the Hindoos burn their dead), and the widow had no alternative but to immolate herself with the dead body of her husband, or sink in the estimation of her caste, and become the family drudge.

In the foregoing crude and imperfect outline, the usages of the two great classes of which the population of India is composed have been sketched. The other races are, for the most part, too insignificant, numerically, or approach in many instances too nearly to the Hindoo and Mussulman, to merit special description in this volume. There are, however, three—the Portuguese, the Eurasians, and the Europeans—who are worth particular notice, and for a sketch of the former we readily avail ourselves of the graphic pen of Mrs. Postans:—

"The Portuguese may be known by his sallow countenance, slovenly gait, and mimicry of European fashion. His garments are the worst-shaped things imaginable, and where colour is admitted, it is of the gaudiest tint; he affects a swagger, and desires to pass as a man of style and taste. Nothing can be more dirty and despicable than the Portuguese of the lower order, nothing more absurd and comical than the affected beau of the upper. The Portuguese loves society and music, dancing and festivity; he is troublesome when holding positions of authority, and offensive in his self-importance when invested with power. Among the natives of India generally, the

Portuguese are held in contempt, and considered capable of all sorts of depravity and wickedness. That he is weak and degenerate is certain, while all that energy and talent which originated the Portuguese government in India is wholly lost. The Portuguese encourage priestcraft, while their religious teachers place their foot upon the necks of the laymen, and, constraining a very sufficient contribution, live in great content and comfort. The Portuguese seat of government, Goa, is beautifully situated, and adorned with palaces and churches, worthy the great city founded by the noble-hearted Albuquerque; but the towns which once equally marked their conquests are overgrown with brambles, while the glossy snake glides among their tombs, and the timid songster of the wood shelters its bright plumage among the rich foliage tangled alike round hall and bower.

"The Portuguese woman, pretty when young, becomes coarse both in form and nature when advanced in age. She loves gaudy colours, the glare of feasts, the incense of admiration. The better class affect sentiment, poetry, and taste, but it is to be feared are very unfemininely deficient in all these, if any opinion may be formed from the alliances that are often considered the most eligible, from their favourite songs, and the striking contrasts adopted in costume.

"The Portuguese, however offensive he becomes when a ruler, weak as he is as a diplomatist, ridiculous as a beau, ignorant as a priest, and useless generally as a member of the native community of India, is yet admirable as a *cook;* and although his deficiency in cleanliness and his love of potent liquors detract somewhat from his merits, yet it must be admitted that the European gastronomist in India is materially a debtor to the Portuguese: unhappily, in this sphere of action, his usefulness ends, and with it his claim to our attention."

The Eurasians, a term invented by the late Marquis of Hastings, but which does not fully express the whole race of half-castes, some of which are of American extraction (though it is now conventionally accepted as embracing all the progeny of *white* fathers and Hindoo or Mahometan mothers), are as much between the Europeans and natives in their habits and pursuits as in their genealogy, and interfere but little with either in the pursuit of sustentation. They are an orderly and intelligent, and in one line, an industrious race of people; but they are devoid of both mental and personal energy, and are unlikely, therefore, to ever make a political class in the state of any weight or importance. In laying down opinions of this kind, we must never be understood as maintaining a proposition to the truth of which there are no exceptions; but we do say, that *if ever* the exceptions to a rule have been of force in establishing the rule itself, they are so pre-eminently in the question now before us. Perhaps there is no class of men, with their educational advantages, and their other facilities for acquiring local superiority (supposing the true mental vigour to exist), who have produced so few men of note in any of the departments from which such men spring in Europe. In painting, in sculpture, in navigation, in law, in arms, in agriculture, in eloquence, in literature, in science, they have not only not acquired the slightest reputation in Europe or in India (with the one or two exceptions of a Skinner* in war, and a Kyd† in the higher mechanics), but they have not even endeavoured to acquire it, because their constitutional temperament is, by nature's own decree, a bar to the endeavour. Clerkships in the public offices is the line of employment which the body of them *look to*, and which is manifestly the one best suited to their quiet and unambitious turn of mind. We are aware that they have laboured, and do still labour, under difficulties of position which might have repressed the advancement of a more aspiring race, and this has shallowly been urged in refutation of the opinion that they are incapable of achieving greatness. But has it ever been observed that they have been incessantly *trying* to elevate themselves in the social scale, or have they not been quiescent, and apparently attached to the sub-official employment which so easily gives them food?‡ It is

* Colonel Skinner, commanding a body of irregular horse, raised by himself and stationed at Delhi. The corps rendered important services in the Mahratta and Pindarree campaigns.

† Mr. James Kyd, the son of General Kyd, constructed dock-yards of some extent, and gave great attention to the mechanical arts.

‡ In reply to this, we may be reminded of their having petitioned parliament to open to them new paths of distinction; but what *were* those paths? Why, the easy and sure ones (for livelihood) of the Company's regular service, which incur no speculative risk, and render *necessary* no greater average of daily labour than they had always performed, and still do perform. The army is in general an indolent life for all who choose to be indolent; but how came it that the Eurasians, *if* a naturally energetic and vigorous-minded race, did not enter the more arduous lines of life, which were always open to them in their several grades? The reason is obvious; and it is no refutation of our argument to shew that they made an effort to be rendered eligible for the Company's service, when they have never as a body

nothing, in the way of argument, to point to a few individual instances of activity of mind, and successful striving against obstacles to advancement. The character of the body at large is to be estimated by the conduct and propensities of the body at large; and it would be as true to assert that Englishmen were neither enterprising nor intrepid, because individuals there are among them who are neither the one nor the other, as to maintain that Eurasians are energetic, or laudably ambitious of that distinction which energy and genius can alone acquire, because a few out of the whole class have evinced those qualities,—but even those few not in a degree which would have attracted wonder in England. Speaking of them merely in the population branch of our argument, however, we think it doubtful whether they will increase in any of the admitted ratios (under the various forms of human life), or whether, if they do that, they will physically improve in like proportion. We incline to the negative side of both these problems, in spite of some appearances which, however, we deem fallacious, on the affirmative side of the former of these questions. It is said that the number given in recently published tables, as the Eurasian census, shews an increase, and it is thence inferred that the same result will be observable at any future time; but the inaccuracy of the old guess-work estimates of population is too notorious to admit of their being depended upon for the establishment of so grave a theory. On the other hand, we are of opinion, that if they were, properly

been found to be active mechanics, industrious agriculturists, enterprising seamen, or daring politicians.

speaking, an increasing and a multiplying race, their numbers would now be far greater than that which they are shewn to be; inasmuch as they live under a state of social affairs highly favourable to such a result. They lead a life of much ease; they have plenty of food, earned without great labour; they live unmolested in their native clime; they are cherished by the government; and they are partial to the marriage state: yet at this late period there are not twenty thousand of them, though numerically augmented to some extent from their original source. But this latter supply will gradually dry up,* as the system whence it issued disappears before the march of matrimony (and it has already almost done so), and then they will be left entirely to their own intermarriages, which, by the course of nature, will not sustain a mixed race in a healthy and vigorous state, but will assuredly produce degeneracy, and eventual decay. Even that source, however, is not left wholly at their command; for it is a notorious fact, that their females prefer to marry with Europeans, and that, of the inferior classes, many are taken as wives by the British soldiery, and by the various English who are in the capacity of assistants, and the like; and in all these instances the real Eurasian people, as a race, are losers. We think, then, upon these considerations, and others, that the class in question will not swell into an essential portion of the Indian community, and that the feelings of both Europeans

* We should here explain that by the "original source" is meant the illicit connections between Europeans and native females, a sort of connection that is happily falling into desuetude.

and natives regarding them will prevent their ever attaining to political importance as a section of our subjects.

The European, by which we more particularly mean the native of Great Britain, may not change his soul with his skies, but his manners assuredly undergo, in India, a remarkable metamorphosis. Accustomed in youth to habits of obedience to authority, deference to superiors, and civility to equals, he cannot support with becoming equanimity the comparatively elevated position in which he finds himself placed. Invested at once with authority, or treated by his personal domestics, and the traders with whom he may traffic, with abject humility, he naturally conceives a much higher opinion of his own merits than he ever entertained before, and hence is begotten an overweening *amour propre,* which thenceforth, more or less, influences his character through life. With this difference, however, and the adoption of a costume and habits peculiar to the climate, the European is much the same as we find him elsewhere. Energetic and active, courageous and speculative, he performs the duties intrusted to him, or carries out his own plans of personal advantage, in a manner which excites the admiration and confidence of the people around him, and serves the country of his adoption. He is the upright and inflexible judge, the brave and adventurous soldier, the dauntless and skilful navigator, and the calculating and enterprising merchant. Even his pastimes partake of the loftiness of his character, for he fearlessly encounters the tiger in his lair, does battle with the wild boar, the bison, and even the untamed elephant, and, "witching the world with noble" equitation, ardently encourages every pursuit that serves to improve the horse, and render him more serviceable to the purposes of man. All that the Englishman might do, or might have done, for the benefit and advancement of the people who have fallen under British rule, has not, however, been accomplished. For more than one half of the period of our dominion, the natives were treated as a people who existed only as ministrants to temporary British interests; we drained the country of its wealth, and offered no compensation for the heavy appropriation. But a better spirit has arisen of late years, and a sound and liberal policy is gradually taking the place of the narrow system of government which erst rendered British rule in the East a bye-word and reproach. The lights of European science are spreading themselves over the Eastern world. Colleges and schools upon a considerable scale are established at all the great towns; offices of trust are rendered accessible to the intelligent and the upright native; Englishmen have unlimited permission to settle in the towns and agricultural districts, and introduce improvements in machinery and culture; the science of medicine is freely taught, and the qualified practitioner in the healing art distributed over the country. But we have elsewhere touched on these matters already, and need not allude to them here, further than to express a hope that every man whose fortune may carry him to India will consider it personally incumbent upon him to return, in some degree, the blessings of ease and competence, which the residence in the country may ultimately confer upon him, by an endeavour to improve the condition of its interesting population.

COMMERCE.

The external trade of India comprehends not only the commercial intercourse between the various ports in Europe and America with the three presidencies of British India, but the trade carried on by the people of the western coasts, from Scinde to Cape Comorin, and thence to the mouth of the Ganges, and by the people of the Eastern Archipelago and the Burmese coasts, China, Siam, Sumatra, the Dutch settlement of Java, &c., with each other.

England sends to India a large proportion of her manufactures—iron, piece-goods, copper, lead, mule-twist, hardware, wines, malt liquors, stationery, haberdashery, books, saddlery, jewellery, glass, cheeses, hams, preserves,—in fact, every sort of production adapted to the wants of civilized life, and to the temperature of the country.

France furnishes wines, preserved meats, millinery, porcelain, and, in a lesser degree, the manufactures of her brilliant metropolis.

From America, India receives timber, sheeting, spermaceti candles, ice, fruits, furniture.

In exchange for these commodities, Europe and America receive such of the vast and various productions of India as are convertible to useful purposes in more northern and western climates. The ports to which their vessels speed are not in themselves sources of merchantable commodity, so much as emporiums for the fruits of other parts of the East, and channels of transit trade, for which their positions so particularly qualify them. It will facilitate the description to place under their respective heads the articles which each is thus enabled to export, instead of enumerating the various sources of supply.

Bombay, as the recipient of the trade of the gulfs of Persia and Arabia, and the northern parts of Western India, supplies cotton and piece-goods from Guzerat; opium from Malwa; tea, ivory, silk, lac, gold and silver filigree-work, from China; cornelians, from Cambay; ghee, grain, oils, putchock, seeds, tobacco, and soap, from the northern coast; shawls, drugs, and horses, from Scinde, the Red Sea, and Bussorah. From the coast of Canara, Bombay derives rice, pepper, betel and cocoa nuts, sarda, cassia, and turmeric; from the Malabar coast, coir, ginger, ambergris, pepper, teak timber, cowries, cardamoms, *coculus Indicus*, colombo-root, elephants' teeth, fish maws, sandal-wood, tamarinds, turmeric, wax, zedoary, coffee, coarse white piece-goods, nankeen; and from the Maldives, dried fruits, tortoise-shell, and some rude and trifling manufactures.

Ceylon yields cinnamon, coffee, cocoa-nuts, coir, oil, wild honey, arrack, areca-nuts, cotton, tobacco, timber, ornamental woods, precious stones, ivory, drugs, dye-stuffs, oleaginous seeds, copperas, pearls, and precious stones of an inferior quality.

Madras is the emporium of the trade from Cape Comorin and the whole of the Coromandel coast. Thence we derive piece-goods, called calamaganzies, aunniketches, &c., made of a hard long-grained cotton; long cloths, palampores (light counterpanes of printed cotton), coarse plain cloths dyed with the chaya root, Chicacole muslins, Ellore woollen carpets, Jehapoor salt, Masulipatam tobacco, Vizagapatam ivory, rice, dholl, wax-oil, and a proportion of the produce of the Straits of Malacca.

CALCUTTA, the head-quarters of the trade of Bengal, Behar, and Orissa, and of the provinces east, north, and north-west of those extensive districts, exports indigo, saltpetre, sugar, rice, annatto, arrow-root, opium (chiefly sent to China), wheat, *terra Japonica*, tamarinds, talc, sugar-candy, raw silk, silk piece-goods, flax, ghee, hemp, ginger, hides, horns, lac, lac-dye, oil of roses, rum, safflower, dried fruits, munjeet, black salt (*bit nober*), borax, castor-oil, chillies, cochineal, coriander, and piece-goods, such as baftas, cossas, dorias, mamoodies, &c., from Patna, Allahabad, Lucknow, Central India, and lower Bengal.

At the four above-mentioned ports the external trade of all India may be said to be concentrated. We have enumerated the productions of the continent, but every part of the coasts and islands to the eastward and the south are also tributary to their stores in a greater or lesser degree. For example, she receives from—

Arracan—Rice, elephants' teeth, wax, wood-oil, and coarse piece-goods.

Pegu—Teak timber, in balks; keel-pieces, mast fishes, planks, and sheathing boards (all from Rangoon); precious stones, iron, copper, tin, lead, wood-oil, earth-oil, wax, dammer, elephants' teeth, cutch, silver, naphtha, and asphaltum.

Andaman and Nicobar Islands—Timber for building purposes, masts of ships, dyes, cocoa-nuts, oil, birds' nests, tortoise-shell, ambergris, &c.

Malay Peninsula and the Islands of Singapore and Penang—Tin, *biche de mer*, bees' wax, birds' nests, fish maws, rice, rattans, shark fins, areca and pepper, gold dust, camphor, and all the produce of China, Cochin China, and Siam.

At the last-named islands, also, the produce of the Eastern Archipelago may be obtained; but as this is for the most part transmitted either to India or to China, for consumption there, it is scarcely necessary to include it in the commerce with Europe. To complete the description of the productions of the gorgeous and wealthy East, the main items of this local trade from port to port may be enumerated, but the reader is requested to bear in mind, that, to avoid repetition, many articles are omitted which may be found in common at each of the islands:—

Agal, argus feathers, balacharry, or agapi (shrimp caviar), gourd-seed, gum benjamin, black wood, kyapootee oil, canes, clove bark, copper, cossumba, ejoo, gambia, shells, lignum aloes, rattans, sago, wood-oil, dragons' blood, patch leaf, brimstone, silks, sugars, ivory, salt, betel-nut, tobacco, indigo, from Java and Manilla; nutmegs, oil of nutmegs, and mace, all from Banda; cloves and oil of cloves, from Amboyna; birds of paradise, missoy bark, pearls, pearl shells, tortoise shells, and many curious birds, which the Papuans (of Mysol, New Guinea, &c.) have a particular way of drying; diamonds, gum copal, civet, and timber, from Ternati, Timor,

Borneo, &c.; sapan wood, precious stones, copper, and tutenague, from Siam.

The value of the exports of merchandize from India to the United Kingdom, France, and America, the gulfs of Persia and Arabia, and different parts to the eastward, not including China, is about seven millions sterling. In addition to this, treasure to the amount of half a million sterling is annually exported. The declared annual value of British produce and manufactures imported in that quarter, including China, is about six millions sterling. It has increased progressively to that amount since 1833, when the trading privileges of the East-India Company were abolished. At that time, the value was not more than three millions and a half.

The trade with India is carried on in various descriptions of craft. The French and Americans employ vessels of from 300 to 600 tons burthen. Liverpool and the Clyde send out vessels of similar tonnage, while those built and employed by the London merchants range from 400 to 1,200 tons. The trade between Bombay and China employs teak-built ships of 500 to 700 tons measurement; that from Calcutta to China is carried on in a small description of vessel, ordinarily denominated a clipper, and constructed for the reception of chests of opium and tea. They are, for the most part, very fast-sailing craft, well manned, and skilfully commanded. The coasting trade between Cambay, on the shores of Guzerat, to the termination of the Malabar coast, is carried on in rude, ill-fashioned native boats, called *pattamars*, with high poops, and a similar description of vessel, called a *dhony*, voyages between Madras and the points of the Coromandel coast. The vessel in chief use in the straits of the Eastern Archipelago is called a *proa*, and much of the trade with the Persian and Arabian gulfs is borne in buggalows and dows.

The number of vessels employed in the carrying trade between the United Kingdom and the ports within the limits of the East-India Company's charter is about eight hundred. Of this number there were entered inwards from—

Calcutta, in 1842	224
Madras	18
Bombay	107
Ceylon	33
Singapore and Penang	47

The number of vessels which sailed in the same period *to* India was—

Calcutta	164
Madras	28
Bombay	124
Ceylon	30
Singapore and Penang	51

The inland trade of India comprehends the intercourse between one portion of the British dominions and another; the trade of the latter with the tributary and independent states of Hindostan, and the commerce along a land frontier of 2,000 miles in length. Scinde, Cabul, the Punjab, the states of Nepaul and Burmah, can obtain few foreign or tropical productions but through their commercial connection with us. Corn, cotton, oil-producing plants, and sugar are the principal articles of this inland trade. Rice, which is grown in such vast abundance up to the twenty-fifth degree of latitude, and the millet and pulses cultivated beyond those limits, are chiefly consumed upon the spot. The cotton-plant, which is of almost universal production in India, from Ceylon to the Himalaya Mountains, furnishes material for a prodigious variety of fabrics; and the sugar-cane, which for the most part is grown in the valley of the Ganges, supplies a sugar which is consumed in very considerable quantities in the form of sweetmeats. Besides these main articles, there are a great number of others, such as indigo, salt, opium, silk, tobacco, saltpetre, oils, and oil-skins, drugs, hides, lime, timber, &c., which are objects of the inland trade. These various commodities are paid for by the productions of the coasts, such as spices, teak-timber, sandal-wood, and coarse piece-goods; in the productions of foreign tropical countries of Asia, and in the produce and manufactures of Europe and China. The tropical or foreign commodities which are obtained in exchange for the Indian produce consist of the areca-nut, spices, metals—iron, zinc, tin, copper, and lead—woollens and cottons. The extent of the inland trade, in other words, the amount of home manufacture and home consumption, it is extremely difficult to ascertain. The odious tax which formerly existed, under the denomination of transit-duty, and which furnished a clue to the computation, has been abolished, and nothing now remains to check the spirit of industry, and bring forth the choicest fruits of the generous soil of India, but the government monopoly of the manufacture and sale of salt, and the culture of the poppy, for conversion into opium for the

China market. There is no doubt, however, that, in proportion as facilities for the transport of goods from one part of the vast country to another are augmented, and the charges of trade thereby lessened, an additional impulse will be given to enterprise. At present, excepting the rivers Ganges, Berampooter, Jumna, Gunduk, Casi, Gagra, Goomtee, Soane, Betwah, Chumbul, Taptee, Nerbuddah, Mahe, Sabrematta, Godavery, Krishna, Cavery, the Indus, and the Irrawaddy, the greater part of which, by the way, are only suited to canal-navigation, few effective channels of inter-communication exist. There are not many good carriage-roads in any part of India; the bridges are generally small, and few in number, though the rivers or streams over which they are thrown are very numerous; the ferries are rude, unsafe, and by no means numerous. The carriage of the inland trade is as imperfect, slow, and expensive as the ground over which it traverses is rough and impracticable. Uncouth and primitive carts, drawn by oxen, the strength of eight of which animals is only equivalent to that of a good English cart-horse; pack-bullocks, camels, pack-horses (in the north-west), small horses and jackasses (in the hills), comprise the means of land transport; and on the rivers, large boats, of a burthen varying from 15 to 150 tons, with rude and coarse sails, oars, and track-ropes (when wind and tide are adverse), constitute the ordinary craft. On the Ganges, iron steamers, the property of the government and of private associations, ply between Calcutta and Allahabad, but the rate of freight is so high, and so large a proportion of the space appropriated to cargo is occupied by baggage and special supplies for the Europeans in the interior, that they can scarcely be included in an enumeration of the river trading-vessels.

The standard currency of continental India consists of silver, in coins of the value of about two shillings, and called the rupee. There are copper coins, called *pice* (four of which represent the anna, the sixteenth part of a rupee), and *four-anna pieces*, which constitute the quarter of a rupee. Of gold, there is scarcely a single coin in circulation. The *mohur*, which is represented by sixteen rupees, may occasionally be obtained, and certain coins in existence in the southern parts of India, called pagodas and fanams, may also be seen from time to time, but the exceeding rarity of all these monies authorizes the assertion that in India gold forms no part of the currency. In native transactions, use is made of the cowrie, an exceedingly small shell of the *Cyprea* species, imported as an article of trade from the Maldive and Laccadive islands. Five thousand one hundred and twenty cowries go to the rupee, whence an inference may be drawn of the extreme poverty of the natives. Paper-money forms a very small proportion of the Indian circulation. Bills of exchange, termed hoondees, are employed as a means of remittance, and are obtained from the native bankers, or shroffs, who are to be found in all the large towns. They are generally written upon small pieces of glazed yellow paper, in a character not easily decipherable by any but the parties whom they more immediately concern, namely, the agents and correspondents on whom they are drawn, and who are scattered in every part of India, the Punjab,

Affghanistan, and Persia. The rest of the paper-money consists of Treasury notes, bills which the government permits its civil officers to issue, for an equivalent, to facilitate the remittable operations of their own servants and others who may wish to avail themselves of the accommodation. The paper-money which circulates in India in the form of bank notes amounts to a very inconsiderable sum. The banks at the several presidencies are permitted to issue notes, but as they are not all regarded as legal tenders in payment of revenue, the great channel into which, if generally current and recognized by the government, they would ultimately flow, their circulation (comparatively small under any circumstances) is materially restrained.

The large capital employed upon the commerce of India is drawn from a variety of sources. England contributes a very large proportion ; her merchants depute parties to establish mercantile houses at the several presidencies and ports, and supply them with the means of purchasing produce, encouraging agriculture and local manufactures. The natives, as banians or dubashes (a species of broker to the European houses), or as merchants on their own account, furnish the remainder of the resources. Formerly, all these parties added the business of banking to their other pursuits, and thus derived immense appliances for commerce from the aggregate deposits of their constituents ; but the rashness of speculation, the prodigality of personal expenditure, and the incautiousness with which loans were afforded to parties in all classes of society, and involved in every description of business, led to a bankruptcy that was almost universal, scattering injury far and wide, and striking a fearful blow at the credit of the Indian merchant. Banking, therefore, is now, with comparatively insignificant exceptions, confined to institutions established exclusively for the operations understood by that term. There are now six banks in India,—the Bank of Bengal (chartered), the Union Bank of Calcutta, the Madras Bank (chartered), the Agra Bank, the Bombay Bank, and the Bank of Western India; and while we write, efforts are making to establish a seventh, whose head-quarters are to be at Calcutta. The chartered banks are, to a certain degree, connected with the state, and are, in part, managed by government officers; the joint stock banks rest their claim to support upon the ground of a wealthy co-partnership, each member of which is liable, to the full extent of his means, for the claims upon the institution.

MONETARY SYSTEM.

The following Table exhibits the scheme of the British Indian Monetary System.

Gold mohur.	Rupee.	Anna.	Pysa.	Pie.
Calcutta 1	16	256	1024	3072
Madras and Bombay 1	15	240	960	2880
	1	16	64	192
		1	4	12
			1	3

Small shells, called cowries, are also still partially made use of for fractional payments, and are reckoned as follows; but their value is subject to considerable fluctuation, and they are now nearly superseded by the copper currency.

4 Cowries make	..	..	..	1 Gunda.
20 Gundas ..	..	..	..	1 Pun.
5 Puns ..	..	..	..	1 Anna.

EXCHANGES.

For the conversion of the rupee into the equivalent currency of other nations, it is necessary to take into consideration the fluctuating relative value of the precious metals *inter se*, from the circumstance of gold being in some, and silver in others, the legal medium of circulation.

It is also necessary to take account of the mint charge for coining at each place, which adds a fictitious value to the local coin. The *par of exchange* is, for these reasons, a somewhat ambiguous term, requiring to be distinguished under two more definite denominations: 1st, the *intrinsic par*, which represents that case in which the pure metal contained in the parallel denominations of coins is equal; 2nd, the *commercial par*, or that case in which the current value of the coin at each place (after deducting the seignorage leviable for coinage) is equal; or, in other words, "two sums of money of different countries are *commercially* at par, while they can *purchase* an equal quantity of the same kind of pure metal."*

Thus, if silver be taken from India to England, it must be sold to a bullion merchant at the market price, the proprietor receiving payment in gold (or notes convertible into it). The London mint is closed

* Kelly's Cambist., iii. 13.

against the importer of silver; which metal has not therefore a minimum value in the English market fixed by the mint price, although it has so in Calcutta, where it may always be converted into coin at a charge of two per cent. On the other hand, if a remittance in gold be made from India to England, its out-turn there is known and fixed; each new Calcutta *gold mohur* being convertible into 1·66 or $1\frac{2}{3}$ sovereigns nearly; but the price of the *gold mohur* fluctuates as considerably in India as that of silver does in England, the natural tendency of commerce being to bring to an equilibrium the operations of exchange in the two metals.

The exchange between England and India has, therefore, a two-fold expression; for silver, the price of the sicca rupee in shillings and pence; for gold, the price of the sovereign in rupees. To calculate the out-turn of a bullion remittance in either metal, recourse may be had to the following

Tables of English and Indian Exchanges.

The *data* for the calculation of these tables are:

1st. One *mun* (or 100 lbs. troy) of silver ($\frac{1}{12}$th alloy) is coined into 3,200 Company's rupees, of which 64 and 60 respectively are taken as mint duty; being at the rate of two per cent.

2nd. 100 lbs. troy, of English standard silver ($\frac{18}{240}$ths alloy), are coined into 6,600 shillings, of which 400 are taken as seignorage or mint duty; being 4*s*. per lb., or nearly six per cent.; but the mint is not open to the holders of silver bullion, which is only purchased through the bank when required for coinage.

3rd. The sovereign ($\frac{1}{12}$th alloy) weighs 123·25 grains troy, and no duty is charged on its coinage. 100 lbs. of pure gold yield 5098·3 sovereigns, =3069·5 new *gold mohurs*, =3041·4 old *gold mohurs*, =3490·9 Madras and Bombay *mohurs*.

The par of exchange with other countries may be estimated from the intrinsic and mint produce of their coins; thus, assuming the Spanish dollar to weigh 416 grains troy, and to be 5 dwts. worse in assay, we have for

Spain and America.

100 Dollars	=231·111 tolas in weight.		
	=225·858 Fd. rupees,	or, deducting duty of 2 per cent.	221·341 Fd. rs.
	=211·742 Sicca rupees,		207·508 Sicca rs.

The Spanish dollar forms also the currency of the Straits of Malacca and of Manilla; and it is extensively known in the colonies of England, Ceylon, the Cape, Australia, &c.

For the British colonial possessions, however, an order of council was promulgated on the 23rd March, 1825, extending to them the circulation of British silver and copper money, and directing all public accounts to be kept therein. Where the dollar was, either by law, fact, or practice, still a legal tender, it was to be accounted equivalent to 4*s.* 4*d.*, and *vice versâ*. For the Cape of Good Hope, where the circulation consisted of paper rix-dollars, and Ceylon, where it consisted of silver and paper rix-dollars, as well as a variety of other coins, it was provided that a tender and payment of 1*s.* 6*d.* in British silver money should be equivalent to the rix-dollar. The Company's rupee is allowed circulation at 1*s.* 11*d.*, and the 5-franc-piece at 4*s.* These regulations are still in force in Ceylon, Australia, Van Diemen's Land, the Cape, Mauritius, and St. Helena.

France.

The French *kilogramme* of standard silver ($\frac{1}{10}$th alloy) is coined into 200 francs, and the *kilogramme* weighs 85·744 tolas; therefore—

100 Francs	= 42·872 tolas in weight.		
	= 42·092 Co.'s rupees,	or, deducting duty of 2 per cent.	41·250 Fd. rs.
	= 39·462 Sicca rupees,		38·673 Sicca rs.

The coinage duty on silver at Paris is $1\frac{1}{2}$ per cent., or $\frac{1}{2}$ per cent. less than in India; hence it will be found, that

100 sicca rupees realize almost precisely 250 francs at the Paris mint.

Minted gold in France is worth $15\frac{1}{2}$ its weight of minted silver, or the *kilogramme* is coined into 155 *Napoleons*, or 20-franc-pieces; the seignorage on gold is only $\frac{1}{3}$ per cent.

One kilogramme of pure gold yields 81·457 gold mohurs, or (deducting two per cent. mint duty) 79·828 ditto, therefore—

100 Napoleons	= 55·319 tolas in weight.		
	= 47·315 old gold mohurs,	or deducting duty of 2 per cent.	46·369 old gold mohurs.
	47·757 new ditto,		46·802 new ditto.
	= 54·313 Madras and Bombay gold rupees,		53·227 Madras & Bombay gold rupees.

CHINA.

As the Chinese have no gold or silver coins, but make payments in those metals by weight, it is sufficient to state the value of the *tael* of the sycee and dollar silver usually current with them.

100 tacl of sycee silver aver. 15 dwts. Br. ..	= 322·135 tolas in weight = 120 oz. 16 dwts. English.		
	= 344·108 Comp. rs.	or, deducting duty of 2 per cent.	337·226 Fd. rs.
	= 322·602 Sicca rs.		316·150 Sa. rs.
100 tael of dollars 5 Wo.,	= 314·811 Comp. rs.	or, deducting duty of 2 per cent.	308·515 Fd. rs.
	= 295·135 Sa. rs.		289·233 Sa. 3 rs.

BRITISH INDIAN WEIGHTS AND MEASURES.

The unit of the British Indian ponderary system* is called the tola. It weighs 180 grains English troy weight. From it, upwards, are derived the heavy weights, *viz. chitak, seer,* and *mun,* or *maund;* and by its subdivision the small, or jeweller's weights, called *mashas, ruttees,* and *dhans.*

The following scheme comprehends both of these in one series:—

MUN.	PUSSEREE.	SEER.	CHITAK.	TOLA.	MASHA.	RUTTEE.	DHAN.
1	8	40	640	3200	38400	307200	1228800
	1	5	80	400	4800	38100	153600
		1	16	80	960	7680	30720
			1	5	60	480	1920
				1	12	96	384
					1	8	32
						1	4

The *mun* (or that weight to which it closely accords in value, and to which it is legally equivalent in the new scale) has been hitherto better known among Europeans by the name of *bazaar maund;* but upon its general adoption, under Regulation VII., 1833, for all transactions of the British government, it should be denominated the *British maund* (in Hindee, *Un-*

* The advantages of this system are—

1. That the maund formed from the modified weight would be precisely equal to one hundred English troy pounds; and

2. That thirty-five seers would also be precisely equal to seventy-two pounds avoirdupois; thus establishing a simple connection, void of fractions, between the two English metrical scales and that of India.

grezee mun), to distinguish it at once from all other weights in use throughout the country.*

The *pusseree* is, as its name denotes, a five-seer weight, and therefore should not form an integrant point of the scale; but, as its use is very general, it has been introduced for the convenience of reference.

The *seer*, being the commonest weight in use in the retail business of the bazaars in India, and being liable, according to the pernicious system hitherto prevalent, to vary in weight for every article sold, as well as for every market, is generally referred to the common unit in native mercantile dealings, as "the seer of so many *tolas*" (or siccas, barees, takas, &c.); the standard, or *bazaar seer*, being always eighty *tolas*.

The *chituk* is the lowest denomination of the gross weights, and is commonly divided into halves and quarters (called, in Bengalee, *kacha*); thus marking the line between the two series, which are otherwise connected by the relation of the seer, &c., to the tola.

The *tola* is chiefly used in the weighing of the precious metals and coin; all bullion at the mints is received in this denomination, and the tables of bullion produce (as seen in the foregoing pages) are calculated per one hundred tolas. It is also usual at the mints to make the subdivisions of the tola into annas (sixteenth) and pie, in lieu of mashas and ruttees.

* In the same way the Madras, Bombay, and Furakhabad rupee (when the sicca rupee is abolished, and an English device adopted) may be called "the *British rupee*," and in the native languages, *rupya Ungrezee*.

Mashas, ruttees, and *dhans* are used chiefly by native goldsmiths and jewellers. They are also employed in the native evaluation by assay of the precious metals; thus ten mashas fine signifies ten-twelfths pure, and corresponds to "ten-ounce touch" of the English assay report or silver. There is a closer accordance with the English gold assay scale, inasmuch as the ninety-six ruttees in a tola exactly represent the ninety-six carat grains in the gold assay pound, and the *dhan*, the quarter grain.

British Indian Weights.		English Troy Weights.					French Weights.
		lbs.	oz.	dwts.	grs.		grammes.
One Maund .	=	100	0	0	0	=	37320·182
One Seer ..	=	2	6	0	0	=	933·005
One Chitak .	=	0	1	17	12	=	58·310
One Tola ..	=	0	0	7	12	=	11·662
One Masha .	=	0	0	0	15	=	0·972
One Ruttee .	=	0	0	0	1·875	=	0·122

Comparison with troy weights.

For the conversion of English troy weights into those of India, the following scale will suffice, since the simplicity of their relation renders a more detailed table unnecessary:—

Lb. Troy.	Ounce.	Pennyweight.	Grain.		Tolas and Decimals.
1	12	240	5760	=	32·0000
	1	20	480	=	2·6666, &c.
		1	24	=	0·1333, &c.
			1	=	0·0055, &c.

The accordance of a *mun* weight with the 100 lbs. troy of England affords a ready means of ascertaining its relative value in the standards of other countries employed in weighing the precious metals, since tables of the latter are generally expressed in pounds troy.

Linear and Square Measures of India.

Place.	Denomination.	Value in Eng. mea.
Agra, Presidency,	Standard Ilahy guz, assumed at	33 inches.
	Standard Beega of Western Provinces = 60 × 60 guz. = 3600 *guz*.	.. 3025 sq. yds. ($\frac{5}{8}$ acres).
	Local *guz*. varies from 32·8 to 33·25, aver.	.. 32·625 inches.
Batavia,	*Ell* = 27$\frac{3}{4}$ inches, *foot* =	.. 12·36 ditto.
Bombay,	*Hath* = 18 inches, the *guz* =	27 ditto.
Calcutta,	*Beega* = 20 cottahs of 16 chittaks	1600 square yards.
	Cottah	.. 720 sq. ft. = 80 sq. yds.
	Chittak	.. 45 sq. ft. = 5 sq. yds.
China,	Mathematical foot ..	.. 13·12 inches.
	Builder's ditto	.. 12·7 ditto.
	Tailor's ditto	.. 13·13 ditto.
	200 *lis* = 1 degree ..	.. 69·166 miles.
Goa,	Portuguese *corado* ..	.. 26·66 inches.
Madras,	*Mauney*, 60 × 40 feet ..	.. 2400 square feet.
	Cawney = 24 mauney ..	.. 1·3223 acres.
Malwa,	*Guz* (from 28 to 32) ..	.. 30·00 ditto.
	Beega, of 20 wusas ..	.. 2 roods nearly.
Mocha,	*Cobid* = 19 inches ..	.. 25 ditto.
Persia,	*Guerze*, royal	.. 37·5 inches.
	Common measure	.. 25·0 ditto.
	Parasang, twentieth of a degree at the equator.	
Siam,	*Vouah* (2000 = 1 league)	.. 75·75 inches.

THE GOVERNMENT OF INDIA.

THE jealousy with which the legislature watches over the exercise of political power when delegated to British subjects in distant dependencies, and the extreme difficulty of managing an immense extent of territory abroad through a single secretary of state, have created a mass of gubernatorial machinery for British India, which is as costly as it is unwieldy. That it moves at all, is rather owing to the boldness of the local governors, who often act as emergencies dictate, preferring future obloquy to the evils of present delay, than to any particular harmony in the arrangement of the component parts of the complex mechanism.

The political government and patronage of India are placed by charter in the hands of the directors of the East-India Company. They are twenty-four in number, chosen by the proprietors, and are usually selected from the members of the civil, military, or maritime services, or from among the merchants who have acquired knowledge and fortunes in India. Each director must hold £2,000 of the Company's stock, and the proprietors who elect him are only eligible on possession of £1,000 stock, which carries with it a single vote. A larger share gives a greater number of votes, but not in a proportionate degree, £10,000 merely conferring the right to four votes.

There are about two thousand six hundred proprietors, a proportion of whom have only an interest in the stock to the extent of £500, which gives no power to vote at an election, although it enables the proprietor to debate at the meetings of the court. Six of the directors retire annually by rotation, and are eligible for re-election after twelve months' absence.

The Court of Directors enjoy full initiatory authority over all matters in England or India relating to the political, financial, judicial, and military affairs of the Company. But their proceedings are subject to the superintendence of a board of commissioners appointed by the Crown, to the parliament of Great Britain, and in several matters to the approval of the Court of Proprietors.

In addition to this home establishment, there are local governments in different parts of India. A survey of the map of India will at once satisfy the most cursory observer that it would be perfectly impossible to govern so vast a tract of country from any single point, however advantageously situated such a position might be. From Cape Comorin in the south, to Simla, in the Himalayan Mountains, in the north,—from Munneepore, in Assam, in the east, to Kurrachee, the chief sea-port in Scinde, in the west,—a distance comprising twenty-two degrees of latitude and twenty-five degrees of longitude, or an area of 1,076,590·7 square miles,—every inch of ground acknowledges British rule, or is, directly or indirectly, subject to British influence. Hence the necessity for placing the territory under several distinct governments, all, however, subordinate to one supreme ruler or governor-general, aided by a council, who in their turn are controlled by the home powers mentioned above.

The five governments have their seats respectively

in Bengal, Madras, Bombay, Agra, and Hyderabad, in Scinde. The Bengal government, which exercises a supervision over the rest, has its head-quarters at Calcutta, and administers the affairs of the countries lying between Saugor in the west, Cuttack in the south-west, Arracan in the south-east, and the Nepaulese frontier to the north; and between the territory of Assam in the east to the nearest boundaries of the kingdom of Oude in the north-west. The management of the affairs of Bengal Proper is, however, exclusively intrusted to a deputy-governor, as they are found to interfere too seriously with the business of directing the affairs of the empire at large to allow of their entering into the consideration of the governor-general. The territory west of Oude, from Allahabad to Agra, and due north from Agra as far as Simla, is designated "the North-western Provinces," and is ruled by a lieutenant-governor without a council, excepting when the governor-general himself visits the provinces, and then the entire control is assumed by him. The Madras government exercises authority over the space embraced between Ganjam, on the coast of Orissa, to Cape Comorin, in the extreme south of the Peninsula, and from Masulipatam in the east to Saddashegarh on the opposite, or Malabar, coast. The intermediate state, from Mostoor, south, to Ellichpore, north, is ruled by a native prince, denominated the Nizam, but he is subsidized by the British, who keep several of their own (Madras) regiments in the neighbourhood of his capital,—Hyderabad. To the government of Bombay, constituted like that of Madras, is intrusted the management of the districts lying between Vingorla on the Malabar coast, south, and Palunpore in Guzerat, north, and between Bombay, west, to Asseerghur, east. The limits of the government of Scinde are not at present exactly defined, but its head-quarters are at Hyderabad, and the whole country acknowledges its rule. The extent to which it may be necessary to carry British authority will doubtless be adjusted when the legislature has had time to consider the question of the recent conquest.

Besides these five divisions of the government of the continent of India, there are separate governments for the islands to the south and south-east, which form part of the appendages to the British crown, namely, Ceylon (exclusively a British colony, and totally independent of the East-India Company's authority), Penang, Singapore, and Malacca; to which may be added the Burmese coast as far as Moulmein, where affairs are administered by political commissioners.

The various governments above enumerated are composed as follows:—

THE SUPREME GOVERNMENT OF INDIA.

Governor-General and President in Council.

Two members drawn from the civil service.

One member from the military service of the East-India Company.

One military member, who is likewise commander-in-chief of the army; almost invariably a general officer in the royal service.

One ordinary member, who is not in any service, and generally selected for his legal attainments.

A due proportion of secretaries and assistants.

There is no legislative assembly of any kind to assist the government in its deliberations, or to represent the interests of any class of the governed; but the right of the community at large to express its sentiments upon measures immediately affecting its interests is recognized, by implication, in the publication of all *drafts* of laws for general information. Such publication often elicits opinions, either communicated to the government direct or through the medium of the press, which are not without their weight occasionally, in leading to a reconsideration, or even an abandonment, of the draft before it passes into an act.

To assist the supreme government of India in fulfilling its important trust, a highly-educated civil service, consisting of about four hundred members, is placed at its disposal by the home administration. Of this number, one-fifth is generally absent, from sickness or other causes; the remainder, therefore, insufficiently perform the offices of revenue collection, the administration of laws in the interior of the country, the management of political relations with native states, &c. The army which the government has at its immediate disposal consists of about one hundred thousand men, principally natives of India, commanded by European officers, and divided into seventy-six regiments of regular infantry, ten of regular cavalry, several corps of irregular and local horse and foot, and a due proportion of artillery, engineers, and sappers. The police duties are performed by large and well-trained bodies of natives, guided and directed by British officers, selected from those most remarkable for courage, intelligence, and a knowledge of the native character.

THE GOVERNMENT OF FORT ST. GEORGE (OR MADRAS GOVERNMENT)

Consists of

A Governor	... ...	President, and
A Commander of the Forces	}	Members of
Two civilians	... ... }	Council.

This administrative body is supported by a civil service, two hundred in number, and an army of about three-fifths the strength of that of Bengal.

THE BOMBAY GOVERNMENT

Is constituted exactly like that of Madras, with, however, only one hundred and twenty-five civil officers, and thirty-five thousand troops, regular and irregular.

THE GOVERNMENTS OF AGRA, SINDE, PENANG, MALACCA, ETC.,

Consist each of a single officer, aided by one or more secretaries, aides-de-camp, a due proportion of troops, drawn from the other presidencies, and an adequate police force.

The manner in which the business of government is carried on will appear to those who are familiar with the method of proceeding in England tedious and changeable, almost all transactions being conducted through the medium of official correspondence, carried through a variety of channels. But this is the unavoidable result of the responsibility of the local administration to the two supervising authorities in England. When every thing has to be formally reported to the controlling power, every thing must necessarily be placed on record; and, as reference may continually have to be made to the official communications on the spot, the original documents are retained, and copies, in duplicate, forwarded to the Court of Directors and the Board of Commissioners for the Affairs of India. The voluminous correspondence between the government and its officers is, therefore, multiplied by four, and sometimes oftener, thus rendering the machinery of the *secrétariat* extremely cumbrous and costly.

The method of transacting public affairs in India may be thus briefly described. Every officer of government charged with the management of political, financial, military, municipal, revenue, police, ecclesiastical, judicial, marine, medical, or other matters, either addresses the authorities direct (advising, reporting, or soliciting instructions and assistance), or through the functionaries and boards intrusted with the immediate control of the several departments of the executive. These communications, amounting to many scores per diem, are laid by the respective secretaries to the government before the Council Board, and they are duly discussed, and orders issued thereupon, in conformity with the sentiments of the majority of the members. The initials of the council on the back of the letter of the authority addressing them *direct*, are, in the majority of instances, a sufficient guide to the secretarial officers; but where the question discussed is of importance enough to elicit elaborate or precise expressions of opinion, the members of the government place on record separate minutes, from the aggregate of which the decision or ultimate resolution is deduced. On these latter occasions, where the council is much divided, the governor-general, or governor, has power to adopt his own views, even though they may be at variance with those of the whole body of his colleagues; but this is a prerogative exercised only in cases of great emergency, the more ordinary course in such circumstances being, to refer the disputed question to the arbitrement of the home authorities.

It will be obvious, from this concentration of the government of so vast an empire, that the members of the administration must be men of very considerable and varied attainments; for though they may not originate the multitudinous measures carried into effect almost daily for the good of the country and the integrity of the British possessions, they must possess a capacity for determining upon the propriety of yielding assent to propositions submitted for their consideration. Care, therefore, is taken to select for the functions of government as great a variety of ability as so small a council is susceptible of containing. The governors are generally chosen from the statesmen in the mother-country who have manifested a taste and capacity for public business, and to whom Indian affairs are not entirely caviare, or from the public servants of the East-India Company, whose high character, long services, and extensive local experience point them out as peculiarly fitted for the important trust. The commanders-in-chief, in almost every instance, have earned distinction in the wars of Europe, and are familiar with the science of organizing and disciplining large forces. They carry with them to India a thorough knowledge of the principles of civilized warfare, and an acquaintance with the interior economy of an army—qualities which, combined with a stern sense of duty and a lofty chivalry, atone for the temporary absence of local knowledge, and enable them, while acquiring requisite information, to impart a wholesome spirit to the legions intrusted to their command. The other members of the council are gentlemen of the civil service, who have served for many years in revenue, judicial, political, or secretarial offices,—or in all of those branches,—and acquired therein a high official reputation. In the Supreme Council there are two additional members, one of whom is selected from the senior officers, for his superior acquaintance with the affairs of the Indian army, and his regard for its interests, and the other for his legal attainments and familiarity with the principles of British polity. The salaries of all these officers are liberal, but not more than sufficient for the degree of state which is almost inseparable from exalted life in India, and for the annual contribution to useful and charitable public objects. The Governor-General receives £25,000 per annum, and is provided with a splendid palace at Calcutta, and a rural residence at Barrackpore, sixteen miles from the presidency. The governors of the other presidencies (Madras and Bombay) receive £12,000 a year, and are similarly domiciled. The Governor of Agra £12,000; the Governor of Scinde £7,000. The members of the Supreme Council receive each £10,000 per annum, of Madras and Bombay, each £6,000; the Commander-in-Chief, £10,000, in addition to which he enjoys the pay of his rank in the army, and very often the off-reckonings of a regiment, of which he may be the colonel.

We may conclude this sketch with a few particulars concerning the relative powers of the several governments of India.

All subordinate governments send abstracts of their weekly proceedings for the inspection of the supreme government. All extraordinary outlay of public money by the subordinate governments requires the confirmation of the supreme government, pensions likewise; and here it may be noticed, that on one occasion, in answer to a question of the governor in council, inquiring with reference to the provision of the pension rules, whether the local government was not competent of itself to sanction such pensions, it was stated that the terms of the 59th section of Act 3rd and 4th Wm. IV. cap. 85, were too precise to admit of any latitude of interpretation. Its provision is conclusive against the power of the subordinate government to make any increase without the previous sanction of the government of India. Where pension is claimable under distinct rules passed by the government, and approved by the Honourable Court, such sanction is sufficient; but in respect to pensions to the families of persons killed in the performance of their duty, though the rules recognize the claim to pension, they do not specify the amount, and a reference to the government of India would seem to be necessary.

The new charter provides for most matters relating to the constitution of the government, but we may here notice the following :

The senior member of council, when the commander-in-chief stands appointed to that situation, becomes president of the council during the temporary absence of the governor-general, but does not succeed to the position, in consequence of such seniority, when permanently vacated, even if no provisional appointment exists.

Members of the supreme council may be selected from any member of the Hon. Company's service of twelve years' standing. Ordinary councillorships of the subordinate presidencies, must be civil servants of those presidencies of twelve years' standing. Retired servants may also hold seats in the supreme council, if annuitants drawing their annuities, under 77 cl. 3 and 4 Wm. IV., cap. 85.

Members of council proceeding to sea or elsewhere within limits, do so without creating a vacancy or forfeiting their allowances. But if the council owing to such absence be incomplete, i. e. if there are less than three members present, the number required to pass any act, the provisional member shall be called in.

The above relates to the supreme council.

In the subordinate council the provisional member is called in at the discretion of the governor.

All memorials to the home authorities must lie twenty days on the council table before transmission to England, and if not coming through the proper channels they are always liable not to be received.

The fourth ordinary member of the council of India is declared not to be *entitled* to sit or vote in the council, except at meetings for the making of laws and regulations. The law, however, does not *preclude* him from sitting in council, or prohibit his aid being always made available without his vote; He accordingly does attend every council. He, however, signs no despatches, except those relating to laws and regulations.

NATIVE STATES.

Classification of Native States, with which the British Indian Government is in Alliance.

	Square Miles.
The area of the native states in alliance with the British Government is	449,845
That of the territory under British rule, with the remaining small states and jageerdars	626,746
Superficial area of all India	1,076,591

The extent of coast from Cape Negrais to the frontiers of Sinde is 3,622 British miles; the breadth from Surat to Silhet, 1,260 miles.

The native states of India may be classed under the three following heads:

I.—*Foreign*, viz. Persia, Senna, the Arab tribes, Siam, Acheen.

II.—*External, on the frontier*; viz. Ava, Nepal, Lahore, Cabul.

III.—*Internal*, which are those included in the present list. All of these have relinquished political relations with one another and with all other states. They are, according to the nature of their relations or treaties with the English, divided into six classes.

First Class.—*Treaties offensive and defensive: right on their part to claim protection, external and internal, from the British government: right on its part to interfere in their internal affairs.*

	Square Miles.
1. Oude, containing	23,923
2. Mysore	27,999
3. Berar or Nagpore	56,723
4. Travancore	4,574
5. Cochin	1,988

Second Class.—*Treaties offensive and defensive: right on their part to claim protection, external and internal, from the British Government, and to the aid of its troops to realize their just claims from their own subjects: no right on its part to interfere in their internal affairs.*

	Square Miles.
6. Hyderabad, containing	88,884
7. Baroda	24,950

Third Class.—*Treaties offensive and defensive: states mostly tributary, acknowledging the supremacy of, and promising subordinate co-operation to, the British Government; but supreme rulers in their own domains.*

8. Indore, containing .. .. 4,245 square miles.

Rajputána States.	Square Miles.		Square Miles.
9. Oudeporc ..	.. 11,784	19. Pertabgurh	.. 1,457
10. Jeypore ..	.. 13,427	20. Dungarpore	.. 2,005
11. Jodhpore ..	.. 34,132	21. Kerolee ..	.. 1,878
12. Kotah ..	.. 4,389	22. Serowee ..	.. 3,024
13. Boondee ..	.. 2,291	23. Bhurtpore	.. 1,946
14. Alwar ..	.. 3,235	24. Bhopal ..	.. 6,772
15. Bikaneer ..	.. 18,060	25. Kutch ..	.. 7,396
16. Jesalmeer ..	.. 9,779	26. Dhar and Dewas ..	1,466
17. Kishengurh	.. 724	27. Dhalpore ..	.. 1,626
18. Banswara ..	.. 1,440		

		Square Miles.
Boghelkhund and *Bundelkhund*	28. Dewar	.. 10,310
	29. Dhattea, Jhansi, Terhee	.. 16,173
	30. Sawantwaree	.. 935

Fourth Class.—*Guarantee and protection, subordinate co-operation, but supremacy in their own territory.*

		Square Miles.
31. Ameer Khan	Tonk .. .. 1,103; Seronee .. 261; Ninbahara .. 269	 1,633
32. Patiala, Khytal, Naba and Jeend	.. .. ..	.. 16,602

Fifth Class.—*Amity and friendship.*

33. Gwalior	.. 32,944

Sixth Class. *Protection, with right on the part of the British Government to control internal affairs.*

	Square Miles.
34. Sattara	.. 7,943
35. Kolapore	.. 3,184

Of the above states, four are Mohammedan; viz. Hyderabad, Oude, Bhopal, and Tonk. Of the Hindoo states, eight are Mahratta; viz. Sattara, Gwalior, Nagpore, Indore, Banda, Kolapore, Dhar, and Dewas.

Nineteen are Rajpoot; viz. Oudeepore, Jeypore, Jodhpore, Boondee, Kotah, Kutch, Alwar, Kikaneer, Jesalmeer, Kishengurh, Banswara, Pertabgarh, Dungerpore, Kerolee, Serowee, Rewah, Dhattea, Jhansi, Terhee.

Six are of other Hindoo tribes; viz. Mysore, Bhurtpore, Travancore, Sawantwaree, Cochin, and Dholpore.

Besides these allied states, there are the following inferior Rajships and Jageerdarees: viz. Chota Nagpore, Sirgoojer, Sumbhoolpore, Singhbhoom, Munipore, Cacheir, Assam frontier. Tanjore, the Bareich family, Ferozpore, Merich, Tansgaon, Nepanee, Akulkote, and those of the Saugur and Nerbudda country; also Sikkim and the states of the northern hills and the Tributary Mehals of Kutuk.

FOREIGN RELATIONS.

PERSIA.—The relations of England with Persia arose altogether from our position in India. At one time we apprehended designs on the part of France against our possessions there, and at another, on the part of Russia. Several embassies were sent to Persia at the early part of the present century, laden with valuable presents, and finally an envoy from the home government was established at the capital of Persia, while a subordinate resident was located at Bushire. Subsequently, British officers were employed to drill a part of the Persian army, and the alliance became, to all appearance, firm. The conduct of the present king of Persia, however, in prosecuting the siege of Herat against the Affghans, led to a temporary dissolution of our connection with the Iranee empire, which has only been recently resumed. Consuls now reside in Persia, in addition to the envoy and minister; and active endeavours have been made to introduce a commerce between Persia and England *viâ* the Black Sea and Asia Minor. Our military connection is at an end, and scarcely any British officers now hold trusts in the Persian army.

ACHEEN.—With the sovereign of this place, England has entered into a treaty, which secures to her subjects a free trade to the ports of the kingdom, and allows of the residence of a British agent, and the exclusion of all other European powers, and likewise of all Americans.

SIAM.—Amicable relations subsist between the British government and the monarch of Siam, for which we are indebted to the idea of our power derived from the hostile operations in Burmah in 1824-25. There is no accredited English agent residing at the Siamese court, but occasional missions have been received in the best spirit; and our commerce is upon a secure, liberal, and well-defined footing.

BURMAH (AVA).—The treaty entered into with this state at the termination of the war of 1824-26 ensured the payment, by the Burmese, of certain sums of money; their abstinence from all interference in the affairs of the states on their frontier which had fallen under the protection of the British; the residence of a political agent at the principal port; and the unrestricted ingress, into all the ports, of vessels under British colours. The relations have, at times, since then, been partially disturbed, owing to changes in the dynasty, low intrigues, and misrepresentation; and there is no longer a representative of our government residing within the Burmese territories, but the terms of the treaties remain substantially intact, and trade is carried on uninterruptedly. The possession by the British of the coast of Arracan, and the Tenasserim provinces, added to the facilities with which troops can be sent from Bengal to Rangoon, and thence up the river Irrawaddie, effectually forbid any apprehension of serious ruptures with the sovereign of Burmah.

NEPAL.—A resident, armed with political powers, is accredited at this court. The treaty imposes upon the rajah the obligation of refraining from aggressions upon the frontier of the British empire contiguous to his state. He is likewise bound to allow British traders to travel unmolested through his territories; to surrender criminals who may take refuge therein; and to respect the agreement under which he ceded certain portions of his kingdom, and recognized the independence of his neighbours.

LAHORE.—The recent commotion in this capital, terminating in the wholesale destruction of sovereign, lineal successors, minister, &c., has unsettled our relations with the Punjaub, and leaves it, while this volume passes through the press, uncertain what our position will be in the course of a few months.

CABUL.—The relations with this place—the principal town in Affghanistan, and generally the seat of government—are as yet undetermined. Dost Mahomed Khan, so recently prisoner in the British territories, has reason to be friendly to his former custodians; but until the permanency of his rule is assured, all intercourse with Affghanistan must remain in abeyance.

THE CIVIL SERVICE.

For a considerable number of years after the East-India Company had acquired large territorial possessions in India, the gentlemen sent out to fill the various civil offices of the government were selected without any peculiar references to qualification. A writership was considered a provision for life, if not a source of large ultimate fortune; for if the salary was not liberal, the opportunities of gain, by means of trade and other less honourable proceedings, were numerous; while a knowledge of languages and of official business would, it was considered, be acquired in due course of time. The evil working of this loose system, however, at all times partially obvious, was the more apparent as the demand for talent augmented, and rigid integrity and an independence of native connection became a *sine quâ non* of good government. It was then that the Company began to devise plans of home education, for parties aspiring to serve them in the civil departments abroad. Character, connections, and a certain stock of knowledge, were declared the essential concomitants of a writership, though merely preparative to other qualifications, of which the candidate was to possess himself in India. This declaration was a material step towards the improvement of the service; but it was not until the year 1809, when the college of Haileybury, in Hertford, was founded, that the education of the future civilian resolved itself into a system, the adherence to which has since been uniform. With the rare exceptions of young men who have earned much distinction at some of the great public schools or colleges, and who are honoured with presentations of Indian appointments by Presidents of the Board of Control, or Chairmen of the Direction, who are more anxious to promote individual merit than to dispense their patronage to friends and family connections, the civil officers in the service of the East-India Company receive instruction at the Haileybury College, the nomination to which is dependent upon the following regulations and preparatory instructions.

NOMINATION OF STUDENTS.

Regulations and Preparatory Instructions.

No candidate for the college can be nominated thereto until he has completed the sixteenth year of his age. And no person who has been dismissed from the army or navy, or expelled from any place of education, will be nominated to the college.

The parents or guardian of every candidate for the college will be required to address the following letter to the nominating Director :—

Sir :—I beg to assure you, on my honour, that my ————, to whom you have been so good as to give a nomination to the college, has not been dismissed from the army or the navy, and that he never has been expelled from any place of education.

I have the honour to be, &c.

Candidates for the college must produce the undermentioned documents, previously to their being nominated as students:

An extract from the parish register of their birth or baptism, properly signed by the minister, churchwardens, or elders; and, in addition thereto,

A certificate, agreeably to the following form, signed by the parent, guardian, or near relation:

I do hereby certify, that the foregoing extract from the register of baptisms of the parish of ———, in the county of ———, contains the date of the birth of my ———, who is the bearer of this, and presented for a nomination as a student at the East-India College, by ———, Esq.; and I do further declare, that I received the said presentation for my ——— gratuitously, and that no money or other valuable consideration has been or is to be paid, either directly or indirectly, for the same, and that I will not pay or cause to be paid, either by myself, by my —, or by the hands of any other person, any pecuniary or valuable consideration whatsoever, to any person or persons who have interested themselves in procuring the said presentation for my ——, from the Director above mentioned.

Witness my hand, this ——— day of ——,
in the year of our Lord ——.

In the event of no parish register existing or to be found, a declaration of such circumstance is to be made before a magistrate to the following effect, viz.

I, ———, presented as a student for the East-India College by ———, do declare, that I have caused search to be made for a parish register whereby to ascertain my age, but am unable to produce the same, there being none to be found; and, further, I declare, that from the information of my parents (and other relations), which information I verily believe to be true, that I was born in the parish of ———, in the county of ———, on ———, in the year ———, and that I am not at this time under the age of sixteen, or above twenty-one years.

Witness my hand, this —— day of ——,
in the year of our Lord ——.

The parent, guardian, or near relation, must then add his certificate as to the truth of the declaration, which must be similar to that ordered to be annexed to the extract from the parish register.

The above-mentioned certificate (and declaration, in cases where a declaration shall be required) are to be annexed to the petition to be written by the candidate, and they are to sign a declaration thereon, that they have read these printed instructions. The same declaration is to be signed by the parent, guardian, or near relation of the candidates respectively.

Candidates will be interrogated in an open committee as to their character, connections, and qualifications, conformably to the General Court's resolution of the 6th July, 1809. The nature of this interrogation may be known on application to the clerk of the college department. And the following rules and regulations are to be observed with respect to the examination of candidates:

Each candidate shall produce testimonials of good moral conduct, under the hand of the principal or superior authority of the college or public institution in which he may have been educated, or under the hand of the private instructor to whose care he may have been confided; and the said testimonials shall have reference to his conduct during the two years immediately preceding his presentation for admission.

Each candidate shall be examined in the four gospels of the Greek Testament, and shall not be deemed duly qualified for admission to Haileybury College, unless he be found to possess a competent knowledge thereof; nor unless he be able to render into English some portion of the works of one of the following Greek authors:—Homer, Herodotus, Xenophon, Thucydides, Sophocles, and Euripides; nor unless he can render into English some portion of the works of one of the following Latin authors: —Livy, Terence, Cicero, Tacitus, Virgil, and Horace; and this part of the examination will include questions in ancient history, geography, and philosophy.

Each candidate shall also be examined in modern history and geography, and in the elements of mathematical science, including the common rules of arithmetic, vulgar and decimal fractions, and the first four books of Euclid. He shall also be examined in moral philosophy, and in the evidences of the Christian religion as set forth in the works of Paley.

It is, however, to be understood, that superior attainments in one of the departments of literature or science, comprised in the foregoing plan of examination, shall, at the discretion of the examiners, be considered to compensate for comparative deficiency in other qualifications; and also that the examination shall be so conducted as to give to each candidate reasonable time to prepare himself for the said examination.

A student publicly expelled the college will not be admitted into the Company's civil or military service in India, or into the Company's Military Seminary.

No person can be appointed a writer in the Company's service whose age is less than eighteen or more than twenty-three years, nor until he shall have resided four terms, at least, in the college, and shall have obtained a certificate, signed by the Principal, of his having conformed himself to the statutes and regulations of the college.

On a student's appointment to be a writer, after he has left the college, a legal instrument is to be entered into by some one person (to be approved by the Court of Directors), binding himself to pay the sum of £3,000, as liquidated damages, to the Company, for breach of a covenant to be entered into, that the student's nomination hath not been in any way bought, or sold, or exchanged for any thing convertible into a pecuniary benefit.

The rank of students leaving the college is determined by the certificate of the Principal, which is granted with reference to the industry, proficiency, and general good behaviour of the student.

Such rank to take effect only in the event of the students proceeding to India within six months after they are so ranked.

TERMS OF ADMISSION FOR STUDENTS.

One hundred guineas per annum for each student, a moiety whereof to be paid at the commencement of each term, there being two in the year, besides the expense of books and stationery.

Students to provide themselves with a table-spoon, tea-spoon, knife and fork, half-a-dozen towels, tea-equipage, and a looking-glass; also, with not less than two pair of sheets, two pillow-cases, and two breakfast-cloths.

Ten guineas to be paid on leaving college by each student for the use of the philosophical apparatus and library.

COLLEGE TERMS.

First commences 19th January, and ends 30th June } in each year.
Second commences 10th Sept., and ends 15th Dec. }

The days for receiving petitions at the East-India House from candidates for admission into the college, are the two Wednesdays immediately preceding the 10th January and 1st September in each year.

N.B. *The students are to provide themselves with proper academical habits.*

The terms comprise instruction in the classics, mathematics, history, political economy, and law; and in the Hindee, Hindoostanee, Mahratta, Arabic, Persian, Sanscrit, and Teloogoo languages. Prizes, medals, and other honourable distinctions, are conferred on the students at the examinations, especially when they are leaving college to proceed to India. On the arrival of a writer at either of the presidencies, he is allowed a twelvemonth to master one of the languages principally required in the transaction of public business. During this interval he draws the unemployed salary of three hundred rupees per mensem, and a small sum for a moonshee. When the period allotted, or supposed to be allotted, to special Oriental studies has expired, the student presents himself to a local board of examination. If he passes with tolerable credit, he is pronounced qualified for the public service, and is at once "attached," in a subordinate capacity, to the establishment of a judge, a collector, or a magistrate, or, in remarkable instances of *great interest*, to the *secrétariat*, customs, or accountant-general's department, at the presidency to which he may be nominated. Should the candidate, however, fail to obtain a certificate of qualification from the examiners; in other words, should he, through natural incapacity or indolence, be unsuccessful in displaying the requisite amount of Oriental learning, he is sent back to his studies for six weeks, at the end of which period he must either establish the possession of the requisite qualifications, or he is shipped to England, as a hopeless subject, and deprived of his appointment in the Company's service.

When we consider the immense extent of the territorial dependencies of the East-India Company, and the circumstances of the vast population by which they are occupied, it is not difficult to conjecture that the civil officer who desires to acquire honour for himself and his masters, and to make his native fellow-subjects participate in the blessings of good government, has an awful and an arduous task imposed upon him. He has frequently to exercise authority over a district comprising an area not inferior in extent to three or four of the largest provinces in Great Britain (in some instances a space as large as the whole of Ireland has been under the control of one man); and as he has only two or three European assistants, and a body of native functionaries—on the trustworthiness and activity of which latter, by the way, no reliance whatever can be placed—his heavy responsibility and severe labour may be tolerably well understood. It is true that he has his head-quarters at some central station, whither suitors, land-rent payers, applicants for redress, &c., repair in crowds; but the importance of personal investigation into the affairs of a district begets the necessity for locomotion, and as India does not as yet, offer the same facilities for rapidity of movement as Great Britain or the United States, the judge, magistrate, or collector, is compelled periodically to travel dawk into remote, and often unhealthy, parts of the country; living in tents, and regaling on such fare as the neighbouring villages can supply, or he may have been enabled to transport from his permanent domicile.

But the civil service has its *agrémens* as well as its inconveniences. The salaries are large, varying from £500 to £10,000 per annum; and the furlough allowance and retiring annuity handsome and all sufficient. The leading civilian is the acknowledged head of the society of whatever place he may be stationed at, while the juniors are regarded, as much from their position as their generally superior attainments, with deference and respect. The sports and pastimes peculiar to the country (hunting, shooting, racing, &c.) are accessible to him upon a scale of magnificence and affluence unknown to the English sportsman, who ranges the fields with his gun and a brace of pointers, and seeks no nobler game than the partridge or the hare. If he is in the political line, occupying the office of resident at a native court, he holds a position neither less honourable, less responsible, nor less associated with the elegancies of life (rendered accessible by his large salary), than a British ambassador on the continent of Europe. In this, and indeed in all the other offices of trust, he acquires a fitness for serious avocations elsewhere; and this capacity, supported by the renown he has earned, frequently recommends him for responsible offices upon his return to England.* But of all the advantages of the position of the civilian, none are so enviable as the opportunities afforded him of spreading happiness amongst the thousands of human beings placed under his protection. Through his instrumentality, the cause of education, and, therefore, of Christian enlightenment, may be advanced—his charities, judiciously dispensed, will save myriads from starvation—and the encouragement he has it in his power to give to the labourer by building bridges, constructing roads, and draining lands, will confer the blessing of employment upon the industriously disposed, while it gives an impulse to the internal commerce of the country, and diffuses health in regions of disease.

A vague allusion has been made above to the furlough and retiring advantages of the civil service. A more particular description of them seems called for. At each presidency there are funds to which civilians contribute a per-centage upon their salaries, and other public emoluments, to entitle them to retire after twenty-two years' actual service in India, upon an annuity of £1000. Should they be compelled

* The appointment of Sir C. Metcalfe to the government, successively, of Jamaica and Canada, is one of the best illustrations of the fact.

by ill-health to quit the service before the expiry of that period, they receive lesser sums, 250*l.* per annum for more than ten and less than fifteen years' service; £500 for upwards of fifteen years, and less than the full regulated period. And if sickness drives them permanently to England before they have even completed ten years' service, they are paid a donation of £500. After ten years' service, a civilian is allowed a furlough to Europe for three years, receiving, during that interval, 500*l.* per annum—always supposing that the number of gentlemen who may avail themselves of the privilege does not exceed a prescribed limit (seventeen annually from Bengal, nine from Madras, six from Bombay); but should he be obliged to seek a restoration to health before the expiry of the specified period, he then receives only £250 per annum, and £200 on account of passage-money.

In addition to these provisions, all of which, it should be remembered, are accompanied by conditions duly set forth in sundry codes of regulations, there are funds which particularly provide for the widows and children of deceased civil functionaries, upon a scale sufficiently liberal to remove all scruples concerning settlements from the minds of hesitating spinsters, in the first instance, and to relieve husbands and fathers from any anxiety upon the subject of their widows and orphans, in the second.

In conclusion, it may be mentioned, that any civil servant who, on proceeding to England on leave of absence, shall fail to return to India before the expiry of five years, is disqualified for further service, unless it be found that such continued absence was the result of sickness or infirmity, or unless his return is sanctioned by a vote or resolution passed at a meeting of the Proprietors of East-India Stock.

Another circumstance which involves the penalty of dismissal at any period during the service of a civil officer is, the discovery that his appointment in the first instance was obtained by any pecuniary or other corrupt arrangement with the party in whom the presentation lay. The only exception to the penalty is, the free and voluntary disclosure of the transaction when a Director of the Company has been implicated therein.

THE ARMY.

It has been contended of late years, by some public writers, that we hold India entirely by the force of opinion; that is to say, that we are permitted to rule simply because the principles of justice and equity, and a respect for the religious usages of the thousands under our sway, are carried out to the fullest extent compatible with human frailty. On the other hand, it has been argued that our empire is held entirely by the sword; and our wars, victories, and their political results, have been pointed at as evidence of the soundness of the theory. Truth lies, in most cases, between extremes, and there seems little reason to doubt that such is its proper position in the present instance. The highest opinion that might be entertained of our character as governors, would of itself, we apprehend, avail but little in the retention of the country against the schemes of disaffected or designing men, if it were not backed by a well-organized and judiciously-distributed physical force. If there were no descendants of the countless chieftains who once held possession of the country, eager, upon any pretext supported by opportunity, to assert fanciful claims to territory or to privileges; if there were no frontier foes, whose incursions it were necessary to resist or prevent, as much for the sake of the peace and happiness of the people as for the maintenance of British supremacy; there would still be evil powers within the heart of the empire against whose machinations the greatest amount of political integrity could not successfully contend. The Hindoo and the Mussulman are priest-ridden; the Hindoo and the Mussulman are alike avaricious. What elements more potent than priestcraft and avarice to excite a populace to rebellion? While the Zemindar's disinclination to pay his rent ignited the spark of insurrection, on the one hand, there would not be wanting the ambition and the self-interest of the Brahmin, and the savage religious fervour of the Moollah, to fan the flame, upon the other. The sword, therefore, is an indispensable agent in the retention of India; and it is a happy thing for the populace of that empire, that the mercy and humanity which distinguish the administration of the civil government attemper the steel by which the sedition of the disaffected and the incursion of the foreign foe are invariably chastised.

A rough statement has been given above of the strength of the armies of the several presidencies. A more precise estimate is essential in a work of this description.

THE INDIAN ARMY—the most remarkable phenomenon in the history of the world, since conquerors thought of making the vanquished the means of their own perpetual subjugation—consists, in round numbers, of two hundred and fifty thousand men, of all arms, thus divided:—

Regiments in her Majesty's service, lent to the East-India Company, infantry and light dragoons, comprising (men and officers)	20,000
BENGAL PRESIDENCY—	
Three brigades of horse artillery	1,100
Seven battalions of foot ditto	2,250
Ten regiments of native cavalry	5,150
Two regiments of European infantry	1,900
Seventy-four regiments of native infantry (sepoys)	88,600
Sappers and miners, and engineer officers	890
Surgeons	120
Assistant surgeons	230
Veterinary surgeons	18
Native doctors	222
Ordnance and commissariat warrant officers	46
MADRAS—	
One brigade of horse artillery	400
Four battalions of foot ditto	1,420
Eight regiments of native cavalry	4,160
Two regiments of European infantry	1,800
Fifty-two regiments of native ditto	44,200
Engineers and sappers	500
Surgeons	73
Assistant surgeons	160
Veterinary surgeons	10
BOMBAY—	
One brigade of horse artillery	400
Two battalions of foot ditto	750
Three regiments of native cavalry	1,500
Two regiments of European infantry	1,800
Twenty-six regiments of native ditto	30,000
Engineers and sappers	400

Surgeons	50
Assistant Surgeons	105
Veterinary ditto	6

The remainder of the army consists of irregular and local corps, body guards, militia, &c., officered from the line, and amounting to some forty thousand men. There is a considerable body, also, of invalids and veterans, but as they cannot, in fairness, be included in the physical strength of the government, there is no necessity for taking particular account of them.

Out of the two hundred and fifty thousand men who compose the East-India Company's troops in India, not more than four thousand eight hundred and thirty are European officers; and of this number at least seven hundred are generally absent on furlough, and a great many are on the staff, or in charge of local corps, or otherwise employed. The proportion of regimental effective officers is therefore extremely small; and although they are aided in the ordinary routine duties of a garrison by the native commissioned officers, and experience little trouble in managing the happy and tractable sepoy in cantonments, their numerical deficiency has exposed armies to serious risks in the field, where the example of European intrepidity has been of the last consequence in rallying native troops at a critical juncture. In the very last pitched battle fought in India, it was remarked by the commander of the forces engaged (Sir C. Napier), that the fall of a European officer was invariably the signal for sepoy-faltering, and that if others had not been at hand to at once supply the place of the stricken leaders, the action must have had a different and far less glorious termination.

The emoluments of the officers of the Indian Army doing regimental duty are accurately set forth in the annexed table:—

TABLE OF PAY AND ALLOWANCES, FOR A MONTH OF 30 DAYS.

	In Garrison or Cantonment.							In the Field.					
	Pay.	Gratuity.	Tent Allowance.	House Rent, if only in Receipt of Half Batta, and not provided with Quarters.	Horse Allowance.	Half Batta.	TOTAL.	Pay.	Gratuity.	Tent Allowance.	Horse Allowance.	Full Batta.	TOTAL.
	Rs. a. p.	Rs.	Rs. a.	Rs.	Rs.	*a* Rs.	Rs. a. p.	Rs. a. p.	Rs.	Rs.	Rs.	Rs.	Rs. a. p.
European Infantry.													
Colonel, not a general officer on the staff ...	*a*300 0 0	—	100 0	—	*d*30	*c*750	1180 0 0	*a*300 0 0	—	200	*d*30	*a*750	1280 0 0
Lieutenant-colonel ...	240 0 0	—	75 0	100	30	300	745 0 0	240 0 0	—	150	30	600	1020 0 0
Major	180 0 0	—	60 0	80	30	225	575 0 0	180 0 0	—	120	30	450	780 0 0
Captain	120 0 0	36	37 8	50	—	90	333 8 0	120 0 0	36	75	—	180	411 0 0
Lieutenant	60 0 0	24	25 0	30	—	60	199 0 0	60 0 0	24	50	—	120	254 0 0
Ensign	48 0 0	12	25 0	25	—	45	155 0 0	48 0 0	12	50	—	90	200 0 0
Surgeon, as captain ...	—	—	—	—	—	—	333 8 0	—	—	—	—	—	411 0 0
Assistant-surgeon, as lieutenant	—	—	—	—	—	—	199 0 0	—	—	—	—	—	254 0 0
European Artillery.													
Colonel of a battalion ...	300 0 0	—	100 0	—	30	*c*750	1180 0 0	300 0 0	—	200	30	750	1280 0 0
Lieutenant-colonel ...	240 0 0	—	75 0	100	30	300	745 0 0	240 0 0	—	150	30	600	1020 0 0
Major	180 0 0	—	60 0	80	30	225	575 0 0	180 0 0	—	120	30	450	780 0 0
Captain	*b*140 0 0	36	37 8	50	—	90	353 8 0	*b*140 0 0	36	75	—	180	431 0 0
1st lieutenant	*b* 70 0 0	24	25 0	30	—	60	209 0 0	*b* 70 0 0	24	50	—	120	264 0 0
2nd lieutenant ...	*b* 60 0 0	12	25 0	25	—	45	167 0 0	*b* 60 0 0	12	50	—	90	212 0 0
Surgeon and assistant-surgeon	As in the European Infantry.												
Engineers (the same as the Artillery.)													

Native Cavalry.													
Colonel	b397 8 0	—	200 0	—	120	c750	1467 8 0	b397 8 0	—	200	120	750	1467 8 0
Lieutenant-colonel ...	b278 4 0	—	150 0	100	120	300	948 4 0	b278 4 0	—	150	120	600	1148 4 0
Major	b232 13 4	—	120 0	80	120	225	777 13 4	b232 13 4	—	120	120	450	922 13 4
Captain	b179 6 4	36	75 0	50	90	90	520 6 4	b179 6 4	36	75	90	180	560 6 4
Lieutenant	b109 8 0	24	50 0	30	60	60	333 8 0	b109 8 0	24	50	60	120	363 8 0
Cornet...	b 97 5 4	12	50 0	25	60	45	289 5 4	b 97 5 4	12	50	60	90	309 5 4
Surgeon, as captain ...	—	—	—	—	—	—	520 6 4	—	—	—	—	—	560 6 4
Assistant-surgeon, as lieutenant	—	—	—	—	—	—	333 8 0	—	—	—	—	—	363 8 0
Veterinary surgeon ...	—	—	—	—	—	—	—	97 0 0	24	50	48	122	341 0 0
Native Infantry.													
Colonel, not a general officer on the staff ...	300 0 0	—	200 0	—	30	c750	1280 0 0	300 0 0	—	200	30	750	1280 0 0
Lieutenant-colonel ...	240 0 0	—	150 0	100	30	300	820 0 0	240 0 0	—	150	30	600	1020 0 0
Major	180 0 0	—	120 0	80	30	225	635 0 0	180 0 0	—	120	30	450	780 0 0
Captain	120 0 0	36	75 0	50	—	90	371 0 0	120 0 0	36	75	—	180	411 0 0
Lieutenant	60 0 0	24	50 0	30	—	60	224 0 0	60 0 0	24	50	—	120	254 0 0
Ensign	48 0 0	12	50 0	25	—	45	180 0 0	48 0 0	12	50	—	90	200 0 0
Surgeon, as captain ...	—	—	—	—	—	—	371 0 0	—	—	—	—	—	411 0 0
Assistant-surgeon, as lieutenant	—	—	—	—	—	—	224 0 0	—	—	—	—	—	254 0 0

(*a*) Pay and Batta are per diem allowances. (*b*) The same for any month.

(*c*) Colonels in Regimental Rank are allowed full Batta at any Station.

(*d*) Horse Allowance only granted to Field Officers of Artillery, Engineers, and Infantry, while in the actual performance of Regimental Duty. Officers of inferior rank, when actually commanding Corps of Infantry, will continue to draw Horse Allowance, as heretofore sanctioned.

N.B. Tent Allowance is not allowed to the Chief Engineer, or Adjutant of Engineers.

Situations on the general staff, to which officers are eligible after four years of actual service in India, and a passage through the ordeal of an examination in one of the native languages, are handsomely endowed, the salaries varying from two thousand to forty thousand rupees (£4,000) per annum; the incumbent, however, in some cases relinquishing a proportion of his regimental emoluments. In former times, and especially upon the settlement of a newly-conquered country, military men were frequently selected to fill the important civil offices of revenue collectors, magistrates, superintendents of police, political agents, &c., but the very natural jealousy of the civil servants, and the demand for the professional services of soldiers, caused the selection to be discontinued as a system. The government, however, still finds it necessary to avail itself of the aid of military officers in the civil branch, more particularly in the departments of police, in tracts of country recently evacuated by regular troops. But apart from these offices, the staff provides honourable and lucrative employment in a variety of ways. The departments of the adjutant, auditor, quartermaster, surveyor, paymaster, judge-advocate, and commissary general; the offices of brigade-major, aide-de-camp, barrackmaster, secretary to the military board, clothing agent, superintendent of studs, &c., are all filled by officers withdrawn from regimental duty; and it is very rare (excepting in instances of field service, when every officer is required to join his corps), that the appointment passes from the hands of the fortunate possessor until his promotion to exalted regimental rank disqualifies him for a subordinate occupation on the staff.

To narrate the achievements of the army of India, from the hour when mere handfuls garrisoned the factories on the Coromandel coast two centuries ago, down to the time when China humbled herself to the British crown and Sinde became a part of our dominions, were to fill volumes historically descriptive of the rise and progress of the British empire in the East. The task must therefore be abandoned, that our available space may be devoted to the more immediate purpose of representing things as they are. It is sufficient to record, that the army has attained, with the gradual augmentation of its strength, the highest point of military discipline and efficiency; that the sepoy has uniformly, and under the most trying circumstances, proved faithful to his salt; and that never, even when assailed by countless numbers of foes at various points, has the British flag been tarnished, excepting when treachery conspired with inclemency of climate to render a retiring force helpless, and therefore an easy prey to the murderous assaults of masses of savage, determined, and rapacious enemies.

For the guidance of all candidates for military service in India, under the auspices of the East-India Company, we here transcribe such rules and regulations as may at once aid them in obtaining admission into the army, and of acquiring a knowledge of some of the conditions and advantages of their future profession. It should be premised, that for the infantry and cavalry branches of the service, education at the Military College is not indispensable, though it is very advantageous; while, for the artillery and engineers, it is a condition of the presentation of a cadetship that the candidate should have gone through a regular course of instruction at Addiscombe.

(*By a Resolution of the Court of Directors of the* 16*th January,* 1828, *all Cadets at the Military Seminary, and all subsequent nominations thereto, are deemed for general Service until brought forward for public examination.*).

TERMS OF ADMISSION.

Conditions and Qualifications for a Candidate.

1. No candidate can be admitted under the age of fourteen, or above the age of eighteen years.

2. Every candidate must produce a certificate of his birth taken from the parish register, and signed by the minister, and countersigned by the churchwardens; or, if born in Scotland, by the sessions' clerk and two elders, accompanied by a declaration from his father, mother, or nearest of kin, the forms of which may be had in the military department. In the event of there being no register of his birth or baptism, the candidate will be furnished with the form of a declaration to be taken by him previously to his being appointed.

3. No candidate will be admitted without a certificate that he has had the small-pox, or has been vaccinated; nor without a certificate, in the prescribed form, to be given by two practising surgeons, that he has no mental or bodily defect whatever to disqualify him for military service.

4. Every candidate must produce a certificate of good conduct from the master under whom he has last studied.

5. Every candidate must deliver the names and addresses of two persons residing in London, or its vicinity, who engage to receive him if he shall be dismissed from the seminary, or removed from sickness or any other cause.

6. It is an indispensable qualification that the candidate write a good legible hand. He will be required to write down a sentence from dictation by the head master; and if he should be found deficient in his handwriting, or in his orthography, his reception into the institution will be deferred for such length of time as the head master shall report to be necessary.

7. No candidate will be admitted who cannot read and construe Cæsar's Commentaries, and who is not expert in vulgar and decimal fractions.

8. Every cadet upon his admission is considered a *Probationary* pupil for the first six months; at the end of which period the public examiner will be required to report to the military committee, on the probability of the cadet being able to pass for the artillery or infantry in the required period of four Terms. Should this appear improbable, either from want of talent or diligence, the cadet will then be returned to his friends.

PAYMENTS, &c.—1. The parents or guardians of the gentleman cadet are required to pay 50*l.* per term· towards defraying the expense of his board, lodging, and education; also an entrance subscription of 2*l.* 2*s.* to the public library; which payments include every charge except for uniform clothes, books, and pocket-money, as hereafter specified.

2. Such articles of uniform dress* as may be considered by the military committee to be necessary, shall be provided at the cost of the cadet. The amount of pocket-money issued to him at the rates† fixed by the rules of the seminary is also to be defrayed by his parents or guardians.

3. The following class-books will be provided at the public expense, the mutilation or destruction of which to be chargeable to the cadets, viz.:

Hindustani Dictionary
Latin do.
Woodhouse's Spherical Trigonometry
Inman's Nautical Astronomy
Do. Nautical Tables.

4. The cadets will, on their first joining Addiscombe, be supplied with the following books, the cost of which will be charged to their parents or guardians, viz.:

Cape's Mathematics
Straith's Treatise on Fortification
Hindustani Grammar
First Vol. Hindoo Selections
Fielding's Perspective
French Grammar
Do. Dictionary
De la Voye's French Instructions
Cæsar's Commentaries
Jackson's Military Surveying

Any books not included in the above enumeration, or which may be hereafter required at the seminary, to be paid for by the cadets.

* Viz.: Jackets, waistcoats, stocks, foraging-caps, trousers, shoes, gloves, together with a proportionate share of the expense of any other periodical supplies, and the repairs of the same. The average cost is £6. 6*s*. per term.

† Viz.: 2*s*. 6*d*. a week, with 1*s*. additional to censors, and 2*s*. 6*d*. additional to corporals.

5. A cadet entering in a term, at whatever part of it, must pay the regulated sum for the whole term in which he enters, which will count as one of the four terms of his residence; and no return of any portion of the advance will be made in the event of a cadet's quitting the seminary.

6. Previous to the cadet's admission, his parents or guardians shall furnish him with the following articles, viz.:

Twelve shirts (including three night-shirts), eight pairs of cotton stockings, six pairs of worsted ditto, six towels, six night-caps, eight pocket-handkerchiefs, one pair of white trowsers (to be repaired, or, if necessary, to be renewed by the parents or guardians at the vacation), two combs and a brush, a tooth-brush, a bible and prayer-book, a case of mathematical instruments of an approved pattern, to be seen at Messrs. Troughton & Sims, 136, Fleet-street; Mr. Gilbert, 138, Fenchurch-street; Messrs. Reeves & Sons, 150, Cheapside; and at Mr. Jones's, 62, Charing Cross.

7. The payment of the fixed charges for each term is to be made in advance; and the payment for clothes, pocket-money, and books for the preceding term, is to be made previous to the cadet's return to the seminary.

PROHIBITION.—The cadet must not join the seminary with a greater sum in his possession than one guinea; and a further supply from any of his relations during the term may subject him to dismission from the seminary.

VACATIONS.—Midsummer commences about the middle of June, and ends 31st July.

Christmas commences about the middle of December, and ends 31st January.

At the close of every vacation, the cadet must apply at the Cadet Department, Military Office, East-India House, for an order for his re-admission, and all sums then due to the Company must be paid up. This order will express that he is only to be re-admitted upon his returning with the same number of books and instruments which he took home with him, that his linen is put into proper repair, and that he is in a fit state of health to renew his studies.

Notice to Parents and Guardians.

The friends of every cadet are hereby informed, that provision being made for furnishing him with every requisite, he cannot really want a supply of money to be placed at his disposal while at the seminary; and if they do, notwithstanding, think proper to furnish him with money, they put it in his power to commit irregularities, which must always retard his studies, and may eventually lead to his removal from the institution.

The parents and friends are further particularly desired not to attend to any application from the cadet for money, under the pretence of his having incurred any debts at Croydon, or elsewhere, or for the purpose of subscribing to public charities, or any other pretence whatever.

It having become known that cadets have been in the habit of writing to their friends for money, under the pretence that there were so many stoppages from their weekly allowance that they had scarcely any money left, the Committee have ascertained that these stoppages have arisen, not only from wilful and wanton destruction of public property, but in a considerable degree from the postage of letters, and the carriage of parcels addressed to the cadets. It has in consequence been ordered, that no letter or parcel shall be admitted into the seminary unless the postage or carriage of such letter or parcel shall have been previously fully paid for by the person sending the same. It has also been ordered that every parcel shall be opened in the presence of one of the orderly officers and the cadet to whom it is sent; that should it contain wine, or any thing prohibited by the regulations, the parcel, upon the first offence, will be returned to the person sending the same; and that upon the second offence, the cadet will be ordered home, and will not be re-admitted until a written apology has been sent to the Committee by the person who has committed a breach of this regulation.

Extract from the Standing Regulations of the Seminary, Sec. 1, *Clause* 1.

"No professor, master, or other person in the institution, shall receive from the cadet, or the parents or friends of any cadet, any pecuniary present or consideration, on any pretence whatever."

Extract Resolution of Court of 12*th March*, 1823, *and Military Letter to Bengal, dated* 30*th of August*, 1826.

"That all persons nominated in future as cadets, be required, as a condition to their appointment, to subscribe to the military funds of their respective presidencies."

MEMORANDA.

The gentlemen cadets educated at the Military Seminary are eligible for the corps of engineers, artillery, and infantry. Admission to the two first of these branches, viz. the engineers and artillery, is only to be obtained by these cadets, none others being eligible. Those who are most distinguished are selected for the engineers, according to the vacancies in that branch. Those immediately following in order of succession, are promoted to the corps of horse and foot artillery.

Those cadets for whom there is no room in the engineers, but who are reported to have attained to a high degree of qualification, receive honorary certificates, and their names are announced to the governments in India, and published in general orders to the army, as meriting particular notice. They have the privilege of choosing the presidency in India to which they shall be stationed. The cadets not appointed to the engineers or artillery, are, when reported qualified, posted to the infantry, and rank together according to the rank which they obtained at the seminary.

The gentlemen cadets may pass through the seminary as rapidly as their attainments and qualifications will enable them to pass after a year's residence, provided that they are of the age of sixteen years on or before the day of their final examination. Their stay at the institution is limited to four terms.

The cadets educated at this institution take rank in the army above all other cadets who are appointed from the commencement of three months previously to the date of the seminary-cadets being reported qualified; and all the time passed by them at the institution after they attain the age of sixteen, counts as so much time passed in India in calculating their period of service for retiring pensions on full pay.

ASSISTANT-SURGEONS.

Regulations for their Admission into the Company's Service.

AGE.—The assistant-surgeon must not be under twenty-two years, in proof of which he must produce an extract from the register of the parish in which he was born, or his own declaration, pursuant to the Act of the 5th and 6th Gulielmi IV., cap. 62, and other certificates, agreeably to forms to be obtained in the office for cadets and assistant-surgeons.

QUALIFICATION IN SURGERY.—The assistant-surgeon, upon receiving a nomination, will be furnished with a letter to the Court of Examiners of the Royal College of Surgeons, to be examined in Surgery, and their certificate will be deemed a satisfactory testimonial of his qualification: but should the assistant-surgeon be previously in possession of a diploma from the Royal College of Surgeons of London, or of the Colleges of Surgeons of Dublin or Edinburgh, or of the College and University of Glasgow, or of the Faculty of Physicians and Surgeons of Glasgow, either of them will be deemed satisfactory as to his knowledge of Surgery, without any further examination.

QUALIFICATION IN PHYSIC.—The assistant-surgeon will also be required to pass an examination by the Company's examining physician in the practice of physic, in which examination will be included as much anatomy and physiology as is necessary for understanding the causes and treatment of internal diseases, as well as the art of prescribing and compounding medicines; and Dr. Hume will then require him to produce satisfactory proof of his having attended at least two courses of lectures on the practice of physic; and above all, that he should produce a certificate of having attended diligently the practice of the physicians at some general *hospital* in London for six months; or at some general hospital in the country (within the United Kingdom) for six months, provided such provincial hospital contain at least, on an average, one hundred in-patients, and have attached to it a regular establishment of physicians as well as surgeons. No attendance on the practice of a physician at any *Dispensary* will be admitted.

The assistant-surgeon is also required, as a condition to his appointment, to subscribe to the military or medical and medical retiring fund at his respective presidency.

The assistant-surgeon is required, by resolution of Court of the 21st of May, 1828, to apply at the cadet-office for his order for embarkation, and actually proceed under such orders within three months from the date of being passed and sworn before the Military Committee; he will then be furnished with an order to obtain the certificate of his appointment, signed by the secretary, for which he will pay a fee of £5 in the secretary's office.

CAVALRY OR INFANTRY CADETS.

Cadets nominated for either of the above corps must be sixteen years of age, and under twenty-two, unless they have held a commission in her Majesty's service for one year, or in the militia or fencibles when embodied and have been called into actual service, or from the company of cadets in the royal regiment of artillery, they are then eligible if not more than twenty-five years of age; and they must procure similar certificates and vouchers to those prescribed for cadets entering the seminary.

No person who has been dismissed the army or navy, the Royal Military College at Sandhurst, the Royal Military Academy at Woolwich, or who has been obliged to retire from any public institution for immoral or ungentlemanly conduct, will be appointed a cadet direct for India.

No person will be appointed a cadet direct for India, without producing to the Military Committee a certificate, signed by two practising surgeons, that he has no mental or bodily defect whatever to disqualify him for military service.

CADETS AND ASSISTANT-SURGEONS.

At a Court of Directors, held on Friday, the 27th Feb. 1818—Resolved, that cadets and assistant-surgeons be in future ranked according to the seniority of the Directors nominating them, from the date of sailing of the several ships from Gravesend, by Lloyd's List; and that those who may embark at any of the outports be likewise ranked upon the same principle from the date of the ship's departure from such outports by Lloyd's List.

At a Court of Directors held 21st May, 1828:—Resolved, that all the cavalry and infantry cadets and assistant-surgeons who shall fail to apply at the Cadet Department for their orders for embarkation within three months from the date of their being passed and sworn before the committee, or shall not actually proceed under such orders, be considered as having forfeited their appointments, unless special circumstances shall justify the Court's departure from this regulation.

By a resolution of Court of the 4th Dec. 1833, all direct cadets appointed or sworn in between the 10th March and 10th June, or between 10th Sept. and 10th Dec. (or the days which may be fixed on for the public examination of the seminary cadets), do rank after the seminary cadets who may pass their said examinations, provided the latter sail for their respective destinations within *three* months after passing said examinations.

After five years' absence from India, on leave in the first instance, an officer, below the rank of colonel, is removed from the service, unless satisfactory proof be given that such protracted absence has arisen from sickness or infirmity, or some inevitable accident; and if it be proved at any time, during the service of an officer, that his original appointment was obtained by purchase, or any corrupt pretence whatever, on his own part or that of his friends. his commission is liable to be cancelled, and himself returned to England. A timely disclosure of the manner of such corruption is, however, accompanied by a remission of the penalty of indirect participation.

The following regulations respecting the retirement of officers from the service cannot be abridged.

OFFICERS RETIRING FROM SERVICE.

Regulations respecting Military and other Officers retiring from the Company's Service.

Officers who have served less than three years in India, and have lost their health there, are entitled to an allowance from Lord Clive's Fund, if the Court of Directors shall adjudge them to be proper objects of that bounty, to the extent of—

If a second lieutenant, cornet, or ensign, two shillings a day, or £36. 10*s*. a year; if a lieutenant, two shillings and sixpence a day, or £45. 12*s*. 6*d*. a year; provided they are not possessed of, or entitled to, real or personal property, to the extent of, if an ensign £750, if a lieutenant, £1,000.

Officers who are compelled to quit the service by wounds received in action, or by ill-health contracted on duty after three years' service in India, are permitted to retire on the half pay of their rank, viz.:

If a second lieutenant, cornet, or ensign, three shillings a day, or £54. 15*s*. per annum; if a lieutenant, four shillings a day, or £73. per annum.

A subaltern officer, or assistant-surgeon, having served six years in India, is permitted to retire on the *half pay of ensign*, if his constitution should be so impaired as to prevent the possibility of his continuing in India.

A lieutenant having served thirteen, or a second lieutenant, cornet, or ensign, nine years in India (including three years for a furlough), may retire on the *half pay* of his rank, in case his health shall not permit him to serve in India.

Regimental captains, majors, and lieutenant-colonels, who have not served sufficiently long in India to entitle them to retire on full pay, and whose ill state of health renders it impossible for them to continue to serve in India, are allowed to retire from the service on the half pay of their respective ranks, viz.:

Captains, seven shillings a day, or £127. 15*s.* per annum; major, nine shillings and sixpence a day, or £173. 7*s.* 6*d.* per annum; lieutenant-colonel, eleven shillings a-day, or £200. 15*s.* per annum.

All officers who have actually served twenty-two years in India, or twenty-five years (including three years for a furlough), are allowed to retire on the full pay of their respective ranks.

Officers are also allowed to retire on the following pensions without reference to the rank they may have attained, if they have served for the undermentioned periods, viz.:

After twenty-three years' service in India (including three years for a furlough), on the full pay of captain, viz. £191. 12*s.* 6*d.* per annum; after twenty-seven years' service in India (including three years for a furlough), on the full pay of major, £292. per annum; after thirty-one years' service in India (including three years for a furlough), on the full pay of a lieutenant-colonel, £365. per annum; after thirty-five years' service in India (including three years for a furlough), on the full pay of colonel, £456. 5*s.* per annum.

Members of the Medical Board, who have been in that station not less than two years, and not less than twenty years in India (including three years for one furlough), are permitted to retire from the service, and allowed £500 per annum; or, in the event of ill-health, they may retire on that pension, after any period of service as member of the Medical Board. If they have served *five* years, or are obliged, after three years' service in that station, to retire, from ill-health, they are allowed £700 per annum.

Superintending surgeons, who have been in that station not less than two years, and whose period of service have been not less than twenty years (including three years for one furlough), are permitted to retire from the service, and allowed £300 per annum; or in the event of ill-health, they may retire on that pension, after any period of service as superintending surgeon. If they have served five years, or are obliged, after three years' service in that station, to retire, from ill-health, they are allowed £365 per annum.

All other surgeons and assistant-surgeons attached to the military are permitted to retire from the service on the pay of their rank, after having served in India not less than twenty years (including three years for one furlough).

When officers on furlough retire upon the pay or half pay of their rank, they are only entitled to claim the benefit of the rank held by them at the expiration of one year from the date of their landing in the United Kingdom.

A veterinary surgeon is allowed to retire on seven shillings a day after twenty years' service (including three years for one furlough); five shillings and sixpence a day after thirteen years' service (including three years for one furlough); and three shillings a day after six years' service, in the two last cases, provided his health shall not permit him to continue to serve in India.

A chaplain (appointed previously to the 1st of September, 1836), after eighteen years' service in India, including three years for one furlough, is allowed to retire on the pay of lieutenant-colonel, £365 per annum; after ten years (if compelled by ill-health to quit the service), on the half pay of lieutenant-colonel, £200. 15*s.* per annum; after seven years, on the half pay of major, £173. 7*s.* 6*d.* per annum.

If appointed subsequently to that date, according to the following scale, viz. after eighteen years' service (including three years for one furlough), the pay of major, viz. £292 per annum; after ten years' service (if compelled by ill-health to quit the service), on the half pay of major, viz. £173. 7*s.* 6*d.* per annum; after seven years, the half pay of captain, viz. £127. 15*s.* per annum.

A commissary or deputy commissary of ordnance, not being a commissioned officer, is allowed to retire on full pay, if he has served twenty-seven years in India, of which twelve must have been in the ordnance department; twenty-five years, fourteen of which in that department; or twenty-two years, seventeen years of which in the ordnance department.

A conductor of stores is allowed to retire on £60

per annum, after twenty-five years' actual service in India.

Officers retiring from the service will be considered to have retired from the date of their application for leave to retire; or from the expiration of two years and a half from their quitting India, whichever shall happen first.

FURLOUGH REGULATIONS.

Officers (of whatever rank) must be ten years in India before they can be entitled (except in case of certified sickness, and as hereafter specified) to their rotation to be absent on furlough; and the same rule is applicable to assistant-surgeons and veterinary surgeons. The furlough to be granted by the commander-in-chief at each presidency, with the approbation of the respective governments.

Officers who have not served ten years in India, but whose presence in England is required by urgent private affairs, may be allowed a furlough for one year, without pay.

A chaplain (appointed previously to the 1st Sept. 1836), after seven years' residence in India, is allowed to come home on furlough and receive the pay of major, £292 per annum. Should he come home, from sickness, prior to this period of service, he is allowed the pay of captain only, viz. £191. 12*s.* 6*d.* per annum.

If appointed subsequently to that date, after seven years' residence in India, the pay of captain, viz. £191. 12*s.* per annum; and if compelled by ill-health to come home prior to this period of service, the half pay of captain, or £127. 15*s.* per annum.

A conductor of stores is allowed furlough pay only in case of coming home from sickness.

Officers coming to England on furlough, are required immediately to report their arrival by letter to the secretary, stating the name of the ship in which they came, and their address, forwarding, at the same time, the certificates they received in India.

The period of furlough is three years, reckoning from its date to the day of the return of the officer to his presidency.

Officers are required to join the establishment to which they belong at the expiration of the three years' furlough, unless they shall have obtained an extension of leave from the court, six months before the expiration of that period. No furlough will be extended, except in cases of sickness, certified in the manner hereafter mentioned; or in cases, in which it shall be proved to the court that a further residence in Europe is indispensably necessary.

All officers finding it necessary to solicit a further leave of absence on account of sickness, must, if resident in London or its vicinity, appear before the Company's examining physician, Dr. J. R. Hume, 9, Curzon-street, who will report to the Court of Directors his opinion on the state of such officer's health. And if resident in the country, in any part of the United Kingdom, they must transmit, with their letter of application for such leave, a certificate according to the following form, signed by at least two gentlemen, eminent in the medical profession, viz.:—

I hereby certify, that I have carefully examined (state the nature of the case as well as the name of the party), and I declare, upon my honour, that, according to the best of my judgment and belief,

——————— *is at present unfit for military duty, and that it is absolutely necessary, for the recovery of his health, that he should remain at least* ——————— *longer in this country.*

Also, previously to such extension of furlough being granted, such further proof shall be adduced by personal examination, or by such other evidence as shall be deemed satisfactory.

Officers abroad in any part of Europe, applying to remain a further time from their duty on account of sickness, are to furnish a certificate of two eminent physicians, *in the above form,* with the attestation of a magistrate, that the persons who signed the certificate are physicians.

Officers having obtained an extension of furlough to a given period, must, at its expiration, apply for permission, either to return to their duty or to reside a further time in England.

No officer who has failed to obtain an extension of furlough, will be considered eligible to return to the service after five years' absence, under the Act of 33 Geo. III. cap. 52, sect. 70.

Every officer upon leaving India will receive a printed copy of the general order on this subject, published agreeably to the court's instruction, and the plea of ignorance of the regulations will not be admitted as any justification of the breach of them; officers therefore, who shall come home on furlough and who shall not in due time apply, so as to effect their return to the presidency to which they belong within the period of three years from the commencement of their furlough, will subject themselves to the loss of the service, unless they shall be permitted by the court to remain a further time in Europe.

No officer on furlough can receive pay for more than two years and a half from the period of his quitting India until he returns, excepting colonels of regiments, and those of the rank of lieutenant-colonel regimentally, when promoted to that of major-general; the latter are then allowed to draw the pay of their brevet rank beyond the above period.

OFFICERS RETURNING TO INDIA.

Regulations as to the Charge of Recruits.

Whenever a detachment of Company's recruits, to the extent of thirty men, shall be embarked on any one ship, they be placed in charge of the senior Company's officer, not exceeding the rank of a field officer, who shall have obtained permission to return to his duty on the ship, within at least seven days of the period fixed for embarkation :—That the officer proceed with the men from the depôt; that, as a remuneration for this service, he be granted the passage-money of his rank, payable to the commander of the ship.

LORD CLIVE'S FUND.

Regulations for the Admission of Pensioners.

Every petitioning officer and soldier must produce a certificate from his commanding officer of his being an invalid, and rendered incapable of further service in India, together with an approbation of such certificate by the governor and council of the presidency where he shall have served.

Every commissioned officer must previously make oath before the governor and council, viz.: A colonel, that he is not possessed of, or entitled to, real and personal property to the value of £4,000. A lieut.-colonel, £3,000. A major, £2,500. A captain, £2,000. A lieutenant, £1,000. An ensign, £750. Officers' widows must produce proof, on affidavit, that their husbands did not die possessed of property as above.

Petitioners residing in England may be admitted if the Court shall adjudge them to be proper objects.

All commissioned, staff, or warrant officers, to have half the ordinary pay they enjoyed whilst in service, viz.

	Per ann.				Per day.	
Colonels	£228	2	6	or	12s.	6d.
Lieut. cols. and mem. med. board ..	182	10	0		10	0
Majors, senior chaplains, and sup. surgeons	136	17	0		7	6
Captains, chaplains, and surgeons ..	91	5	0		5	0
Lieutenants, and assistant surgeons ..	45	12	6		2	6
Ensigns	36	10	0		2	0
Conductors of ordnance	36	10	0		2	0

Their widows one-half the above, to continue during their widowhood.

Serjeants of artillery to have ninepence per day, and those that have lost a limb one shilling per day. Gunners of the artillery sixpence per day, and those that have lost a limb ninepence per day.

All other non-commissioned officers and bombadiers to have fourpence three farthings per day.

Officers and privates to be entitled from the period of their landing in England.

Pensioners neglecting to claim the pension for three half years will be considered as dead; and no arrears for a larger period than two years back from the date of application for admission or re-admission, as the case may be, will be allowed either to claimants or to pensioners after admission.

The foregoing comprise the advantages conferred by the Government upon their officers when unfitted temporarily or permanently for effective service. The provisions, however, were manifestly so insufficient, that several years ago, the officers of the different armies formed military, medical, and retiring funds of their own, contributing certain donations and monthly subscriptions, in view to benefits in the form of passage money, furlough allowance, equipment, pensions to families, &c. All these have worked well, excepting in the case of the retiring funds, which have for the most part failed, in consequence of the difficulty of reconciling the jarring interests of officers placed in different circumstances. But even the failure of the retiring funds as a system, has, in a measure, been modified by the permission accorded to officers to receive from their regimental brethren a sum of money in consideration of retirement from the service, and consequent acceleration of regimental promotion.

INDIAN NAVY AND MARINE DEPARTMENT.

About half a century ago, when the Coromandel and Malabar coasts were visited by pirates and French privateers, and the trade between the Persian and Arabian Gulfs and India was interrupted by rovers who hoisted the black signal of the professional freebooter, or the scarcely less suspicious blood-red flag of the ostensible Arab trader, the

East-India Company kept up a flotilla of gun-brigs. They were called, for the most part, cruisers; and their officers and crew composed a body, then known by the name of *The Bombay Marine*. The men were, for the most part, drawn from the merchant-vessels in the harbour—the officers were sent out by the Court of Directors as midshipmen, whence they rose by gradation to the rank of captains.

The history of our trade in India, and of our political occupation of the country, presents many brilliant proofs of the skill and prowess of the Bombay Marine, whether in conflict with hordes of desperate pirates, or in more organized operations, in conjunction with other sea and land forces, against the strong holds of enemies on the shores of India, Persia, or Burmah. But there is no question that the state of discipline on board those cruisers was low; the rank of the officers, relatively with that of the members of other warlike professions, was undetermined; the pay and allowances were insignificant; and altogether there was a deficiency of that pride and self-respect, without which no service can acquire the esteem of the rest of civilized mankind, or advance its own consequence amongst contemporary professions. To remedy this state of things, an effort was made, and with complete success, during his late Majesty William the Fourth's occupancy of the office of Lord High Admiral, to exalt the character of the marine by giving it the title of *The Indian Navy*, and honouring it with the control of an experienced officer of the British navy. In all respects—uniform, emoluments, rank—it was placed upon a just level with the royal service; and although this salutary change came at a time when maritime war in the East had ceased, and steam had begun to facilitate the communication of the eastern with the western world, and therefore to demand of the naval officer science and moral courage, in addition to, if not in substitution of, prowess, there is no doubt that the service very largely benefited by the experiment.

The Indian navy now consists of 150 officers, of whom six are captains, twelve commanders, forty-eight lieutenants, and the remainder mates, midshipmen, and pursers. The staff-officers, and the situation of superintendent, are filled, at the pleasure of the home government, by experienced members of the British navy, or retired officers of the famous mercantile marine of the East-India Company *of Merchants*. The fleet, officered and commanded by the Indian navy, amounts to forty vessels, of which more than one-half are armed steamers variously employed in keeping up the communication between India and China, India, the Red Sea, and the Persian Gulf, China and the Red Sea, Bombay and Sinde, and in the navigation of the Indus. The remainder of the vessels are sailing-sloops, brigs, and schooners, employed on surveys, or in the protection of trade in the western gulfs and the Straits of Malacca. Great and important service has been rendered in the survey department by officers of the Indian navy, amongst the most illustrious of whom stand the names of Captain Lloyd and Captain Moresby; to the former, the merchant-service is indebted for some invaluable charts of the dangerous approaches to the shores of Bengal, and of the intricacies of the mighty Ganges; while to the former belongs the honour of having ascertained and proclaimed the full extent of the perils of the Red Sea, the Maldives, and the Malabar Coast, and rendered that plain sailing which had previously been avoided as difficult and hazardous navigation.

The pay and allowances of the Indian navy, and the rules which regulate their furloughs, retirement, &c., are subjoined.

Table of Salaries to Officers in the Indian Navy and Marine Department, under the Presidency of Bombay.

Appointment.	Salaries.			Remarks.
	Rs.	a.	p.	
Superintendent	2500	0	0	In addition to the net pay of his rank.
Assistant Superintendent ..	450	0	0	
Master Attendant	1250	9	0	
1st Assistant do.	600	0	0	
2nd do. do.	570	0	0	
3rd do. do.	400	0	0	
Pilot, Senior	200	0	0	The pilots residing in the Fort are allowed, in addition, Rs. 80 per month house-rent, and those at Colaba, Rs. 50 per month, if not occcupying public quarters.
Do. 2nd Class, each	120	0	0	
Do. 3rd and 4th do. each ..	108	0	0	
Store Receiver and Accountant	380	0	0	In addition to the pay of purser, Rs. 120.
Inspector	250	0	0	
Master Builder	800	0	0	
2nd do.	680	0	0	Includes an allowance of Rs. 80 as [Draughtsman of the Dockyard.
1st Assistant	130	0	0	
2nd do.	110	0	0	
3rd do.	75	0	0	
Asst. Scy. Milty. Board (Marine Branch).. ..	650	0	0	Inclusive of naval pay and allowances.
Draughtsmen	300	0	0	
Indian Naval Storekeeper ..	1285	12	11	
Assistant Storekeeper ..	330	0	0	Draws in addition to net pay of purser, [Rs. 120.
Signal Officer at Light House	120	9	0	
Sup. of Dockyard Steam Engine	200	0	0	Rs. 4 per day, in addition to the pay of an [invalid Lieut.
Assistant ditto..	100	0	0	
Surgeon Indian Navy.. ..	467	0	0	
Commodore at Surat.. ..	1390	0	0	Includes Rs. 90 house-rent, and Rs. 20 palankeen allowance. Pay.. .. .. .. Rs. 900 Table allowance .. .. 400 House-rent 90 1390
Commodore in Persian Gulf..	1300	0	0	Pay.. .. .. .. 900 Table allowance 400 1300
Persian Interpreter to do. ..	200	0	0	In addition to the net pay of his rank.
Commodore's Clerk	90	0	0	
Superintendent of Pattemars .	60	0	0	

Table of Pay to Officers of the Indian Navy.

Rank.		Amount.			Rank.	Amount.		
WHEN EMPLOYED AFLOAT.		Rs.	a.	p.	WHEN EMPLOYED AFLOAT.	Rr.	a.	p.
Captain, 1st rate } Do. 2nd do. } ..	A.	900	0	0	Assist. Surgeon in charge of ship	306	10	0
Com. 3rd do. } ..	B. {	800	0	0	Servants' wages	12	0	0
Do. 4th do. } ..		600	0	0	Do. when unemployed ..	206	10	0
Do. 5th do.		400	0	0				
Lieut. 1st fifteen		175	0	0				
Do. all other		145	0	0	WHEN UNEMPLOYED.			
Pursers, 2nd rate		270	0	0				
Do. 3rd do.		250	0	0	Captain	400	0	0
Clerk in charge, pay .. Rs. 50					Commander	300	0	0
Allowance .. 50					Senior Lieut. first fifteen on the list	150	0	0
		100*						
Mates	C.	50	0	0	Junior ditto	120	0	0
Midshipmen		50	0	0	Pursers	120	0	0
Captain's Clerks		50	0	0	Midshipmen	50	0	0

Iron Steamers.

	Rs.	a.	p.		Rs	a.	p.
Indus Flotilla.				Second-class Vessels.			
Commander	600	0	0	Acting Master	225	0	0
† Lieut.	145	0	0	Second	100	0	0
† Assistant Surgeon	306	10	0				
† Purser	250	0	0	Third-class Vessels.			
First-class Vessels.				Acting Master	200	0	0
Acting Master	250	0	0	Second	100	0	0
Second	100	0	0				

NOTE.—Officers sick on shore allowed house-rent as follows:

Lieut. and Purser	90	Rs. 3 per day.
Midshipmen	60	2 do.

A. If employed on shore .. .. .. Rs. 600.
B. Ditto .. .. 422.
C. In addition to the net pay of their rank.
* With additional half batta.
† In addition to full batta.

Regulations respecting Retirement and Furloughs in the Indian Navy.

RETIREMENT.

Every officer who has actually served twenty-two years or upwards in India is permitted to retire from the service with the following pay :—

The master-attendant and the commodore, after having served five years in either of those capacities, £450 ; a captain £360 ; commander £290 ; lieutenant £190 ; purser £190.

Every officer retiring from ill-health, after ten years' service, and before they have completed that of twenty-two years, is granted the following retiring allowance :—

A captain £200; commander £170; lieutenant £125; second lieutenant £70; purser £125.

FURLOUGHS.

A certain proportion of the officers (to be determined by the government, with a due regard to the exigencies of the service), are allowed to come home on furlough for three years, with the pay only of their rank.

No officer under the rank of captain, who has not actually served ten years, can be permitted to come home on furlough, unless in cases of ill-health, under the like certificates as required from military officers.

If the commodore is permitted to come home on furlough, he is to be allowed the pay of a captain only. Half the remainder of his allowance to be drawn by the senior captain in the service, who is to act as commodore during his absence, in addition to the pay of his rank as senior captain.

The regulations for drawing pay on furlough and retirement by the officers are, as far as circumstances will admit, the same as those for the military officers.

The remainder of the maritime establishment of the East-India Company consists of a body of pilots employed to navigate the Hooghly, a master attendant's establishment at Calcutta, and another at Madras (with subordinates on the coasts), whose business it is to preserve beacons and landmarks for navigators, assist vessels in distress, regulate transports in government service, control the pilots, &c.; and a few steam-vessels which ply between China, Arracan, Moulmein, the Malacca Straits, Madras, and Calcutta, for the occasional rapid conveyance of packets, treasure, stores, troops, or great state officers.

THE PROTESTANT ECCLESIASTICAL ESTABLISHMENT.

As good morals are essential ingredients in good government, and a well-endowed, active, and pious body of Christian ministers necessary to the maintenance and encouragement of sound morality, the ecclesiastical establishment of British India is properly regarded as one of the most important arms and instruments of the executive. The principle of protection to the Protestant church, so long recognized by the government of Great Britain as indispensable to the common weal, is therefore carried out in India to the fullest possible extent. While the British legislature limits itself to the preservation of Protestantism in the person of the sovereign, the endowment of Protestant institutions, the selection of members of the Protestant persuasion to fill great public offices, and the enforcement of taxes for the partial support of the church, the government of India builds churches at its own expense, and takes upon itself the *entire* support of the English and Scotch (established) clergy. Three bishops, as many archdeacons, and upwards of one hundred Protestant chaplains, are spread over British India; and their several incomes, varying from £600 to £2,000 per annum (the Bishop of Calcutta receiving as much as £4,000 per annum), are paid monthly from the state coffers. The chaplains generally receive their appointments at the hands of the Court of Directors in England, but it is within the competency of the Bishop of Calcutta to admit to holy orders young men who have studied at the college on the banks of the Hooghly, founded by Bishop Middleton in 1820, and to nominate them to share in the duties which devolve on the chaplains generally. The number who have been thus admitted is, however, small, as the college scarcely supplies enough to fulfil its own original purpose, namely, the propagation of the gospel among the heathen by means of missionaries.

The duties of the British clergy in India are by no means light: excepting at the chief towns of Calcutta, Madras, and Bombay, and the great military cantonments of Cawnpore, Meerut, Secunderabad, and Bangalore, but one chaplain officiates at each station; on him, consequently, devolves not merely the performance of all the parts of divine service, but the ceremonies of baptism, marriage, and burial; the duties of visiting the hospital and the chamber of the sick man at places very remote from head-quarters; the superintendence of schools and charitable institutions; the assisting missionaries of the Church of England in the translation and diffusion of the Scriptures (but this is not a compulsory duty); and generally affording co-operation in every description of good work within his sphere. These combined offices severely tax the time of the Christian minister, leaving him but little space for reflection or recreation; but it does not appear that temperate and systematic men sink under the accumulation, even in so fierce a climate as that of India; and there is this comfort in store for the district clergyman—that every vacancy in the senior ranks places him higher on the list, and brings him nearer to the enviable possession of a chaplaincy at the presidency, with comparative leisure, and a harvest of marriage, burial, and christening fees.

The regulations for the admission of chaplains into the service of the East-India Company, are as follow:—

Candidates for appointments as assistant-chaplains must have been two years in orders, and must not exceed forty years of age; and at the time of appointment are required to produce their letters of orders, deacon, and priest, as well as testimonial, signed by three beneficed clergymen, and a medical certificate; the appointments are made subject to the approval of the Archbishop of Canterbury or the Bishop of London.

Chaplains are required to enter into covenant, and to give a bond for £500, jointly with two sureties for the due fulfilment of the same.

Under the deed of covenant, chaplains are required to subscribe to the Military Fund at the presidency to which they may be attached.

Chaplains must proceed to their destination within six months from the date of the Court's resolution by which they were nominated; and in failure thereof, without leave obtained from the Court, their appointments will lapse.

The salary of an assistant-chaplain, which position is generally retained for about seven years, does not exceed £600 per annum; and for the first year several deductions are made on account of donations and subscriptions to certain funds from which he, or his surviving family, should he die prematurely, will ultimately derive particular benefit. After eighteen years' service, including three years for one furlough, a chaplain is permitted to retire upon the pay of a major, viz. £292 per annum; after ten years' service (if compelled by ill-health to quit the service), on the half pay of major, viz. £173. 7*s*. 6*d*. per annum; and after seven years, the half pay of captain, viz. £127. 15*s*. per annum. When a chaplain has served seven years, he is allowed a furlough to England, receiving during such absence the pay of captain, viz. £191. 12*s*. per annum; and if compelled by ill-health to return to England before he has served seven years, he receives the half pay of captain, or £127. 15*s*. per annum. The Military Funds allow to subscribers a sum for their passage money and equipment, if they are not in a position to incur expenses on these accounts from their own purses, or entitled to draw upon the government treasury; and to the widow of a chaplain, who is not in possession of a certain specified sum, they allow passage money, and a pension, varying according to the presidency to which the chaplain may have belonged, from £120 to £205. 6*s*. 3*d*. per annum.

LAWS, POLICE, THE PRESS.

WHILE a body of experienced lawyers and well-informed civil servants are engaged in the preparation of a code of laws applicable to India, and pending the completion of their labours, procure, from time to time, the passage of enactments, which provide for temporary difficulties, we must consider the system of judicial administration in our Eastern possessions as in a partial state of transition. Enough of the intentions of the law commissioners has, however, been shadowed forth, to warrant the impression that the great framework of the laws will be left intact; that the system of jurisprudence now extant will only be modified to suit the improved state of society, and that simplification will supersede the complexity which at present obtains.

The laws which prevail at this moment in India are based upon the Mahomedan code, excepting at the three presidencies, and the islands of Penang and Ceylon, where, within certain narrow limits, the British laws are administered upon precisely the same principles, and regulated by the same statutes, as govern our courts in England. Much of the ancient Hindoo law having reference to questions of title, inheritance, succession, marriage, adoption, and caste, has entered into the Mahomedan system, but no separate and well-defined Hindoo code has existed from the date of the consolidation of the Moslem power. But two distinct systems of laws are therefore current throughout the length and breadth of British India.

The Supreme, or Queen's Courts, at the three presidencies and the islands, consist each of three judges,* selected by ministers from the practising barristers in England. The selection has often been eminently judicious. Sir William Jones, Sir James Mackintosh, Sir Francis Macnaghten, Sir Edward Hyde East, and Sir Charles Grey, have acquired a reputation which has not died with the termination of their services in the East. The advocates of the courts consist of men who, having been called to the bar in England, are induced, by the hope of realizing an independence, to transport themselves to India. They are, for the most part, men of average capacity; but there have been instances of great talent adorning the courts, especially that of Calcutta; and it is to the honour of the profession that when public questions have arisen, in which the government and the governed were antagonistic, the Bar have almost invariably been found ranged on the weaker side, employing their eloquence and their energy to baffle oppression, and wring from the executive the concession of great privileges. To the brilliant exertions of Messrs. Turton, Dickens, and Longueville Clarke, of the Calcutta bar, the Indian community are indebted for effective resistance to an iniquitous stamp act, for the liberty of the press, for the free ingress of intelligent and independent Europeans; and, in point of fact, for very many advantages, unconnected with the laws, which have

* There are but two judges at present sitting in the Bombay Court, and as no disposition has for some time past been shewn by the home authorities to appoint a third, it is supposed that the number will henceforth be permanently limited to two.

inspired the natives with a greater degree of self-respect, and rendered Englishmen as secure of their birthrights in India as they are in their native land. The attorneys, like the barristers, have, for the most part, received their education and served their apprenticeship in London; but of late years a good many have been admitted who began as articled clerks in local offices; and it must be confessed, that if they are deficient in the higher qualities which distinguish a solicitor, their familiarity with the character and language of the natives gives them advantages which their competitors are many years in acquiring.

The extent of the jurisdiction of the Supreme Courts is not so exactly defined as to silence all discussion upon the point, but, generally speaking, their respective charters have settled their powers as to the nature of the law they are at liberty to administer. These are extensive. Every case, which in London would be heard either in the Court of Queen's Bench or Common Pleas, Admiralty or Ecclesiastical Courts, Courts of Chancery, Exchequer, or Insolvency, comes under the cognizance of the Supreme Courts in India, and from their decision there is no appeal but to the Queen in Council. How far the extension of English law to every part of the Indian empire would be satisfactory to the natives, is a question we are not called upon to discuss in these pages; but it is right to say, that wherever it prevails, it is regarded, both in its principles and its operation, as a security and a blessing. Unlike the judges of the Company's courts, the administrators of the law in the Queen's courts are totally independent of the local government. Brute force might, in extreme cases, be opposed to the execution of their decrees; but their offices cannot be taken from them, on the one hand, as a punishment for the stern and upright execution of their duty; nor, on the other hand, could they be tempted by any thing the highest authorities have it in their power to bestow, to deviate from the straight path chalked out to them by the dictates of conscience and the obligation of their oath.

The Company's judicial establishments in the interior of Hindostan consist of a great number of courts, of various degrees of power and responsibility. At each presidency are Supreme *Native* Courts, consisting of four judges each, chosen from the most experienced officers in the judicial line. At the principal stations are courts of circuit; in every zillah, or district, and in each great and populous city, there is a single judge. Besides these, there are assistant judges, registers of zillahs, who hold courts; and many native petty judges, under the appellations of sudder ameens and moonsiffs, the former term signifying "chief arbitrator," and the latter "a justice," or one who distributes justice. From the inferior courts lie appeals to the courts of circuit, and from the courts of circuit to the presidency courts, in all civil causes of any considerable amount, in questions of real property, and even in personal actions involving a certain sum of money; and from the courts of circuit references are necessary to the superior tribunal, in criminal convictions involving life or transportation. The Mahomedan law (as we have said above), modified by innumerable regulations, rules, and ordinances, passed by the government from time to time, is the law of all these courts; and if it were possible to carry out its provisions to the letter, the people would have less ground for the complaint that justice, as administered therein, exists merely in name. But the obstacles to a correct administration of the law are immense. The ignorance of the native pleaders; the corruption of the *omluh*, or native officers of the courts; the prevalence of perjury among all classes of native witnesses; the impossibility of checking oppression in the execution of decrees; the consumption of justice in the progressive system of appeal from the lowest upwards, which holds out a temptation to litigation by multiplying the chances of success; the imperfect knowledge possessed by the Anglo-Indian judges of the multitude of dialects, and of the customs, manners, and ideas of the natives—constitute so many serious impediments to the healthy course of law, that justice, to use the words of an enlightened writer upon the subject, becomes a "perfect *caput mortuum*, not worth the having."

The causes which chiefly engage the attention of the judicial officers in India arise out of failure to pay revenue, disputed succession or inheritance, breach of contract, debt, and trespass. The crimes they have principally to try are larceny, robbery on the highway, burglary, murder, forgery, piracy, and perjury. The punishments which they are competent to inflict are death, imprisonment, labour on the roads, transportation to the Straits of Malacca, and confiscation of property. Juries, composed of Europeans, Eurasians, and educated natives, are empannelled to try criminal causes only in the presidency Queen's courts; but the institution is unknown in the interior, excepting in the form of a *punchayat*, or jury of five individuals, who are occasionally called in to aid the judge, as assessors, in cases of doubt and difficulty.

The police in India is probably the worst preventive or detective establishment of any in the world. The activity and zeal of magistrates and superintendents are almost entirely neutralized by the apathy, cowardice, and corruption of the *posse comitatus*. The force is sufficiently large, consisting, as it does, of thousands of thannadars, chokeedars, burkundauzes, pykes, &c. &c., with all the grades of rank and pay that can stimulate activity and preserve discipline, and armed well enough to encounter any number of brigands, and suppress any popular mutinies; but the inherent defects in the native character, minimize the utility of the officers, and render them, in many parts of the country, more of a curse than a blessing to the myriads of the poorer orders. Bound by the ties of caste, apprehensive of the vengeance of a culprit's relatives, greedy of the *douceurs* which can be wrung from an offender, or a reluctant witness, unmindful of truth, constitutionally indolent, and secure, by distance, from the immediate *surveillance* of their superiors, they volunteer no steps that militate against their individual interests, and execute no imposed duty with independence, integrity, or alacrity. Thus, the difficulty experienced by the judges in administering the law is materially enhanced, and the people pay a heavy tax for the maintenance of an institution with which, under present circumstances, they could, with rare exceptions, most easily dispense. But one remedy for this state of things appears to exist, and that is, the employment of some hundreds of Europeans as inspectors and superintendents of police in all the districts. Well-disciplined and intelligent soldiers would be the fittest persons for this description of office, which would, at the same time, be a reward for good conduct, and a motive for the enlistment of young men from the respectable classes now struggling for existence in England. At the presidencies there are a few European constables and bailiffs, and their great efficiency supplies an unanswerable argument in favour of the extension of such description of control to every town and populous village in the country.

So much of the improvement that has taken place, and is still on the advance, in the administration of the law in India, is ascribable to the newspaper discussions, that a notice of the Indian press may not be inaptly introduced in the present section.

THE INDIAN PRESS.

The first English newspaper published in India, made its appearance in Bengal on the 29th January, 1780. It assumed and long enjoyed a latitude of discussion scarcely paralleled by any part of the English press at the present day. This, however, the Government found it necessary to check, and a censorship was established, supported by penalties, which continued in operation for nearly thirty years. The governing party, who, for a long time, were almost the only *European* party in the state, dreaded lest the communication of too much information* might place a weapon in the hands of their active foes, the struggling princes and their French allies, which might be turned to the disadvantage of British interest. The progress of conquest, however, and the complete annihilation of all European power in India, save that which the English possessed, diminished the fears arising from the general diffusion of news. Accordingly, in or about the year 1816, the propriety of freeing the press became the subject of frequent debate. But the executive opposed any alteration upon totally new grounds. It was now pretended that our dominion mainly rested upon the respect in which the government was held, and that that respect, according to the authorities of the time, could only be maintained by adding a tender regard for the infirmities of public men to the pompous displays which the revenues were employed to keep up. Regulations were therefore made, protecting from public comment the acts of bishops, judges, governors, commanders-in-chief, and numerous other functionaries; and by way of extending the shield of protection over the whole fry of *employés*, a clause was ingeniously introduced by some governments prohibiting all discussions which were calculated to

* Before the parliamentary committee which sat on Mr. Buckingham's claim to compensation for the sacrifice of his newspaper property by the Indian Government, curious evidence was given of the nature of the orders issued to the conductors of papers from time to time during the war with Tippoo Sultaun. Even the announcement of the arrival and departure of ships at the Indian ports was at one time prohibited.

interfere with the harmony of society!—a comprehensive term, the purport of which was not misunderstood. Under the operation of these restrictions, the press of India was for a long time a mere receptacle for advertisements, innocent extracts from English papers (in which police reports and trials for crim. con. enjoyed a marked preference over political disquisitions), shipping arrivals, details of balls, *fêtes*, and reviews, criticisms on amateur theatricals, the government gazettes, and occasional letters deprecating some small local nuisance. About the year 1820, however, the papers began to wear a new aspect. The legitimate purposes of a public press were first asserted, it is believed, by Mr. Buckingham; and influenced by his example—though not approaching him in boldness of tone—the Calcutta press began to question the wisdom of some of the acts of government, and the immaculacy of sundry of its favoured officers. The sensation occasioned by this sudden assumption of moral and political power, in a community of whom passive obedience to orders and tacit submission to laws were from habit and necessity the chief characteristics, may be imagined. The Europeans, all at once reminded that freedom of opinion was an inalienable birthright, hailed Mr. Buckingham as a deliverer; and in the ecstasy of their delight at being liberated from the shackles which bound their tongues and pens, they forgot that there was scarcely one amongst them who might not sooner or later feel the inconvenience of too much publicity. Not quite so regardless of the consequences of this bold emancipation were the elderly gentlemen who held responsible offices under the government. To them, the operation of the freedom of the press presented itself in its most fearful colours, and they immediately applied the whole weight of their personal and official influence to a counteraction of the assaults of this formidable hydra. But the Marquis of Hastings, then governor-general, had publicly declared that a good government had nothing to fear from the light;—he avowed that he courted or dared investigation into his public acts; and thus, while his bearing gave no countenance to the anxious endeavours of the *bureaucracie* and staff by which he was surrounded, it animated with fresh courage the spirited Buckingham and his now numerous and intrepid adherents.

Mr. Buckingham, and the fate of his efforts to assert the freedom of the press of India, have been so often before the public, that it is needless to recapitulate them here. Suffice to say, that, after two or three years of unexampled success as a journalist, a timid *locum tenens* of the reins of government deported him to England, and for a time checked the *adolescent* press. But the darkness that followed was not of long duration. Lord Amherst allowed the editors of his day a tolerable latitude of expression. Lord William Bentinck, his successor, permitted them during his seven years' administration to say or publish any thing they pleased, and declared that he considered the press a valuable adjunct of the government; yet, with singular inconsistency and littleness, to the last moment of his rule he clung with unaccountable tenacity to his power of "*coming down* upon the press." Sir Charles Metcalfe, who temporarily succeeded Lord William, at once and *sans façon* freed the press; Lord Auckland, the succeeding governor-general, not only recognized the act of his predecessor (though the court of directors gave him, it is said, power to annul it), but, in a variety of ways, promoted its prosperty and enhanced its utility. Lord Ellenborough's merit is negative; he does not aid the press, but he does not venture to curb it.

Of the character of the Indian press, it is not easy to speak in *unqualified* terms of satisfaction. Unlike the press of other free countries, it is the organ, not of the people, but of the executive and (with slight exceptions) the handful of Europeans scattered throughout India as merchants, tradespeople, lawyers, and indigo planters. Nor can it well be otherwise, if the object of its conductors be to increase rather than to destroy their capital. Readers must be looked for amongst the intelligent few—not the masses of millions to whom even their own written language is a sealed book: and the "intelligent few," who betake themselves to India either to make fortunes, or to eat that bread which the difficulty of obtaining employment denies them in England, care little, generally speaking, for the interests of the country at large. It hence becomes the unavoidable policy of the editorial fraternity to render their columns subservient to the welfare and amusement of the army, the civil service, and the other classes of Europeans; and if they do occasionally discuss the merits of those acts of government which are intended for the good of the empire at large, it is not because they expect thereby materially to serve the thousands of tax-payers, but because it is becoming in a public journalist at least to make an effort to acquire an influence over the councils of the rulers, and to appear to be alive to their proceedings. A press to be powerful must have a large and enlightened public at its back—or (for whether it leads or follows the community is still a question) it must be the representative of thoughts and wishes which can ultimately ensure their own realization by some constitutional—or, we had almost written, brute—power. The Indian press has nothing of this. It rests for support chiefly on the *services* and the handful of Englishmen above referred to; and in proportion as it brings their interests prominently before the government, and promotes a discussion of their views, its proprietors are rewarded in their outlay of capital.

Notwithstanding, however, the necessity, which we have thus pointed out, of the Indian press conforming to the tastes of the great majority of its readers, the European inhabitants of India, it would be unjust not to admit that it has done good service to the natives. It is, perhaps, impossible for an Englishman not to sympathize with the oppressed, and our Indian editors have not only constantly opened their papers to complaints of oppression from all quarters, but have also, almost uniformly, strongly advocated the cause of the sufferer. In this they have occasionally been misled by false statements, and have, perhaps, let their indignation overrun their discretion; but in general they have exercised a sufficient caution in receiving statements which affect those in power, and a sufficient boldness in publishing and commenting upon them, when authenticated.

They have thus been of some service, in checking abuses of authority, and exposing misconduct which might never have reached the ear of government. Their utility in this respect will, however, receive a vast increase, when the English language is more generally understood, and the people consequently become able to comprehend the ready method of making known their complaints which the press affords them.

Having thus sketched the history and character of the Calcutta press, it may be as well to present a detail of its circulation, and furnish some idea of its cost, profits, &c.

There are three daily papers now published in Calcutta, the *Englishman*, the *Hurkaru*, or Messenger, and the *Star;* and one of these, the *Hurkaru*, issues a smaller edition three times a week, under the designation of the *India Gazette*, once a separate and independent daily paper. The weekly papers are six in number, viz. the *Bengal Herald*, the *Eastern Star*, the *Planter's Journal*, the *Church Magazine*, the *Christian Advocate*, and the *Catholic Herald*. Besides these, there is a paper entitled the *Friend of India*, published at the neighbouring settlement of Serampore, but Calcutta is too glad to class that journal among her own offspring, for it more completely fulfils the true purposes of a press than any other published in India. It ministers to no interests but the interests of religion, humanity, and good government.

The Madras press boasts of no daily papers. The journals are published once, twice, or thrice a week. They are seven or eight in number; but the *Athe-*

næum, the *Spectator*, *United Service Gazette*, *Examiner*, and the *Evening Mail*, are the only ones that deserve mention. At Bombay two papers are published half-weekly—the *Times* and the *Courier*, and one daily—the *Gentleman's Gazette*. A paper is published at Delhi, and another at Agra (both twice a week); while Penang, Ceylon, Singapore, Malacca, and Moulmein, all have their hebdomadals.

It is difficult to compute the exact circulation of all these papers, for the tendency to exaggeration on the part of proprietors is as rife in India as in England; but it may be safely asserted, that the number of subscribers of the dailies, weeklies, &c., combined, does not exceed 10,000, of whom eleven or twelve hundred take the Calcutta *Englishman*, and twelve or thirteen hundred the *Friend of India*, and about the same number the *Bombay Times*.*

The character of these papers, with the exception of the three or four professedly in the interests of religion, is pretty much the same. The editors are for the most part educated and independent gentlemen, who, having no interests but the cause of truth, and the welfare and entertainment of society to promote, and being perfectly unconnected with the government, freely express their sentiments upon every public question that may arise. The contents and order of arrangement of the papers are tolerably uniform. One-fourth, or rather more, of each journal is appropriated to advertisements; these are followed by local correspondence, extracts from contemporary publications, the government general

* Assuming that each paper circulates among five persons, there are 50,000 readers in India.

orders announcing appointments, promotions, &c., acts of the legislative council, &c. Next we have two or three columns devoted to editorial lucubrations upon the topics of the day; and these are succeeded by items of Indian news, or news from China, the Cape of Good Hope, New South Wales, Mauritius, &c., winding up with copious extracts from the English papers. Indeed, such is the avidity with which the Indian exile devours intelligence from his native country, that when an overland packet arrives from England, the editors find it their best policy to exclude almost every thing for two or three days, in order to make room for abundant selections. The public appetite, however, is soon satiated, and the dailies then fall into the old track.*

The monthly publications in the City of Palaces are seventeen in number, three of which are partial reprints from the daily papers, for transmission to England by the overland mail. The others are devoted to science, Christianity, commerce, and the *coups d'essai* of unfledged scribblers, hot from the Calcutta schools and colleges. There are, moreover, an *Army List*, a *Sporting Magazine*, and a *Journal of Natural History*, published quarterly, and half a

* As an instance of the necessity for supplying instantaneously the demand of the public for English news, it may be mentioned that papers are now printed in London, embracing the whole of the news for a month, and despatched by hundreds, *viâ* Bombay, to the address of the country subscribers to the principal Indian papers, and to a large number of persons who do not separately receive the latter. Of these London papers, the *Monthly Times*, well conducted by Mr. John Blackburn, is deservedly at the head. The agents of the proprietary, Messrs. James Barber & Co., present it gratis to all subscribers to the separate agency of the latter firm.

dozen Guides, Souvenirs, and Directories, issued annually. There are thus six-and-thirty periodicals, of all denominations, published in Calcutta in the English language. At Madras and Bombay there are only two or three monthlies, chiefly scientific and religious.

There are several presses in India which limit themselves, almost exclusively, to the printing of books, pamphlets, &c.; and as they are chiefly directed by experienced Englishmen, they seldom turn out works inferior in their typography, paper, &c., to the best offspring of the London publishers. Of these establishments the Bishop's College Press, at Calcutta, unquestionably stands at the head. It was originally set up for the purpose of reprinting the Holy Scriptures in the native languages, and other works tending to the enlightenment and conversion of the Hindoos; but as these did not occupy the entire time of the printers, an extension of its business was suggested, and it now prints books and periodicals, provided their tendency be not immoral.

The native papers constitute a remarkable feature of the Calcutta press. They owe their origin to Mr. Marshman, the son of the celebrated Dr. Marshman, who, some twenty or thirty years ago, started the *Sumachar Durpun*, a weekly paper, in the vernacular language. The large support which it immediately received from the natives led to its publication in the Bengalee and English languages (each alternate column being a translation of its neighbour); and in the year 1837, the proprietor was encouraged to put it forth three times a week. But in the meanwhile other native papers had started into existence. Some attacks upon the Hindoos, in the columns of the *Durpun*, originated the *Cowmoody*, of which the late Rajah Rammohun Roy was one of the editors. It defended the Hindoos, while it endeavoured to instruct them. But the Rajah was not sufficiently orthodox for his colleagues: he soon began to oppose himself to some of the rites and ceremonies of the Hindoo religion, which, if not actually enjoined by the shasters, or sacred books, had been hallowed by custom. Amongst other usages, he assailed the suttee, or self-immolation of widows upon the funereal pile. This led to the withdrawal of one of the staunchest of his *collaborateurs*, who immediately established a third paper, the *Chundrika*, having for its object that pure conservatism which resists the progress of intelligence, and maintains the worst absurdities and most odious tyrannies in all their time-honoured integrity. The *Cowmoody* expired on the departure of Rammohun Roy for England. The impulse, however, had been given to the native press, and a multitude of journals were consequently soon ushered into existence, some of them originating with the ex-students of the Hindoo college, who had been imbued with rather extravagant notions of political freedom; and others springing from the orthodox party, or from sycophants who had learnt that something was to be gained by publicly chanting the praises of sundry rajahs; or from libellers who panted for a channel of vituperation; or from the necessitous, who found, in the circulation of a paper, the means of subsistence and the opportunity of literary distinction. About twenty papers, which sprung into existence under such auspices, have since expired, after a brief and unsatisfactory career. Eight only are now before the public, circulating, weekly, about 2000 copies altogether. This is, indeed, but a very small drop of civilization in the vast ocean of ignorance and superstition, but it is idle to suppose that it is altogether without its beneficial effects. From the extreme parsimony of the natives, it may be conjectured that all these papers are subscribed for by clubs, and that, consequently, the 2000 copies have, on an average, 20,000 readers. To inoculate this number with habits of reflection, to draw their attention to higher objects than the accumulation of money, the indulgence in sensual pleasures, or the study of the superstitions and ceremonials of a misguiding religion, is something gained to the cause of humanity. The character of the native press, setting aside the heats and personalities of controversy, is creditable to its conductors. There is an evident anxiety on the part of each journalist to render service to the cause of good government. The honest, and active, and philanthropic civil functionary receives his due meed of praise, while the iniquities of the unjust steward, and his crowd of corrupt omlah,* are boldly exposed and animadverted upon in the strongest terms permitted by the law of libel. That more of the purposes of a press are not fulfilled by the native editors, is owing principally to the poverty of the young men who have embarked in the journalists' profession. There can be no doubt, however, that, in process of time, the wealthier classes will become alive to the great im-

* The native officers of the courts of law and revenue.

portance of supporting the press; and we shall find large capitalists yielding the means of establishing correspondence with all the districts in India, of translating large proportions of the best English journals for transference to the columns of the native papers, and of maintaining the integrity and independence of the editors.

There are a considerable number of native presses extant, which are limited to the printing of almanacs, books, catalogues, handbills, &c. Of these no particular account is necessary.

There are also several lithographic presses, one of which belongs to the government, and is used to multiply copies of official correspondence, maps, &c. The others are private property, and are kept in constant employ; but we are not aware that they have hitherto yielded their proprietors good returns.

The native papers at Madras and Bombay are very few in number and insignificant in circulation and influence.

PREPARATIONS FOR THE OUTWARD VOYAGE IN A SAILING VESSEL, *VIA* THE CAPE.

As a person unacquainted with Indian shipping, that is to say, with the vessels which habitually sail between England and India, will have considerable difficulty in making a good selection, and may, moreover, be too much occupied with bidding farewell to friends, to be able to spare time for the superintendence of all the details connected with the embarkation of baggage, fitting-up a cabin, &c., it is advisable that he should at once betake himself, either to Messrs. James Barber & Co., the East-India agents; or to Messrs. Grindlay & Co., and enter himself as a subscriber to their agency; or to any of the agents whose address is at the end of this volume. This proceeding will save him a world of trouble. Captain James Barber, the head of the first-named house, has had large experience of the Indian trade, and is personally acquainted, not only with the qualities of each desirable vessel, but with the characters, tempers, and *savoir faire* of their respective commanders. We would, however, earnestly recommend passengers desirous of quiet and comfort, to give injunctions to the agent to select a cabin on the *lower* deck of a ship; for though not so light and airy as the upper cabins, especially in bad weather, there is no disturbance from the continual walking and shuffling over-head, the dropping coils of rope, &c.; and, besides, the cost of the lower cabins is somewhat less. On the *homeward* voyage the upper cabins are preferable in every way, as the vessels are then deeply laden, and it is scarcely safe to open the port-holes of the lower deck for the admission of air and light.

The passage being engaged, and the average price, £100,* duly paid, the next object which engages attention is the purchase of cabin furniture and the outfit. In the selection of these, the passenger will

* A single man in a side-cabin below seldom pays more, though £120 is generally asked. An upper, or poop-cabin, costs, for one person, £150, and the stern cabins, which accommodate a married couple and a child, pay in proportion to the number of persons.

be prudent always to keep in mind the possibility of converting them to useful purposes in India. Thus, a sofa, with drawers beneath it, is preferable to a swing-cot, because it can be rendered serviceable in a house, whereas the uses of the latter terminate with the voyage. But, perhaps, the following list, applicable to almost any condition of life, will sufficiently indicate the absolute necessities of the traveller. We will merely premise, that it will be good economy to require of the agent that the cabin furniture and fittings-up shall be procured of the upholsterers at the East-India Docks, in preference to any of the professional outfitters:—

A sofa, with mattress, pillow, and a chintz covering for the day-time.

A folding-chair, or camp-stool.

A wash-hand stand, complete, with ewer, basin, soap-dish, &c.

A hanging lamp.

A looking-glass, with sliding cover.

A swing-tray.

A chest of drawers, in two pieces, the upper part having a ledge around the top, for the purpose of holding a small collection of books, or preventing articles from falling off.

A foul-clothes bag. A cylindrical cane basket is better, but it generally occupies too much room in a side cabin.

An oil-cloth, or carpet, for the cabin. This is merely for the sake of appearances. The bare deck is cleaner, cooler, and offers a firmer footing when the ship is rolling or pitching.

Equipment of a single man for one hundred and twenty days, something above the computed duration of a voyage:—

Ten dozen shirts.

Four dozen night ditto.

Eighteen pairs of sheets (size of the sofa).

One dozen and a half of pillow-cases.

One blanket.

One counterpane.

Six dozen towels.

Three dozen silk pocket-handkerchiefs.

Six pairs of loose cotton drawers, for sleeping or bathing in.

A couple of brown holland blouses.

A blue camlet jacket.

Two pairs of merino, camlet, or gambroon trowsers.

Two dozen pairs of white jean trowsers.

Two dozen white jean jackets.

Two dozen white jean waistcoats.

Three dozen pairs of cotton socks.

Cloth coats, trousers, and waistcoats, at discretion. The stock in possession of a passenger when he is leaving England will suffice.

A hat, in leathern box, for Indian wear.

A straw hat.

A blue cloth forage-cap.

Two black silk stocks, or cravats.

A dozen pairs of white kid gloves. (These articles are very dear in India: those which may be obtained for 1*s.* 6*d.* in the Strand, cost three rupees in Calcutta.)

A couple of morning gowns.

Two pairs of shoes.

Two pairs of boots.

One pair of slippers.

A boat-cloak, of cloth or camlet.

A dressing-case and Russian leather writing-case, suitably filled.

Three pounds of Windsor soap.

Six pounds of short wax candles.

A bucket and rope (serviceable in drawing up salt water whenever wanted).

A brush-case and blacking, boot-hooks and shoe-horn.

A sponge and sponge-bag.

A japanned jug, basin, soap-dish, and tooth-brush tray. These are preferable to a China set, which is liable to break, or to pewter vessels which soon look dirty and are not easily cleaned. General instructions to the tradesman from whom the wash-hand stand may be bought, will ensure its being fitted up with every convenience.

The foregoing list embraces the *actual necessaries*

of a bachelor on the voyage to India by a sailing vessel. For purposes of pastime or study numerous additions may be made, suitable to the means and inclinations of passengers. Fowling-pieces, rifles, fishing-tackle, colour-boxes, musical instruments, books, scientific instruments, telescopes, cards, chess and backgammon boards, are taken, and an outline map of the route, published by Messrs. W. H. Allen & Co., Leadenhall Street, is often added;* but were it considered expedient to enumerate all the articles that fancy, taste, artificial wants, or peculiar pursuits may suggest, our list may be swelled illimitably.

Some guide-books recommend that water, soda-water, brandy, lucifer-matches, raspberry-vinegar, jams, and a score of similar superfluities be carried; but there can be no occasion for any of these in a well-found ship. Abundance is the ordinary characteristic of the supplies on board; prompt and obliging attention the distinguishing feature of the domestics.

The trunks in which clothes for the voyage may be packed, should depend upon the capacity of the traveller. If he be a military or medical man, and therefore liable to march about the country, bullock-trunks, specially made and sold at the outfitters', are preferable, as they are permanently useful. But for persons in the civil service, indigo-planters, merchants, clergymen, &c., the portmanteau or tin box,

* Marking the track and progress of the voyage on this map every day, after the captain has taken his observation *and made it twelve o'clock*, is a common and by no means uninstructive amusement.

eighteen inches square, would answer all purposes. The tin boxes can be carried in India by the bunghy-bearers, or running-porters, who accompany palankeen travellers across the country.

Of the money which a passenger may carry with him, sovereigns should always be preferred, even to the extent of the £200 required at first starting in India. For all beyond that, if any be necessary, a letter of credit had better be taken.

Letters of introduction, to which so much importance was once attached, are now of comparatively little account in India. The establishment of hotels and boarding-houses has rendered persons on their first arrival less dependent than they formerly were upon the accommodating spirit of the resident community. Add to this, the great ease with which people of respectability get acquainted with one another at those places of entertainment, and at other public reunions; to say nothing of the *entrée* to the government-house, which is promptly accorded to all who are entitled by their rank in the social scale to leave their cards; and it will be readily understood that even for the purposes of agreeable intercourse no introductions are essential. Those who imagine that letters of recommendation will tend to their professional advancement, form an erroneous estimate of their utility. Neither governors, judges, nor commanders-in-chief, are much in the habit of paying attention to the particular requests of absent friends, unless the latter are very anxious to see their *protégés* put forward, and *have the means of reciprocating the civility of the authori-*

ties abroad. A prime minister, perhaps, would not ask a favour of a governor in vain; nor would a wealthy merchant in the city be likely to have his injunctions disregarded by his own agent.

In the above instructions regard has only been had to the wants of a single man proceeding to India. To a certain extent the same suggestions will apply to the other sex, for there can be little variety in cabin furniture, and the principal accessories to the toilette. But in regard to costume, distinct details are obviously necessary, as there is scarcely any thing in the attire of one sex which corresponds with the garments of the other. The following, therefore, may be regarded as a fair and reasonable wardrobe for a lady, but can be augmented, if necessary, according to the affluence or wishes of the party :—

Six dozen chemises.
Four dozen night ditto.
Four dozen pair of drawers.
Four dozen pair of thin cotton stockings.
Two dozen, &c. of silk stockings.
Eight flannel petticoats.
Three pairs of stays.*
Six white dressing gowns.
Six coloured ditto.
Two dozen night-caps.
Five dozen pocket-handkerchiefs.
One dozen of net neckerchiefs.
Four dozen of towels.
Six pairs of black silk stockings.
Four printed morning dresses, worn at breakfast.

* A visit to Mrs. Wise, 31, Saville Row, Conduit Street, Bond Street, will insure to the lady passenger some valuable advice, and a description of corset of inestimable utility in a relaxing climate.

A black silk dress at dinner.

A slight coloured silk, or any cheap material, for dress on Sundays: as these dresses generally become unfit for wear after the voyage, the less cost in the purchase the better.

Black silk or cotton petticoat for every day's wear.

An ordinary cloak, and common straw bonnet, to wear on deck.

Shoes and dressing slippers.

Small silk neckerchiefs.

Collars, caps, gloves, and mittens, according to taste.

Quilling-net and piece-net; ribbons of low price and different colours; hair powder; pins of various sizes; needles, buttons, hooks and eyes, tape and bodkins, cotton-reels, scissors; a good supply of papillote paper.

Windsor-soap and wax-candles, pomatum, smelling-bottle, hartshorn, aromatic-vinegar, aperients, and a case of Cologne-water.

A dressing-case and writing-desk, both properly furnished.

The pastimes and employments of ladies depend so much upon taste that it is impossible to offer any but general hints regarding the implements of entertainment most suitable to the leisure of a voyage. Knitting and netting,* carpet and crochet work, drawing, books, and music, constitute the ordinary occupations, which, however, may be varied *ad libitum*. Musical practice will much depend upon the presence of a piano-forte. If there be not one in the vessel, belonging to the captain, we do not recommend a female passenger to allow of her own, supposing her to possess one, being unpacked for cabin use. The damp sea air and the motion of the vessel are calculated to seriously damage the delicate machinery of a Broadwood or Zeitte, even though it be clamped and fastened and *clothed*, to suit the climate of the tropics.

* For these purposes silver needles are recommended, as the moisture of the fingers at a high temperature is calculated to rust the implement.

THE VOYAGE TO INDIA.

The prospect of an imprisonment on board a ship for three or four months, with no more agreeable view, externally, than a vast expanse of sea and sky, is to many minds perfectly appalling. Those who have been accustomed to much confinement in town or country, from the nature of their business or the inclemency of the season, have still found time pass lightly in the midst of profitable occupation, the companionship of books, or the centre of a happy family circle; but in the narrow limits of a trading vessel, cast amongst strangers, deprived of the necessity for labour, and oppressed with the painful feelings attending a separation from home and valued friends and relatives, they anticipate a wearisome and monotonous existence. The picture which fancy draws is, however, found, on close inspection, to be much less charged with gloomy objects than it appears to be in the distance. The excitement and bustle ever attendant upon the business of a ship, the common interest and sympathy which draw people together who, otherwise, would maintain towards each other the characteristic reserve of Englishmen, the evanescent nature of the griefs which assail the youth of both sexes at the commencement of a career replete with hope and novelty, rapidly create a favourable change in the views of the outward-bound, and prepare the mind for a cheerful endurance of the inconvenience of a protracted voyage. Few, indeed, are the men and women, who in their after-life do not look back upon the voyage to India as one of the greenest spots in memory's waste. For the devotee of science, there is perpetual entertainment in tracing the progress of the vessel, in observing the practical use of the compass, in taking lunar and solar observations, marking the changes of climate, the phenomena of the sea's phosphorescence, the uses of the complex machinery of a ship, &c. The sportsman will find ample employment for his gun when the gigantic albatross and the sportive Cape pigeon carcer around and about the vessel in search of prey, and the fish-hook and the harpoon may not unprofitably be brought into requisition to snare the monster shark or slay the brilliant dolphin. He who is either a votary of science or of sport will resort to books, cards, music, and the various games which exercise ingenuity and produce gentle excitement. These will pleasantly while away many hours of the day; and a walk on the quarter-deck, or a merry quadrille, when the presence of a band and of a sufficient number of lady passengers admits of such an enjoyment, will often consume a long evening in the tropics, and stimulate health while they promote good fellowship. Meals, on board ship, are also more a matter of entertainment than of business, and are prolonged beyond the ordinary duration, because they contribute to the exhaustion of leisure. Then amateur theatricals serve occasionally to diversify existence, and the accidental rencontre of a vessel homeward-bound awakens family recollections and associations, and sends the passenger to his writing-desk to report progress, and proclaim all's well. It sometimes happens that either from previous arrangements, connected with the landing of passengers and cargo, or with the embarkation of fresh accessions of both, or from stress of weather, deficiency of water or provisions, the vessel puts into the port of Madeira, the Cape of Good Hope, or any of the islands which stud the route between the Azores (inclusive) and the Indian coast. There are pleasant breaks in the voyage which may be turned to profitable account by an observant traveller, and at all events serve as a brief recreation and an agreeable souvenir for the irreflective. At Cape Town, Cape of Good Hope, there are hotels and boarding-houses, where accommodation may be obtained at the rate of about a guinea a day, including the expense of a carriage to the villages and vintages within a few hours' drive of the town. There are no "lions," so to speak, at the Cape. A public library offers the means of whiling away an hour; and a ramble about the streets, amidst a motley population of Dutch colonists, British officers, Negroes and Indians, affords entertainment to the eye unaccustomed to diversified costumes and complexions. The ascent of Table Mountain is a feat which some adventurous visitors take pleasure in accomplishing; and if a fine view of the bay and surrounding country is deemed an object of interest, it is certainly to be obtained by the mere trouble of the ascent.

THE OVERLAND PASSAGE TO INDIA.

The passage to India, *viâ* the Mediterranean and the Red Sea, has been rendered so facile of late years by the construction of magnificent steamers, the property of the Oriental and Peninsular Steam Navigation Company, that great numbers of persons give it a preference to the route round the Cape of Good Hope. It has the advantage of being an infinitely more expeditious method of reaching India, and of being less wearisome by reason of the perpetual change of scene which it presents between England, passing the coast of Spain, Gibraltar, Malta, Egypt, Aden (and if bound to Calcutta), Ceylon and the continent of India. In point of expense, there is but little difference in the two routes, for what is saved in passage-money *viâ* the Cape, is spent in the additional outfit rendered necessary by the length of the voyage. One hundred and forty pounds (£140) is the lowest sum paid for a single berth in a cabin in any of the great steamers to Alexandria, for a passage across the desert to Suez in one of the vans, and thence in another magnificent vessel to Ceylon, Madras, or Calcutta. If the party is proceeding to Bombay, a passage is secured (including the trip over the desert) to Suez, and there a Government steamer is monthly in waiting to proceed directly to Bombay. The cost of this partial voyage is about £60; and £60 more, payable at Suez, is the charge of the Bombay steamers for the remaining half. The steamers of the Oriental and Peninsular Company leave Southampton upon the

1st of each month, and passages may be engaged on application at their office, No. 51, St. Mary Axe, or to Captain James Barber, No. 17, St. Mary Axe. The passage money includes an excellent table, wines, liquors, servants' fees, and the carriage of five hundred-weight of personal baggage. Upon the subject of the quantity of baggage, we may be allowed, in extracting the following hints from the *Asiatic Journal*, to repeat ourselves, and to assure the traveller, that a little attention to them will be advantageous to his purse in more ways than one.

"These equipments are always overdone; and as it often happens that what is purchased in London is unserviceable in Calcutta, and the reverse, the travelling public cannot be sufficiently warned against a needless outlay. I will state what I consider would be a very complete bachelor's wardrobe, &c.; premising that, under the present arrangements in the large steamers of the Peninsular and Oriental Company, there is *no occasion* for bed or table linen, a sofa, washhand-stand, looking-glass, boot-hooks, jugs, tumbler, blacking and brushes, writing-desk, or books: all these are provided in the steamers. Take with you only six dozen shirts, three dozen pairs of socks, a couple of brown Holland blouses, two dozen pairs of white pantaloons, a couple of pair of merino or gambroon trousers, six dozen pocket-handkerchiefs, three dozen pairs of long drawers, a forage-cap, a straw hat, shoes, slippers, and your razors and tooth-brushes. I say nothing of waistcoats, boots, cloth coats and trousers, cloak or great-coat, because the stock which a man may have with him when he engages his passage will generally suffice; but it will be prudent to be provided with a mat or rug, a pillow, and a quilted counterpane (or *resai*), for it is very probable that, when the passenger gets into a warm climate he will prefer sleeping on deck, and the steamer bedding is not allowed to be used for that purpose. The best packages are, beyond all question, portmanteaus and a carpet bag; for besides being more easily stowable in a cabin, (*one* may generally be kept there), they can bear a good deal of tumbling about in holds and baggage-rooms, on camels' backs, and in river-steamers, while the wooden chest or trunk is very liable to get knocked to pieces or wetted through."

Ladies who may proceed by the Southampton steamers to Alexandria, *en route* to India, will proportion their equipment accordingly. If they will go back a few pages to the list of articles suggested for the sea voyage, and divide that list by two, they will arrive at something like a reasonable conclusion as to what may be really necessary for them.

Some parties prefer going through France and Italy on their way to India. There is no doubt that the pleasure of the trip is greatly heightened by taking such a route, if the countries have not been visited upon any previous occasion, though it is not unattended by inconvenience. In the event of the adoption of such a route, all the baggage requisite for the sea trip, upon the Red Sea side of the isthmus of Suez, should be sent previously by the Southampton steamer, consigned to some reputable house at Alexandria. There is a material difference in the charge for luggage, if it is understood that the Indian half of the journey will be accomplished in one of the

Oriental and Peninsular Steam Navigation Company's vessels. After going through France, if the traveller purposes terminating his land journey at Marseilles, he will find French steamers leaving every ten days, or more frequently, for Malta, whither he can proceed to await the Southampton steamer, or go on at once in the French vessel to Alexandria. In the event of a possible detention at either place, and he has his option, we would recommend his proceeding to Egypt without delay, as the time of detention there may be more profitably spent, though possibly not more agreeably, for an introduction to any respectable parties at Malta insures the visitor much hospitality. Should the outward-bound traveller extend his journey to Italy, he may calculate on finding Neapolitan steamers either at Genoa, Leghorn, or Naples, once, or oftener, every ten days, and in one of these he will obtain a quick and comfortable passage to Malta, touching at one or more of the ports in Sicily. The cost of the passage for a single man from Marseilles to Malta is about £10; from Naples to Malta about £4; a French steamer charges £11 more, independently of the table, from Malta to Alexandria; and the Oriental and Peninsular Company £17. 10*s.* for the latter trip, the English vessel supplying a liberal table and wines without further charge.

If persons who are on their way to India, having at some previous time seen Italy and France, are now desirous of extending their knowledge of Europe in another direction, it will be competent for them, on paying the whole amount of their passage to India to the Oriental and Peninsular Steam Navigation Company, to proceed free of charge in the Company's weekly Peninsular steamers, to the coast of Spain and Portugal, visiting Vigo, Oporto, Lisbon, Cintra, Cadiz, Seville, &c., joining the Alexandria steamer at Gibraltar.

No description of places so well known as Malta and Gibraltar can here be necessary; but as some particulars of the attractions of Egypt, the manner of getting across the desert, and of proceeding from Suez to India, may be of interest and value, we will again draw from the *Asiatic Journal* a portion of the description of an *Overland Trip,* recently written by the author of this compilation, immediately after the journey had been completed. To render it more intelligible to the outward traveller, the order of the paper has been somewhat reversed :—

"Arrived at Alexandria, we proceeded, a-donkey-back, to the *Hôtel de l'Europe.* There are two tolerable hotels at this place—the *Hôtel de l'Orient* and the *Hôtel de l'Europe.* The charges are much the same (fifty piastres per day, wine not included,) at each; but at the former the style of living is French; at the latter, things are conducted more upon English principles. Dismissing your donkeys, *do not pay their drivers* (we foolishly did), neither should you do so going from Boulac to Cairo. These charges are borne by the Transit Company; it is part of the contract for the '*right-through*' passage to England. At Alexandria—where, when you have seen Pompey's Pillar, Cleopatra's Needle, the Pacha's palace and dockyards, and useless vessels of war, you have seen all—you will prepare for embarkation in the long, narrow, covered boat, in which you will be towed up the Mahmoudie canal by a small steamer, fitted with the Archimedean screw, to Alexandria. This is the only part of the whole trip from India that is positively disagreeable. There is no room for lying down in the canal boats, unless you take possession of the narrow tables or the floor beneath the tables, and then you are assailed by vermin. With this uninviting exception, it is your doom to sit bolt upright, on a hard seat, and keep yourself awake with talking, or get a crick in your neck by falling asleep without a support for your head.

"At Atfé you are transfixed to one of the little steamers navigating the Nile, and carried, in twelve hours, to Grand Cairo.

"We dismounted at the 'Great Eastern Hotel,' the head-quarters of the Egyptian Transit Company, who own the vans, horses, and boats, which transport passengers to and from Suez and Alexandria. Two-thirds of the passengers remained at this hotel, the remainder betaking themselves to Colombe's Hôtel de l'Europe. The latter is on every account to be preferred by future travellers. The rooms are cleaner and more spacious—the table is more sumptuously provided—the attendance infinitely better. The charges are, in the aggregate, the same at both hotels. Fifty piastres (the piastre is 2½*d.*) per diem include breakfast, luncheon, dinner, tea, and bed, with *café noir* in the morning. Candles are charged ten piastres, and five piastres (a shilling) are included in the bill for porterage. The wines are good, of their kind, and not very expensive. Marsala, the best and most commonly drank, costs fifteen piastres per bottle; claret, thirty piastres; champagne, fifty piastres. Bottled ale (Bass's and Hodgson's) is drank at ten piastres the bottle.

"The opportunity for sight-seeing in Cairo varies with the arrival of the steamer which is to carry the traveller the *other* half of his trip. If you find, on your arrival at Alexandria, that the steamer from India *awaits you* on the other side of the isthmus, the time allowed you by the Transit Company for running about is limited to the few hours which the camel will occupy in carrying your baggage across the strip of desert, in anticipation of your journey in the Cairo mail-coach; and *vice versâ*, on your reaching Suez from India, the English steamer being in waiting at Alexandria. On the other hand, if you are some days in Egypt in advance of the relay steamer, you may visit the pyramids, the Pasha's palace at the citadel, and his gardens at Shoubra, the petrified forest, the slave-market, the mosque of Sultan Hassan, the mint, manufactories, chicken-ovens, &c., at a cost of fifteen piastres per diem, the donkey which bears you and the *bakshish* to the guides included. A journey to the pyramids is particularly good fun, apart from the antiquarian enthusiasm which a man insensibly *gets up* on these occasions. The ride thither occupies two hours and a half; and should you fortunately be in Egypt while the corn is growing, the scene of your journey is particularly cheerful. Every inch of the ground to within two or three hundred yards of the base of the pyramid of Cheops, at Djeeza, is cultivated. The perfume of the crisp, fresh air is delicious; the lark rises from beneath your feet, the grasshopper (the locust?) disports across your path. As you approach the pyramid, Arab cultivators are seen running from different quarters of the field to offer you their services as guides to the summit. Keep them at arm's-length, or your purse and your pocket-handkerchief will speedily change owners. Your dragoman, or servant and interpreter, will select a proper escort when you have reached the termination of the journey.

"The first view of the Great Pyramid is rather disappointing. It does not augment in size as distance diminishes, nor can one form any correct notion of its stupendous bulk by comparison with any other neighbouring object 'upreared of human hands.' Its neighbours, Cephrenes, Philista, and Mycerinas, approach it too nearly in magnitude, and bear too close a family resemblance for purposes of contrast. They form a cluster of solitary monuments, insignificant in proportion to the vast extent of the desert cemetery which lies beyond and around them; and when the visitor reaches the base of 'Cheops,' the impression of its grandeur vanishes altogether, for the passage to the summit slopes so much, that little is visible beyond the first few stones, which invite, by their resemblance to a flight of steps, the ascent of the adventurers.

"It is advisable, if you are bent on mounting to the summit, to disencumber yourself of all but your shirt and a pair of hose trousers, for the journey upwards must be taken rapidly, and cannot easily be accomplished with warm and tight clothing. A couple of Arabs leap on to the stones immediately above you, and offer you each a hand, while a third follows to give you an impetus from behind, and catch you in case of a slip. Up you go, panting and toiling, as you mount step after step (each three feet in height), and stopping every four or five minutes to take breath and receive the cheering congratulations of your rude guides. '*Good, good, Inglese, berry good!*' and then, in an under tone, and with an impudent grin and extended hand, '*Bak-sheesh!*' Arrived at the top, and relieved from your fatigue, for it *does* try the sinews and disarrange the bellows, you sit to contemplate the prospect. Now you begin to be sensible of the altitude of the pyramid. From the apex of no insignificant building could you behold so much of the works of nature and the efforts of man. Before you lies Grand Cairo, with its cupolas, fortifications, minarets, and cypresses; beneath you, and to the very walls of the town, is spread a carpet of softest green, fringed by the silvery Nile. To the extreme right, and to the left, and for the whole space behind you, is the vast and apparently illimitable world of sand, where myriads of minute crystals glitter and sparkle in the sun, relieving the dead and dreary monotony of the boundless expanse. You insensibly fall into a reverie, while the scenes of the mighty past flit before you, like so many 'dissolving views.' The history of the twelve kings, the discovery of Moses in the bulrushes, the adventures of Joseph and his brethren, the loves of Antony and Cleopatra; the more modern events, in which Napoleon and the French army, Mahomed Ali and the Mamelukes, have figured, successively occupy your musings. In a moment, the vision is dissipated, your guides are at your elbow, and while one whispers the eternal '*buk-sheesh,*' with a leer, another draws from his bosom a rude porcelain imitation of a mummy, and hints, '*Antique! antique! you buy? Bedouin berry good.*'

"The descent from the summit of the Great Pyramid is rather more fatiguing than the ascent. Perhaps neither the one nor the other would weary an athletic man of temperate habits; but a month's confinement in a steamer, and its concomitant animal indulgences, do somewhat impair the climbing faculties. The intending traveller in Egypt should bear this wholesome fact in mind, and carefully resist the wiles and blandishments which, in the form of basins of mock-turtle and flagons of iced champagne, woo him to obesity.

"At the foot of the pyramid, on the slope of a hill, are certain subterraneous excavations, which answer the purpose of resting-places, refectories, and dormitories, for the visitor. The Bedouins, who people a village in the neighbourhood, have established a proprietary right to these desert hotels, and claim a few piastres for permitting you to lodge therein. Pay the sum asked, and keep the fellows and their sheiks from your threshold, or you may hunt, and hunt in vain, for the silver fork and spoon which you have probably brought in your pocket, to assist at the breakfast and luncheon table.

"There is another pyramid, popularly called Belzoni's, in the immediate neighbourhood of that which bears the name of Cheops. A few yards from the apex of this second monument, the stones are glazed, which renders the ascent a feat of dexterity very few travellers can boast of accomplishing. The Arabs will undertake to reach the top in five minutes, for the bonus of half a dollar. Of the two, it will, perhaps, be more agreeable to let these gentlemen scale the height, at the cost proposed, than to attempt it yourself, unless you particularly wish to *say* you have been at the summit; and even in such case Tom Sheridan's advice conveniently comes to your aid.

"After bivouacking a couple of hours in the rocky hollows, consuming half a dozen of the minute chickens and diminutive doves, which form the *toujours perdrix* of a Cairo dinner, we strolled out to see the Sphynx, and some recently-discovered sarcophagi. The Sphynx is said, by certain travellers, to wear a peculiarly benignant expression of countenance, and to retain many traces of the beauty of the original sculpture. There is no ascertaining, at this date, whether the travellers who so spoke of this remnant of antiquity were gifted with powerful imaginations, or adhered religiously to matter of fact: it is certain, however, that age, or that neglect which imparts, in time, a vinegar aspect to the countenance of the most comely belle, has bereft the Sphynx of her benignity. To my perception, the colossal head (all that now remains) very closely resembles, when seen in profile, a cynical doctor of laws, with wig awry, suffering strangulation per tight cravat.

"Seven or eight miles beyond the pyramids of Djeezah, lie the smaller pyramids of Sercara, and the celebrated mummy-pits. These tempted some of our party to linger another day in the desert, while the rest returned to Cairo. For the peculiar guidance and information of those who may wish to creep into mummy-pits, and to wander in darkness and foul air, amidst dust, and slime, and ordure, saluted with occasional flaps from the wings of disturbed owls and confused bats, I would beg to refer to Mr. St. John's interesting book, *Egypt and Mahomed Ali.* The other sights of Cairo and its neighbourhood, after the pyramids, are the Pasha's palace, in the citadel (where rich damask curtains and satin hangings, *à la Françuise*, are associated with coarse arabesques and wretched attempts at perspective by a Greek, and divans and sofas, *à la Turque*), the country-seat at Shoubra (where myrtles under severe restraint, box disciplined to represent ships and peacocks, and pavilions built in humble imitation of the Trianons, remind one of the French gardens, *siècle* Louis XIV.), the Mint, the chicken-ovens, Joseph's Well, Hassan's Mosque, the hospital, the slave-market, the petrified forest, and the obelisk at Heliopolis. All these, and other points of attraction, including Mahomed Ali himself, have been so frequently described, that it is unnecessary to speak particularly of them in this place. The Mint, intended to shew how far the Pasha of Egypt is in advance of other Oriental potentates, merely demonstrates how much his machinery for coining is in arrear of that in use in England and in India. Joseph's Well, curious for its depth, confuses people who associate it with an incident in the history of one or other of the Scriptural Josephs, instead of ascribing its construction to the vizier Yusuf, who lived in A.D. 1100; while the *chicken-ovens* leave the curious traveller in amaze that such a hatching process should be resorted to when the natural course could be adopted with smaller risk and cost, and the certainty of a larger and better breed of birds being produced. To the other objects of interest at Cairo, accessible to those who will be at the trouble of soliciting the privilege of inspection, I may add the private museum of Dr. Henry Abbott, the secretary to the Egyptian Literary Association. There are many curious antique remains in this collection; coins, gems, household deities, implements of daily use among the Egyptians, MSS., ornaments, &c., which would be a prize in the British Museum, and for which the French government would pay *any* equivalent. Amongst the reliques, the doctor shews his visitors a piece of *virtù*, evidently of Greek origin, for the Egyptians never could conceive of any thing so perfectly natural and beautiful. It consists of two bronze figures of lizards, as large as life, engaged in mortal combat. One has seized the other by the middle of the body, pressing down his head with a fore-paw, and the root of his tail with a hind-paw, while the lower parts of the two rival tails are entwined and distended by muscular exertion. Nothing can be more true to nature than the representation of the sinews of the animals in the fury of the contest. The prostrate lizard's head and neck, however, exhibit helplessness and suffering. Pressed by the vigorous claw of his antagonist, his upper extremities appear quite paralyzed, and it is obvious, that if he can be held in that attitude for many minutes, the victory is assured. The convolutions of the bodies of these figures, and the development of the muscles in a state of violent action, are worthy of a comparison with the famous Laocoon.

"The slave-maket at Cairo will disappoint the visitor who expects to behold ranges of romantic Circassians, poetical Greeks, and voluptuous Georgians, inviting purchasers by the display of their charms and the glances of their black eyes, or exciting sympathy by the cruel helplessness of their condition. Instead of this interesting spectacle, the stranger will be fortunate if he sees half a dozen forbidding Nubians and Abyssinians, as black as jet, and possessing no other recommendation than their obvious capacity to undergo the drudgery to which they may be subjected by their future proprietors.

"A bath at Cairo, after a voyage, is an *agrément* which few will deny themselves. It is neither as elaborate nor as effective an affair as a Persian bath, but, like Mercutio's wound, 'it will serve.' The soft coir, or fibrous matter, which is used instead of flannel or the hair-glove, is not by any means so efficacious as the latter in removing the sodden matter, or *papier maché*, which covers the human cuticle. Then there is neither shampooing, nor joint-cracking, nor mustachio-dying; nevertheless, it is pleasant to *get into hot water* after a month's exclusion from the indulgence, even though some of the accessories to the hummaum are wanting.

* * * * *

"Our baggage having been sent forward to Suez on camels, we prepared to cross the desert. The uninitiated reader will doubtless picture to himself a complete Oriental *cortège*, such as we find in the illustrations of the works of Buckingham and Burckhardt, turbaned travellers, long strings of camels, rude tents, guards bristling with arms, a flaring sun, drought, privation, a single palm-tree, and the apex of a pyramid in the distance. Ah, *nous avons changé tout cela!* Thanks to the exertions of the British agents and associations, who make it their business to promote the intercourse with India, there is little difference now between travelling seventy miles over a post-road in England and going over the same space of ground on the isthmus of Suez. Forty vans, each drawn by four good horses, and driven by an Egyptian jehu, carrying from four to six inside and none out, transport the living contents of two crowded steamers across the arid and desolate plain which divides Cairo from the Red Sea. Some of the vans have arched roofs, like those of common waggons, waterproof, and painted green. They are all light, but very strong, and capable of bearing, without damage, the violent collisions with lumps of stone and rock, to which they are exposed in some parts of the road. The passengers sit, omnibus-fashion, at the sides of the vehicles, entering at the back; an arrangement, that is unavoidable from the height of the wheels (a single pair), which reach half-way up the body of the van. The seats are carpeted, and the whole thing is roomy and commodious. At the end of every ten or twelve miles, horses are changed at a sort of road-side stable-inn, erected for the purpose; at two or three of which the traveller will get a capital dinner, or breakfast, or luncheon, of eggs, mutton-chops, roast pigeons, stewed fowls, potatoes, bread, and good bottled ale, with tea or coffee, if he prefer them. Midway, and at the halting-place, twenty miles from Cairo, there are divans, or sofas, all round the chief apartment, and bed-rooms for ladies and married people. At one of these it is as well to sleep for a few hours, for sixteen hours' continual travelling in the vans will be found *de trop* by people unaccustomed to great fatigue. From all this it is obvious that the day has gone by for grand desert, or, as they call it, overland preparations. Let the traveller, therefore, shun the tempting advertisements of outfitters and guide-books. All the urgent recommendations, that people should provide themselves with camel-saddles, canteens, bottles of water, parasols, braces of pistols, green veils, carpets, &c., are superfluous. Dress yourself lightly for the day, carrying a cloak or great-coat for the night. Put a tooth-brush, a clean shirt, and a couple of dollars into your pocket, and you are completely equipped for the trip.

"Suez is not very inviting externally, and when you get fairly within its walls you are satisfied that its exterior has not deceived you. Every thing, excepting the court-yard of the Caravanserai, which does duty for a custom-house, and contains numerous bales of silks, drugs, grain, &c., denotes poverty and wretchedness. The houses, built of rough-hewn lumps of rocks cemented by mud, or a clay composed of sand, water, and coarse lime, have a dun-coloured exterior, in capital keeping with the dirty faces of the people and the soil on which the town is built. Still, there is enough in Suez to interest, at the first view, a traveller who has never before beheld a purely Mahomedan town. The place is thickly inhabited by Arabs, Egyptians, Copts, and a few Turks. Caravans of camels, which have just arrived, laden with merchandize from Cairo, or awaiting recumbent their loads of wealth from the farther East; mules and donkeys saddled for travellers; an occasional horse covered with gay trappings; the long dark bazaar and the lofty minaret; the veiled and masked female, and the swarthy, bearded male, present a picture nearly new even to the man who has just left Cairo.

"A six days' trip from Suez, with fine weather and pleasant breezes, carries you to Aden, and you have now had a good opportunity of judging of the accommodation and capabilities of the steamer. The *Hindostan* is a very fine steamer, of nearly 2000 tons burthen, with engines of 500-horse power. She has a magnificent saloon, or cuddy, where eighty persons can dine with comfort in cool weather. They might be equally at their ease in warm weather if the space now consecrated to fanciful pictures of the Nile were devoted to port-holes. The cabins are numerous, and in each of these are two berths and a horse-hair sofa (convertible into a third berth), a wash-hand stand, a mirror, and a pair of boot-hooks. When one person has a cabin to himself, it is only very disagreeably warm and confined; when two are located in the same closet, it is unspeakably hot and inconvenient; and when there are three 'cribbed and confined' in the same *endroit*, it is—but the thing may be conceived by persons who have been accustomed to dwell upon the sufferings of the captives in the Black Hole. There is a shower-bath and a plunge-bath on the starboard side of the vessel, and you may stand upon the grating near the paddle-boxes and be deluged with buckets of salt-water by an obliging seaman. The two former are the most agreeable methods of performing an ablution, but when you have sixty male fellow-passengers all equally anxious with yourself to dabble and splash in the cool fluid, it is sometimes unavoidably necessary to have recourse to the third process. The larboard side of the *Hindostan,* from the end of the cuddy to the gangway, is appropriated to the ladies, who have cabins, baths, and a small saloon to themselves. The library on board is select, and well adapted to the instruction and entertainment of the traveller in Egypt, Syria, India, &c. And as for the table!—I have here transcribed the bill of fare on one single day, and will trouble the greatest *gourmet* of the City of London Corporation to say if he could add any thing to the *carte:*—

"Mock turtle soup and bouilli—boiled legs of mutton—roast ditto—jugged hare—roast capons—corned pork—pigeon pies—roast geese—stewed breast of mutton and green peas—boiled and roast turkeys—ham—roast shoulder of mutton and onion sauce—harricot—boiled capons and tongues—stewed ducks and green peas—roast beef—curried mutton and chickens—rice—potatoes, boiled and baked—pickles and sauces of every description—jam puddings—gooseberry, plum, currant, and cherry tarts—stewed pippins—maccaroni and cheese—rice puddings. A dessert of almonds, raisins, brandy—fruits and preserves, oranges, plaintains, biscuits. At dinner, sherry, claret, champagne, ale, and porter. At dessert, port, madeira, and sherry.—The wine well iced. The breakfasts were (and are still, I dare say) on the same scale of liberality. Then there was luncheon, and tea and coffee in the morning while decks were washing, and a fusillade of soda-water kept up from nine A.M. until nine P.M. In truth, meals were so numerous, and blended into each other so felicitously, that life on board the *Hindostan* was one vast *monstre* refection. In a word, if she were better ventilated, and every two cabins thrown into one, and lighted, the *Hindostan* would be an unexceptionable vessel. No steamer can be easier and smoother on the water; the action of her machinery is almost inaudible—there is no tremulous motion perceptible when the paddles are at work—the crew and engineers understand their duty, and do it, and Captain Moresby is an excellent man. It may be added, that abundance of steam-water is allowed the passengers for washing purposes, and the bed-linen, towels, &c., required on board, being found by the Oriental Steam-Navigation Company, there is no occasion to take any with you. The *Bentinck* is, if possible, a finer vessel than the *Hindostan*, certainly cooler and more roomy.

"Aden presents us with one of those phenomena which the giant 'steam' is every day and everywhere achieving. Barren rocks, and a few yards of sandy shore, once tenanted only by the sea-gull and the crab, are now covered by cheerful domiciles, and animated by a small but busy and contented population, who live by unloading the fuel-ships, storing and protecting the coal, and embarking it upon the steamers. Upon the shore of a little bay, formed by a small belt of rocks, stands a spacious and commodious building of wood, wattle, and dab, covered within and without by whitewash, and duly matted and thatched, which serves the purposes of an hotel. Some enterprising Parsees from Bombay started and maintain this establishment, where the steam-boat traveller will find an excellent and (all things considered) not expensive table and cellar, clean beds, white linen, and excellent attendance. Fire-wood and sweet water, being brought from a considerable distance, must necessarily be dear; but they do not constitute special items in the bill, unless you indulge in a fresh bath, when four shillings, or two rupees, are payable. Donkeys and their attendant vagabond owners are available by scores, and it is usual to hire one for a ride to the Arab town of Aden, four miles from the anchorage, and inspect the scene of many a bloody strife, before our troops established their present footing on the soil of the Ishmaelite. We were regaled with excellent fish, including oysters, during our stay at Aden. But, indeed, there was no deficiency of any of the necessaries of life. Every thing that reasonable men can desire is obtained in abundance from the interior; and, judging from the specimens of grain and vegetables daily brought in on camels' backs, there can be no doubt of the richness and fertility of the soil of Arabia. It was singular to see every Arab in and about Aden unarmed. On the opposite coast, and on the shores of the Persian Gulf—nay, from Bussorah to Constantinople, from Bushire to Tabreez—you rarely meet a man without his matchlock, his kundjur, or his scimitar, and sometimes with all three, and a lance and pistols into the bargain; but here you would fancy that the Moslem had ceased to war with his fellow, for if his hand *be* against every body, it is at Aden an *empty* hand! This restriction upon the use of arms has originated with the political agent, and is no doubt intended as a protection against treachery. There is not, however, much of that to be apprehended now. The people are evidently more than reconciled to British authority, for they flock to Aden in numbers totally unknown during the government of the Sultan. From six hundred to a thousand souls inhabited the town before our conquest and occupation : at this moment there are not less than 20,000 living there !"

From Aden the steamer goes to Ceylon, *en route* to Madras and Calcutta. If, however, the traveller is bound to Bombay, he embarks at Suez in one of the smaller steamers belonging to the East-India Company, and proceeds to his destination direct. The Bombay steamers are neither so commodious nor so expeditious as those belonging to the Oriental and Peninsular Company, but they are sufficiently comfortable for a short trip, and are seldom crowded with passengers.

We now arrive in India; for a description of the principal places in which, the reader is referred to the Itinerary.

TRAVELLING IN INDIA.—LAND TRAVELLING.

There are but two methods of travelling by land in India, on horseback or in a palanquin. The former method is tedious if only one or two horses be used, and even with relays can only be safely and comfortably prosecuted during the mornings before sunrise, or in the evenings when the sun has much declined, while the latter enables the traveller to pursue his journey unintermittingly throughout the twenty-four hours. Nevertheless, the horse is very generally used for economy's sake, by officers proceeding to join their regiments, and often from the necessity of accompanying detachments of corps on duty; and in very short trips it is frequently adopted from choice, especially when the distance can be accomplished with a single halt, if relays of horses are provided by friends. In marching—as the travelling on horseback by daily stages of twelve, fifteen, or twenty miles is called—it is customary to send on your servants one march in advance, with tent, bedding, tent-furniture, canteen, &c. &c., so as to give time for your tent to be pitched and your breakfast to be prepared by the time you may reach the ground yourself. In the different villages, no difficulty is experienced in procuring fowls, eggs, milk, rice, and the common vegetables of the country; but every thing else, such as tea, coffee, dried or preserved meats, sauces, spices, wine, beer, &c., must be procured at one of the principal towns in sufficient quantities to last a week, or even much longer; for though these things can be obtained on the route, they are necessarily more expensive, owing to the cost of carriage from the presidency. Food and fodder for your cattle are always available, at prices varying with the character or fertility of the country in which the halt may be made. Having arrived at your ground, and refreshed yourself with a nap or a meal, or both, you may, if the sun be not too powerful, proceed, gun in hand, to a neighbouring jheel or tank (lake or pond), or piece of stubble-land, and shoot for a few hours. Snipe, wild fowl, quail, partridges, and hares, abound (according to the season) in most parts of India, and not unfrequently the sportsman's toil is rewarded with a florican, a jungle-cock, or even a bustard. No particular costume, differing from the dress of every-day life in India, is requisite on the march, but it will be prudent to wear a sola topee, or hat composed of the soft pulp of a tree, or a straw hat covered with white cotton cloth or feathers; and a pair of jack-boots will be serviceable as protecting the legs while riding, and also in wandering in covers or along the edges of swamps or tanks. Should the traveller possess nothing of the sportsman's ardour, he may advantageously spend a little time beyond the walls of his tent, in inspecting the temples, serais, and other works of art in the neighbourhood, or in observing the usages of the people in the surrounding villages. He must be scrupulously careful, however, of committing any act of aggression, or of violating any of the prejudices of caste or religion; for though the people are, generally speaking, civil, if not obsequious and timid, they will not scruple to assemble in a body and assault a solitary and unprotected individual, if provoked thereto by an offensive interference with their usages. Injury done to a cow, the death of a monkey or a peacock, or entrance into a temple booted and spurred, are amongst the outrages of which the Hindoo, in different parts of India, is peculiarly intolerant. Travelling by *dawk*, or post, as the trip in a palanquin is designated, involves more fatigue and expense than the method of moving across the country just described, and is by no means so independent, seeing that all the stoppages must be settled beforehand and adhered to; but it has the advantage of very superior expedition. Preparatory to setting out on a journey, a palanquin must be purchased, and fitted up so as to enable its tenant to have a few books, his shaving and washing apparatus, a canister of biscuits, a bottle and glass, a drinking-cup, a little additional night clothing—a few books and his writing materials always at hand. A good strong palanquin may be procured for less than 100 rupees (£10), and can always be disposed of at the end of the journey, if the owner have no further occasion for it. The clothes of the traveller and such articles as he does not immediately require, are carried in tin boxes, or wicker baskets, called pettarahs, by separate bearers, who run ahead or alongside of the palanquin; and these pettarahs may be procured in any number at the chief towns and stations at a very slight cost. Of money it will be necessary to carry in *silver* as much as will be required for the expenses of the entire journey, especially if the route lies through different territories, for the civil officers of the respective presidencies, and the residents (envoys) at native courts, have no pecuniary relations with each other. It will be also advisable to carry a considerable number of the smaller coins of eight and four annas, as gratuities to boatmen who ferry you across the small nullahs or rivers, and to the palanquin-bearers (called hammals at Bombay), at each stage; for in many parts of the country these latter people are paid so irregularly, or kept so much in arrears, that their very subsistence depends upon the bounty of the dawk traveller. Eight annas (one shilling) at each stage for the entire set of bearers, is, however, as much as is ever expected in the way of bonus. When the traveller is prepared to set out, his first business is to write to the postmaster-general, stating how many bearers he would like to have (twelve is the usual number, but it is sometimes reduced to eight when no great expedition is requisite), how many banghy-bearers for his pettarahs, where he proposes to stop, and for how many hours. The postmaster then writes to the different villages and post stations, ordering relays to be posted at the appointed hours, and intimates to you the amount to be paid to the limits of the presidency, including a deposit (afterwards refunded), on account of possible demurrage. A mussaul (called in Bengal a mussalchee), or torch-bearer, is added to the number, and his duty is to carry a flambeau during the night. The flambeau is composed of twisted hemp, fed with oil from a hollow bamboo, likewise carried by the mussaul.

RIVER TRAVELLING.

Although several of the rivers in India are navigable for boats of considerable burthen, those alone on which Europeans are accustomed to travel are the Ganges and its tributaries (the Hooghly, the Bhauguruttee, the Jumna) and the Indus. Running as does the first through a populous and most important section of the British dominions in India, it connects many of the principal civil and military stations with the seat of the Supreme Government; while the Indus affords an easy channel of communication between the extreme point of the north-west possessions and the island of Bombay, passing the provinces and chief towns in Scinde. The traffic on these rivers is immense. By the Ganges the entire produce of Europe, Southern India, the Eastern Archipelago, and China, is distributed upwards between Calcutta, Benares, and Allahabad, and carried from the latter town to the great north-western cities of Lucknow, Agra, Delhi, and the stations of Cawnpore and Meerut, &c., &c.; while the return boats convey to the capital and the cities on the river's banks the raw cotton, piece goods, rich stuffs, grain, horses, indigo, sugar, and the thousand smaller commodities and fabrics produced in the interior. The boats on the Indus are freighted, on their voyage from the mouth of the river to the frontier station of Ferozepore, with the commerce of the Persian and Arabian Gulfs, Cutch, Western India, and so much of the products of Europe and of China, procurable in the Bombay market, as are available to Scinde, the Punjaub, and Upper India. The downward cargoes consist of the produce of the three latter states and provinces, and of Affghanistan and Cashmere. There are two methods of travelling on the Ganges, namely, the flat-bottomed vessels towed by iron steamers, and by pinnaces or budgerows, constructed much after the fashion of the royal or civic barges which float on the Thames, but with the addition of a mast and sails, and sometimes boasting a schooner rig, or the more ambitious equipment of a Lilliputian brig. The rapidity with which the steamer-led flats effect their voyages gives them a preference over the sailing-boat, a preference which is somewhat strengthened by the attractions of society; but where great expedition is not a material object, and where it may be of importance, or a matter of inclination, to visit the principal stations on the river-route, or necessary to convey a family and a large quantity of baggage, the budgerow or pinnace should be selected.

The flats, or accommodation-boats, consist of sixteen cabins ranged on either side of the vessel. These are divided into three classes, and cost respectively for the entire trip from Calcutta to Allahabad (at the confluence of the Ganges and Jumna), three hundred, two hundred and fifty, and two hundred rupees. The charge for the downward trip is much less, because the course of the stream assists the progress of the vessel and essentially shortens the voyage. Besides the sum paid for the cabin, the passenger is charged three rupees per diem for his table, which consists of a substantial breakfast, a luncheon, dinner, and tea. All wines, beer, spirituous liquors, &c., are paid for separately, and at rather exorbitant rates. The baggage and furniture requisite for the trip (there is none of the latter to be found in the government boats), must be carried in the cabin; the remainder, to the extent of five cwt. only, is placed below in a species of hold, and is not available until the end of the voyage. The superior cabins, however, are sufficiently spacious to contain all that the traveller may require, those of the first class being between twelve and a half feet long, the second nine and a half, and both eight and a half in breadth. The third class cabins are but five feet and a half in length, and are consequently only adapted to persons of an inferior grade of life. Every passenger is allowed to take with him one servant free of cost for his passage; his diet, if he be a Mussulman, being paid for to the master of the flat, at the rate of four annas (sixpence) per diem. Hindoo servants diet themselves, to which end they disembark every evening when the vessel comes to an anchor. The ordinary length of the entire passage of these boats is three weeks. They stop every three or four days at different stations on the river's banks to take in coal, which is carried in the steam tug only, and deliver and receive packages. This affords the passengers a brief opportunity of seeing a little of the country beyond what can be discerned from the deck of the vessel during the trip. The steam tugs attached to the accommodation or flat boats are of iron, and propelled each by two engines of thirty-horse power; they are connected with the flat by hawsers and a beam, five-and-twenty feet in length, and a foot in width, which answers the double purpose of a medium of communication between the two vessels at all hours, and a protection from the risk of collision when the steamer happens to ground or to slacken her speed too suddenly. The greater part of these steamers and their attendant flats are the property of the government, at the office of whose superintending officer passages should be engaged; but the great demand for conveyance to the interior by vessels of this kind, and the enormous prices charged by the government for freight and passage, has led certain private individuals to place other steamers upon the same line, which will doubtless be less expensive. The experiment of competition has been too recently tried to enable us to say if it has succeeded, or to mention the cost of travelling by such means; there can be no difficulty, however, in ascertaining these points upon the spot.

Parties who, for the reasons given above, prefer effecting their voyage to their appointed station in a budgerow or pinnace, will do well to address themselves to any of the boat-agents in Calcutta, Messrs. Kemp, Strickland and Co., or Holmes and Co., stating the number of persons requiring accommodation (more than three will be inconvenient), the distance to be travelled, the quantity of baggage to be taken. The expense varies with the number of oars required. A twelve-oared budgerow costs three rupees eight annas per day:—

	Rupees.	Annas.
Fourteen oars	4	12
Sixteen oars	5	12
Eighteen oars	6	4

Two or three officers engaging the largest description of boat will find the cost of the native trip, whithersoever they may be bound, fall short of the boat-allowance granted them by the government. The clubbing together is, therefore, not merely agreeable, as ensuring social intercourse during a long and somewhat wearisome pilgrimage, but commendable as a piece of economy. In addition to the budgerow, a dinghy, or covered native row-boat, is required as an attendant kitchen; for the culinary process on board the budgerow would be both disagreeable and inconvenient.

The furniture of the boat should be of a permanently valuable quality; that is to say, it should consist of articles convertible to useful purposes after the voyage has been completed. Accordingly, the soldier would do well to provide himself with a camp-table, a camp-stool or folding-chair, a charpoy or bedstead, the bottom of which consists of broad tape or sacking, laced and stretched crosswise, and, therefore, not only less liable to injury than a cane or wooden bottom, but more easily replaced when worn out, and at all times susceptible of washing; a copper basin (called a guindy at Bombay, and a chillumchee in Bengal), and folding tripod for its support; a narrow carpet, or rug; a hanging lamp (that which he had on board of ship, if he had gone to India in a sailing vessel, will do); a canteen; bullock or camel trunks, a *chaise percée*,* and one or two morahs, or stools. All articles beyond these, in the furniture way, are positive superfluities. Of the articles requisite for the table, the toilet, and the pastime of the *voyageur*, it is not easy to give general instructions, because, beyond the mere necessaries of life, the quantity and description of these things will so materially depend upon individual taste and means. A good head-servant, or *khitmutghar*, will take care to provide poultry, eggs, milk, rice, spices, and vegetables, as the boat reaches towns and villages on the river's banks; but every thing else must be procured at the starting place; and it should be borne in mind, by persons going upwards from Cal-

* H. Pratt, of New Bond-street, has fabricated a light and compact article of this description, which will be found of great utility on the march.

cutta, that it is good economy to lay in store for the entire voyage, inasmuch as all articles, the produce of Europe, augment in price in proportion to the distance from the metropolis whence they are carried. Wines, malt and spirituous liquors, preserves, cheeses, pickles, &c., sealed meats, hams, tongues, pickles, &c., cost, at Benares, double the price paid at the presidency, treble when they are sold at Cawnpore, and so on. The *ennui* consequent upon the confinement on board a budgerow, during the entire day, makes the possession of certain articles, otherwise luxuries and superfluities, a matter of essential importance to the traveller. Thus, a good double-barrelled fowling-piece will be requisite to ensure a little sport on shore before sunrise and after sunset. Drawing materials will serve to while away a few hours in sketching the scenery on the banks, the costumes of the people, the boats in the river.

Books, a chess and backgammon board, and musical instruments, supply endless entertainment; and it will be no bad plan if the beginner were to apply himself to the study of the language of the country, with the help of Gilchrist and Shakespear. The boatmen and native servants do not speak the purest Hindostanee nor the least exceptionable Bengalee; but there is nothing lost by acquiring a familiarity with a *patois*, which, in the common intercourse of life, is perhaps of more importance than the undefiled language taught by the best philologists, and used at courts, and in the transaction of public business.

With respect to costume, money, and the attention which it is important to pay to native prejudices and customs, the same remarks hold good as have been offered in the section of hints for dawk travellers and persons on the march; it is needless, therefore, to repeat them. One word only: in the treatment of native servants on the river voyages, it is advisable to combine the greatest strictness with the most perfect forbearance. Look well into the khitmutghar's accounts; trust him with no more money than is really wanted at the different halting-places; insist upon the most deferential and respectful demeanour, neither permitting familiar speech nor a disregard of cleanliness and propriety of costume; require a correct return every evening of your plate, table-linen, and dusters, and exact payment for every piece of crockery or glass carelessly broken, and every article or other fabric alleged to be lost. The neglect of these matters at the commencement renders servants dirty, impertinent, and dishonest, and involves more serious loss than would at first thought be conceived. On the other hand, be careful of striking a servant for *any* offence he may commit; for, in the first place, it is cowardly to raise a hand to one who is incapable of physical retort; and, in the second, it places the offending servant in the advantageous position of a prosecutor for a species of assault which is always severely visited by the Company's courts of law. Another disadvantage attending a resort to the *argumentum baculinum* is the tolerable certainty of the servant's quitting the boat under cover of the night, leaving the inexperienced traveller perfectly helpless, at a great distance from any station where the services of the man can be replaced. You must bear patiently with the offending domestic on the occasion of misconduct, reserving vengeance for a suitable opportunity of appealing to a local magistrate and of supplying the place of the discarded servant.

A voyage up or down the Indus is accomplished, at present, with less comfort and facility than a trip on the Ganges, by reason of the ignorance of the boat-owners of European ideas of comfort, the comparative rarity of the trip, the destitute state of the scattered villages upon either bank, and the free-booting propensities of the people of Scinde and the Punjaub. Small steamers now and then ply on the Indus; but, apart from their occasional detention on the business of the government by whom they are maintained, they are liable to get upon some of the numerous sand-banks with which the river abounds, and to remain there for a considerable time. A resort to the Sutledge boats (when the voyage is to be made downwards) is, therefore, prudent, if not unavoidable. These are long and clumsy, and are not propelled at a greater rate than one mile an hour, if so much, while the current carries them two miles per hour. A late author, who made the voyage down in one, describes their form as resembling that of a Thames coal-barge. The stern, however, is greatly elevated, and the steersman stands thereon working a broad paddle as a rudder, assisted by two men, who use oars. The passenger occupies the entire length of the boat between the stem and the stern, in a rude apartment made of bamboos and strong grass, thirteen or fourteen feet in length, and rather more than half that space in breadth. The boats carry one mast and a sail, removable at pleasure, and when the wind is foul, they are tracked along shore by the boatmen; a usage, by the way, equally common upon the Ganges. The boat-hire averages five-and-forty rupees per mensem, and it is always made a condition by the owners, that the boat be engaged for a period sufficiently long to enable her to return to her starting-point: thus, a voyage of a fortnight's duration will cost as much as if it lasted three months; and if it be engaged down to the sea, it is charged for at the rate of a six months' trip. The price paid includes the charge for the crew, and, "indeed, every expense but the thatching, which costs the traveller twenty rupees in addition." In respect to the supplies requisite during the voyage, rather more foresight will be requisite than in the case of a Ganges trip, for, excepting Bhawulpore, Sukker, and Hyderabad, there is not a place on either side of the rivers Sutledge and Indus where any thing can be procured. Rice, eggs, flour, oil, milk, and butter, must, in the Sutledge, form part of the traveller's original stock, as they are not to be obtained at the miserable villages of Scinde and the Punjaub. In respect to the furniture of the boats, and the articles generally requisite, the suggestions offered above may be considered entirely applicable, with this addition, that when on the Sutledge and Indus fire-arms are perhaps useful; on the Ganges they are by no means necessary.

TRAVELLING BY SEA.

The occasion for this mode of transit from one part of India to another is so rare that it scarcely seems necessary to offer any special advice.

It is only when gentlemen are proceeding from port to port on the Malabar and Coromandel coasts that it becomes essential, in the absence of a steamer, or a sailing free-trader, or country ship, to engage a pattamar, or large sea-going boat. When such are resorted to, the provision to be made will resemble that which has been recommended for the river voyages, though on a much more moderate scale, as the trips along the coast seldom occupy many days. The amount of passage-money will materially depend upon the circumstances of the vessel. If the pattamar be already laden with cargo for the coasts, the proportion of accommodation set apart for the passengers will not cost so much as if the boat had been specifically engaged to carry a party from one port to another. Water and fuel are always included in the charge for the passage in either case, but all else must be taken on board.

In proceeding by a sailing vessel or steamer to join a regiment or a civil employment (the only occasion on which duty will call any public servant from the continent of India), at Moulmein, Arracan, Penang, Malacca, or Aden, the officer will be furnished with a passage by the government, and this will include cabin, table, &c., in the same degree, and after the same manner, as in the case of a voyage from England in a sailing vessel. The sole care of the passenger will be to furnish himself with such articles as may be scarce and dear at the station to which he is ordered, more especially those which are produced in England; for the prices thereof, always high at the several presidencies, become exorbitant when the charges of further exportation and the profit of the retailer come to be added.

SOCIETY, SOCIAL HABITS, AND DOMESTIC EXPENDITURE IN INDIA.

In the great majority of instances, it happens that those of our countrymen who go to India to seek their fortunes, do so at a period of life too early to have allowed of their seeing much society at home, and consequently with too little experience of it to have formed any judgment that can enable them to compare it with the social system which they find established in the land of promise to which they have been led. But to those who do visit India in the maturity of life, and who have been accustomed to move in the good circles of England, the contrast must be striking, and, we apprehend, unfavourable to the Anglo-Indian community. The stranger's eye will at first, indeed, be dazzled by a showiness and profusion, which have the semblance of grandeur, but he will speedily miss the elegance and comfort of an English gentleman's establishment, and above all he will miss, at the presidencies, that cordial hospitality which in our own land ever follows a proper introduction. In fact, it is not speaking too strongly to say that, in the acknowledged sense of the word in England, there is *no* society in India. People meet together, it is true, and dine together; but the nameless charm is ever wanting, and this deficiency is, in our opinion, as easily accounted for, as to the observant eye it is early visible.

The men and women who chiefly compose the society leave home in their immaturity. The conditions of the Company's service render this, for the most part, indispensable, as regards their own servants; and the residents, whose daughters are being educated in the parent country, have a double inducement for getting them quickly out; first, the great cost of maintaining them at home, and secondly, the fear that, if they are old when they arrive, there will be "nobody coming to marry them;" and that, consequently, the life-provision, which was looked forward to, will have passed beyond their reach for ever and for ever. The men and women of Indian society, then, may be said to leave the home of their fathers as merely boys and girls, green in mind though blooming in person, and almost totally deficient in the knowledge of society, and what constitutes either its conveniences or its charms. Then, there is no such thing in India as a class of persons of easy fortune, who depend not on any kind of daily labour for their bread, and who need only concern themselves in public business as far as it suits their dispositions or their fancy so to do, but who have the means of commanding the literary and social *agrémens* of life, and the talent to thoroughly appreciate the former mental luxury, and even of adding to the abundance of its supply.

But in all that we have said, it must be borne in mind that we are comparing the Indian presidencies with London, and that they *must* lose most grievously in the comparison. Rarely revisiting their native land (though the power of steam is gradually obviating that disadvantage), residents in India necessarily degenerate, in an intellectual sense, and also in what are regarded as good manners and social habits in England, and their minds and judgments become contracted by a life of monotonous routine, in respect to European subjects of mental cultivation, so that they are at last not only backward, but bigoted, in many such respects; and are looked upon, whenever they do revisit their native land, as conceited and ill-informed beyond what they really are. From having long ceased to see and know the *best* of every thing in sciences, arts, and the minor elegancies of life, they come to have an incompetent standard by which to estimate things in these various departments; and thus the best painter, the best singer, the best actor, the best scholar, the best horseman, the best musician, the best speaker, the best any thing, in fact, in *India*, is taken to be the best of the kind respectively in the world; and we have known old Indians, by no means deficient in understanding, who, even after a visit to London, could not bring their minds to see the superiority of really superior things, because they had been so long accustomed to meaner criteria of perfection.

Another circumstance which prevents the tone of the Anglo-Indian's mind from acquiring strength or his mind itself from preserving its elasticity, is the humdrum nature of the only society he has.

Dine where you will in Calcutta, Madras, or Bombay, you are sure to meet either the same people, or some of the same people, or, all in all, the same description of people; so that your faculties have no new exercise, nothing to polish or to keep them keen; no new range, or species, of intellect to encounter; and thus they become either rusted, or stiffened, or worn, by one kind of constant use, into such unwhetstonable bluntness, that they are past all renewing by the time they come into collision with the better-exercised minds of England, and are bewildered, or soured, or stupified, by the too-late discovery. The intending adventurer, therefore, who shall peruse these passages, may lay his account in meeting with but a second-rate society, in regard to manners, customs, and even intellect (save in respect to local affairs), on his arrival in India; but there is this comfort in store for him, namely, that he will inevitably get used to it, and, without greater exertion than is usually employed, he will find his English mind subsiding to the Anglo-Indian level; and, forgetting the standards of excellence which he leaves behind him, will in time, like the rest of his expatriated countrymen, deem that the best which is the best he knows.

Regarding those divertisements of society which are strictly social without being strictly private, and without which mere private society would languish to the death in any quarter of the world, Calcutta, at least, is not without its variety, and even its abundance. Of these, the re-unions, held during the cold season in the Town-Hall, are the first in rank, as being the most exclusive. Subscribers to them must belong to the Government-House list—a range of admission which varies under every new reign —or be passed by the "Committee of Reference," which is empowered to decide upon all claims, and which is rigid in its scrutiny. Besides these, there occur in the course of every cold season some events which are deemed important enough to deserve especial celebration. Some locally great personage is going away, or some new governor is arriving, or some domestico-political anniversary is coming round, or the bachelors think the ladies should have an entertainment, or something or other there is sure to be, which will serve as a peg to hang a public dinner or a public ball upon. Then there are the races, and the amateur theatre, and concerts, and fancy fairs; and as these shows are always well attended by the temporary visitors, whose new faces also serve to allure the listless residents of *pseudo* ton to the same haunts, the city may be said to be a scene of great vivacity and amusement between November and March—indemnifying people, in some measure, for the lethargic in-door lives they have led during the previous months of caloric, and re-energizing them to again sustain the same infliction during the season which is approaching. At Bombay, the pastimes of the cold weather nearly correspond with those of Calcutta, excepting that they have no amateur theatre. At Madras, the entertainments, bating the races, are purely private.

Recurring to the *agrémens* of private life, we may comprise them in one word—a dinner; and as to that chief auxiliary to society, they are, in India, far behind the home *cuisine* in every material respect. The native servants have no inherent taste, and no conception of elegance of arrangement. Their sole idea of a good dinner is a plentiful and a coarse one; and a joint of meat between every two people would be, in their eyes, a festival which the late Lord Sefton himself would be a perfect madman to turn up his nose at. During the past few years, the kitchen schoolmaster has somewhat improved this hecatomb system into comparative elegance; but the *tout ensemble* is still, in the majority of instances, far removed from the perfection attained to in the "tight little island." The beautiful table-cloth, the brilliant glasses, the highly-polished silver, which adorn the tables of almost every private family in England, and not only of the wealthy, are almost *unknown* in India, and the *fault* of never changing the glasses on the removal of the cloth, is so much a part of the *system*, that it is no more considered as a solecism there, than would be the appearance of the most delicate oyster patty as a part of the refection. In little appertaining to the table, in fact, is the *comme il faut* thoroughly understood; the wines in use are inferior in quality to the same wines in England (the long sea voyage being detrimental to the finer French wines), and there is nothing like the variety of them which characterizes every good cellar in the motherland.

In India, almost every man is a man of business —of laborious daily business, so great, that it amounts almost to a physical miracle how in such a climate the work can be performed by the natives of other lands—and he at last becomes so mentally interwoven with his official duty, that he can think of nothing else in the hours when he is disengaged from the drudgery of his desk; thus, "the shop" forms the staple of his social converse, and virtually banishes the superior orders of intellectual recreation. At the presidencies, there are two distinct *classes* of society, though each have various intermingling branches; those are the persons having the right or privilege of public *entrée* to the Government Houses, and those who neither possess the right, nor are allowed the privilege. All persons in the civil and military services of the Queen or East-India Company have the *right* here mentioned, without any reference to their several ranks or salaries; and the *privilege* is more or less extensively disseminated throughout the principal merchants, the law profession, the gentlemen of the Press, the uncovenanted servants, the East-Indians, and the natives themselves. This grand line of demarcation, however, has no avowed practical influence in the arrangements of the general society; where individuals constantly meet at private tables, who can never see each other at the Government-House assemblies. Again, the gentlemen of different classes meet on terms of intimacy in cases where the ladies of the higher grade will not mingle with the wives of their husbands' occasional companions in the lower—an exception which holds in London as well as in Calcutta, and which necessarily arises out of the intercourse of business. But the "trail of the serpent," which is all over Indian society, is the official *hauteur* of men who in England would be esteemed as very ordinary persons, but who have the weakness to imagine that the extrinsic circumstance of their being counsellors, secretaries, judges, magistrates, or staff officers, is sufficient to exalt them in the social scale, and to command a deference to which their intrinsic qualities would give them no extraordinary title.

But it must be confessed that, even where society is not infested by these important personages, it falls, intellectually, far below the festive or other social re-unions, which render London and continental society in various ways so charming. The labours of the day have wearied the body, and there is no new stimulus to invigorate the mind. No critical political question in agitation, on the decision of which hangs the fate of a minister, and which for the time excites the hopes and fears of some and the curiosity of all, and flings a dash of manly energy into the evening discussion where men do congregate. No delightful new novel, or biography, just steaming from the press, and forming the cynosure of tongues in acute criticism or pleasing compliment. No enlivening anecdote of the day, or current piece of wit, or gay badinage, or unpedantic disquisition. No learned leisure, or "lettered ease," and no *lion* to be seen or discoursed of. The pursuits of the official day are uppermost in all men's minds; and opium, indigo, or banking; Government regulations, decrees, or correspondence; military orders, appointments, or allowances; or something or other immediately connected with the political or commercial proceedings of the period, form the heavy staple of after-dinner talk, bringing the honey-heavy dew of slumber on the weary lids of the new arrival, and sending him home convinced or informed of nothing but that the party had been dull, and that the intercourse of tongues had not added one grain of wheat to his intellectual granary. Subjects of light conversation are of great rarity. Exhibitions, operas, plays, fair *débutantes*, literary or fashionable gossip, and the encounter of wit which these topics call forth, are nearly all wanting to the Indian community, every one of whom is known to every one in such a degree as to leave nothing tellable about men in any way locally eminent which all do not know already, or which the few who happen not to be on a par with the rest in that species of knowledge care much to know, because they are familiar—by sight and name at least, and generally by acquaintance, or constant official or other business intercourse with the parties referred to, and have no longer that curiosity about them with which the eminent characters of London society inspire the mass of the conversational community. There is nothing, in fact, to dissipate the languor which is induced by the drudgery of the day, and the constitutional depression which is a consequence of the climate, for the monthly packet of overland news from Europe brings seldom any thing to long interest the public mind of India; and of books, the novelty and freshness are worn off before they reach India, by the reviews and other criticisms which always precede them, and make them appear stale to the transoceanic reader before he has an opportunity of giving them a perusal.

Yet, with all this characteristic (for, alas! it is not merely occasional) dulness and uninstructiveness of social life, it need not appear paradoxical to the reflecting reader if we assert, that in no community of like numerical proportion, is a greater amount of general ability, strong sense, and individual cleverness to be found, than exists among the European gentry of our eastern capital.

Almost every one who comes to India, in the rank of life to which alone our observations are to be understood to apply, has the means of procuring introductions to one or other of the regular inhabitants, and these introductions will always serve to procure him one or more opportunities of making his observations on the social habits of the new people among whom he has been cast. He will be invited to dinner by those to whom his letters are addressed (he may find exceptions, however, even to this rule of hospitality), and according as they chance to be married men or bachelors, so will be the phase of the social life which he will for the most part see. If his introduction be to a bachelor "well to do," his fortune will be greater than if he carry credentials to married people only; for, in the former case, he will, in all probability, be offered a domicile, which in general means a corner-room, were he will have to bring his own bed, and be attended by his own servants; but in the latter event, he will be almost sure to be left at one of the hotels, or in his bare-walled and unfurnished barrack-room, as the case may happen to be; and if he be invited by his friend's friend to dinner, he will most likely be very glad to get back to his temporary home again, and will care little how seldom the honour may be repeated. If he be an officer in the Queen's or Company's service, his sojourn at the capital will necessarily be brief—say a month at the utmost, unless his regiment be stationed there—and in that case it would be lost labour to endeavour by a round of visits (nine-tenths of which would never be returned) to establish himself among the permanent residents on terms of equal sociality. He will, even if he have no introductions, soon form acquaintances among those of his own class, and will receive the hospitality of the mess in the barracks,* or of some brother sub, who will instruct him in cigar-smoking, auction and bazaar purchases, horse-flesh, dogs, and the coarser species of local scandal—in the "life," in fact, of that warm-hearted, careless, and practically philosophical section of the Anglo-Indian people. If he be of the class who are at once permanently settled at the presidencies, and who are at the same time admissible to the well-defined, yet apparently confused, circle of society to which we are adverting—if, for example, he be a member of the bar, and properly introduced as such, he will make his round of calls (for the stranger, excepting at Bombay, must call on the residents, by way of a beginning) on the principal inhabitants, and will in due course find the civility returned, and that again followed by the formal procedure of an invitation to dinner; after which he will naturally fall into a mixed society of his own professional *kith*, and the less constantly busy, and consequently more accessible, persons of the various services, the merchants, &c., and may lead "a very merry, hey down derry, sort of life enough," and yet one which shall not interrupt his proper pursuits of business. Strictly speaking, there are no "idlers"

* At each presidency there is a fortress containing barracks for two or three thousand men.

at either Calcutta, Madras, or Bombay, unless it be the few officers who are on leave of absence, and the young writers who are studying the language!

The Indian hospitality, in its olden phase, has almost totally disappeared, and consequently there are not now any of those sheep-and-bullock dinners, round which from forty to eighty guests assembled, and which certainly had an air of grandeur to the unaccustomed eye, and which was supported at an expense totally incompatible with the more modern system of living, and, alas! of means. Now-a-days, a party of twenty (excepting at a mess) is considered large, and the usual number varies from eight to sixteen—the medium quantity being, perhaps, the one oftenest collected. Nor are even these so unlike angels' visits as the traditionary belief in England of Indian munificence might lead the reader to suppose. They are rife enough, it is true, contrasted with similar demonstrations in any other civilized quarter of the British empire; but, compared to the almost ceaseless and open-door hospitality of the olden time, they are, it must be confessed, not so plentiful as blackberries, where blackberries *are* plentiful.

The wane of hospitality, which introduced respectable hotels, made at the same time an opening for boarding and lodging houses—things unheard of even in Calcutta twenty years ago; but they are not (or the exceptive cases are extremely rare) made subservient to the purposes of the permanent inhabitants, among whom the practice is for even bachelors to keep house, each for himself, the *chumming* system occasionally varying the monotony; while the "publics" above mentioned are, as elsewhere, the resort of the occasional visitants, who find good accommodation in them, on reasonable terms, and are thus saved "a world of woe" in establishing themselves on their own accounts for the few months, or perhaps weeks, of their oppidan existence. The interiors of the private houses are all so alike, in the arrangement of the rooms, the verandahs, and the portion of furnishing, that he who has seen two or three of the medium size and style will find scarcely any variety in an inspection of the rest, though great novelty, and, to the unaccustomed eye, discomfort, and even the uneasiness arising from a mixture of the fine and the shabby, when his mind's eye contrasts what is before him with his recollections of the elegance and comfort of home domestic arrangement. The houses of the richer classes may contain better chairs and couches than those of their less affluent fellow-citizens—mahogany instead of imitative toon, jackwood or blackwood, or the lighter-coloured but polishable and well-grained teak; and the punkahs of Dives may be more elaborately gilded than those of the poorer householder; while the silk or damask of his couches may parade it somewhat more finely than the chintz of the inferior. The wall-shades, too, may be better (probably not proportionately more numerous), by having drops to them, or double branches, and richer chandeliers may aid in illuminating the rooms of the wealthier inhabitant; but *the way of doing the thing* is the same in all, and the want of what in England is considered perfect elegance is as observable in the Government-Houses as in the more limited mansion of him whose monthly income (for in India all incomes, whether yearly or otherwise, are paid *by the month*) may vary from five hundred to a thousand of the Company's rupees.

Works of art, as the term is properly understood in Europe, can hardly be said to exist in our eastern cities. The prints which are hung up to hide the nakedness of the "whitened walls" are seldom of the higher class of engravings—the best impressions not always finding their way out to India; and of pieces of *vertu*, ornaments in bronze and alabaster, or even beautiful japan-ware, there is a plentiful lack, though the best which are on the spot appear in the eyes of the possessors as good as the best which are anywhere else. Every person who keeps house has his service of plate—more or less extensive, according to his station; but well-cleaned plate is a thing not to be met with among high or low. We do not mean to insinuate that it is dirty, but the servants have not the method of imparting to it that brilliancy of polish which causes it in England to add so greatly to the beauty of a dinner-table; and the same remark is applicable to the glass-ware, which, generally speaking, is in all respects inferior to that in use in England, even among the humbler-fortuned classes of the gentry. So much for an outline sketch of the domestic economy.

In regard to apparel, a few remarks will suffice. From March till October, the European clothes himself in white cotton jacket, like a barber's or a footman's in the morning—and decorates himself in broad-cloth for the remainder of the twelvemonth, though there are some gentlemen who have been so thoroughly sun-dried, that they can wear the woollens all the year round without serious exudation. As to the general nature of his other habits, if he reside in town, or at one of the large stations, it is pretty accurately as follows:—He rises early—the lark having no start of him—and in the cold season proceeds to take a fresh air gallop, or, if he be a subscriber to a hunt, he "goes to the dogs" in that way. In the warm weather, as he must return home soon after the sun is up, he usually undresses, puts on his *pajamas* (the loose Turkish trouser), drinks iced soda-water, lies down on the couch, novel or newspaper in hand, and in all human probability goes to sleep, in spite of all the cawing of crows (for India is as full of them as a rookery is of rooks), the creaking of wheels, the shrill cry of kites, and the general native bustle; rises, bathes, and dresses, so as to have breakfast over by ten—the said meal consisting, at all seasons, of rice, fried fish, eggs, omelette, preserves, tea, coffee, &c., more in the fashion of a Scotch than an English matutinal recreation—and soon after goes to the counting-house or office, and there labours assiduously till four or five o'clock in his vocation, when he returns home and undresses himself (after a little more lounging on the couch than is really necessary for his bodily refreshment), to prepare, by a new course of bathing and toiletting, for the evening drive, to see "the order of the course." Every one keeps a horse, and most men a plurality of that various quadruped, which is to be had of all sorts, sizes, and prices, from the pony (familiarly called *tat*—corruption of the native name for the small animal, *tattoo*), at from thirty up to two hundred rupees, to the horse, *par excellence*, of which the price varies from the last-mentioned sum, or, by'r lady, even less, up to two, five, and even ten thousand rupees, according to his qualities and the uses for which the purchaser may intend him. Also do all men keep buggies, at the least—a buggy being a one-horse vehicle, combining something of the advantages and appearance, with but little of the style, of the Stanhope cabriolet—and, in addition to this, a singly-blessed merchant, or government official, keeps unto himself a palankeen carriage (called, at Bombay, a shigrampo), which carries him to and from office, and is just a larger (not always even a larger) sort of palankeen, mounted on wheels, and drawn by one horse, or by two horses, instead of being carried upon four men's shoulders. Married persons of even minor condition keep their carriages, which are not thirty pounds per annum more expensive than the buggy, and which are constantly to be had for private sale, or at auctions, horses and all, for from about a hundred and fifty to three hundred pounds. The evening drive has no recommendation beyond that of passing the most disagreeable hour of the day in inhaling coolish air, for you meet the same faces, the same equipages, and receive and make the same formal bows, almost every evening, and the mind derives no refreshment, save what goes to it through the body. The drive is succeeded by a languid sort of dinner, and the whole community are asleep before eleven.

In England, where business of every kind—political, commercial, and miscellaneous—is in so great a measure (as is known to be the case) carried on by means of oral communications, it will excite surprise to learn how little is thus transacted in the metropolis of India; and any mercantile man arriving there and at once entering upon his vocation, would at first not comprehend the necessity for the apparently time-wasting system which we are going to describe, and which we shall denominate the CHIT-SYSTEM. The word *chit* does not signify in India, as it does in England, we believe, a saucy little girl, but is a corruption of the Hindee term *chit hee* (loosely pronounced *chitty*), which in English means "a letter," be the same short or long, for they have no such epistolary distinction there as corresponds with our "notes," "letters," &c., all kinds of letters being indicated by the one common epithet. Throughout the British eastern territories, then, verbal messages, by servants, are almost totally unknown, and wholly so on matters of any importance; so that *chits* are flying about the town all day, and a particular class of servants, called peons, or sepoys, are kept in very constant employment as the bearers of these despatches. Written generally in haste, not commonly on matters of consequence, many having to be written every day, and the bearers being unable to master their contents, a slovenly habit has been naturally fallen into of despatching them carelessly folded, written on scraps of paper, and despatched unwafered or unsealed; whence it happens that persons in the way of receiving a multitude of them daily sometimes open the *chits* designed for other people, which the stupidity of the peon, or the careless directions of his master, may have been the means of leading to the unintended house; and in this way curious secrets have sometimes been arrived at in a very innocent spirit. The system itself is, we apprehend, inevitable, for the climate does not admit of the constant running about of Europeans themselves: their Eurasian clerks cannot go a hundred yards without incurring the cost of a palankeen. The English can rarely speak the native language well enough to enable them to intercommunicate by means of native servants, and there would be various objections to trusting a native with the purport of such communications, even where some of the baboos, sircars, purvoes, and others of that genus, can converse with sufficient comprehensiveness in English for the purpose. In the cold season, more, of course, is done by personal intercourse than in the *housing* times of the year; but even shopping of all kinds is principally carried on by *chits*, and for borrowing a book, as much as for borrowing a thousand rupees, a *chit* has to be written, and a *chit* answer returned, in the event of the loan not being accorded. Where a *chit* requires no answer, or where an affirmative rejoinder needs no explanation (such as where one accepts a friendly invitation to dinner), then the word *salaam*, sent by the messenger to his master, serves the several purposes of an acknowledgment of, or a receipt for, the *chit*, and an acquiescence in the request it contained; but so firmly based in usage and social convenience is the old system of *chit* circulation, that although an anna post, on the principle of the London twopenny one, was made a speculation of by a sanguine individual in Calcutta, it was not found in any degree to supersede the use of private peons; and, indeed, no such establishment could be effectual for its purpose, which had not a "delivery" every quarter of an hour, at the seldomest rate of transaction.*

We have hitherto been speaking of the gentleman *chit* affairs; those of the ladies are the same in principle, but, oh! how dissimilar in practice! We think we do not exaggerate when we say that every lady of *ton* at either presidency has to write, on an average, two thousand *chits* per annum; but in theirs is observable none of the slovenliness which characterizes the bulk of the masculine dealings in the same industrious line. Neatly written, neatly folded, on pretty paper, and either sealed with all the discretion of Donna Julia's own, or else so cunningly implicated into cocked hats, twists, and other sacred involutions, that to make wax itself "render up its trust" would be far less trouble than the unfolding of such missives by unpractised fingers.

But the stranger will long be sorely perplexed by that branch of the system (and it is a most important branch) which concerns the name and whereabout of the particular gentleman with whom he wishes to communicate. A Johnson, Smith, Brown, Jones, or Robinson will be as so much caviare to the multitude of peons, if referred to under the principles of English orthoepy. The identification, to be of any utility, must be made thus:—Janseen, Ismitt, Burroon, June, or Rabbyseen; and as these are among the easiest specimens of our nomenclature, let the bewildered exile judge, *ex pede*, of the difficulties

* Men of business send their *chits*, for the most part, in a book, in which is written the name of the *sendee*, who puts his initials opposite thereto, and thus supplies a voucher of the safe delivery, in case he answers not the communication on the instant.

which await him, when he shall come to encounter the various tailed Macs, Os, Fitzes, and the poly-syllabic and crackling designations which Britons are wont to hold, and some of which are not inferior to the Russian breakers,

Of twelve consonants apiece.

Then, as to the localities; albeit there are some streets with pure English specifications, not only have almost all such got a native denotement also, but the others have aboriginal distinguishments only, and unless the tongue and memory of the new inhabitant can master them, he may as well whistle for his correspondent as attempt to send a servant to his "local habitation," and in a knowledge of his "name." His only resource must otherwise be some of the old stagers, or their servants, until custom shall have familiarized him with these peculiarities.

Another usage, which cannot fail to strike a newly-arrived emigrant to Calcutta with surprise, but which he will find to be in many respects convenient, and scarcely at all perplexing, is the extent and variety of street-traffic which will be forced upon his notice as he lolls in his palankeen. In London, there is a species and degree of this retail trade, to be sure, in the shape of fruit-stalls, stick-exhibitions, oyster-stands, old-book temptations, and wandering Jews; but they are only tolerated by the municipality; whereas in Calcutta there is no right of interference with the out-door race, and as regards "Europe" articles, they are all perambulatory. Hats, stocks, boots, shoes, books of all descriptions —new and old, standard and ephemeral, costly and cheap; prints, boxes of every species of the Geneva writing-desk, tea-caddy, and work-box; jewellery, forest-birds, looking-glasses, toys, guinea-pigs, foot-stools, dogs, ivory articles, whips of all sorts, fringe-work, shells, pedlary, perfumery—in a word, almost every portable thing, after its kind, is to be had from the street-venders, at rates which seem to baffle all doctrines of production-cost, and as good as the same kind of wares, &c., can be had in the native shops. The very centre of the street is the part where they most do ply, and they are so civil, patient, and insinuating, that it is rather an amusement than an annoyance, as you go along, palkee-borne, to haggle in a quiet way for whatever takes your fancy; and as the venders all smatter English, they are as acceptable to the griff on that score as he is to them, on account of the inexperience whence they can extract three rupees for the article which the old hand could obtain for eight annas, or just one-sixth of that amount.

As we speak of the sporting amusements of Calcutta in the portion of the Itinerary devoted to that capital, we shall in this place only mention one or two of the recreations which belong to the class called pic-nics, and which occasionally break through the business monotony of a Calcutta life. A day at Barrackpore Park, which is a lovely piece of ground, and in which the Government keep up a menagerie and aviary, allows the mind a holiday which it often stands in need of; and as the settledness of the weather between November and March is uniform enough to almost insure a party of this kind against the *contretems* of a ducking, and the temperature so pleasant as to involve no other risk to health from the unusual exposure of the skyey influences, there is a great deal of cordial cockney enjoyment derivable from such excursions, where the party is well assorted, and where it is understood that a spinster may be spoken to more than once by a bachelor without his being thereby involved in the inferential "offer," which, on more formal occasions, would be taken to be comprised, or at the very least intended, in such very deep familiarity. The party can go by land and return by water, or *vice versâ*, and thus obtain a variation of travel which, in returning especially from these exciting excursions, is well adapted to keep the mind from flagging, or feeling jaded, by its long and unusual state of joyous excitation. In the opposite direction—to wit, *down* the river Hooghly—the Company's Botanic Gardens are a favourite resort of all classes of the community upon Saturdays and Sundays.

But what are termed the Doorga Pooja holidays, which usually commence about the middle of September, and last eight or ten days, form the period of time which admits extended excursions of almost all classes of men of business from the metropolis, and there is as much deadness then in Calcutta as there is in London at or near the same time of the year. The Hindoo natives lay aside all kind of business, save what daily necessity renders it indispensable to pursue, and shops and offices are shut up, or their tradeful hum and bustle all but stagnated, while that great religious ceremonial is in course of being observed. Then the European merchant, the clerk, the official, the lawyer, the shopkeeper, and artisan, all absent themselves; some for several days, and some for a few weeks, in the certainty that competition cannot be active while they are gone, and that the general stagnation is such, that little could be profited by their remaining at their business. Pinnaces and budgerows are then hired for trips into the Mofussil, and the exploring citizen, who gets a hundred miles inland, feels from that hour at liberty to relate, when he revisits England, that he has travelled into the interior of India, and surveyed men and manners in the ruralities of our empire! At all times and seasons there are recreative lounges, fit to occupy an hour or two, within the precincts of the city, and which a justly-proud or good-natured "Ditcher" will, like his compeer of London, occasionally take a Mofussil "Cousin" to behold, or, as Pierre expressed it to Jaffier, to "gaze with wonder at, and envy." Such are the rooms and museum of the Asiatic Society, where you will see strange armours of Oriental and savage people, the sight of which would do good to the eyes of Sir H. Meyrick, and the possession of which would gladden his heart for ever; and where curious birds, beasts, and fishes are in a state of admirable preservation. Then there is the Mint, with its fine and ample machinery, to which the politeness of the Mint and Assay Masters insures easy access; a visit to some rich argosy in the river, or a ship-launch at Kidderpore, together with the fancy fairs and other devices, which assist greatly in their employment those whose labour it is to kill the time, or who, in a pure love of employment, are hunters of the lions in every part of the world.

The holiday amusements of the residents at Bombay are more limited than those of the inhabitants of Calcutta; but they are very delightful of their kind. The island of Elephanta, and its curious subterranean temples, the islands of Salsette, Gorabunder, and Bassein, all abounding with picturesque scenery, antiquities, and remains of the Portuguese dominion, are reached in two or three hours' sail, or in a land journey of the same duration. Livery-stable-keepers supply excellent carriages and horses to those who have not cattle of their own; and beautiful roomy boats, called bunder-boats, are obtainable at the piers, by application over-night. At Madras, the cold weather brings the opportunity for rural trips into the interior, where the diversions of shooting and hunting afford the toil-worn man of business a pleasant annual relaxation.

The important question of general morals, which in a disquisition on the social states should not be wholly overlooked, may be justly decided in favour of an Indian residence over a London one, as regards a young man just entering into life in search of his own subsistence. In our Oriental cities there are none of those lures and haunts which prove so attractive and fatal to the young Londoner. His Indian contemporary almost *must* spend his evenings in a decorous manner, for not only would he soon become marked if he frequented such scenes of debauchery as there are, which are of the very lowest description, and where common soldiers, sailors, and the absolute blackguards of the place resort; but there is not that field for "lark" which tempts the London spruce apprentice, and youths of higher degree, to take to the streets in search of such adventures. Drinking, too, is a practice not at all encouraged or countenanced in the Anglo-Indian community. It used to be so, but its pernicious day has long gone by, and the very, very few who are still victims to its brutifying power, are looked upon with mingled pity and contempt by all other classes of their fellow-citizens, and are morally mischievous, not from any bad influence which their vice can exercise over their own countrymen, but from the degree to which their sad propensity risks the degradation of the English character in the eyes of the native community, among all but the dregs of whom (and even among them the crime is rare compared to its spread among our own lower orders) drunkenness is looked upon with detestation and disgust. On the whole, whatever bugbear-born apprehension fond parents may entertain of sending their junior offspring to India, on account of fever, liver, cholera, sun-strokes, and Thugs, we may conscientiously assure them, that, whether in the Company's service or the mercantile or miscellaneous line of adventure, their morals are in infinitely less danger of contamination than they are in life in England; and other portions of this work, relating to the climate, and to the constitutional effect which it has upon foreign residents, will be sufficient, we think, to calm the fears of maternal hearts upon that score, and to convince them that Englishmen can live long comfortably and respectably in India, unless their own impropriety shall nullify their advantages.

Although we shall now lay down a full establishment, such as is kept up by a person of local rank or mercantile affluence at the presidencies, yet our details will be designed for the information and guidance of those who go to India to seek their fortunes, and whose mode of living must, or in prudence should, be rather in accordance with their immediate means and near prospects, than with any air-located castles which they may amuse themselves with raising, or even with any *certain* prospective advantages which many of them (writers, cadets, &c.) must possess—if they only live long enough, and continue in the service.

The few persons who are sent to India at years of discretion, and with their fortunes, rank, and stations ready cut out for them—such as members of council, commanders-in-chief, bishops, judges, law commissioners, and a few more of the same description—are at no loss about their domestic settlements; nor will it inchoate *their* ruin to expend a few rupees more than an accurate calculation of comforts might allow; whereas if the cadet, the merchant's clerk, or the tradesman were to *begin* imprudently, the consequences to them would be the "bread of sorrow" in after-days, when reflection, coming too late, could only serve for punishment. Young men who enter the civil service, and cadets, have a fixed and regularly-paid monthly salary from the day of their landing—the former having Rs. 300 and the latter Rs. 200 *per mensem;* with this farther difference, that the former, if a diligent student of the native languages, may in two years, or even less, acquire a material addition to his original income, while the latter may, and usually does, remain from six to twelve years in rank and emolument exactly where he started. They who come out in a good mercantile connection are also generally provided for at once, as clerks or assistants; but the tradesman or mechanic has to rely on the produce of his brow's sweat from the beginning, unless he chooses to eat into his little capital, which is just the last sort of meal we should advise him to make.

With reference to the mention of the local coin which the nature of this section will render it necessary for us to make, we may state at once that, although the rupee fluctuates in exchangeable value (in remittances to England) from 1*s.* 11*d.* to 2*s.* 1*d.*, and is sometimes lower and higher than these two points, respectively; yet it will give the reader a sufficiently correct estimate of our price-current observations, to consider it, in round numbers, as representing two shillings sterling. This scale will keep him, commercially and arithmetically speaking, very nearly right; but it will not (and nothing but local experience will) make him accurately acquainted with the great difference in what we may call the moral value of money in England and in India. A rupee is constantly given where even one shilling would be hesitated about by the better home economist, and is very frequently expended where even a sixpence would serve the turn in England; but the grounding of the adventurer in this description of unconveyable knowledge must be the work of experience and observations on the spot. Book learning will not assist him. If the "young gentleman" get into a Mess, or to *chum* with an old hand, it will be financially much the better for him at the outset, if he have common sense and ordinary prudence; but if circumstances so shape his lot that he shall have to keep house for himself, he will then find some benefit from remembering the information we design to supply. As a general rule, we recommend to him worthy Mrs. John Gilpin's accomplishment—" a frugal mind"—and with that aphorism, we shall proceed to set out a list of the expenses attending an Anglo-Indian establishment upon an entire scale, and subsequently point out the reductions in it which are applicable to inferior conditions of white mankind in the East. The cost named is the monthly cost.

ANGLO-INDIAN ESTABLISHMENT.

BOMBAY.	CALCUTTA.	MADRAS.	
House	House	House	Rs. 30 to Rs. 600.
Butler	Khansama	Dobash	Rs. 10 to Rs. 50.
Boy	Khidmutgar	Boy	Rs. 6 to Rs. 8.
Mussal	Musalchee	Musalchee	Rs. 4.
	Cook		Rs. 7 to Rs. 20.
Bearer	Sirdar-bearer	Head-bearer	Rs. 6.
	Mate-bearer	Bearer	Rs. 5.
Hammals	Palkee-bearers		Rs. 4 each.
Puckaulie	Bheesty	Puckally	Rs. 5.
Jaroo-wallah	Mihtur		Rs. 3 to Rs. 4.
	Dhobee	Washerman	Rs. 6.
	Tailor	Durzee	Rs. 6.
Sepoy	Peon or chupprassy	Peon	Rs. 5.
Gora-wallah	Syce	Ghirawallah	Rs. 5.
	Grasscutter		Rs. 3.
	Coachman		Rs. 8 to Rs. 20.
	Ayah		Rs. 7 to Rs. 16.
	Mihturanee	Tarrycatch	Rs. 5.
	Abdar		Rs. 8 to Rs. 12.
	Hookahburdar		Rs. 8.
Purvoe	Sircar or baboo	Dobarh	Rs. 10 —*up* to any thing.

Now we shall endeavour to give such a description

of each of these human items as shall convey to the tyro an intelligible, if not a very vivid, notion of their several duties and peculiarities; but before entering upon the "humanities," let us offer two or three hints concerning the domicile. As in almost every town "where men do congregate," so at the presidencies, there are houses in as great variety, in size, situation, and rent-charge, as there were dogs, after their kinds, in Islington, at the time Oliver Goldsmith classified the canine species of that ancient place into

> Mongrel, puppy, whelp, and hound,
> And cur of low degree;

and, of course, in this variety of dwelling-places, the purse may be suited even at the lowest ebb which will allow its possessor a roof over his unhappy head at all; but it is not easy for any respectably-situated person to procure a tenement which will insure him the lowest degree of comfort, with reference to the skyey influences, for a less rentage than fifty rupees a month; and such a house will probably be deficient as to convenience of site for any one whose daily business requires his presence in the town. Certainly, two, or even more, young men may take a house among them, even if circumstances should not allow of their living together throughout; but the adventurer who comes to India in a state of double-blessedness, or who imprudently gets into such a state too soon, financially speaking, afterwards will find himself compelled to put up with but sorry accommodation, compared with what the lowest Calcutta or Madras rent for a decent European—say thirty rupees a month, or nearly forty pounds per annum—would obtain for him in most parts of England. Houses, in fact, are very dear at each presidency, the higher class letting, without an atom of furnishing, at from £400 to £800 per annum, and no really respectable abode being to be had, in a convenient position, under £250 or £300 per annum (paid, like every thing else connected with the "domicile," in rupees, monthly), though without the addition, to the *renter*, of any description of municipal taxes. And now for the menials.

The khansama, or butler, acts the part which, in a moderate English establishment, is acted by the mistress and the cook together; that is to say, he markets, prepares the pastry and the made dishes, makes preserves, superintends the whole kitchen arrangement, and in general leaves nothing to the cook but the actual cooking. It is the custom to think him a rogue, and the theory is discreet, inasmuch as it induces a strict scrutiny of his accounts; but to infer from it that he is less honest than an English servant would be under like facilities, were to libel the khansama. In the first place, a poor or only a middling rich man—one of the happy *juste milieu*,—has no business to have this functionary upon his establishment at all. He is a luxury for the rich, and in their houses he has such scope for "knavish tricks," that his not plundering his employer on a large scale is to be noted to his credit, under the head of the virtue denominated abstinence. He is entitled by prescriptive right to charge the round rupee for any thing which falls but a little short of it: thus, as there are sixteen annas in the rupee, he would debit "master" with the integral coin, though he might have obtained the article for fourteen annas; and, in addition to this, he obtains, as a matter of course (the rule in all native dealings), what is termed *dustooree,* which means 'custom;' and this is levied from the vender at the rate of half an anna out of every rupee, so that, in every thirty-two rupees, the purchaser gains *one,*—being upwards of three per cent.,—and we believe there are cases where the exaction is extended to double that amount. Scarcely any but the lower orders of Anglo-Indians go to market for themselves. In even the humblest establishments, where a butler, as such, is no more dreamt of than any other philosophy of grandeur, the solitary khidmutgar, or boy, will dub himself, and be dubbed by his inferiors, by that much-usurped culinary title; but in houses of degree, where he is an avowed functionary, his wages are according to his cunning in his art, and one who is an Ude among the numerous members of his tribe will get fifty rupees a month, though that rate is rare: ten, twelve, and sixteen rupees may be taken as the running averages of the species. They are always intelligent, respectful, and well-mannered men—Mussulmans, or Parsees—and have much influence in the house, being treated very familiarly (within perfectly becoming bounds) by their masters and mistresses, of whose interests they are usually watchful against all depredators but themselves.

The khidmutgar, or boy, is of the khansama genus, and often assumes the title, where no regular one is kept. His own business, however, is (in a full establishment) solely to lay the table, bring up the dinner, and wait during the meal. A couple "well to do" would probably keep three or four of these menials, and more than that if the domestic quiver were full, for the children of such magnates have servants of their own. General honesty, amid much temptation and many facilities for a lapse from virtue, cannot but be conceded to them; for they have constant access to the plate, wines, tea, table linen, and similar valuables, and might decamp with various spoons under all reasonable chances of impunity, as the police is rather inferior to that of Paris when Fouché had its management. The khidmutgar is a clean and smart-looking servant, not at all *mal-adroit* in the practice of waiting, though inferior in nimbleness to the true English waiter, to whom, however, it must be remembered, there is no necessity for his being equal, because, as at all Indian parties every guest brings his or her own attendant (and seldom so few as one apiece), the entertainer's servants have little or nothing to do with that part of the convivial business. Small people, if bachelors, are for the most part content with one khidmutgar, and dream not of a khansama; but whether there be one or half a dozen, the breakfast and dinner table exhibits the same fanciful neatness of arrangement. All the spoons in the house are displayed in the centre of the table, in various tasteful ways, and are interspersed with wine-glasses, flowers, silver forks, &c., while in the midst rises the butter-pot—of cut glass or silver, as the case may be—in which the butter appears like a piece of beautiful carved work, and, with the appliance of sparkling ice, is really tempting to behold. Indeed, the khidmutgar contrives to lay out a very enchanting breakfast with sufficiently simple means. The snowy whiteness of the daily-clean cloth, the green chillies floating in the clean water of the half-filled wine-glass, the eye-refreshing mustard and cress, the silver (which might be brighter), the pots or glass-ware recipients of various preserves, and lastly, the substantials—the omelette, the rice, the fish, the muffins, the *chitnee*, the cold meats, and the fresh and fragrant tea—all have a tendency to create an appetite beneath the ribs of death, and to render gaunt famine, or penurious scarcity, quite impossible visitants.

Next in descent to the above-described "obedient humble servant" comes the musalchee (at Bombay called a mussal), who is like unto the scullion in British households, but who looks to being one day a khidmutgar, and who has even attained, though in rare instances, the khansamaship itself—just as a clerk in the treasury *might* rise to be a lord of it, or the cook of the home old bachelor get exalted into ruling the *whole* roast of the establishment. The analogy between the musalchee and the scullion, indeed, is not complete in all its parts; for the former cleans knives, plates, spoons, glasses, &c., and does, in a word, the underwork of the butler's pantry, which is somewhat above the performances of the nymph of the scullery.

The cook, or *bawurchee*, called *bobberjee* by the English, who are the vilest corrupters on earth of both foreign languages and their own, is in a rank by himself, and composed of himself solely, unless he has a *mate* (not meaning a wife), as in large houses he has. To the establishments of the smaller orders he is not essential, for the khidmutgar and musalchee will there manage that business very creditably between them; and where he is kept, he is paid according to his excellence. Pity 'tis that neither he nor any of the rest, who have a hand in the preparation of the meals, will ever taste any thing, though, under that disadvantage, it is "most wonderful, and after that out of all whooping," to see how accurate they are in the flavourings of the various dishes. Still, it bars them from attaining to that delicacy of touch and variety of savour which the cook at the Clarendon knows well enough; but if the said Clarendon cook were suddenly, by fairy power, wafted to, and set down in, an Oriental kitchen, and there told to prepare a dinner, consisting of every delicacy in fish, flesh, and pudding, for twenty people, by seven o'clock P.M., his first emotion would have a direct tendency to suicide, and his eventual calmness would be nothing more comfortable than a settled despair. Nothing that *he* would call a spit, a grate, an oven, or any one convenience would meet his wildered eye; and he might as well go to the Highlands to look for knee-buckles, as there to search for a dripping-pan, or a roller; sieves, dredgers, cullenders, and such like would be just as plentiful as blackberries are in Hyde Park, and even a dishclout would be very difficult to procure. Yet the indigenous cook will, out of this nettle, deficiency, pluck the flower, good dinner.

But, leaving the culinary precincts, let us proceed into the body of the house, and there we meet, at

Calcutta at least, with the dignitary called the sirdar, or chief of the bearers, who is the person equivalent to that European functionary in whose eyes no man seems a hero—so levelled are we all by our mortal imperfections! The sirdar-bearer, called *sirdar*, in brevity, is, among other things, the valet-de-chambre. He prepares—he and his mate, if a mate be kept—the evening lights, a duty which naturally involves the furbishment of the candlesticks, glass shades, and snuffers, and which, at Bombay, is performed by the mussal, and at Madras by the matee. He also polishes the shoes, boots, straps, and so forth, of his master. Moreover, he rubs tables into brightness, with coco-nut shell and wax-cloth, makes the beds (for housemaids are things unknown), and performs a variety of little nameless items, which need not to be enumerated.

Among the upper classes (the upper in point of salary we mean), there are four or six palankeen-bearers retained, besides the sirdar and mate; but the two latter are to be found in almost every house, and may be considered indispensable. The former of these carries an immense bunch of keys at his girdle, and whether his master have boxes enough to demand a large bunch or not, such bunch there is sure to be, for the dignity of the office.

The bheesty (properly *bihishtee*) provides the water for the use of the whole establishment; hanging a sheepskin on his recreant *hip*, and carrying it along with apparent awkwardness, though with real ease. The duty, at Bombay, devolves on a puckalee, who carries the water in copper vessels, attached to a bamboo slung across the shoulders.

The mihtur—a word signifying "a prince!"—is the pariah of the establishment, but has no small opinion of himself, and is wise enough to eat of the crumbs (a phrase including every good thing) which fall from his master's table. He sweeps the house, cleans out the bathing-room, and does all the dirty work, in fact, as well as takes care of a dog or two, if necessary, and is usually the happiest and often the sprucest and the most prettily-wived of all the domestics.

The dhobee, or washerman, is fully explained to the English reader by his English name, though he differs in some respects from the English washer-woman, as well as in being of a different sex. For instance, while she is up to her elbows in a wash-tub, he is up to his knees in a tank, or may be in a river; while she rubs her knuckles into a shrivelled and blistery-looking skin, he bangs the linen raiment of master, mistress, and child, against a serrated log, or a roughened stone; while she is all suds, the frothy article is scarcely known to him, and yet he is well off for soap, but the *modus operandi* is unfavourable for the accumulation of the frothy pile; while she mangles, he is ironing, with an enormous brazen iron, of which the weight has an effect equivalent to mangling, on the cloth; and finally, while she brings home her linen as yellow as saffron, he brings his home as white as snow. The dhobee of a bachelor gets the pay opposite to his name in the foregoing list; but where there is a lady in the case, his wages are at least doubled, and increased also by a rupee or two for every child.

The durzee, or tailor, is an indispensable adjunct,

his business being to mend the clothes as fast as the dhobee tears them, and for this purpose, chiefly, he works daily from morn till dewy eve—from nine o'clock till five, at the presidency, but from sunrise till sunset in the upper provinces, or (more comprehensively) in the Mofussil. A lady's tailor gets from eight to ten rupees a month, and has no very quiet life of it; but the scolding is systematic, and he cares little about the matter, though he never may have "heard great ordnance in the field." But the bachelor's tailor hath a life of ease and pleasure, working half the time for the servants, who pay him for that same.

The peon, chuprassy, peada, sepoy, or messenger, carries letters, runs by palankeens, stands behind carriages, and is altogether a functionary of consequence. When forming part of the official establishment of a civil servant, he is feared, hated, and outwardly reverenced, by the natives of the district —for then he acts as bailiff, process-server, and all manner of hateful things; and invariably turns his power into a source of unlawful profit, from exactions and general corruption.

The syce, or groom, does what his translated name denotes; but in a way very different from his English namesake. Smart and vigorous grooming is unknown in India, and, judging from the fair condition of the horses, would not appear to be needed. He, moreover, runs behind the horse, or vehicle, as the case may be; and will keep up with the latter for miles, without any apparent effort, as also with a horse going at an easy canter. He is a good and generally trustworthy servant.

The grasscutter is, nowadays, more a Mofussil appendage than a Presidency one; for in the latter place, grass or hay is purchasable; whereas in the former regions the grass has to be daily rooted up for the horses, and this labour is, in the dry and hot months, especially severe.

The coachman (in native corruption, *coachwaun*) would be out of his element in the crowded streets of London, or in a throng at the Opera, but he is sufficiently expert for his vocation in the East, where crowds of carriages are almost unknown, and where all cart-drivers, &c., are forced to get out of the way. He has no great delicacy of *rein*-touch, and not the smallest pride in his harness or other appointments, which, if the master chooses, will go dim and dirty enough. Indeed, the best Anglo-Indian turn-out is but a poor affair compared to the second-best London one. The entire cost of a carriage and pair—including not only the above-named stable-servants, but the periodical repairs, varnishings, &c.—is calculated to come within a hundred rupees a month, or about £100 sterling per annum.

The abdar (literally "keeper of the water") is he who used to cool the wines, water, &c., with saltpetre, before the enterprise of the Americans afforded the delightful luxury of ice; and his services are still called into requisition when the non-timely arrival of the ice-ships throws back the citizens upon their old resources. The abdar now manages the ice, but it is only in wealthy establishments that such a servant is retained, as the khidmutgar and sirdar-bearer, between them, can manage well enough.

The hookah-burdar is a domestic fast *going out*, in

consequence of the gradual, or indeed fast, supersession of the hookah by the cigar.

The ayah, or lady's maid, has no innate taste for dressing, but can usually plait hair well, and contrives to fasten a hook, and to stick in a pin so that it shall soon come out again. She is often the wife of one of the khidmutgars, and then the double wages make the service valuable to the worthy couple. Frequently, she is an Indo-Portuguese woman, and though a sad and ugly drab, is in most respects superior to the Mussulman women.

The mihturanee is usually the sweeper's wife, is more intelligent than the ayah, and does the slop-work of "my lady's chamber;" but is often, where there are no children, the only female on the establishment; in which case her wages are raised a rupee or so, and the arrangement answers very well. Where children are, then the women of both classes are multiplied in a concatenation accordingly.

The sircar, baboo, purvoe, or whatever he may be called, is the chancellor of the exchequer, and it is not unseldom (in the olden time it was always the case) that his master is his debtor—and then the mastership is but a *vox*. They are a shrewd, intelligent race, of most respectable appearance and demeanour, talk English, and manage every thing for you so easily and so delightfully, that where you feel you can always meet the day of reckoning, a sircar or purvoe is the most delightful servant you can have. They are almost always honest, in the sense of never absconding with your money, even where they give no security; because their great profit is made by commissions and small surcharges upon every thing you buy, and *dustooree*, or custom (per-centage, taken from the native seller), upon every payment you have to make. All men in business have sircars, but a mere private family, such as that of a military man, for example, seldom retains and does not require them. They are a strange compound of easiness and strictness, usuriousness and liberality, honesty and fraudulence, patience and importunity.

Such is an Indian household; a motley assemblage, and yet harmoniously enough conducted. Hindoo and Mussulman pull well together, and where good service is not done, it is oftener the fault of the employers than the employed.

DESCRIPTION AND ITINERARY

OF

THE PRINCIPAL PLACES IN INDIA.

DEPARTING from the plan usually adopted by gazetteers, who give the names of places alphabetically, and necessarily mention a great many which are of very small account, we have in the following confined our descriptions to towns, villages, stations, &c., to which the business of Europeans will carry them, or which they may be induced by curiosity to visit. Almost every locality will be named, and their relative distances duly set down, but such only will be minutely described as present some peculiar features of interest.

Taking the presidencies of India in the order of their importance, we begin with

CALCUTTA.

GENERAL DESCRIPTION.—The first view of Bengal-India gives the longing voyager a dreary pang of disappointment, owing to the low, ugly, and inhospitable shores of Saugor Island, with scarcely a sign of cheering civilization, or any tokens of a thickly-populated land. This desolate appearance, and the corresponding sensation which it excites in the stranger's breast, arise from the peculiar circumstance of there being no town at the mouth of the river, nor any mark of one as far as the eye can reach. Arriving at Madras, for instance, the city, fortifications, and all oppidan appurtenances, burst upon you while you are yet at sea, and you at once feel that you are cast among a civilized community; but Bengal frowns upon you, and you experience no temptation to explore her farther. Sail on, however, in the true hope which should always sustain those adventurous spirits who go down to the sea in great ships, and you will be richly rewarded for your primary disappointment. Viewed from the magnificent bend of the river, denominated Garden Reach, where the town first opens on the approaching vessel, the *coup d'œil* is one of various and enchanting beauty. Houses like palaces are studding the bank on the proper left of the river, and a verdure like that of an eternal summer, renovates the eye, so long accustomed to the glitter of the ocean. Anon, on *your* left, appears the semi-gothic Bishop's College; and in front of you, every moment growing more distinct, are beheld a forest of stately masts, a noble and beautiful fortress, a thousand small boats, of shapes new and undreamt of by the visitant, skimming over the stream; the larger vessels of the country, pleasant to look upon even for their strange dissymmetry and their consequent unwieldiness; the green and goose-shaped budgerow, lying idly for hire, and the airy little bauleahs, with their light venetian'd rooms, which seem fitted for the water-bowers of lovers on some of the lakes of those sunny isles which poets are wont to sing of, and where the breezes are never stronger than can be borne by silken sails. There cannot be a scene more beautiful, connected with the bustle and business of life, and the heart of the traveller feels light within him as he views it. He experiences undefinable emotions of joy, and he imagines he is in a country in which he could dwell unrepiningly for ever, voluntarily debarred from the prospect of ever again beholding the gloomier shores of England.

In the year 1757 occurred the memorable capture and plunder of Calcutta by Sooraj-ool-Dowlah, the Nawab of Bengal, and the attendant atrocity of the Black Hole sacrifice; an event with which even English children are familiar, and the horrors of which need not be detailed or farther alluded to here. The fate of his countrymen was signally revenged by the great Lord Clive; and from that period may be dated the stable foundation of our Indian empire, with the growth of which Calcutta has to this day kept pace in every description of metropolitan prosperity. The original boundaries of the city, indeed, continue as they were; because the circumscribed area was not for a long period, nor can it scarcely yet be said to be, occupied with urban fulness or regularity; for in the olden time there was no rule by which to guide the buildings, but every one was allowed to erect his residence where and how he pleased, so that there was never a uniformity in position or architecture, nor any unity of general design; a negligence of which the city will probably never get rid of the ill effects. As the inhabitants thickened, however, by births or immigration, much was gradually done in remedy of the evil, though probably not at first with that particular intent, and thus the greater portion of the originally allotted space has been formed into streets and squares; and though the houses are in general considerably apart from each other, and spots of unoccupied ground still here and there exist, yet Calcutta may be described as having long been completed,—that is, no change can be made in its external character or its construction as a city,—and, like other overgrown towns, to have flowed over into its suburbs. It is built on an almost dead level, which is the character of the far-surrounding country, so that it is calculated to be raised hardly so much as one foot above the mean of high water, though there is a slight fall from the bank of the river to the eastward, in the direction of the already mentioned salt-water lake. The soil is a rich alluvium, mixed with micaceous sand, and resting, at some depth below the surface, on a blackish clay; and such is its aptitude for imbibing and retaining moisture, that in spite of the heat of the climate, the earth is always damp, and the air in general humid.

This metropolis of British India, and emporium of eastern commerce, is situated in lat. 22° 33′ 54″ N., long. 88° 20′ 17″ E., on the eastern bank of the river Hooghly, which is merely a branch, being the most westerly one, of the Ganges, and is at the distance of nearly one hundred miles from the sea. The breadth of the stream, which is deep, muddy, and rapid, is about equal to that of the Thames at Gravesend, and ships of from twelve to fourteen hundred tons anchor abreast of the city, either in six or seven fathoms, near mid-channel, or at the chain moorings within a few yards of the shore, where they are fastened, head and stern, so as not to swing with the tide.

Topography.—We have said that the *coup d'œil* from the river impresses the beholder with an idea of magnificence in regard to the width of the streets and the splendour of the houses in external architecture; but although the bare facts which justify the inference remain, upon a nearer view of the objects, which have still the characteristic grandeur of spaciousness in their respective ways, yet the first impression, which is derived from the mind's belief in the existence of unqualified splendour, is, on the nearer view, discovered to be in a great measure illusory. The houses continue, indeed, to be justly considered by the stranger superior "in complement extern" to the great majority of the town residences in the principal capitals of Europe; but the eye is soon offended, and that grievously, by the admixture of mean and dirty huts, which abound in some of the finest streets, and come almost into contact with the colonnaded mansions; or as a humorous poet once described it:—

> "Where the palaced house stands, cheek by jowl,
> By the hut from the dunghill plaster'd;
> Like the china vase by the crockery bowl,
> And taste is by gain o'ermaster'd."

These mean and wretched-looking buildings are occupied, principally, during the daytime only, as shops, by the native venders of commodities connected with the consumption, or the petty handicrafts of the people; but as the ground belongs, for the most part, to native landholders, and yields a lucrative rent when thus parcelled out into small allotments, for the purpose above specified, it is likely to continue the sordid cause of the solecisms we have alluded to in the architectural character of the town.

For municipal purposes, the city of Calcutta is quartered out into four divisions as follows:—

1st, or Upper North Division, bounded on the north by the Mahratta Ditch; south by the Mutchooa Bazaar-road and Cotton-street, to Meerbhur Ghaut; east by the Circular-road, and west by the river Hooghly.

2nd, or Lower North Division, bounded on the north by the Mutchooa Bazaar-road and Cotton-street, to Meerbhur Ghaut; south by the Boitakhanna-road, Bow Bazaar, and Loll Bazaar, to the Custom House Ghaut, and east and west as above.

3rd, or Upper South Division, bounded on the north by the Boitakhanna-road, Bow Bazaar, and Loll Bazaar, to Custom House Ghaut; south by Dhurrumtollah-street and Esplanade-row, to Chandpaul Ghaut, and east and west as above.

4th, or Lower South Division, bounded on the north by the Dhurrumtollah-street and Esplanade-row, to Chandpaul Ghaut; south by the Lower Circular-road, to Kidderpore-bridge, and Tolly's Nullah, to the river Hooghly, and east and west as above.

To each of these divisions a magistrate is appointed, who, however, does not reside, nor even hold his sittings, within the precincts of his *beat*, as the only police-office in the place is situated in the Loll Bazaar, near the north-western extremity of the English part of the town.

The conventional divisions of the city, which are but two, are tolerably well defined, and are describable as follows:—A line drawn from Beebee Ross's Ghaut, on the river-bank, due east, to the Upper Circular-road, and from Hastings's-bridge, on the Tolly's Nullah, in a north-easterly direction, to the Lower Circular-road, will include the whole of the space occupied by the Christian part of the community; while a similar process of demarcation, commencing at Beebee Ross's Ghaut and running eastward as above mentioned, including all the streets northward as far as Chitpore-bridge and the boundary of the Mahratta Ditch (a now useless and unseemly excavation, commenced in the middle of the eighteenth century, and encircling the city from its northern extremity to a point on its opposite boundary, called Bridgetullow), will comprehend the greater portion of the city which is occupied by natives. There is, however, this material difference to be observed in the two localities, namely, that a considerable part of the European division is occupied by natives—chiefly Mussulmans and the lower castes of Hindoos—while very few Christians have their abode in the native quarter. In this latter, with but a few exceptions, the streets are, like those of most Oriental towns, exceedingly narrow, and the houses lofty, the lower apartments being used for shops or store-rooms, while the more strictly domiciliary parts of the building, above, are primitively garnished with loop-holes instead of windows, and the backs of the houses are for the most part to the streets. Some dwellings, indeed, there are which have the convenience of windows, and even of balconies, but even those are, in general, most sorry imitations of the European style, and from being commonly unpainted, and never kept in good repair, present that mean and dilapidated appearance which is a characteristic of the native architectural constructions, both public and private—the dwelling-house, the temple, the ghaut, serai, and bridge.

And from this sweeping condemnation of the thriftlessness and want of taste of the people of Hindostan, can be excepted only the very few houses belonging to certain opulent natives in Calcutta, who have grafted the European customs on their own, and whose residences are fitted up with considerable elegance and judgment; and there are many, also, among the native upper classes, generally, who, though they cannot totally wean themselves from the customs of their country, are ambitious of having their houses furnished and decorated in the English way, which, however, ill assimilates with the confined dimensions and dark interiors incidental to the style of eastern architecture. Hence an incongruity which makes apartments, thus bedizened, look paltry amid magnificence, and tawdry and disarranged, though every article in them may be costly and, in its individual character, free from meretriciousness; and hence, too, a manifest and a certain sign that such apartments are intended rather for show than for enjoyment. But to revert to our topography.

The business part of Calcutta, or what in England would be termed "the city," and which in India is known by the designation of "the town," is comprised between Chandpaul Ghaut and the New Mint, on the river-bank, eastward; and from the former to the head of Cossitollah-street, at its junction with the Dhurrumtollah and Chowringhee roads; and in a similar direction from the New Mint to the Burra Bazaar, a line drawn from the latter to the Cossitollah completing the definement. The fashionable, or what may be figuratively, though not geographically, called the *west* end, is at Chowringhee; but as Calcutta is made up of an official and a mercantile community, and can boast of no exclusive circle in resemblance to the "fashionable" one of London, the distinctive appellation bestowed on the quarter just mentioned has originated more in the circumstance of its being locally apart from the "busy hum of men," about the traffic-hives of warehouses, and yet near enough to the scenes of both commercial and official business, to render it a convenient residence for high functionaries and wealthy merchants, than from any difference in their social modes of life from the practice of their fellow-exiles.

A few of the streets in the European town are of great dimensions; as the Chowringhee-road, for instance, which is nearly two miles long, and in average width not less than eighty feet; but, as its name of "Road" would import, it has houses on only one (the eastern) side, facing the extensive plain, or *maidan*, which separates it from the river. The Dhurrumtollah is nearly equal, in dimensive character, to this; and being on each side bordered by a row of houses of good elevation, and many of them even splendid in their outward appearance—with but comparatively few native hut-edifices on its line —it would claim to be considered a first-rate street in any western capital. A short way down this road is the Chandny Bazaar, where the street is usually much crowded by retailers of cloth and various other articles, who seriously encroach on the public thoroughfare, and obstruct the free passage of vehicles to and fro, as the police make no effort to vindicate the public right of way either there or in any other part of the town,—a fact than which there is no other single one more demonstrative of inefficiency in the named department, in whatever town the remark can be rightly made. Wellesley-road would be acknowledgedly a fine street, were it not lined, almost continuously, with native huts, and exposed to the greater nuisance of the Kalassee, or native seamen's quarter, which is situated about the middle of it—near the spot at which it intersects the Jaun Bazaar-street—and is inhabited by a debauched and otherwise totally demoralized mass of people, composed chiefly of those who are out of employment, or who live on the fruits of barefaced prostitution. The Upper and Lower Circular roads, which nearly encompass the city on its eastern or landward side, are long and of noble proportions; but the paucity of houses gives it a straggling and here and there a desolated appearance; while that before-named opprobrium of the city, the Mahratta Ditch, with much jungle in the back-ground, forms a drawback to its perfection, which, until the whole line of road shall be cleared, to the extent of some hundred feet beyond the boundary, and the ditch itself filled up, will tend to retain it in that stationary condition (while improvement is elsewhere active) in which it has now for so many years continued. In the Chowringhee quarter, there are many fine though not long streets; among which the one called Russell-street, debouching at either end into Park and Middleton streets, respectively, takes rank among the best. Camac-street is also a very good street, but has as yet few buildings, and towards its southern extremity has numerous huts, and much unoccupied ground; both of which circumstances are destructive of true town beauty, and give an appearance of mingled wretchedness and desolation, which detracts from the effect of even adjacent completeness. Park-street is a somewhat long, but disproportionately narrow street, having some good houses on its line, and has always been considered an abiding-place of the first respectability. But it has one great disadvantage in being the thoroughfare for funerals to the English Protestant cemetery, which is situated at its eastern termination; and as the *cortège* on these solemn and sombrous occasions is always considerable, and in general beyond what in England would be deemed commensurate with the rank in life of the deceased; and, moreover, as the processions occur, alas! almost every day, the place is objected to as a residence by many people, who think they should not enjoy such frequent intimations that they are in the high road to the grave, or who care not to be reminded, like the ancient monarch, once in every four-and-twenty hours, of their mortality. For although it may be tacitly admitted, upon pure ethical authority, that—

> "Death is the privilege of human nature,
> And life without it were not worth the taking;"

yet it is surprising what a disposition there is practically evinced, on the part of mankind, to postpone the use of the "privilege" to an indefinite and far-off period, and to rest satisfied with its long remaining, unappropriated, in the distance! Loudon-street, which is near the eastern end of that just delineated, has several good houses of recent erection; but it, too, is disfigured by unseemly and barbarous hovels.

Until recently, Calcutta was destitute of one architectural feature which marks all towns in England (and in various other parts), in which the national mass of commerce is circulated through the whole body-social by the veins which are kept open for it in the system of retail. We allude to the plan of regular shop-fronts, which distinguish the place of business from the private abode, and which, when tastefully designed, and sample-adorned, as in London, yield an ornament to the streets, and eloquently proclaim the prosperity of the country. Calcutta is still deficient, when compared to English towns, in this pleasing and convenient system, and from climatic difficulties must probably remain so; for goods exposed to the heat and glare in a window would speedily deteriorate, and meanwhile there would be no pedestrian customers to be attracted by the display. But of late, there have been shop-fronts added to the lower stories of several of the houses in Council House-street, Cossitollah, and other streets, and the propensity towards this kind of improvement is daily increasing among the European tradesmen. Still, however, the fenestral exhibition, above alluded to, is wanting, and the shops must be entered ere goods can be beheld; and thus the place, though in reality the theatre of a most extensive commerce, has not, as far as the exterior of the trades houses is concerned, any thing of the bustling and busy look, and none of the "busy hum," which are characteristics of European seaports. Another cause of this outward dulness consists in the isolation of the houses, as contrasted with the contiguity of buildings in, for instance, a London street; and from each traffical residence having its warehouses, or *godowns,* inside a court-yard, which is closed with gates, so that the passenger is little aware, from any mark or likelihood which meets his eye, of the ceaseless activity which is going on within. To a person, however, of very ordinary power of observation, the number of vehicles, describable and indescribable, which *navigate* the streets (for the "rules of the road" are in desuetude in India), including quantities of laden bullock-carts; and the concourse of employed natives which on every side he must perceive, would be adequate proof of the place being an emporium of first-rate consequence, even did not the abundance of shipping, and the shoals of concomitant small craft of every form and pressure, sufficiently of themselves give assurance of the fact.

Calcutta has no walls, barriers, or other outward appliances of a fortified town—for the circumvallation, called the Mahratta Ditch, merits no such rank; nor is there need of such defences, not only in the improbability of its ever being attacked, but from the vicinity of Fort William, which commands the circumjacent country, and which, on an emergency, could contain the whole Christian population, and in the face of which no enemy could retain a footing in the town. Its principal defect, as a place besieged, would consist in its being, from internal resources, unsupplied with drinkable water, save from a tank, or pond, on the southern glacis, within only a few hundred feet of the ramparts.

There are several neat, yet spacious religious edifices, and other buildings devoted to public purposes, the principal of which are the Town Hall, the Hindoo and Madrissa colleges, the Metcalfe Building, the Sans Souci Theatre, and the Supreme Court; and though, like other capitals, it can boast its bazaars, yet the reader who pictures these mart-places in his mind, according to any pattern taken from the Pantheon, Baker-street, Soho-square, or other similar establishments in London, will be no nearer a correct conception of the reality than if he were to imagine a house in the Chitpore-road from his inspection-derived impression of Buckingham Palace. True, there are various articles sold by various retail traders, congregated, yet independent of each other, in both bazaar institutions; just as there is a river in Macedon and a river in Wales;

> "But there all likeness ends between the pair,"

who then become fairly representable by the classical illustration of Hyperion and the Satyr;—the English bazaar being a place of beautiful arrangement, defined charges, delicate merchandize, and respectable conduct; and the Indian one being a scene of riot, knavery, prostitution, and filthiness, exhibiting, moreover, the mercantile incongruity of the costliest manufactures in the merest dens, and the often disgusting necessaries of the native culinary department, such as rancid and uncleanly ghee,* and bad and bitter oil, attainting the air, which is at the same time impregnated by the Sabæan odours of uttur, frankincense, and aromatic spices. With shame also it is that we feel compelled to proclaim that the City of Palaces is, with rare and recent exceptions, most wretchedly lighted by means

* Clarified butter.

of sordid oil-lamps, supplied with material of so inferior a description that even the inside of the lamp is scarcely illuminated, and placed at the respectable distances of the corners of streets, or other wide intervals, which make them appear as few and far between as did the angels' visits of the poet's illustration. Neither is the city watched, or paved, or efficiently regulated in its municipal relations, in all pertaining to which it is considerably behind a second-rate English provincial town. Within the limits of the city itself there are no bridges, for the sufficient reason that there is no intersection of the place by running streams; but it is by this circumstance deprived of one of the most effective sources of architectural ornament—the magnificent bridge—which, wheresoever viewed from, presents a beautiful object to the eye; and which, by joining together the water-severed sections of the spreading town, is the apparent means of a union in partition, and of a safe and easy intercourse.

There are, however, some very neat suspension bridges—a description of pontifice which must, in the first instance, have imbued with astonishment even the Hindoo's apathetic mind—over the creeks and canals (at either end of the town) which debouch into the river Hooghly.

The city of Calcutta is supplied with good drinking-water from a considerable number of large ponds (called tanks), for the most part situated towards the Chowringhee quarter; but the one which gives the name to Tank-square lies in the business part of the town, and contains a fine reservoir of water, which covers an area of about three acres, and which is twenty feet deep at the place of its greatest depth. It is, unfortunately, however, liable to be rendered occasionally brackish, in consequence of its vicinity to the river, from which, in dry seasons, it is now and then replenished; and this deterioration is the more to be lamented, as the tank in question forms the only local source of supply to a very thickly-peopled portion of the city. In these junctures, most of the European families, and several of them, indeed, uniformly, procure the water for their table uses from the tanks on the plain, of which there are several, and all containing water of excellent quality; but that which bears away the elemental palm from the rest of the temperance fountains, is a tank in the Free School grounds, which has the advantage of land-springs. All the tanks obtain "annual supplies" from the periodical rains; and therefore, in seasons when these happen to be scanty, much distress is endured, ere their recurrence, by the general population; and this distress is especially great during the ensuing hot months, when the ponds come to their lowest ebb, and their then remnant of water becomes turbid, in consequence of the incessant drain which is made on it at that parching period.

Calcutta has extensive, irregular, and thickly native-peopled suburbs; but the Europeans, thereabouts, are few, and their houses far apart. Of these suburbial localities, that of Garden Reach, about four miles to the south of the town, is by far the most important, and, indeed, magnificent; some of the buildings being on a scale of much grandeur and elegance, and surrounded by extensive grounds, laid out in miniature representations of the beautiful parks of England. These used to be the residences of the *élite* of the metropolis; but latterly, in consequence of the place's salubrity having been said to be impaired, but perhaps more owing, in reality, to the greater activity of both official and mercantile life, brought about by the more stirring character of the times, the locality has come to be less and less frequented, excepting at the driest periods of the year, when every house has its tenant.

Eastward of Garden Reach, are Allipore and Balligunge, both considered healthy spots, and the latter having a few good houses round an extensive plain, in which are placed the lines of the Governor-General's body-guard. After a long interval, and in a northerly direction, comes Entally—a suburb branching out from the eastern side of the Circular Road, opposite its junction with the Dhurrumtollah. It contains many houses, which are inhabited, principally, by the middling classes, and which, being on the outer side of the Mahratta Ditch, have the advantage, in common with the other suburbs, of being exempt from the jurisdiction of the Supreme Court of Judicature in cases of civil process. Still farther to the north, at the head of the Boitaconnah or Bow Bazaar Road, lies the Sealdah or Baliaghaut Road, leading to the Salt-water Lake, where there are a few good residences; and thence, stretching to a great extent to the north-west, are Simlah and other suburbs, entirely occupied by natives, and interspersed with the garden-houses, or suburban retreats, of the wealthy merchants and other men of fortune among the aborigines.

In regard to climate, Calcutta may be described

as subject to the extremity of moisture, and nearly to that of heat; which atmospheric characteristics, joined to that of a tolerable degree of cold, divide the "rolling year," into the seasons sufficiently well defined to be classified with that distinctness. But upon this point, and in regard also to the diseases peculiar to India, we have said enough in preceding pages.

Population.—A belief had long been prevalent, that Calcutta was a thickly-populated town, and some estimates made the number of inhabitants amount to nearly half a million, while, in the looser language of conversation, we have known double that number mentioned as being within the truth. Recent and accurate surveys, however, have sufficiently established the fact, that its resident population does not much exceed two hundred and twenty thousand, comprised within the proper limits of the city, which stretch for a distance of four miles along the banks of the river, and to about one mile and a half, at the greatest extension, inland. The old errors upon this subject, whence flowed so much exaggeration, arose, no doubt, from an observation on the part of the calculators of the immense number of day-sojourners, whom they uninquiringly took for regular inhabitants, instead of discovering them to be the result of the vast influx of people from the adjacent villages, who have employment in town, or who attend the bazaars with the produce of their gardens or fields, and to procure for themselves those necessaries which, in the first instance, are all swept into the Calcutta markets. From this cause the place appears to be swarming with population; and as, besides, the men who happen to be unemployed are more in the habit of lounging or lying about the streets than of keeping within their houses, the observer, who trusted to his eyes merely for the formation of a census, would arrive at a far higher calculation than the more systematic investigator into censual truth. The following tabular estimate, made not long since, upon the recognized principles, by the superintendent of police, exhibits at one view the number and classified description of the then population :—

English	3,138
Eurasians	4,746
Portuguese	3,181
French	160
Chinese	362
Armenians	636
Jews	307
Western Mahomedans	13,677
Bengal Mahomedans	45,067
Western Hindoos	17,333
Bengal Hindoos	120,318
Moguls	527
Parsees	40
Arabs	351
Mugs	683
Madrassees	55
Native Christians	49
Low Castes	19,084
Total	229,714

Among this great variety of the human race, there is little or no collision in the important struggle for the obtainment of subsistence; and hence, in a great measure, arises the blessing of internal public tranquillity, which is uniformly experienced in this magnificent, yet motley-peopled capital. No one class interferes in any objectionable way with the pursuits of another, but, on the contrary, the course of occupation causes each class to assist the others, for the promotion of its own individual interest; and caste, climate, and prejudice, effect as true and politic a division of labour as meditation and design have been able to do in England. In India the system has its evil as well as its good. The evil is, the prevention of competition and improvement in the different professions to which the natives incline. In England, every man can follow any trade he pleases; but in India, the son of the tailor may not become a shoemaker; nor must the family of the blacksmith recruit the ranks of the carpenter. If a washerman were starving for want of employment, he would never dream of turning barber, though in his neighbourhood there might be a paucity of the chattering tribe; nor would a starving barber seek a livelihood by starting as a water-carrier. We have here spoken of the *classes of tribes;* but among the tribes themselves there is nearly the same separation of pursuits, and the same variation of means for attaining the one great and common end—subsistence.

The Calcutta English, who are not in the East-India Company's service, may be divided into the three main classes of the mercantile, the retail dealers, and the artisans. The numerically minor bodies belonging to the church and the law, several of each of these last sections being also in the Company's employment, it is not necessary, for the purpose of the present exposition, to notice particularly; and the seafaring persons form, of course, properly, no portion of the residentiary British community.

Of these three major divisions of our own peculiar people, the artisans are those whom the uninitiated reader might, at the first blush, suppose inevitably instrumental in causing a clash with the native artificers, and thus demonstrating the fallacy of our proposition on that subject. But the fact is, that the British mechanics in Calcutta are all in the capacities of master-workmen, and are not, in the English understanding of the term, actual labourers in their crafts at all. The tailors, shoemakers, house-builders, coach-makers, carvers and gilders, cabinet-makers, and the like, are practically no more than supervisors of the work (including instruction to some extent), in the laborious part of which, or what is literally the manufacturing department, natives are employed as journeymen; and thus, instead of being jostled out of employment by the introgression of Europeans, they have employment secured to them at a better rate of wages than their own master-manufacturers could afford to bestow. On the other hand, the native master-artisans lose little or no custom by the similar speculations of their pale-faced brethren; for the shoes and clothes of the aborigines are of a peculiar kind and quality, and such as the emigrants would be incapable of producing at the uniform market price; while of such articles as are suitable for European wear or other use, many are sought by our countrymen from the native on account of the immediate cheapness, as it is often more convenient to renew a cheap article, at comparatively frequent intervals, than to pay largely down for such as may last you longer. Of many English trades there are no branches at all in India. Hatters, saddlers, gun-makers, cutlers, hosiers, brewers, perfumers, and an infinity more, are unknown in India; though the several commodities produced by them are on sale there as importations, and by persons, sometimes, who belong to the particular trade (such as gun-making), though their Indian work in it is confined to repairing, and that chiefly by natives under their inspection.*

To the English trader, manufacturer, or vender, we recommend Europeans invariably to apply in preference to resorting to the natives. "Europe shops," as they are called, are so nearly on a level with those of the China bazaar, that there is little to be gained, where there used to be much, by having recourse to native dealers, especially if we take into account the extra trouble of the process, and the higgling about the cost. Moreover, among the tradesmen of Calcutta, as a body, there is much real

* It was anticipated by the friends of free trade and colonization, that the abrogation of the East-India Company's monopoly and of the prohibition of European resort to India, would cause an influx of British capital and skill; and many thought that the immigration of labourers and artisans would take place to an extent to interfere with the pursuits and happiness of the natives. Few of these anticipations have been fulfilled. That *trade* has increased to a very considerable extent, since the abolition of the monopoly, is beyond all question, but in no other respect have the provisions of the present charter been of much service to India. Scarcely a single practical agriculturist, with money enough to cultivate a hundred acres, has made his appearance; while the artisans remain numerically about the same. The only people who have resorted to India in considerable numbers have been composed of that very useless class (colonially considered) who have followed the occupation of clerks and gentlemen's servants in England—people who have no qualifications for employment beyond those possessed, perhaps in a superior degree, by the Eurasians and Hindoos already on the spot.

liberality of dealing, and a spirit of great indulgence towards those whose extravagance or misfortune may have placed them in their legal power; and when it is considered how often their just and decorous applications for payment are either treated with silent contempt or replied to in terms of ill-mannered arrogance, the wonder should be, that they are systematically so forbearing, instead of that they occasionally retaliate upon combined rudeness and neglect, through the medium of a document from the sheriff's sanctum.

Of the entire mass of Mahomedans and Hindoos, exclusively of the degraded castes of the latter, which forms a recognized portion of the inhabitants of Calcutta, and which may be estimated in round numbers at two hundred thousand, it is probable that a full moiety are in the service of the Europeans and Armenians, and that of this moiety the far greater division may be ranged under the head of domestic servants, and the remainder described as employed in the government and mercantile offices, in the capacity of under-clerks, messengers, and the like inferior, yet trustworthy employments. The other half of the entire number subsist themselves by what may be termed street or river labour, in contradistinction to that which is rural, and find employment in carrying palanquins as bearers, and parcels as *coolies*, or porters. The employments are perfectly distinct, and though each is pursued by Hindoos, yet neither would interchange the *modus operandi*—it being against the prejudice of caste for a bearer to carry any weight upon his head, or for a coolie to do so on his back or shoulder. The honesty of the coolie is proverbial over India. Paid at a rate not exceeding at the utmost threepence sterling a day, and often at a lower rate than that; and employed to convey parcels of value and of easy appropriation from place to place, we are not aware of many instances of a coolie having been found guilty of a breach of trust, even in circumstances where detection was next to impossible and the temptation great. You may employ one of these men (and they constantly are employed) to carry packages of about half a maund—that is forty pounds—weight, for a distance of a thousand miles, and for a six weeks or two months' journey, and they are rarely known to fail; nor even, weather and health permitting, to be otherwise than punctual to their covenanted time of arrival, calculating the average daily progress, with the burden borne on the head, at about two and twenty miles! As a body, they are under no sort of police regulation, being neither badged nor ticketed, nor having their hire adjusted by municipal law. On a rumoured attempt to arrange them, in those respects, they all left Calcutta, and would not have returned to it had the design not been abandoned. Formerly, the palanquin-bearers were equally uncontrolled, and they soon struck work, on the introduction of a regulating system; but as they *could* have been done without, and their places supplied by the rival body of up-country bearers, the plan was persevered in, the bearers had to yield, and now the hack, or as they are called *teeka,* palanquins, are regulated in like manner, and in principle as are the hackney coaches and similar vehicles in London. Such as remain to be mentioned, after the deduction of these two principal classes from the aggregate, gain their livelihood as boatmen, dealers in grain, oil, cloth, and other articles of every-day consumption by the population at large; and as workmen in the various trades which are requisite to supply the household demands of their multifarious fellow-citizens.

The rest of the inhabitants of Calcutta are sufficiently described in the section appropriated to the population of India generally.

Public Buildings.—From the high reputation Calcutta has acquired for the palatial character of her buildings, it might be supposed that the city boasted of many noble public edifices. This, however, is far from the fact. It is upon the number of superb private mansions that Calcutta must rely to bear out the character she enjoys, for it is only within the last half-century that her inhabitants have considered it incumbent upon them to erect buildings for particular public objects. The practice has been, when an institution has been formed, to locate it in the first instance in a spacious private dwelling, and only to give it a special habitation when the purposes of the establishment have been extended or the funds increased to an amount that would admit of the extra outlay. Thus, there are not more than eighteen erections, not including places of worship, in the town, which deserve to be called "public," on the score of their having been originally built for the reception of a public establishment; these are:—

The Government House, the Town Hall, the Writers' Buildings, the Metcalfe Hall, the Hindoo

College, the Madrussa or Mahomedan College, the General Assembly's Institution, the Sans Souci Theatre, the Medical College, the Mechanics' Institute, the Orphan School, the General Hospital, the Ice House, the Ochterlony Monument, the Martiniére, the Race Stand, the Asiatic Society's Rooms, and the Mint.

THE GOVERNMENT HOUSE.—The Government House was built about the year 1804, at the instance of the late Marquis of Wellesley, then Governor-general. The architect was Captain Wyatt, of the corps of engineers, and the expense of erection about thirteen lacs of rupees, or about (in those days) one hundred and fifty thousand pounds sterling. The building with all its faults may be considered a noble one, and particularly well adapted in its plan and interior arrangements to the climate. The external view is grand and imposing, notwithstanding its numerous windows and its want of height. The same altitude, divided between a basement and two floors, would doubtless have had a better appearance, but this would not have been effected except at a great sacrifice of interior space, which, it is presumed, the architecture would not admit of. The verandahs are rather mean for so large a building. The columns have angular Ionic capitals. The grand entrance is on the northern side, by a handsome flight of steps leading to the first floor. It is seldom used, owing to its being entirely exposed, the entrance underneath the stairs being preferred by those who have occasion to go to the house. The position of the dome has often been objected to, and not unjustly: it is situated between the southern wings, and excepting when seen from the south it always appears out of place, from not being in the centre of the whole building. The wings on the southern side are surmounted by the royal arms: those on the northern are ornamented by the Honourable Company's. The greatest credit appears due to the architect for the interior accommodation. It may be considered perfect, as far as convenience is concerned, and splendid in every respect, with the exception of the staircases, as a fit and proper residence for the supreme ruler of our Indian possessions. Had the staircases been improved, the accommodation would have been less, and the architect did wisely in sacrificing splendour to comfort. The centre of the building consists of three large rooms. The ground-floor, being low, is chiefly occupied with offices, &c. The centre of the first floor is a grand marble hall, formed by the three rooms, the entrance of which has a row of columns. They are used on occasions of entertainment as the dining and supper rooms, according to the extent of the company. Above them are the ball-rooms. The floors are of varnished teak neatly laid ; the ceilings are ornamented and covered, so as to conceal the beams; the gilding is tasteful and neat. From the roof are suspended numerous chandeliers, while the sides of the rooms and between the windows are lined with handsome mirrors. The *coup d'œil*, when lighted and filled with company, is certainly splendid, and would do credit to any country.

The four wings, which may be considered as distinct houses, are connected in the centre by means of commodious galleries. They are every way convenient and comfortable, and are occupied by the Governor-general and his suite. All the out-offices are detached and in no way interfere with the view of the room. Upon the whole, the building may justly be viewed as doing great credit to the architect. That it has faults, in architectural purity, must be allowed; but these faults are counterbalanced by the conveniences which proceed from them, and were doubtless known to the architect, and a decision to this effect made. The place altogether is a splendid conception, and few men forty years ago (at any rate, in India), excepting the architect himself, would have elicited from their own invention any thing so complete and satisfactory.

HINDOO COLLEGE.—This excellent and highly interesting institution was projected near the close of the year 1815. It owes its origin to a most zealous advocate for native education, the late Mr. David Hare. He it was who first conceived the idea of such an establishment, which occurred to his mind in the course of a discussion, at the house of the celebrated Rammohun Roy, on the best means of improving the moral and intellectual condition of the people of India. Having written down his thoughts on the subject, the paper was shewn to several individuals, amongst whom was a native gentleman, who without communicating his intention to Mr. Hare, handed it directly to Sir Edward Hyde East, then Chief Judge of the Supreme Court, soliciting his patronage and support of the scheme under consideration. The learned judge was so much pleased with Mr. Hare's suggestion, that he entered immediately into almost all his views, and after having proposed a few trifling alterations in that gentleman's plan for the establishment of the college, he convened a meeting of respectable natives at his own house on the 5th of May, 1816, for the purpose of carrying so happy and noble a design into speedy execution. As Sir Hyde East has been very generally regarded as the sole originator of the Hindoo College, it has been thought due to Mr. Hare's memory to make especial mention of his share in the undertaking.

After various meetings upon the subject, it was resolved "that an institution for promoting education be established, and that it be called the Hindoo College of Calcutta, and that the Governor-general, and the members of the Supreme Council for the time being, be requested to accept the office of patrons of this institution." It was also resolved, that Sir Edward Hyde East should be requested to accept the office of president, and the then chief judge of the Court Sudder Dewanny and Nizamut Adawlut, that of vice-president. A committee was appointed, consisting of both native and European gentlemen, and to these were added an English and a native secretary.

The primary object of the institution was the tuition of Hindoo children in the English and Indian languages; and in the literature and science of Europe and Asia. The committee hired a building in a populous part of the town as a temporary school-house, and on the 20th January, 1817, the school was opened. On that day there were but twenty pupils, but a learned native who was present expressed his hopes that the Hindoo College would resemble the *bur*, the largest of trees, which yet at first was but a small seedling. In less than three months the number of boys was sixty-nine, including sixteen free scholars, all of whom made English their principal study. The funds of the college amounted at this time to upwards of 70,000 rupees. Notwithstanding, however, this auspicious commencement, the expenses connected with the establishment not being regulated with a due regard to economy, were soon discovered to be much beyond the means at the disposal of the management, and, as a consequence, some appointments that were almost sinecures were abolished, and certain extravagant expenditures were reduced. Though so much active interest had been exhibited in the early infancy of the college, the novelty, however, soon began to wear away, and if it had not been for the indefatigable labours and persevering expostulations of Mr. Hare, the founder, the whole undertaking might gradually have dwindled into nothing. The school had been removed from one house to another, and began to exhibit any thing but a flourishing appearance, when the few individuals who still had its success at heart appealed to the government for assistance. Pecuniary aid was immediately granted; and the Governor-general in Council having determined to found a Sanscrit College in Calcutta, for the special purpose of reviving native literature, it was deemed advisable to erect a large and handsome building that might accommodate all the classes of both institutions. A lac and twenty thousand rupees was allotted to the purpose. The foundation stone of this edifice was laid on the 25th of February, 1824. The present building was opened for the reception of the classes of the two institutions in the month of May, 1827. The centre part of the building was to be devoted to the Sanscrit students, and the two wings to the senior and junior departments of the Anglo-Indian school. The two institutions have been kept totally distinct. The Sanscrit College has always been entirely under the superintendence of Government, but the Hindoo College, until the erection of the common edifice, was under the superintendence of native management. With the consent of the native managers, the government appointed Mr. Horace Hayman Wilson, Vice-president of the committee and visitor of the college, and at the same time nominated sundry lecturers and teachers, selecting them from the ablest men whose services were available. The government likewise presented an excellent library to the Hindoo College, and have for some years contributed two thousand rupees per mensem towards the general expenses of the college. A wealthy Rajah presented a donation of 20,000 rupees, which was devoted to the institution of scholarships, the object of which was, by a monthly bursary of sixteen rupees, to induce the pupils of the first class, who would otherwise be obliged to quit college in search of a livelihood, to remain longer and finish their education.

In 1829, the failure of the house of agency, in which the college funds, to the amount of 60,000 rupees, had been placed, plunged the college into great embarrassment; but by the excellent arrangements of Dr. Wilson, the institution was rescued from the very serious injury which so great a loss was expected to occasion. There was an increase in the number of boys, all of whom paid five rupees per mensem for their education (with the exception of those of the first class who had received scholarships), and by enforcing a more regular system of payment of the monthly bills for instruction, and a proper attention to economy, the college soon recovered, in a great measure, from this heavy blow. An unhappy drawback from the popularity of the institution occurred about this period. A Mr. Derozio, an East-Indian, who had acquired some degree of local celebrity as a poet, was one of the masters, and being fond of conversing with the students, he sometimes touched on religious questions with too much freedom, and alarmed the parents of the youths. It was asserted that he taught them atheism, and also insisted upon the necessity of disobeying their parents on all matters connected with liberty of discussion. He positively denied the truth of these charges, and of several others of a similar nature; but as many of the parents had indignantly removed their children, and there was a general impression amongst the natives that the Hindoo faith was the subject of ridicule of the Hindoo College, and that even the great principles of morality and natural religion were attacked by Mr. Derozio, the native management thought it absolutely necessary, as a matter of policy, to dispense with his services as a teacher. The visitor and founder of the college were both of opinion that the charges against Mr. Derozio were unfounded, but they were obliged to give way to the native managers in a matter so peculiarly affecting their own feelings and the interests of the college.

Soon after Mr. Derozio left, the excitement ceased, and the institution recovered the confidence and good-will of the native community.

In 1831, the government authorized the appointment of a Professor of Law and Moral Philosophy, and the General Committee of Public Instruction engaged a gentleman who was a Protestant minister to fill that office; but the native managers expressed their decided objection to the appointment of a clergyman. In consequence of this objection, to which the government attached due weight, as according with their policy of non-interference with the religious prejudices of the natives, the office was changed to that of lecturer on law and political economy, and assigned to a practising barrister of some eminence. On this gentleman's resignation of the office, as incompatible with his practice, it devolved successively on others of less capacity.

In 1835, owing to the retirement or resignation of some of the professors, and the difficulty of filling their places satisfactorily, a new distribution of duties took place. The office of lecturer on mathematics and English literature, which had hitherto been united, was now divided. Subsequently, a principal was appointed in the person of Captain David Lester Richardson, author of "Literary Leaves," &c. The system works well; and if the college cannot be said to have attained the maximum of perfection, it certainly never was in a higher state of prosperity than at the present moment.

The Hindoo College is one of the handsomest buildings in Calcutta. It is of the plain Grecian Ionic order. The grand entrance is on the north, and a flight of stone steps leads to a portico supported by four lofty columns. The portico leads into a square open court, on the east and west sides of which are colonnades, which form the entrance into the lower apartments devoted to the Sanscrit classes. At the south-west corner of the western colonnade is the principal staircase, which leads to the large upper hall of the centre building. This hall, as well as the one beneath it, measures eighty-four feet by twenty-six. In the upper colonnades, east and west of the court, are galleries forming passages into the several side apartments, one of which is devoted to the college library, which contains a large supply of the best works on the literature and science of Europe, with many of the most approved translations from the Greek and Roman classics. A book, in which the titles of the works borrowed and the names of the borrowers are kept, affords an interesting illustration of the taste and acquirements of the students. European visitors are often greatly surprised, on inspecting this record, to observe how much works demanding serious thought, the closest study, and an exertion of the highest faculties of the mind, are voluntarily sought after by these aspiring boys, most of whose parents are as ignorant as their forefathers five thousand years ago. On the south side of the building is a large portico, supported by six columns, on a well-raised pediment. The two wings are of the same order as the centre building, but of one story only. The eastern wing is occupied with the junior department or lower classes of the Hindoo College, and the western wing is devoted to the upper classes. The professors deliver their lectures in the upper apartments of the centre building. The entire edifice, including numerous out-offices, stands on an area of 470 feet by 190 feet. Within the enclosure, which is defined by a handsome iron rail, is a large circular tank and neat lawn.

Thus much of the college and its purposes. It would be agreeable to follow the student from its portals, and trace the effects of the instruction he has received upon the society with which he thenceforth mingles. But it is much to be apprehended that, at present, the advantage stops short with the student himself.

Many of the students in the first and second classes of the Hindoo College are enabled to procure respectable situations under government, and all of them who require employment find a college education of most essential advantage to them. The certificate of character and acquirements which each boy obtains on quitting the institution, when very favourable, is regarded as an invaluable document, and esteemed of higher importance and utility than any private letter of introduction. Even the more wealthy students who do not seek for employment are proud of the honour of a good college certificate. It is amongst these in rather dependent circumstances that the love of learning is longest cherished. Amongst those who have to spend every entire day in official toil or the pursuits of trade, and return exhausted to the idle converse of their families, the desire for intellectual pleasure very speedily cools, and they lose all that generous ambition to distinguish themselves by their talents or their attainments, which they evince in association with their class-fellows. But those who are not doomed to a perpetual struggle for the means of existence often continue to study very sedulously the books recommended to them when at college; and they sometimes contrive to prolong an acquaintance with their teachers by occasional visits, or even letters. They are, however, in an awkward and unencouraging position, for their parents and immediate associates rarely smile upon their studies, and the English in India are, generally speaking, even yet too aristocratic to meet the advances of the natives in a true spirit of sociality. There is too often a proud condescension on the one side and a humiliation on the other. We cannot expect the natives of India to advance much in the scale of society until we hold out the ready hand of fellowship to all who distinguish themselves by their talents or their virtues.

THE SANSCRIT COLLEGE.—The Sanscrit College is supported entirely by the government, and about twelve hundred rupees per mensem are drawn for its expenditure. This institution was established for the encouragement of Oriental learning; but a few years ago a teacher was employed to teach the students reading and writing the English language. Little progress, however, was made in their occidental studies, and English instruction has been for some time discontinued. But a disposition is again evinced to renew the attempt to introduce the study of the English, and also of the vernacular language, both of which had been very injudiciously neglected. At one period there were about a hundred stipendiary scholars, some of whom got eight rupees, and others five rupees, per mensem; and at the period alluded to, there were about 250 students; but when these stipends were ordered to be gradually discontinued, the number of students fell off considerably. There are now only about fifty stipendiaries, and there are not at this period more than 140 or 150 students altogether, and these include a late addition occasioned by the introduction of the study of the vernacular language, which is of more use to the sons of the poor than the Sanscrit. As at the Hindoo College, with the exception of a very few stipendiary scholars in the first and second classes, all the boys pay five rupees per mensem for their instruction, which is a considerable sum of money to many of the parents, and the continued and increasing prosperity of that college is a proof of its great popularity amongst the natives. The students at the Sanscrit and other colleges under government superintendence at present contribute nothing towards the expenses of the education. The immediate management of the Sanscrit College is under a native secretary of great respectability.

The institution next in degree to the Hindoo College, as being particularly adapted to the instruction of natives in the higher branches of learning, though by no means approaching it in point of utility, is

The Madrussa, or Mahomedan College.—This institution was founded in the year 1780, by Warren Hastings, who, at his own expense, erected a building for the college, and obtained from government, for the support of the establishment, a grant of land, estimated at 29,000 rupees per annum. The object of the founder was to encourage the cultivation of Arabic learning, and to prepare persons with perfect knowledge of Mahomedan law, to act as public officers in the courts of justice. Yet this plan, however wisely conceived or generously supported, failed in effecting the object intended; for in the year 1812, a representation was made to government, that the revenue dedicated to the support of this institution was wasted by indolent and ignorant professors and profligate students, and, that "the institution was wholly useless as to all purposes of education." Some partial alterations were then introduced. But apathy, the child of fatality, and vice, the offspring of idleness, soon triumphed over these temporary expedients, and in the year 1820, government, fully convinced that such an institution would never produce any useful results while under the control of natives, appointed a committee of Company's servants, with a secretary, to direct the studies and enforce the rules which they might deem necessary to establish. From that period the college rapidly improved; learned professors were sought, and the studious were rewarded; the revenue of the college fixed at 30,000 rupees per annum, instead of the original jaghir; and a new building was erected on the north side of Wellesley Square, at the charge of 1,40,537 rupees. In 1829, an English school was attached to the Madrussa; but from the jealousy with which the Mahomedans view English literature and science, and from a belief that the school was formed to undermine their religion and render Arabic literature less pre-eminent, it has been rather opposed than supported by the native influence in the college. Very few of the Arabic students availed themselves of this new source of information, and generally those that attended, did it more as a matter of form than from inclination. Out-students were admitted and dismissed as changes took place in the committee, and nothing seemed certain but that whatever was done one year would be altered the next. A radical reform was, however, introduced, yet not without violent opposition from the most celebrated oriental scholars in the education committee. These gentlemen considered the Madrussa as founded purely for the cultivation of Arabic, and that it would be unjust to divert any part of its funds from the direct track pointed out by its founder; and so indignant did they feel at the proposition of a radical change, that all of them who were on the Madrussa committee resigned, rather than have any thing to do with what they termed the spoliation of a vested right. The general committee paid little attention to this sudden burst of passion, and orders were issued according to their declared intention. These orders were certainly harsh and uncompromising, but they have not proved eventually so pernicious as their opponents had anticipated. If the intention of the general committee was to divert the funds of the Madrussa to the support of other institutions, it must be admitted to have been unjustifiable; but if their object was to give a more extended range of information to the Mahomedan community, it was a measure fraught with benevolence and supported by sound policy. Be that as it may, orders were issued declaring that no stipends should be allowed to students admitted after a specified day, and that when vacancies occurred in professorships, none should be filled up in departments where well informed and large classes did not exist. These alterations excited alarm in the breasts of the Mahomedan community; they considered them as indications of a political attack on the independence and rights of their body in general, and on their learned institutions in particular. A general meeting took place, a memorial was prepared, signed and presented in due form, but without producing any other result than a promise that it should be transmitted to England for the consideration of the authorities in that country. In the report of the general committee of public instruction for the year 1835, it is stated :—"Till lately every boy receiving a stipend from the Arabic department was obliged to learn English an hour or two in the day, and those who did not receive stipends had to pay two rupees a month for the privilege of being allowed to join the English class. The result of this arrangement was that the English school was filled with unwilling scholars, who were too old to acquire correct pronunciation, and devoted too short a time to the study to be able to make more than a very limited progress in it. Under these circumstances the school languished until lately, when a change of system was resolved upon. The Arabic students were no longer compelled to learn English, and any other Mahomedan youths who wished it were allowed to do so without any payment being required from them. The result has been satisfactory. The school is now filled with boys who pursue the study of English with zeal and success equal to any of their Hindoo compeers." From this period the affairs of the college proceeded without any obstruction; opposition died away gradually, and business soon flowed into the common routine. In a late report there appeared to be forty-two paid and seventy-two unpaid students in the Arabic department, and one hundred and fifty unpaid scholars in the English school. The English department would be a great advantage to the higher order of Mahomedan inhabitants of Calcutta, if the Arabic establishment would cordially unite with it in the search after and the diffusion of knowledge, and if the people themselves, so deeply interested, would meditate upon the benevolent efforts of government to place them in as advantageous a position as that of the learned part of the Hindoo population. Unhappily, however, the leading members of this great body, as well as the native functionaries of the college, are hostile to the introduction of western literature and modern science, so that few except the children of indigent parents avail themselves of an establishment, introduced solely for the general benefit of their community. It seems to be a matter of doubt, whether the alteration introduced by the committee is justifiable or not, or whether a power existed, by which new studies might be introduced and old ones modified according to the fashion of the times. But if reform be the order of the day, and utility the principle of action, the only question that can arise is, whether it is more profitable for the Mahomedan people still to pore over the dark pages of imperfect translations from Aristotle, or at once to direct their steps towards light, truth, and modern science. These people would be eminently successful if they would dedicate their minds to any pursuit, for they can readily conceive and easily remember, and although fickle in the extreme, still upon any excitement they can study with intense application. In the Arabic department there are four principal preceptors and four assistants. The course of study includes, in Arabic, general literature, logic, rhetoric, philosophy, Mahomedan law, and mathematics.

In the English, there are three masters and six monitors, the course of study in English embracing grammar, geography, astronomy, history, mathematics, natural philosophy, and general literature.

THE TOWN HALL.—This edifice was raised in pursuance of a resolution passed by the inhabitants of Calcutta, in February, 1804. It is a superb building, applied to the purposes of public meetings, balls, public dinners, concerts, dramatic performances, fancy fairs, annual examinations of schools, &c.

The plan was formed principally from the consideration that such a fabric required a grand double staircase to admit numbers at the same time. The stairs are so placed as not to obstruct the air in the hot season. They are therefore situated to the north, a point from which the wind seldom blows, except in the cold weather. In their construction they are spacious, easy of ascent, and well lighted, so that the projection of these stairs serves as a measure, in a certain degree, to determine the proportions of all the other parts of the building. The whole effectually answers, affording every accommodation likely to be required on a liberal and extensive scale, but nothing useless or superfluous.

The vestibule or entrance, together with the two flights of stairs (which commodiously admit two hundred persons to pass at one time), occupy the space of one hundred feet in length by twenty-seven feet in breadth, forty of which are given to the entrance, and thirty to each of the stairs. The breadth is divided into three parts, two for the steps of the ascent, and one in the centre between for music, affording ample space for two large bands. On the side walls ascending the stairs, there are places for two large pictures meant to afford a choice situation and good light: similar blanks could not be left in other parts without impeding the current of air, to obtain which, in the greatest possible degree consistent with strength and appearance, ought to be the first object of an architect in a hot climate.

To the northern front is added an open portico, under which carriages may drive, and set down their company in rainy weather. Over it is contrived an open verandah or colonnade, which would render the principal apartments dark if it were closed.

On each side of the stairs are two rooms of twenty-one by twenty feet, and adjoining to each of them a bath. At the north-west corner, a spiral staircase to the music gallery renders it unnecessary for the musicians to enter any other part of the house.

Near the western end, at about five feet distant from the centre window of the large dining room, is the statue of Marquis Cornwallis, and at the opposite end that of the Marquis Wellesley. This situation was particularly pointed out by Mr. Bacon, the statuary, in preference to the upper floor, under the consideration that the statues ought not to be set up in an assembly or dancing room; and also that from the great weight of the marble it would be absolutely impossible to secure the floor without building a solid mass of masonry under the statues, if they were placed above stairs; thereby shutting out a great deal of air and light from the dining apartment, and spoiling two rooms, by placing in the upper story what would possibly be considered an unappropriate ornament, and better situated below.

The great saloon, being 162 feet in length and sixty-five in breadth, will conveniently dine eight hundred persons in the lower floor, and accommodate the same number at public entertainments for ladies, on the other story.

The southern front consists of two corner rooms, each very nearly a double cube, being forty-three feet in length by twenty-one in width; and a centre portico, eighty-two feet by thirty. The first-mentioned apartments serve as committee rooms below, and as card-rooms above. The centre forms the grand entrance for those who use palanquins, carriages passing round to the northern front: above stairs it affords a spacious roomy promenade, with a beautiful view of the river, fort, &c. The building is raised six feet in the southern front, and flued throughout. An almost imperceptible slope from the outer gates leads to the northern front, in order to facilitate the entrance into the vestibule of the great staircase. On the south it is formed by twelve stone stairs leading into the lower verandah. The height of the rooms from this level is twenty-three feet under the beam, and paved with marble. The upper apartments are boarded with a teak floor throughout, and twenty-seven feet in height. The ceiling is covered, and all the wood work is of teak. An iron nucleus is placed in the centre of the columns in both the floors, in order to strengthen the building, and render the work secure. On the lower floor it is composed of a cylinder of five inches diameter, of two pieces, each eleven feet in length, to screw into each other, and on the upper story the diameter is diminished to 4½ inches, to screw through the floors into the irons of the lower apartments, which necessarily keep all the columns perpendicular and greatly add to the strength of the building.

The order of the architecture is Doric. It may be observed that the style is very simple, the parts of which it is composed few, but large, and particularly calculated to strike at a distance, and to ornament the town. The plan was not copied from any other edifice, but was composed expressly for the purpose mentioned. It exceeds in height that of the Government House by several feet. The amount which was set apart to build the Town Hall appears to have been seven lacs of rupees.

Writers' Buildings form a handsome row of houses, connected, as in England. They are of two stories high, with one room on a floor, a kitchen, and entrance yard. They were applied, until very late years, to the reception of the writers in the East-India Company's Civil Service during the first year after their arrival in England, but they are at present let as lodgings or counting-houses to private individuals.

The Metcalfe Hall.—When Sir Charles Metcalfe, the present governor of the Canadas, was about to return from India to reside permanently in Europe, the numerous members of the Calcutta community, who had long benefitted by his boundless liberalities, his munificent hospitality, and the wisdom and mildness of his rule as temporary Governor-General of India, determined to pay a tribute of gratitude to their benefactor, by raising a monument that should perpetuate the recollection of his many public and private virtues, and more particularly signalize the last great act of his Indo-political life—the emancipation of the Indian press. Various methods of effecting this great object suggested themselves—the erection of a statue, the foundation of scholarships, the placing a bust, or a picture, with a mural inscription in letters of gold, in some conspicuous public building, &c.; but all gave way to the happier conceit of erecting an edifice which, while it subserved purposes of great utility, should, by its title, commemorate the worth of the excellent Sir Charles. A public library had been for some time in existence, but it had no better local habitation than the lower rooms of the private residence of a friend to the institution. The Agricultural and Horticultural Society was equally destitute of a building adapted to the purposes of official meetings, and the depository of curious models of agricultural implements, seeds, specimens of produce, &c. To combine the objects of these institutions under one edifice, and to give to it the name of the statesman who had long patronised both, appeared to be a rational proceeding, acceptable alike to the public who were interested in them, and to Sir Charles Metcalfe himself. A larger sum of money was, however, necessary, for the erection of a building of fitting dimensions and external beauty, than that subscribed exclusively for commemorative purposes. The deficiency was accordingly made up from the funds of the Agricultural Society and the Public Library, and a piece of ground for THE METCALFE HALL having been applied for, the government granted a site fronting the Strand Road and river on the west, Hare Street on the north, and opposite to the Bankshall, Master Attendants' Office, and Post Office. The foundation stone having been laid, with Masonic honours, in January 1841, the HALL is now rapidly erecting.

The order of architecture is from the portico of the Temple or Tower of the Winds, at Athens, which was chosen for its lightness and durability. A broad flight of steps leads to the portico or colonnade on the west or river front, and there is a covered colonnade entrance on the east, with another and similar flight of steps, which lead up to the lobby and internal staircase.

The building is raised on a solid but ornamented basement of ten feet in height, in which there are no openings, and the columns, thirty in number and thirty-six feet high, rise from this basement and support the general entablature of the building, giving it, externally, much the appearance of a Grecian temple of one lofty story.

The columns and colonnade nearly surround the whole building. They would have been carried entirely round, and a more temple-like form thereby given to the building, but the funds would not admit of it; indeed, the limited amount of the subscription, and the necessity for so much internal accommodation, rendered curtailment of the ornament and outward decoration necessary.

Internally there are two stories; the lower one is to be occupied by the Agricultural Society, and will consist of a hall, sixty-three feet by thirty feet; a seed and specimen-room, thirty-six feet by twenty-four; a museum, or room for agricultural and horticultural implements, thirty-six feet by twenty-four; a secretary's room, twenty-four feet by twenty-four; and a corridor, or passage leading to the main hall, thirty-six feet by twelve. All these rooms are twenty-two feet high in the roof.

The upper floor, to be occupied by the Calcutta Public Library, is reached by a handsome teakwood flight of stairs, in a staircase seven feet wide; and opposite to the secretary's room there are the same rooms above as below, only they are more thrown into one by arches, and the roof will be twenty-six instead of twenty-two feet high, which will admit of galleries and side-lights above.

The lower story, or portion appropriated to the Agricultural Society, will have a colonnaded verandah nearly all round, and the principal hall above will have an iron rail on the river-side, inside the pillars.

In the interior of the building there is to be placed a bust of Sir Charles Metcalfe, which, with an appropriate inscription, will intimate the reasons for the erection of the hall and perpetuate the recollection of the many noble qualities which distinguished the Indian career of the worthy baronet.

THE MEDICAL COLLEGE.—This institution was founded in February, 1834, by Lord William Bentinck. It was one of the last acts of that nobleman's administration in India, and one of the most useful. For some years previous to the establishment of the Medical College, a school of instruction for native doctors, as it was termed, had existed under the successive superintendence of Messrs. Breton and Tytler, two gentlemen of great ability, and much distinguished as Oriental scholars. In that school a number of young men were educated for the service of the government in the capacity of native doctors, a very subordinate and inferior grade of medical assistants. The institution was carried on entirely in the Hindostanee language, aided by a few translations in Arabic. The extent of education was very limited, and in no department was it in the slightest degree practical, except in the mere drudgery of dressing wounds and compounding medicine. There was only one teacher for all the branches of medical science, and the students had received no previous education beyond the accomplishments of reading and writing in their own tongue. They were utterly ignorant of the English language and all European knowledge, and for the most part were young men not above the rank of common servants, often of the meanest class. Besides this school, an attempt was made to convey some instruction in medicine to a few students in the Hindoo and Mahomedan colleges in the shape of a lecture twice a week. The means of instruction were in this instance also confined to plates and books. No great progress could be expected to occur from such desultory instruction, although the teachers were gentlemen of great eminence.

The inefficiency of these native schools soon became apparent. It would, indeed, have been impossible to produce better work with such materials as the teachers had at their disposal, and they certainly deserved much credit for the progress they made with such limited means. In consequence of the failure of these institutions, and urged, perhaps, by some papers upon the possibility of improving the scheme of medical education in India, which were laid before him by one or two gentlemen in the medical service, Lord William Bentinck appointed a committee to inquire into the subject and report to him upon the feasibility of establishing a more improved method of instruction in this department of knowledge. At the end of two years, after considerable labour and very patient investigation, a most masterly report upon the subject shewed the utter impossibility of imparting medical instruction, according to the system of translations, without any means of practical illustration, then pursued in India. It urged upon the government to establish, forthwith, a college of medicine, formed upon a very extended basis, wherein instruction might be conveyed, in the English language, by a number of lecturers having each a separate branch of study under his charge; and it suggested that these teachers should be directed to make their instruction as practical as possible, after the model of similar establishments in Europe, more especially with reference to anatomy and the treatment of diseases.

The report also recommended that a superior class of pupils should be selected who had previously received a good English education, and that the scale of remuneration for government appointments should be increased so as to offer encouragement to these young men to exert themselves. It was urged that such an institution would not only supply the government with well-educated medical assistants, but would be the means of improving the wretched state of medicine among the natives generally, by distributing over the country skilful practitioners in lieu of the miserable quacks who had previously formed the physicians of the native community.

The government, though much gratified with this report, and determined upon adopting its principles, considered the scale upon which it was recommended to form the new college, to be too expensive, and Lord William resolved upon commencing with a more limited establishment, which might afterwards be increased as occasion required.

The following extract from the government order creating the college will exhibit what were his lordship's views :—

That a new college shall be formed for the instruction of a certain number of native youths in the various branches of medical science.

That this college shall be under the control of the Education Committee, assisted by certain medical officers.

That instruction be given through the medium of the English language.

That a certain number of native youths, whose ages shall not exceed twenty years, or be less than fourteen years, shall be entered upon the foundation as foundation pupils of the Institution.

That all candidates for admission as foundation pupils shall be required to present respectability of connections and conduct ; shall be able to read and write English and Bengalee, or English and Hindostanee, and with these qualifications, all natives, between the age of fourteen and twenty, shall be equally eligible, without exception to creed or caste.

That the number of the foundation pupils shall be limited to fifty.

That the foundation pupils shall each receive a monthly stipend from the government of seven rupees, which may be increased according to certain rules.

That the foundation pupils shall be expected to remain at the Institution for a period of not less than four years, and not exceeding six years.

That all foundation pupils be required to learn the principles and practice of medical sciences in strict accordance with the mode adopted in Europe.

That all the pupils who shall have completed their studies according to the form prescribed shall be entitled to have certificates, signed by the Superintendent, to enable them to present themselves for final examination.

That such pupils as shall be deemed qualified to practise surgery and medicine shall receive certificates of qualification, signed by the President of the Committee of Education, and countersigned by the Secretary of that Committee and the Superintendent of the Institution.

That the public service shall be supplied with native doctors from the Institution, and with a view to this object, whatever appointments may happen to fall vacant during the period which intervenes two examinations shall be offered for the acceptance of the students who pass at the examination next ensuing. The selection shall be regulated by the extent of professional acquirement.

That the Superintendent shall be supplied, under the direction and management of the Education Committee, with a certain monthly allowance of stationery for the use of the Institution.

That the formation of a plan of medical education, and the rules and discipline of the Institution, shall be intrusted to the Education Committee.

That in addition to the pupils on the foundation, the benefits of this College shall be open to all classes of native youths, between the age of fourteen and twenty, without exception to creed or caste, provided they possess respectable connections and conduct, and can read and write English and Bengalee, or English and Hindostanee; and that all thus qualified shall, at the discretion of the Committee of Education, be permitted to attend the instruction at the College, subject to its discipline and regulations.

That the Superintendent shall draw a pay bill for the establishment of the Institution, which shall be countersigned by the Secretary of the Education Committee, and shall annex it to a nominal roll of the youths on the foundation of, and establishments attached to, the Native Medical Institution, and the voucher for the payment of the house-rent, both signed by the Secretary of the Education Committee.

A superintendent and an assistant were appointed, on handsome salaries, and required to instruct the pupils in anatomy, surgery, medicine, and pharmacy, and to qualify them for medical charges, civil and military. After the death of the first superintendent or principal, the government altered the arrangement by abolishing the office, and appointing four or five additional professors to the college.

The establishment was at first placed in a house adjoining the Hindoo College, but in the meantime, the present commodious building was preparing for its reception, and the institution, in May, 1835, was located on the site it now occupies. This is situated in the centre of the native town, and covers a considerable space of ground.

The buildings comprise a very spacious and handsome theatre, capable of containing five hundred persons—apartments for the purpose of practical anatomy, a laboratory, museum, and a library and hospital. The grounds are extensive, and afford a fine site for additional buildings, for the reception of midwifery patients, and for the general enlargement of the hospital.

A visit to the Medical College will well repay the curiosity of the stranger. The *materiel* for anatomical pursuits is abundantly obtained, and is kept in perfect preservation by the injection of arsenical solutions into the veins—a method which enables the lecturers and students of anatomy to carry on their labours, during the hot season and the rains, without the least offensive smell being generated in the apartments.

THE MUSEUM.—It cannot be expected that the Museum, of which, in 1837, there did not exist a single rudiment, should be very extensive. Yet, in the very short space of time which has elapsed from its commencement, a number of most valuable preparations have been accumulated, and already it presents many highly interesting features. The great industry and zeal of the first Curator, Mr. Evans, enabled him to surmount difficulties of no insignificant character, and the shelves of this infant collection amply attest the importance of that gentleman's services. The department of pathology may, perhaps, be regarded as the best furnished portion of this museum. Amongst the rest are some preparations and casts of enormous tumours, which have been removed from natives of this country. There are many magnificent speciments of neerosis and eostosis, and a collection of urinary calculi, almost unrivalled in any country. There are many remarkable examples of tropical diseases of the viscera, ulcerations of the intestines, alterations and derangements of the biliary organs, &c., and one most striking preparation of the stomach of an individual poisoned by arsenic, together with a large number of aneurisms, diseases of arteries, and some fine preparations of monstrosities, more particularly one of a complete double fœtus, which lived for some hours after its birth. The purely anatomical preparations are less numerous, but many of them very excellent. There is a fine collection of wax models and numerous full-sized figures of dissected parts of Auzoun, &c. &c. The osteological branch of this department is well furnished, and it is especially rich in skulls of various nations and characters; amongst others, two crania of Suttee women are very interesting to the stranger.

The Laboratory contains, among numerous interesting articles, a magnificent series of galvanic batteries, presented to the college by a public subscription in 1837. These instruments consist chiefly of a set of twelve troughs, each exposing forty-three feet of superficial zinc surface to an equal area of copper. The ignoting and magnetic effects of this battery, when excited by solutions of sulphate of soda and sulphate of copper, are of the most splendid and astonishing kind.

2. A series of 100 cells, each fifteen inches square, adapted to a steam chamber, so that the battery can be heated to the boiling point. This is considered to be the finest instrument in existence for the exhibition of the intensity of the electric fluid, as displayed by its deflagration of metals, the production of the galvanic magnet of flame, and its powers over the living system.

3. A series of 300 galvanic cases of copper and zinc in jars, for the demonstration of the laws of voltaic electricity.

Besides the preceding instruments, the laboratory possesses an enormous electro-magnet, the bars of which are three inches in diameter, by six feet long;

and some very curious models illustrative of the application of electro-magnetic forces to the movements of machinery, propulsion of boats and carriages, and effecting of telegraphic communications.

Fifty pupils are maintained on monthly stipends, ranging from seven to twelve rupees, according to their seniority and deserts. Besides these youths, there is a numerous supplementary class of candidate pupils—natives, East Indians, and members of the subordinate medical department.

On leaving college, the native graduates are employed as sub-assistant surgeons, on salaries ranging from sixty to one hundred rupees per month, in the discharge of the duties of medical attendant on large dispensaries, established in different parts of the country.

That the institution is well calculated to fulfil the objects proposed at its formation, and that the labour of the teachers has not been thrown away upon the undeserving, have been amply proved by the result of the last seven years' instruction, as shewn in the examinations which have annually taken place since November, 1838, for the purpose of granting diplomas. Practical proofs of the advantage and capabilities of the college have been given on each occasion, and it can now be no longer doubtful that Hindoos are as able to master the difficulties of medical science as their European brethren.

In June (1838) the government having called upon the college council to furnish a number of students for employment as surgeons to dispensaries in the upper provinces, a list of candidates was submitted by the latter to the authorities, with a request that they would appoint a committee of examiners to decide upon the qualifications of the students. The college council at the same time reminded the government that the full period of instruction prescribed at the commencement of the institution had not been completed by many months—scarcely three years having elapsed since these pupils began the study of medicine.

In November, a committee of professional men, unconnected with the college, having been appointed by the government, the examinations commenced, and after a very severe trial, which lasted the greater part of six days, five students out of eleven who presented themselves were declared to have passed their examination. These examinations, which were held publicly in the college, were as strictly practical as possible. The candidates were obliged to demonstrate their knowledge of anatomy upon the dead body in the dissecting room, where they also performed many of the capital operations of surgery in the presence of the committee. In chemistry and materia medica the ordeal was equally practical, and the oral part of the examination in the various branches of medical study was minute and searching in the extreme. Indeed, nothing could be a more complete test of the student's professional knowledge than these trials, and the reports of the examiners speak in the highest strain of the acquirements of the young men who were placed before them.

In January, the diplomas were conferred upon the successful candidates by the president of the committee of public instruction, in the presence of a large concourse of spectators—Europeans and natives.

The complete success which has thus crowned the efforts of the professors must be a source of high gratification to them. Theirs is, indeed, a situation of which they may be proud. By the triumphal result of their exertions in developing the resources thus placed at their disposal a new era in the science of medicine has commenced in India. The blessings of European medical knowledge will be gradually extended over the land; and the ignorant, chicaning empirics, who have for so many years served the office of physicians in India, will be supplanted by a race of men who possess the requisite ability and scientific acquirement to treat disease with a reasonable prospect of success. At the same time, some of the most deeply-rooted prejudices of the native mind have been completely overthrown, and a new road has thus been opened for the progress of civilization in India.

La Martinière.—This magnificent institution was erected and is maintained by means of property bequeathed for the purpose by Major General Claude Martine, whose name it bears. The founder was a native of France, having been born at Lyons on the 5th day of January, in the year 1735. He appears to have arrived in India at an early age, and to have been led by the political circumstances of the country to try his fortune at Lucknow, the capital of the kingdom of Oude, and the royal residence. At this place he died on the 13th of September, 1800, leaving behind him a most princely fortune, which he had accumulated with a rapidity by no means singular in those days, but far from common in these less troublous and better administered times.

The sum which General Martine set apart for endowing this noble charity was, as appears from the published extract of his will, 3,50,000 sicca rupees, but this having been placed at interest, had, in October, 1832, reached the amount of 9,62,825 sicca rupees, or nearly £100,000 sterling. The precise objects of the charity were only indistinctly defined by the founder, while no attempt whatever was made by him to fix its internal economy. He acknowledges, indeed, in his will, that "he is little able to make any arrangement for such an institution," and expresses a hope that either the government or the Supreme Court will devise the best institution for the public good. The chief and almost the only points specified by him in his brief reference to the subject are, that it shall be for the good of the town of Calcutta; that children of either sex shall be admissible to it, and, after having been educated, shall be apprenticed to some trade, or married; that it shall bear the title of La Martinière; and that an inscription in large legible characters, bearing that it was established by him, shall be fixed on some part of the building. This vagueness of specification was probably the principal reason why thirty-two years were allowed to elapse before any steps were taken to carry his benevolent design into effect. It ought to be mentioned to the honour of Sir Edward Ryan, the late chief justice of the Supreme Court, that he, when second Puisne Judge, was the first who seriously grappled with the difficulty, and that he drew up the decree, bearing date the 22nd October, 1832, in accordance with which the rules and regulations of the institution were afterwards framed. In terms of this decree, the building was erected. It was completed on the 31st December, 1835, and thrown open for the reception of the wards on the 1st of March, 1836.

The objects of La Martinière, as appears from the published rules, are two-fold, viz. :—To provide gratuitous board, education, &c., to a certain number of indigent children of both sexes, and to furnish a superior education to boys in more favoured circumstances, who may be admitted either as boarders, day boarders, or day scholars, on the payment of a fixed monthly fee.

The number of children on the foundation is never to be under fifty. At present it is greatly beyond that number, and it is supposed the boys' department will gradually receive additions, as the funds are found to admit of them. The foundation children are elected from the Christian population of Calcutta without respect to the religious denomination with which they are connected. They are selected on account of their indigent circumstances; but the selection is made from those who are above the *lowest* class of the population, both because children of this class are amply provided for in the charitable institutions which already exist, and because, as is apprehended, the boarders and other scholars would not so readily or so harmoniously associate with them. The boys are eligible between the ages of four and ten years, and are allowed to remain till they reach the age of sixteen, though they may be apprenticed before that time with the approbation of the acting governors; the girls are eligible between the ages of four and twelve years, and unless they are apprenticed or married, they may remain for life. The education given to the foundation children is of the most liberal and comprehensive character. The boys are taught English, English grammar, writing, arithmetic, geography, the general outlines of history, particularly of the histories of Great Britain and British India, the Hindustani and Bengali languages, and the elements of mathematics, natural history, mechanical philosophy; and, in the case of any of them who discover superior talents, it is competent for the head master to instruct them in such additional branches as shall fit them for holding in after-life a higher situation than that of apprentice to a trade. The girls, again, are educated in all the branches which have been specified, with the exception of mathematics and mechanical philosophy, and are besides taught plain and ornamental needle-work, knitting, and straw-plaiting. It may be worth while to subjoin the reason assigned by a committee of the governors for having sketched such an extensive course of education, as it brings into view one of the indirect ends which La Martiniere may eventually subserve. "The course of instruction sketched out for the boys and girls on the foundation is, your committee are fully aware, more liberal and comprehensive than is in general deemed either necessary or expedient for children in their rank of life; but they have been induced to recommend it, partly by the eager desire which they feel to see introduced into this noble institution many of those improvements on the old educational systems which have been adopted in some parts of the continent of Europe, and which are slowly but surely finding their way into favour in Great Britain, and partly by the conviction which they have that no mean advantage will be obtained if in this way a model of education can be presented to the other schools which either now exist, or may hereafter be opened on this side of India."

The boarders, day boarders, and day scholars at present amount to between sixty and seventy; and, as the number has steadily increased since the opening of the institution, there is every reason to think that it is far from having reached its highest point. The inducements for parents to place their children there are partly the superior character of the education imparted, and partly the comparatively cheap rate at which it is afforded;—the charge for day scholars being only six Company's rupees, and for boarders twenty-five Company's rupees, per mensem. The greatest care is taken to avoid every thing like an invidious distinction between them and the foundation children. They take their meals at the same table and share the same fare, are taught in the same classes, when they have reached the same rate of progress, and associate in their play-hours. The only difference between them is, that they occupy separate dormitories, though these are equally spacious, well-aired, and commodious.

The general management of the affairs of the institution is vested, by the decree of the Supreme Court, in ex-officio governors and in four additional governors selected on account of their presumed qualifications. The ex-officio governors are the Governor-General, the Members of Council, the judges of the Supreme Court, the Bishop of Calcutta, and the Advocate-General.

The four additional governors are chosen annually, and, while they hold office, have equal power and authority with the former. They, along with any of the ex-officio governors, are intrusted with the chief superintendence of the charity, and to them belongs the right of filling up any vacancy that may occur in the foundation department. They meet for the transaction of the current business on the first Tuesday of every month, and each of them in turn, in the capacity of monthly visitor, visits the school, examines the classes, and makes a general inspection of the establishment. A general meeting of the governors is held twice every year, when a report of the affairs of the institution for the previous half-year is drawn up, laws are made to meet any emergencies that may have occurred, and all other matters brought before them are considered and determined upon.

The business of the school is conducted by three masters whose several departments are carefully defined in the rules. They are required to possess superior qualifications, and especially an aptitude for teaching, receive higher salaries than are given in any other educational establishment in India, and have apartments in the school. In addition to them, a Moonshee and Pundit are retained for teaching the native languages; and provision besides is made for engaging other teachers and lecturers, whenever the acting governors may deem them necessary for rendering the system of instruction more efficient and complete. The girls' department, which is kept quite distinct from the boys, is taught and superintended by a head mistress and assistant teacher.

The anniversary of General Martine's death, the 13th day of September, is, in terms of his will, observed with peculiar honours. An appropriate sermon is preached to the children in the chapel of the institution by one of the clergymen of Calcutta appointed by the governors; when the service is closed, a silver medal is given to the most deserving boy and girl in the school; and then all adjourn to the dining-room, where they partake of a sumptuous dinner and drink a toast to the memory of the founder.

The most distinctive circumstance connected with the internal arrangements of La Martinière is the system of religious instruction which prevails in it. A general idea of this system may be gathered from the following resolution which was unanimously adopted by the governors—as a compromise, it is understood, between two other views which almost equally divided them;—"that the public religious instruction given to the children of the school be in conformity with the principles held in common by the English, Scotch, Roman, Greek, and Armenian churches; but that the school be not placed under any particular denomination of Christians, and that no points which are in controversy between the said churches be touched upon in the course of public instruction." A course of religious instruction and a form of prayer for family devotional exercises were framed in conformity with these principles by the

Protestant Bishop of Calcutta, the Roman Catholic prelate, and the principal Presbyterian minister. The plan recommended by them and carried into operation consists of two parts, viz. the public religious instruction and the private supplementary. In the former are embraced the fundamental truths of Christianity, as they are held by the five great existing divisions of Christendom enumerated in the resolution just cited, and which are summed up in the following particulars :—" 1. The Being of a God, his unity and perfections. 2. The Holy Scriptures of the Old and New Testaments,—a revelation inspired by the Holy Ghost. 3. The mystery of the adorable Trinity. 4. The Deity, Incarnation, Atonement, and Intercession of our Lord and Saviour Jesus Christ. 5. The fall and corruption of man, his accountableness and guilt. 6. Salvation through grace, by the meritorious sacrifice and redemption of Christ. 7. The Personality and Deity of the Holy Spirit, and his operations and grace in the sanctification of men. 8. The indispensable obligation of repentance towards God, faith in Christ, and continual prayer for the grace of the Holy Spirit. 9. The moral duties which every Christian is bound to perform towards God, his neighbour, and himself, as they are summed up in the ten commandments, and enlarged upon in other parts of the Holy Scriptures; all based upon the doctrines above specified, and enforced as their proper fruits." Catechisms embodying these doctrines are publicly taught in the school, and the Bible is read as a class-book by all the children, Episcopalian, Presbyterian, and Roman Catholic; the English authorized version being used by the two former classes, and the Douay version by the latter, as often as they learn lessons or receive direct instructions from the Scriptures.

The private or supplementary religious instruction relates to discipline, church government, the sacraments, and other matters on which differences more or less important exist, and is communicated by the ministers of different denominations whom the parents or guardians of the respective children may select, and who attend at the school for the purpose. The fullest latitude is given to them in regard to the catechisms to be used by their respective classes, and doctrines, or tenets, to be imparted to them.

All the foundation children of both sexes, and also the boarders, assemble every morning and evening in the chapel of the institution, when a portion of Holy Scripture and prayers are read by the head master, from a form of prayer extracted from different ancient liturgies. At these family devotional exercises all the masters and mistresses, with all the Christian members of the household, are required to attend.

On Sunday mornings, the foundation children are conducted to their respective churches and chapels, as often as the state of the weather permits them; and in the evenings they meet in the chapel of the institution, when the ordinary family devotions are read with the addition of a suitable sermon approved of by the governors.

The building of the institution, which is near the Circular Road, was commenced in June, 1833, and the entire edifice was completed in 1835. It cost about two lacs and Rs. 30,000, and is two-storied, with a large dome, which is employed as a library. Immediately under this—that is, in the centre of the building—is the chapel, on each side of which are the following accommodations for the children, viz. four large halls on each floor, making in all sixteen, employed as class-rooms, dormitory, and refectory. In addition to these, there are apartments (viz. two rooms on each floor with an antechamber and conveniences) at each extremity or wing of the building intended for the teachers. There are two porticoes, north and south, both leading into the chapel. There are besides three rooms on the ground-floor running the whole length of the south portico, the middle of which is the antechamber of the chapel, and the other two the domicile of one of the masters. Lastly, there are three rooms above these, two of which form the residence of one of the masters, and the third is the office of the secretary.

THE SANS SOUCI THEATRE stands in Park-street, Calcutta. It was erected in May, 1840, and opened in March, 1841. The cost of the building, including scenery, wardrobe, chandeliers, &c. &c., was not much under £8000, of which sum the public subscribed about £1600, the remainder falling upon the lady who undertook the erection of the theatre. The Sans Souci is one hundred and ninety-nine feet in length and fifty-two in breadth. A splendid portico in front, covering a magnificent flight of steps, leads into a spacious saloon, whence the entry into the boxes. The area of the audience part of the house comprises a pit and one tier of boxes, in which are five rows of arm-chairs raised above each other amphitheatrically. Behind the boxes runs a lobby or gallery. The stage occupies within the proscenium twenty-eight feet of breadth and nearly fifty of depth. The space concealed from the audience, above and below, is appropriated to green-rooms, dressing-rooms, wardrobes, &c. The house is admirably ventilated, but in the warm weather punkahs are suspended, so that performances continue throughout the year. The gentlemen performers are for the most part amateurs; the ladies are paid handsome salaries, and one of them, Mrs. Leach, was, for talent and personal attractions, without à rival even in England.

Mechanics' Institution.—This is a small edifice of an oblong form, with a frontage resembling an Egyptian sarcophagus. It was built by subscription, with the view of inoculating the natives and the East Indians with a taste for mechanics. A few lectures were given by different gentlemen, but the means of insuring a continuance of such services have latterly been wanting, and the institution now exists simply as a drawing-school.

The Ochterlony Monument.—A column one hundred and sixty feet in height, with a Turkish capital and an Egyptian base. It stands on the esplanade in front of the town, and was erected to commemorate the public worth of Major-General Sir David Ochterlony, who distinguished himself by his political and military services. The pillar is by no means an ornament to the town; but it furnishes an opportunity to him who will be at the trouble of ascending by the circular staircase, of beholding from the summit an interesting panorama of Calcutta. The cost of the edifice was £3500.

THE BENGAL MILITARY ORPHAN INSTITUTION at Kidderpore, about two miles from Calcutta, is an ornament to the place, as much from the excellent and benevolent intentions of its founders, as from the beauty of its architecture. It was established to afford a home to the orphan children of officers and soldiers; and as its affairs have always been managed by a select committee of officers, who have a brotherly interest in its success, it has been most prosperous. Children are not, however, merely housed, clothed, and educated; their advancement in life is cared for, and sums varying according to circumstances are assigned as portions to girls marrying, or as *premia* to set boys forth in the world.

THE PRESIDENCY GENERAL HOSPITAL.—The premises now denominated the General Hospital, were, in their original state, occupied as a garden-house by an individual, from whom they were purchased by the government in the year 1768, and converted into a hospital. They were subsequently enlarged and surrounded by a wall, and now afford ample accommodation, in separate buildings, for patients and for the medical officers and establishment attached to the institution. The situation of the hospital is airy and healthy, and it is sufficiently far from the city without being inconveniently distant from Fort William, the soldiers from which are its principal inmates.

Strictly speaking, the General Hospital is a military establishment, it having been transferred to the military department in the year 1786, when the medical board was instituted; but besides the sick of the European corps in garrison, on their first arrival from Europe, who are received until their own regimental hospitals are prepared for them, the sick of European recruits, supernumeraries, and invalids of the Queen's and Company's army, the hospital is open for the reception of seamen belonging to her Majesty's or the Company's service, or to private and foreign ships, and also to European paupers. Nor, indeed, are Europeans in any other class of life refused admittance. To those who can afford to defray their own expenses, and for sick men belonging to her Majesty's or the Company's ships or other vessels, a charge of one rupee per diem is made on account of each patient.

The management of the hospital is conducted under the fixed military regulations. The immediate charge of it is intrusted to a surgeon of the establishment, and two assistant surgeons, who are permanently attached to it, and which latter reside on the spot.

The General Assembly's Institution, which stands on the outskirts of the city,. on the road to Barrackpore, was, as its title imports, founded at the instance of the General Assembly of the Kirk of Scotland, for the education and consequent conversion of the Hindoos. It is a plain but spacious and well-contrived building, arranged as a school, having large apartments for the purposes of instruction, illustration, &c., and quarters for the teachers. The missionaries of the Church of Scotland have the superintendence of the establishment, and their system is deservedly so popular, that there are seldom less than one thousand youths receiving education at one and the same time.

THE GREAT JAIL is a large, airy, and healthy building, situated upon the eastern side of the race-ground. The debtors are accommodated in lofty apartments, and the prisoners on the criminal side in apartments upon a ground-floor in the centre of a walled enclosure, sufficiently wide to afford the means of healthful exercise. There is a neat little chapel within the jail where service is performed by one of the government chaplains.

THE ASIATIC SOCIETY'S ROOMS, PARK-STREET.—The Asiatic Society of Bengal was instituted by Sir William Jones, on the 15th January, 1784, during the administration of Mr. Warren Hastings, who became its first patron.

The objects of inquiry, for which this noble society was created, were (to use the words of its distinguished founder) "man and nature," or whatever is performed by the one or produced by the other, confined within the geographical limits of Asia.

On the 19th August, 1796, the first proposition was made to provide an edifice, the expenses of which were to be defrayed by entrance-fees of members, and by a quarterly subscription; also by voluntary contributions; and as the estimates for the present building are dated in 1806, it is probable that it was about that period erected. In 1839, the apartments being found too small for the proper display of the greatly-accumulating objects of natural history and other curiosities, two wings were added to it. A third outer apartment has since been added. There are now ten rooms of various sizes on the ground-floor, including the entrance-hall, in which are the stairs, and five on the upper. The grand or assembly-room extends from end to end of the building, which is very wide, with a fine verandah on its southern face. The museum contains many beautiful objects of natural history, chiefly birds, reptiles, and fishes. There are but few specimens of quadrupeds. There is a fine collection of prepared skeletons of various animals, such as the elephant, rhinoceros, camel, horse, ox, ass, tiger, bear, hog, &c. The largest or centre hall of the lower floor being too dark and damp for other purposes, is devoted to the osteological collection. The museum is particularly rich in both minerals and fossils, all of which have their particular gallery.

There is a great collection of fragments of sculpture found in India, of various ages, the most remarkable objects amongst which are Budhist fragments, and some of Grecian origin. One in particular represents Silenus, supported by a group of well-executed figures, male and female, but much mutilated. It was discovered at Muttra by Colonel Stacy. The sculpture is divided into classes, viz. the Budhist and Brahminical, or Hindoo. In addition to the foregoing are various inscribed slabs, some of very great antiquity; amongst these is a fragment of one of Asoka's pillars, brought from Delhi, which is upwards of two thousand years old, the deciphering of which will immortalize the name of James Prinsep, the late secretary to the society.

In the upper apartments is a great variety of weapons of all Indian nations, and of the South-Sea

Islanders, also many curious relics, musical instruments, &c. There is a fine gallery of pictures; but few of these, however, belong to the society: they are merely deposited for exhibition and security's sake.

The library is considered very valuable. Besides many hundred volumes of European publications in all languages, both modern and ancient, there is a fine collection of Oriental works, both printed and in manuscript; some of the latter are rare and of great value. There are also numerous volumes of Thibetan, Chinese, and Burman manuscripts: the former are very curious, and chiefly printed in large characters with wooden blocks. In the hall are the portraits of Sir W. Jones, Mr. Colebrook, and Mr. H. H. Wilson, the works of Chantrey.

The society holds its meetings every month.

The foregoing comprise all the public edifices, excepting the Mint and the churches, which have been raised for the purposes which they now fulfil. But they do not comprehend a tithe of the institutions which the philanthropy, the policy, the taste, and the ambition of Englishmen in India have, at different times, founded, and which now flourish, to the honour of the city of Calcutta and the great advantage of India at large. We will present a list of them, and afterwards describe such as are not sufficiently indicated by their titles.

Religious.—Diocesan Committee of the Society for Promoting Christian Knowledge, Diocesan Committee of the Society for the Propagation of the Gospel in Foreign Parts, the Bible Association,

Auxiliary Bible Society, Church Missionary Association, Christian Institution of the London Missionary Society, Auxiliary Church Missionary Society, Corresponding Committee of the Church Missionary Society, Bengal Missionary Society, Seamen's Friend or Bethel Society, Christian Instruction Society, Christian School-book Society, Baptist Female School Society, Juvenile Society, Christian Tract and Book Society, Baptist Missionary Society, Ladies' Baptist Missionary Society, Native Christian Protection Society.

Charitable.—The Native Hospital, the European Female Orphan Institution, the Sailor's Home, the Leper Asylum, the Howrah Native Hospital, the District Charitable Society.

Colleges, Schools, &c.—*Established either by Government or the Voluntary Contributions of Charitable Individuals.* — Bishop's College, the College of Fort William, Calcutta High School, the Parental Academic Institution, the Armenian Philanthropic Institution, the Free School Institution, St. Xavier's College, St. James's Schools, the Benevolent Institution, the Principal Catholic Free School, the Branch Catholic School, the Oriental Seminary, the Union Schools, the Indian Academy, the Hindoo Benevolent Institution, the Infant School, the Entally Native Institution, the Lorretto House.

Literary, Scientific, &c. Societies.—The Medical and Physical Society, the Agricultural and Horticultural Society, the Public Library.

Commercial, &c.—The Chamber of Commerce, the Indigo Planters' Association, the Bank of Bengal, the Union Bank, the Agency of the Agra and

United Service Bank, the Assam Tea Company, the Bengal Salt Company, the Calcutta Docking Company, the Steam-Tug Association, the Bengal Steam Fund, the Landholders' Society, the Bengal Bonded Warehouse Association, the Trade Association.

Funds, Insurance Societies, &c.—The Civil Fund, the Civil Service Annuity Fund, the Medical Retiring Fund, the Uncovenanted Service Family Pension Fund, the Universal Life Assurance Society, the Oriental Life Assurance Society, the Indian Laudable and Mutual Assurance Society, the Bengal Mariners and General Widows' Fund, the Bengal Provident Society, and upwards of twenty Marine Insurance Societies.

Considering the extent of the commercial community, the precarious tenure of human existence in Calcutta, and the necessity which a large proportion of the public is under of providing creditors with security against casualties, the number of Insurance Societies, though considerable, is not too great for the demand. There are but four whose operations are confined to life assurance, the *Universal,* the *Oriental,* the *Indian Laudable and Mutual Assurance,* and the *Bengal Provident Society.* They are all profitable and substantial institutions, owing in a great measure to the diminished decadence of human life among the Europeans. Since the actuaries first regulated the premiums upon policies, with reference to the rate of mortality in India, so much has been done to render the presidency of Bengal more salubrious, and to regulate diet and habits by climate, that the per-centage of deaths has very materially decreased. The three offices differ in their rules and in their scales of premiums; but the advantage offered by one is so exactly counterbalanced by the benefits held out by another, that it is difficult to say which merits the preference.

The Marine Insurance societies are between twenty and thirty in number; two of these, the *Union* and the *Alliance*, confining themselves entirely to the assurance of boats and goods proceeding up the river Hooghly; the remainder taking risks upon vessels and cargoes proceeding to all parts of the world. To most, if not to all, of these latter offices a marine surveyor is attached, whose report of the condition of a vessel is generally taken before a policy is granted. It must be confessed, however, that either the societies or their surveyors are occasionally chargeable with a little looseness in their manner of doing business, or we should not so often hear of vessels springing leaks just as they are getting out to sea, or foundering on their voyages, without leaving a single man of the ship's company, or even a stray spar, to tell the tale of their disappearance. The consequence of this laxity has been visible of late years in the accounts of the societies, the debit side of which exhibits heavy total losses, and no inconsiderable number of smaller averages. The affairs of the societies are conducted by four or five directors, with a secretary, the latter office being generally held by a commercial firm, who render accounts half-yearly.

There is not a single Fire Insurance Office in Calcutta. Conflagrations, excepting amongst the native huts, have invariably been so rare that an attempt (originating in the upper provinces of Bengal) to establish such an office, failed from the absence of any apparent necessity for precaution.

LAW.—The Supreme Court of Judicature; the Sudder Dewany Adawlut; the Allipore magistracy; the Calcutta Police Office; the Court of Requests.

MASONIC LODGES.—The Grand Lodge of Bengal; Star in the East; Industry and Perseverance; True Friendship; Humility with Fortitude; Marine Lodge; Anchor and Hope; Courage with Humanity; Saint John's.

We proceed to notice the most prominent of the institutions named above. The College of Fort William comprehends a class of examiners only, for it has ceased to offer a residence to the civil servants, who commence the study of the Persian and Bengalee languages on their arrival. The schools are for the most part devoted to the education of Eurasian, Armenian, and English children, but three or four, conducted by natives, assisted by English masters, receive only Hindoo pupils. St. Xavier's College and the Lorretto House are appropriated to the instruction of the Portuguese and Eurasian children of the Roman Catholic persuasion, though Protestants and others are admitted, and no attempt is made at proselytism. These last-named institutions are conducted by Jesuits and nuns, imported direct from the mother-country.

BISHOP'S COLLEGE.—The first stone of Bishop's College was laid by Bishop Middleton, on the 15th of December, 1820, on a spot of ground presented by the government for the purpose, at the distance of about four miles from Calcutta, on the opposite bank of the river, and immediately to the eastern extremity of the Honourable Company's Botanic Garden.

Bishop's College is an elegant Gothic structure, of a quadrangular form, like most of the buildings of the same character in Oxford and Cambridge, but not joined at the angles, the southern side of the square being also open towards the river; thus exhibiting the buildings of the northern side as the most conspicuous object from the opposite bank. The side of the building is composed of a central tower, which is in height sixty-five feet; in depth from east to west, thirty feet; in depth from north to south, twenty-four feet. The right or western side of this tower is occupied by a building of equal depth, but whose height is but forty feet, and its length from east to west sixty feet, the ground-floor of which is the hall. The upper floor is the library of the college. The left, or eastern side of the central tower, is occupied by the chapel, a building of the same dimensions with the preceding, but in every other respect altogether dissimilar; being, of course, a single compartment, with an arched roof, in its exterior figure and decorations approaching to a miniature resemblance of that superb structure, King's College Chapel, in Cambridge. The ground-floor of the central tower forms an entrance both to the chapel and the hall; the first floor is the vestibule of the library, communicating also with the organ-loft of the chapel; the second floor is the council-room, or visitors' chamber, and opens to the terraced roof of the library. The two wings, extending from north to south, to the length of 150 feet (equal to that of the northern side described above), are allotted to the residence of professors, pupils, and domiciliaries. The edifice cost above £13,000.

The college is founded for a principal and two other professors from the English universities, and as many students as can be maintained, either on the proper foundation of the Incorporated Society, or on the endowment of any other religious society of the established church, or of the local governments, or individuals. The students are educated either as missionaries for the extension of Christianity in its present form, and in the mode of ancient discipline and order which is alone recognized by the Church of England, or as schoolmasters for the dissemination of general and useful knowledge.

THE DISTRICT CHARITABLE SOCIETY is a noble institution. It owes its origin to the benevolent and zealous exertions of the late Bishop Turner. At the period of its organization, the distribution of the public charitable funds was chiefly intrusted to the select vestry of St. John's Cathedral; but as the city had greatly enlarged its dimensions, and much difficulty was experienced in determining who were proper objects of public bounty, committees were formed in the different districts, with power to form sub-committees and appoint visitors and inspectors. The system has worked admirably. Many hundreds of destitute people of all classes, colours, and castes, are now liberally relieved from the ample resources of the society, which have progressively augmented through the spontaneous bounty of many individuals of rank and worth; at the head, however, of whom stands the well-known and esteemed Dwarkanath Tagore.

Almshouses and the leper establishment have been formed from the funds of the District Charitable Society.

THE AGRICULTURAL SOCIETY OF INDIA.—This institution was founded by the late Rev. W. Carey, D.D., who directed attention to the benefits likely to arise from the united efforts of a society, in an address from Mission-House, Serampore, dated 15th April, 1820, which was circulated, and followed up by a meeting at the Town-Hall on the 14th September of the same year.

On that occasion the names of thirty-two individuals were enrolled as members, under the patronage of the Marquis of Hastings and Lady Hastings; and the following among other resolutions were passed:

"That a society be formed to be denominated 'The Agricultural Society of India,' of which the following rules should form the basis:

"That the promotion of horticulture in India be considered as a branch of its main object.

"That gentlemen of every nation be eligible as members; and that all members, after the formation of the society, be admitted by ballot of a majority of the members then present.

"That gentlemen in every part of India be requested to communicate their observations upon the cultivation of the different districts in which they reside, pointing out their merits or defects, and suggesting those improvements which may occur to them.

"That the transactions of the society be published in English, and in two, at least, of the languages of

India, as often as a sufficient quantity of information be collected."

The society in its primitive state, devoted its attention and means almost exclusively to *horticulture*, by awarding medals and high pecuniary rewards to the most successful native gardeners, who were required to give evidence of the locality of their ground, and the extent of cultivation. As a further encouragement, seeds were imported from England and other parts at the expense of the society, and distributed gratis to those who undertook to cultivate vegetables for the Calcutta market.

These measures were attended with very successful results; the natives zealously competed for the prizes, and a surprising improvement soon became visible in cauliflower, cabbage, peas, and most of the principal vegetables of England.

Although the society's means were chiefly devoted to the improvement of the kitchen garden, their attention was called to a higher standard of utility, in a series of queries drawn up by the zealous founder, then adopted, and circulated to such individuals in many parts of India as were likely by their intelligence to contribute information. These queries had especial reference to the then existing state of husbandry throughout India, and were eminently calculated to draw out information, as a groundwork for the exercise of future improvement; but it was premature, and, with reference to the general position of those who could answer such queries, made little or no impression.

In 1822, the society appears to have had in contemplation to form a joint stock of their information with the science of botany; and we find that, in prosecution of this object, an establishment was proposed and authorized by government to be formed at Tittyghur, near Barrackpore, as an appendage to the botanical garden, for the general purposes of experimenting and rearing young men as gardeners on scientific and practical principles; but this establishment does not seem to have been ever properly matured.

In the early part of 1824 we find the society's funds did not keep pace with the zeal of the society to promote the objects they had in view, and it was necessary to become less liberal, and call upon nominal ordinary members, who had forgotten to contribute, for the amount of their respective dues. This movement gave rise to a series of salutary rules; but they do not appear ever to have been enforced, for in 1826 a resolution passed *not* to enforce payment.

A Mr. C. K. Robison, one of the members, now projected the establishment of a splendid garden, which was very properly opposed by wiser men; but the novelty of the garden, holding out the prospect of recreation, seemed to have more weight than the sound arguments of the opponents, and a garden was accordingly determined upon, on a site above all others the worst calculated for the purpose, and gold medals were given to commanders of ships for bringing out apple and pear trees from England.

This useless incubus was nearly the ruin of the society, and gave general disgust to all who were really alive to the *objects* of the society. In April, 1829, after the funds of the society had been exhausted, without sanction, it was resolved that the constitution of the society itself should be improved. This report was adopted, and new office-bearers were elected.

It was thought at this epoch, by many, that the attention of the society had been hitherto too much confined to the introduction of what, with reference to the climate of Lower Bengal and the residence of the majority of the subscribers, might be termed exotics ; they conceived that the efforts and the funds of an Indian agricultural society might be far better applied, and more in consonance with the original draft of proposals for its formation, than they had hitherto been ; and that the sugar, cotton, coffee, silk, and other great staples of commerce, were far more legitimate objects of its special encouragement, deriving, as it did, and hoped still more to do, its chief support from the commercial and agricultural community, than the introduction, at a heavy expense, of European fruit-trees, and other similar pursuits.

In November, 1829, the government granted the society the sum of 20,000 rupees, and authorized the society to establish an experimental farm, allowing for the maintenance of such an establishment the annual sum of 10,000 rupees, exclusive of rent, and 4500 rupees for buildings and stock for the first year.

Some difficulty was experienced in finding an area sufficient for these experiments near Calcutta; but at length five hundred beegahs offered at Akra, about sixteen miles below Calcutta, and the society were obliged, rather from necessity than choice, to adopt that as their site.

Here the society grew cotton from seed sent out by the Honourable the Court of Directors, sugar-cane of the Otaheite species, and various other products; but the soil proved bad, being the site of old salt-works, and that misfortune, added to seed of four years' standing, gave very unsatisfactory results. Upon the whole, however, enough was done to shew that although Akra could not produce cotton equal to that in America, the raw material was infinitely superior to what was produced in the most favoured districts from indigenous seed; and the report of the society, upon experiments made at Akra, satisfied the Court of Directors that the money had not been fruitlessly applied.

In the meantime the health of the president called him to the Cape of Good Hope, and we find the society gradually falling to decay. The crisis which shook the commercial credit of Calcutta to its foundation, diverted attention from every other subject, and the money paid into the hands of one of the great firms, for the benefit of successful competitors in sugar, cotton, tobacco, silk, &c., was swept away with the fall of that house. At this crisis a Mr. John Bell was appointed secretary and collector, who, on taking office, found accounts and the general state of the society's affairs in a deplorably depressed condition. Nothing daunted, he set to work and called in all outstanding debts, striking out all those names who refused to pay up their arrears. This was in June, 1835, and when his accounts were made up, and the names of paying members registered, the society was found to be composed of only forty-three members good and true.

A bold and regular publication of its monthly proceedings in the newspapers soon brought in an influx of new members, and enabled the society to recommence the publication of its transactions; one volume and part of the second only having been printed since 1820. In the space of three years, good paying members increased to 350! This great additional numerical strength, and the increasing interest excited by the society's transactions, enabled the directors to appropriate 12,000 rupees (£1200) annually as premiums. On all hands, the cause of agricultural improvement gained ground; branch societies sprang up in every direction; and a spirit of generous emulation animated the sister presidencies of Madras and Bombay.

When matters had reached this prosperous point, Mr. John Bell, to whose application and judgment, as secretary to the society, the altered state of affairs was mainly owing, died, and he was succeeded by Dr. Henry Harpur Spry. To great zeal in the cause of agriculture and horticulture, Dr. Spry added an agreeable, good-natured manner, which attracted friends to the institution in the shape of members and contributors; and if he had pursued the beaten track, its prosperous career would have continued uninterrupted. But about a month before his demise, which occurred in the early part of 1842, Dr. Spry caused to be carried into effect an alteration in the manner of publishing the transactions of the society, which involved an additional expense to each member, without affording a corresponding advantage. This excited considerable disgust; and when, subsequently, a meeting of the Calcutta members passed a resolution that no residents in the interior should have a voice in the election of a new secretary, the vexation of the latter class reached such a height, that many withdrew their names from the list of members. Whether the parties at present directing the affairs of the institution have succeeded in restoring good feeling, and augmenting the finances (which appear by the latest report to have declined materially), we do not know. They have the cordial good wishes of every friend of India for success; as no one can be insensible to the vast benefits which the well-regulated operations of the society are calculated to confer upon the country at large.

In connection with the Agricultural and Horticultural Society, we give some account of

The Botanical Gardens.—If it required a very extensive knowledge of the profound yet fascinating science of botany, in all its range of practical application, to qualify a writer for the task of giving an external description (so to say) of the magnificent seat and nursery of the art, which is kept at the expense of the Honourable Company within a few miles of their capital, then we should have to forego the attempt upon which we are now entering, and leave our book less perfect than we originally designed. But it is not for scientific instruction that the readers of this work will examine its pages; but only for that fulness and accuracy of topographical, municipal, and social description, which may be calculated to familiarize them with a country and a mode of life with which their fortunes may connect them, and in which most of them will feel an interest, arising from family or other personal associations. We have already mentioned, that among the places of pleasurable resort in the vicinity of Calcutta, the Botanic Gardens were in much favour with the holiday pleasure-hunters; and of all localities for carrying out that difficult and oft-failing adventure denominated a picnic, we should say that the above-named one is that least likely to witness a disarrangement of the project; for if rain should fall, the gardens afford various and effectual shelter; and if the sun should visit the world too hotly, there are trees in *that* part of it under which the party who have migrated can be defended from its "strokes," as effectually as if under a canopy of tenfold umbrellas, or a score of parasols. But let us at once get over the unavoidably dry historical account of these splendid and pleasant gardens.

It is now about half a century ago, since the late General Kyd, of the Bengal Engineers, who chanced to be a great personal favourite of the then Soobadar of Bengal, that "Paradise of Nations," as one of the emperors entitled it, was presented by his highness with the extensive ground on the right bank of the Hooghly, about four miles seaward from the city, which now forms the gardens. Kyd was a man of refined taste and scientific acquirement, and especially delighted in horticultural and agricultural pursuits; an inclination which he encouraged, not merely because of his innate love for the study, but in the philanthropic anxiety to improve a country of which he beheld the great capabilities very much neglected. In this spirited and laudable excitement, he began by expending large sums of money in laying out and clearing the jungly and obstructed ground; hiring, and (what required both skill and patience) instructing native gardeners; and procuring plants from all parts of India, China, and other immediately accessible countries; and in the year 1793, having advanced his project sufficiently to demonstrate its feasibility, he recommended the Company's government (Sir John Shore being Governor-general) to occupy the ground as a public botanical garden, and disinterestedly offered it to them, on condition that it should be accepted as a free gift from himself, and perpetually appropriated to the purposes in question. He farther stipulated for the introduction and cultivation of every thing that could tend to the agricultural improvement of the land, as distinct from what is implied in the mere botanical branch of the general undertaking; and his offer was accepted by the government on the terms and in the spirit in which it was laid before them. They immediately sent round to Madras for Dr. Roxburgh, then high in the medical service of that presidency, and justly celebrated for his acquirements as a botanist, and placed him in charge, as "superintendent" of the gardens, on a munificent, but not an extravagant, salary of fifteen hundred rupees per mensem, and built for him a magnificent residence, such as the climate and situation required, which, originally of but two stories high, though covering what in England would be deemed a very large surface, he was eventually authorized to raise another story, as it was considered of importance that he should constantly reside there, and as the locality was deemed unhealthy in the rainy season, especially when there was no such advantage as a high and airy dwelling. Dr. Roxburgh forthwith set to work (with the skill and diligence of one who understood and took pleasure in his vocation), cutting, grafting, planting, and otherwise furthering and perfecting the object had in view by his appointment, and in a short time laid the foundation of what may be termed the richest garden in the world, spoken with reference to such of the produce of the earth as does not require artificial cultivation. In Europe, the deficiencies, and even positive hostility, of climate are supplied or baffled, as the case demands, by buildings, of which the temperature is, without much difficulty, regulated, by scientific appliances, throughout the year; whereas, in India there are no adequate means of overcoming similar difficulties, and hence a greater degree of credit is due to the successful endeavours of the practical Indian botanist.

The supreme government allowed for the general purposes of the establishment about sixteen hundred rupees (then equal to two hundred pounds sterling) a month; and continued that rate down to the year 1830, when it fell, like many other efficient and creditable establishments, under the indiscriminating and most injurious economical fervour of Lord William Bentinck, and was reduced to within eleven hundred, which has crippled it exceedingly. Dr. Roxburgh died in 1813, and his friends erected a monument to his memory about ten years subsequently—in 1823. This memorial is composed of Chunar stone, a very durable material, and bears an elegant Latin inscription, and is in the form of a truncated column, surmounted by an urn, a favourite monumental ornament of Anglo-Indians. In 1837, his son, Captain Roxburgh, of the Company's military service, with filial piety, caused a very chaste and elegant structure, somewhat in the style of a Grecian temple, to be erected over it, so as to at once protect and adorn the monument; and the whole now forms an object of great beauty, and attracting ornament in the gardens—its very appropriate locality.

On the death of Dr. Roxburgh, the celebrated H. T. Colebrooke was nominated to the temporary charge of the post, and held it till Dr. Francis Hamilton, who had been appointed regular successor to Roxburgh, but had been detained to complete certain statistical inquiries, should be enabled to assume the office, which was not until the close of 1814. This justly-celebrated naturalist and extraordinary man (Hamilton), remained but a few years in a situation which his genius so well qualified him to improve and to adorn, when he was necessitated by an impaired constitution to return to England; and was succeeded by Dr. Nathaniel Wallich, of whom it is but bare justice to say, that he was a worthy successor of those great precursors. He is known to the scientific world as the author of *Plantæ Asiaticæ Rariores*, a work of infinite labour, elegance, and research; and he also assisted the late Reverend Dr. Carey in editing the Flora Indica of Roxburgh. Carey, in speaking of the labours of his learned coadjutor, says, he "feels gratified in bearing testimony to the disinterested and highly liberal manner in which Dr. Wallich has contributed his assistance throughout the whole of this work; and to his generosity in enriching it with a number of plants described by himself. The amount of these especially among scitamineæ and grasses, would have been much more considerable had there been time to insert the recent vast accessions of plants which the garden has received from all parts of India, and which, from his earnest solicitude to promote the interests of this pleasing and important science, may be reasonably expected to bear a far greater proportion to the whole, in each succeeding volume."

This completes the general outline (which suffices for the purposes of this notice) of the garden's history, e'en from its rudest days; and here will be a fitting place to mark the death of its founder, General Kyd, which occurred soon after the munificent donation which he made of it to the state. A monument to his memory stands opposite the principal river entrance to the garden, at the termination of an avenue of sissoo trees (one of the staple timbers of India) which leads through a plantation of teak, the extremity of which, reaching the river, is faced by the famous dock-yard, on the opposite bank, built and for a series of years conducted by his son, the excellent and accomplished James Kyd, and his father. This monument, the work of Bacon, is of marble, and typifies the agricultural taste and philanthropic purposes of him whom it is designed to commemorate.

If the importance of this establishment, in a purely

scientific point of view—the notice it has attracted from, and the benefits it has conferred on, learned societies in Europe—and the interest taken in it by the natives of India themselves—together with the undoubted letter and spirit of the conditions on which it was made over to the Company's government—should not suffice to induce the restoration of its former efficiency, we do earnestly hope that such considerations may prove powerful enough to save it from farther deterioration at the hands of parsimony; and that among the few solid benefits we have as yet conferred upon the country, one of the most important may not be rendered nugatory, as it has begun to be duly appreciated by our native population. India is most rich in all botanic materials. Dyes, plants, timbers, fruits, flowers, are all abundantly supplied from nature's munificent storehouse, and only require skill to bring them to most profitable perfection; while the discoveries of late years, in various parts of the country, have brought to light productions and capabilities of the soil, which were never before suspected to have existence, and which prove that our empire in the East may be made to produce a more abundant revenue than ever it has done yet, by means far surer and more creditable than the rack-rent system hitherto relied on, though it is one so utterly unworthy of a great and civilized nation. The Finance Committee, appointed by Lord William Bentinck, appears to have wrought very much in the narrow spirit of its founder; and it must be recorded to its eternal disgrace, that of these magnificent and useful, and even cheap, botanical gardens (for what was their whole charge—viewing their use to science—in the expenditure of our empire?), its official report was to the effect that "although botany, as a science, had been benefited by their existence, nothing really useful had otherwise emanated from the establishment." This is a line of observation most truly in the sordid spirit of a most sordid mind.

The committee could not perceive that the general improvement of the science of botany must inevitably lead to practical improvement in the cultivation of the vegetable world, and that all esculent roots—on which the poor of the country, nay, nearly all the population, from religious observances, are supported—must be rendered more plentiful, cheaper, and more nutritious, by the application of sound botanical skill to the purposes of daily and seasonal cultivation. It is astonishing to us, how these sages could have so far forgotten their own experience during their years of service, as not to have been struck with the improvement of the vegetable, and mainly as an effect of that advancement, the animal, food upon which they themselves were in the habit of subsisting; for we cannot conceive them being aware, or mindful, of that improvement, and yet being so lamentably ignorant, so incomprehensive, as not to perceive that it was an inevitable consequence of that practical skill, which the natives had derived from our botanical appliances under their immediate observation. Such men as these (may they be few in their generation, and their shadows become less!) would strongly object to the expenses of Sir John Herschel's astronomical discoveries at the Cape, and indeed to the practice of every pursuit which, in the wisdom of *their* peculiar mode of reasoning, should only tend to improve science, *as* science;—*proh pudor!* It is a well-known fact, attestable by Dr. Wallich upon official knowledge, that the natives of India have of late years directed their attention most assiduously to the practice of English agriculture as shewn by the garden system. They constantly apply for plants and seeds, which are furnished gratis; and we have it on the best authority, that in one year only (not selected as a remarkable one), sixteen thousand plants were distributed among three hundred applicants, of all classes, and in all parts of the country; besides forty-two thousand tea plants raised in the garden for Assam. But for the existence of the garden, Indian horticulture would know no advancement; for there could be no private nurseries of efficiency formed in India as there are in England, and therefore, if the government did not uphold a public one, the art of cultivation would remain almost barbaric. The imbuing the native population with a taste so pure and useful as agriculture, is of itself most useful as a state policy; for thus, while the imperfect cultivation of the fields is advanced to greater skill in the hands of the ryots, the landlords themselves—the wealthy zumeendars—are led to encourage, in themselves, a fondness for the *garden* cultivation, which tends to expand their knowledge of the subject generally, as well as to add immediately to their personal enjoyments both of sense and subsistence. In our sincere belief, there is no single science so worthy of encouragement in an empire, such as our Eastern one, as the science of agri-horticulture; and it is our equally sincere belief that no process could so rarely tend to deteriorate the country, as a following out, by governments, of such sentiments as those of their narrow-minded finance committee, in their intellectual endeavour to pronounce upon *utility* as disjoined from *science*.

To the new arriver in India, male or female, the Botanic Gardens will afford unalloyed pleasure, as often as they can be visited, and especially between the months of October and April, but at any time of the year rather than they should not be visited at all. The beauty of their site, the grandeur of their extent, the perfectness of their order, the magnificence of their trees, the very *life* that is in them, and which English gardeners encourage not, birds, squirrels, and so forth—and the feeling of buoyant pleasure in the escape from the town, with a delightful party; all these elements of pleasure combine to make a day passed *there*, but especially a day in December, January, or February, a day to be always remembered in an exile's life, when he shall be far out of the reach of a repetition of the enjoyment.

The Sailors' Home.—This institution has been in existence since July, 1837. Its object was to suppress crimping, and all the evils arising from it, to which owners, commanders, officers, and crews of vessels were subject in the port of Calcutta. This object was sought to be attained, by providing board and lodging for the officers and crews, cashing their advance notes, supplying slops of the best materials and at the lowest rate, and affording a safe place of deposit for the savings of seamen during their stay in Calcutta. We believe that the institution has in many instances realized the purposes for which it was formed; but owing to disagreements amongst the committee, impositions practised upon them by men who made the "Home" a refuge from labour, and the discontinuance of the annual subscriptions of many of the first founders, who have died or left Calcutta, it is not now in a very flourishing state. There is hope, however, that some energetic and philanthropic secretary will make an attempt to revive its drooping fortunes; for there is not a class of men in the wide world who stand so much in need of protection from frauds and artifices as the unsuspecting sailor, who, landing in a foreign country with a handful of money, soon becomes too intoxicated to be on his guard against the designs of the low rascals who haunt the scenes to which "Jack ashore" is most likely to resort.

THE MEDICAL AND PHYSICAL SOCIETY was formed for the pupose of promoting intercourse among medical men. Meetings are held once a month, where questions interesting to the faculty are discussed, and papers on remarkable cases read and recorded. The papers are afterwards published in a volume.

THE PUBLIC LIBRARY was established at the instance of the author of this "HAND-BOOK," with the view of affording to the town the advantages of a library of reference and a circulating library. Numerous donations of books, maps, &c., formed a nucleus, and regular subscriptions and proprietory *premia* have since contributed to enrich the institution. There are between one and two hundred subscribers to the library.

THE NATIVE HOSPITAL, as its title imports, affords

relief to indigent natives afflicted with disease or encountering accidents. About one hundred patients, male and female, are generally found within its walls. The establishment is supported partly by government, and partly by the interest upon bequests, and charitable donations.

THE POLICE HOSPITAL is somewhat of the same character.

THE GENERAL HOSPITAL AND THE HOWRAH SEAMEN'S HOSPITAL afford medical treatment and an asylum to sick seamen of the navy or merchant service; but the former, as the larger establishment, and enjoying government support, receives soldiers whose regiments are not part of the garrison of Fort William, and poor Europeans of all descriptions.

THE CHAMBER OF COMMERCE is a sort of court of arbitration, when disputes arise among mercantile men. It likewise forms a channel of communication between the government and the trading community, and otherwise aids the merchants to act in concert upon points involving a common interest.

THE TRADE ASSOCIATION serves, among tradesmen and shopkeepers, the purposes which the Chamber of Commerce effects for the higher classes of commercial men. The Trade Association was originally formed to check the system of unlimited credit which had filled the books of shopkeepers with bad debts; and it is only just to say that it has worked to a good and useful end.

Besides the public establishments mentioned above, there are several of vast importance which belong exclusively to the government, and others the property of private companies; but, as they have no peculiarly attractive exterior, they have not been classed with the buildings. These are—the Arsenal of Fort William and the Cossipore Foundry, the Docks of Kidderpore and Howrah, the Gloster Mills, &c.

THE ARSENAL.—The foundations of Fort William, as we have elsewhere said, were laid during Lord Clive's government, immediately after the battle of Plassy, in the year 1757. We cannot tell when the fortifications were actually completed.

The Fort mounts 619 guns of various calibres, from 12 to 32-pounders, exclusive of mortars, viz.:—the bastions and redans, 205; flanks of bastions, 89; redoubts, ravelins, and counter-guards, 197; lunettes, 122; and faussebraie, 6.

The earliest records we can find belonging to the Arsenal are for the year 1777. In that year the arms were arranged by order and under the auspices of Warren Hastings, then Governor-General of India, as notified, in gold letters, over the interior of the entrance-door of the armoury. The area within the Arsenal buildings is nearly a square, being 234 feet by 232. The dimensions of the room set apart for the armoury are 315 feet long by 60 feet wide, and it contains about 60,000 stand of fire-arms and 20,000 swords. The store-rooms are extensive, and contain large quantities of camp equipage, entrenching tools, saddlery for cavalry, horse-artillery harness, elephant harness, small-arm equipments, together with different descriptions of stores required for engineering, fitting out ordnance for land and sea service, &c., as well as various descriptions of tools and materials required by artificers in the different departments, and for the supply of field-magazines and depôts at out-posts; besides which there are sheds containing a supply of field and siege gun-carriages, which are ready for service at a moment's notice. Attached to the Arsenal there is a work-yard, called the Artificer's Bankshall, in which there are at present thirty forges constantly at work. The gunpowder-magazines of Fort William are all bomb-proof, and, independent of the Grand Magazine, are made to contain something more than 5,000 barrels, or 500,000 pounds of powder. There are, also, branch or expense magazines in the outworks, also bomb-proof, to hold 200 barrels each. So large a quantity, however, is not deposited within the Fort, the principal depôts being at Duckinsore and Pultah, situated on the left bank of the river above Calcutta; the former at the distance of eight and the latter seventeen miles. The Grand Magazine is appropriated entirely to the reception of small-arm ammunition, and, as before stated, is not included among those (four in number) intended for powder in barrels. The proportion of ready-made small-arm ammunition lodged in the Grand Magazine is 1,200,000 rounds.

The ordnance-yards generally contain, independent of the guns mounted on the works, between 3,000 and 4,000 pieces of iron and brass ordnance, including many heavy mortars. The quantity of shot and shell for the different calibres seldom falls short of 1,800,000 rounds, ready-prepared grape and case shot included, but *exclusive* of *more* than 14,000,000 loose shot, of various diameters, for grape and canister.

THE COSSIPORE FOUNDRY.—The new foundry, established by the Hon. the Court of Directors, for the supply of brass ordnance for the whole of India, was commenced in 1832, and completed in 1834.

This large and important public establishment is situated upon the banks of the Hooghly, at Cossipore, about four miles above Calcutta, and presents a chaste and simple *façade* of the Tuscan order, 178 feet in length. On ascending a flight of steps, the entry is into the instrument-room, in which are arranged the various boring bars, bits, and knives, &c., used in the process of boring and turning the ordnance. Here is also preserved a model of the old boring machinery of four laths, wrought by bullocks, forming a striking contrast with the present extensive and beautiful steam machinery. Right and left of the instrument-room is a suite of rooms for the office, model and pattern department, &c.

Adjoining and extending along the whole length of those rooms is a magnificent boring-room, 170 feet long by fifty feet wide, and forty feet high, lighted by numerous elevated windows, throwing a strong and steady light upon the work to be executed. The roof of this room has been much admired for its lightness and novelty, being formed of iron trusses, covered with planks and copper sheathing. Down the east side of the room is arranged the beautiful mill-work and machinery, sent out by the Hon. Court, consisting of twelve boring and turning lathes for ordnance divided into two parts, which can be worked either together or separately by two small steam-engines in adjoining rooms. Down the west side a range of lighter lathes have been put up for all the small miscellaneous work which the foundry has now to execute.

The ordnance boring and twining lathes are of an entirely novel self-acting principle, by which the piece of ordnance is turned as well as bored by the machinery itself; an invention which reduces the amount of manual labour two-thirds, whilst it ensures a greater accuracy of the line of metal. On the north and south of the boring-room are the rooms for the vice-men, carpenters, and finishing departments.

The water for the supply of the steam-engines is brought from a tank in another yard, at a distance of more than 200 feet, by means of a siphon of five-inch bore made in the foundry, which is believed to be the first instance known of a siphon having been successfully used upon so large a scale.

At a short distance from the boring-room, connected by a covered passage, is situated the casting or smelting-house, furnished with cupola blast furnaces for the smelting of iron, of which a good deal is now manufactured in the foundry, and the large reverberatory furnaces for the smelting of the gun metal, in the construction of which a great improvement has been made, the metal being now melted in about half the time formerly required in the usual description of air furnaces. Adjoining the smelting-house are the moulding sheds and blacksmith's department, together with other store-rooms, forming a spacious square enclosure around the principal building.

THE DOCKS, SHIP-BUILDING, &c.—In India, ship-building for foreign voyages was scarcely known, until the settlement in it of Europeans, under whom it made great progress; the architectural parts being supplied by them, and the principal part of the manual labour performed by native artificers, under the instructions of the former, as in the present day.

Prior to the year 1780, Bengal was almost entirely dependent on Surat, Bombay, Demaun, and Pegue, for shipping. The first vessels built on the river Hooghly were the *Amazon* and *Minerva* cruisers, for the Bengal government service; the former, 138 tons, was launched in 1769, and the latter, 180 tons, in 1770.

The earliest specimen of a regular Calcutta-built ship was produced in the year 1781, by the late celebrated Colonel Watson, and named the *Nonsuch*, measuring 483 tons, and so constructed as to answer as a vessel of war, or a merchant ship: she was lost while heaving into dock at Sulkea, in 1802.

About fifty years ago, a large and successful ship-building establishment (Gillett's) existed on the site upon which the old Mint was afterwards erected. Other yards were established in Clive Street; but all were removed at the formation of the Strand Road.

From 1781 to 1800, twenty-seven ships, measuring 14,714 tons, were built at Calcutta. In 1801, eighteen ships, measuring 9,670 tons (calculated to carry about fifty per cent. more than that tonnage), and the same number of ships in 1813, measuring 8,463 tons. Including the above from 1801 to 1821, there were built at Calcutta and adjacent to it, 223 ships, measuring 101,908 tons, which, reckoned at an average cost of two hundred rupees per ton, makes the enormous sum of two *crores* of rupees and upwards; a considerable part of which sum was absorbed in the payment of wages to native artificers and labourers, to the great benefit of the country.

Since the last-mentioned period, ship-building has greatly declined in Bengal. This is accounted for by an increased influx of ships from Great Britain, in consequence of the free trade, which ships are for the most part constructed and sailed at a cheaper rate than ships built in India, and manned with lascars. The cost of building ships at Calcutta was some years ago calculated at about Rs. 200 per ton; but many large ships cost much more in proportion; the charge has latterly been reduced, owing to a great fall in the price of iron, copper, and other European articles, and to the effects of active competition.

The first dry dock constructed at Calcutta was a small one at the Bankshall, in 1790, for the government pilot vessels; subsequent to which, several large docks were built at Howrah and Sulkea; in 1803, the Kidderpore dock was founded. Previous to the construction of these dry docks, ships were hove down at Calcutta when their bottoms required repair.

Since the formation of the Strand Road, ship-building has been confined, with the exception of the extensive dock-yard at Kidderpore, belonging to the Joint Stock Company, to the western side of the river at Howrah and Sulkea; at either of these places ships and vessels, of different descriptions and magnitude, may at all times be seen in the various stages of completion, and others in dock undergoing repair.

There is no wet dock in Calcutta of dimensions adapted to the admission of vessels of large burthen, but such a thing is at present understood to be in contemplation.

RELIGIOUS EDIFICES.—With the list of these we shall complete the enumeration of all the public establishments and edifices in Calcutta.

THE CATHEDRAL (St. John's), now about to be superseded by a larger edifice erecting at the south end of Chowringhee; the Scotch Church, the Old (mission) Church, St. James's Church, the Free School, or St. Thomas's Church, St. Peter's Church (Fort William), a pretty Gothic building, with a beautiful painted window; St. Thomas's Church, Howrah; the Catholic Cathedral, the Roman Catholic Church (Durrumtollah), the Roman Catholic Church (Boitaconnah), the Greek Church, the Armenian Church of Calcutta, the Loll Bazar Baptist Chapel, the Circular-road Baptist Chapel, the Independent Union Chapel (Durrumtollah), the Hindostanee Church (now building), the Simlah Church (about two miles from Calcutta, where a converted and ordained Hindoo officiates), the Mahomedan Mosque (in Durrumtollah), the Orphan Refuge Church, on the left bank of the Hooghly.

Such is an outline of the prominent public features of the metropolis of British India. Of what concerns the private life of the resident much has been said in the portion of this work appropriated to a description of society, social habits, and domestic expenditure; but much remains to be told of the minor features of Calcutta, which have more or less a bearing upon civilized existence. It is difficult to classify them, or arrange them in any particular natural order; they are, therefore, given in the sequences in which they occur to us.

TRADERS, SHOPKEEPERS, &c.—Some idea may be formed of the quantity of business done in Calcutta, and of the extent to which the wants of civilized residents are supplied, from the following list of people in trade, &c., within the town :—

Of English houses of agency there are 27 ; French ditto, 8 ; Italian ditto, 1 ; and Armenian ditto, 16. Commission-agents, 22. Corn and oil millers, 3. Greek merchants, 4. Jew merchants, 21. Mogul merchants, 12. Arab merchant, 1. Parsee merchants, 7. Banian merchants, 8. Principal Hindostanee shroffs, 26. Principal Bengalee shroffs, 10. Native agents and ship captains' Banians, 33. There are 16 presses (English), besides others of inferior note, with 8 native presses. There are, also, 5 English lithographic presses, not including those worked by natives. Almost all the presses execute copper-plate printing. There are 4 circulating libraries. Of booksellers, 10, with many native. Of bookbinders, 4, with many native. Of paper manufactories, 3. Of public auctions, 3. Of house and land registry offices, 2. Of silk and indigo marts, 4. Of bakers, 8, with many native. Of surgeons (unconnected with the service), 5. Of surgeon-apothecaries, 7. Of surgeon-dentists, 2. Of chemists and druggists, 8. Of midwives, 8, with numerous native. Of soda-water manufactories, 8, with a few native. Of artists, 7. Of musical instrument repairers, 12. Of professors of music (violin), 5; guitar teachers, 2; violoncello ditto, 2; piano-forte ditto, 5. Of dancing-masters, 4. Of band suppliers, 3, with several others of an inferior grade. Of music warehouses, 3. Of ship-builders, 6. Of engineers, millwrights, &c., 2 (civil). Of ship-chandlers and rope-manufactories, 4. Of house-builders, 8, with numerous native. Of coach-makers, 14, with many native. Of cabinet-makers, 4, with many native and Chinese. Of general shopkeepers, 14, with a host of native. Of general hardware stores, 1, very many native. Of wine merchants, 27, with a very great many native. Of bakers, provisioners, oilmen, &c., 14, with numerous native. Of cigar manufacturers, 7, with very many native. Of boarding-houses and hotel-keepers, 18, besides a vast number of private, and those of inferior note. Of chop-houses, 5. Of jewellers, silversmiths, &c., 5, with very many native. Of watchmakers, 15, with several native. Of gun-makers, 3. Of carvers and gilders, 8, with a few native. Of milliners and dress-makers, 14. Of tailors and habit-makers, 10, with many native. Of hairdressers and perfumers, 3, with very many native. Of boat-agents, 3, with a few native. Of veterinary surgeons and stable-keepers, 12, with many native of the latter. Of boot, shoe, and harness makers, 18, with very many Christian Chinese and native. Of leather manufacturers, 5. Of undertakers and stonemasons, 8.

STEAM MACHINERY.—Formerly the exportation of machinery from Great Britain was prohibited; but for some years past articles of this nature have been freely imported into India. Steam-engines of different powers, with all their appurtenances, and various other machinery imported from Great Britain, for the manufacture of sugar, oil, saltpetre, paper, and other purposes, are now procurable in Calcutta at reasonable prices.

The Bengal government set the first example of introducing extensive machinery, in the erection of the new Mint at Calcutta, which is filled with the best specimens of the skill and genius of Watt.

The first steam-engine set up in Bengal (it is believed) was that on the bank of the river, at Chaundpaul ghaut, for the purpose of raising water from the Hooghly, to lay the dust of some of the principal streets of the city contiguous to the Government-House. The fluid passes from the engine-well into a large brick-built reservoir, and from it into aqueducts constructed on one side of the road.

On approaching Calcutta, the smoking chimneys of steam-engines are now seen in every direction, on either side of the river, presenting the gratifying appearance of a seat of numerous extensive manufactories, vying with many British cities. The principal establishments on the banks of the river, where steam-engines are in use, are the Akra Farm, the Cotton Screws, the foundries of Messrs. Jessop & Co., and Mr. Calder, the biscuit bakery and flour mills on the Strand and at Cossipore, the Gloster Silk Mills, the paper manufactories at Serampore, &c.

The Sports of Calcutta.—The English have been famous throughout the civilized world for carrying with them, as the snail does his shell, their own country sports and amusements, nor does the City of Palaces, despite all obstacles of climate, form an exception to the general rule. Accordingly, Calcutta can boast of its race-course and its hunt; cricket, archery, and rackets also have their votaries. Regattas occasionally enliven the banks of the Hooghly, and a four-in-hand or tandem varies the monotony of the evening drive. Of these sports, however, the turf is pre-eminent in popular estimation; and, as such, a short sketch of its origin and present state may not be unacceptable in the present work.

The first record of the existence of racing in Calcutta may be dated from the origin of the Bengal Jockey Club, in 1808, from which time, until the cessation, caused by the general stagnation of every thing owing to the great failures in the year 1832, there were annual race meetings in December of each year, a continuation of which was held at Barrackpore, in January following. In 1832, however, they entirely ceased, until their regeneration in 1836, since which period one, and in some instances a second, meeting has been held annually. The total absence in India of the class "black-leg," or indeed of any class of persons who look to turf speculations as a means of livelihood, which is the bane of all racing in Europe, contributes not a little to enhance the general popularity of the races; and in fact the supporters of the Indian turf are composed exclusively of gentlemen, either members of the civil or military services, or wealthy individuals whose pleasure it is to encourage sport. The race-course itself forms part of the esplanade surrounding the glacis of Fort William, and is adorned with a handsome race-stand, where, on a cold race morning in January, the beauty and fashion of Calcutta delight to congregate, and around which the motley groups may vie in point of singularity, though not in number, with Epsom on a Derby day. The wealthy Hindoos in their carriages, and the stately, sedate-looking Mussulmaun, are alike present to view the *tumasha*, as it is called : strange contrasts indeed are there, as in one corner may be seen the slim wasted form of a Newmarket jockey, elbowing a fat ghee-fed Baboo; in another, the grandson of Tippoo Saib conversing familiarly with the owner of a favourite.

The races, like other amusements in the East, commence at sunrise; and unless retarded by the fogs, which occasionally during the cold season envelope the whole plain until dispersed by the sun's rays, are usually over by ten o'clock; thus enabling all classes, from the Governor-General to the sircar, to attend and enjoy the sport without trenching upon their daily avocations,—a circumstance which, in a place where none are idle, contributes mainly to the support of the turf. In former years, racing was discountenanced by the higher authorities, even to such an extent that any servant of government engaged in the turf was compelled to adopt a *nom de guerre*, to prevent his being a marked man; and so it remained until the administration of Sir Charles Metcalfe, who, with that liberality extended alike to all classes, took off the ban, and in the year 1835-36 the handsome gift of a piece of plate by the Governor-General was announced. This example was annually followed by Sir Charles's successor, Lord Auckland, who, with his family, made a point of attending the races.

The class of horses most generally employed on

the turf is the Arab, of which numbers are annually imported from the Persian Gulf to Bombay, and thence to Madras and Calcutta. Their chief characteristic as race-horses is their bottom and powers of endurance, rather than actual speed, rendering them peculiarly adapted for the description of races in vogue in Calcutta, which are seldom less than two miles, and often extend to three-mile heats. Of imported English cattle, there are but few specimens, but little encouragement being held out for their importation, as a succession of years has proved them so superior with any weights or distances to any other class of horse in the country, that competition with the slightest chance of success is nearly useless. From the Cape of Good Hope, horses are also occasionally imported, though very rarely with sufficient success to warrant repetition of the experiment. New South Wales has also furnished a few competitors, and from the general *progression* of all matters in that colony, it appears probable that India will be indebted to it for horses inferior only to the imported English.

The breeding of horses in an Indian climate for turf purposes has been attempted in various instances by private individuals, though with very rare success; the transitory nature of the residence of gentlemen in that country being obviously opposed to the success of an undertaking which, to bring it to perfection in the Indian climate, would consume many years; the necessity also for constant renewal of the blood, whether English or Arab, without which the breed degenerates into weeds, renders the affair expensive, while its necessary tediousness forbids hope of reimbursement within a reasonable time. From the government studs of Haupper, Ghazeepore, &c., horses occasionally make their appearance on the turf, though from the impurity of the blood, which is never pure through more than three generations, they generally fail in endurance, though instances have been seen of extraordinary speed, for short distances. The uncertainty of temper, of which all horses bred in the country more or less partake, is also against them. Maugre all these obstacles, a large breeding stud has been maintained for a considerable period by Mr. Sawers (a gentleman who lately retired from the medical service), though not with the success so enthusiastic a votary of the sport of the turf deserved; this gentleman having regularly run horses both at Calcutta and in the province for the last thirty years. The Indian turf has also numbered among its supporters a gentleman well known as one of the best gentlemen race-riders in England,—Colonel, now Major-General, Gilbert, whose judgment in the selection of Arabs, and in matching them, was allowed to be unrivalled. Mr. James Barwell, for many years sub-treasurer of the presidency of Fort William, was also a staunch friend to the sports of the turf, as his brother, Mr. C. Barwell, was of the hunt. General Sir Robert Stevenson, K.C.B., was also celebrated, and justly so, for the excellence of the country-bred horses he produced—though of late years his attention has been confined to the meetings in Upper India. In later days, the late much-lamented Captain Cockerell stood forth pre-eminently as a munificent patron of the turf; indeed, the re-establishment of the races in 1836 was mainly owing to his influence and support.

Hunting, properly so called, on the footing of fox-hunting in England, is, though a complete exotic in the East, extensively pursued throughout Bengal. Every large station, whether in Bengal itself or the Upper Provinces, usually boasts its pack of hounds. To the "Calcutta hunt," however, the palm of superiority has been awarded, both from the better adaptation of the country about Calcutta for hunting, and from the style in which the hunt club is maintained. The hunt itself has existed since the year 1820, and is composed and managed, like the turf, exclusively by amateurs. The kennels, situated at Alipore, the southern suburb of Calcutta, both in convenience, extent, and appearance, might vie with the best in the mother-country : thirty couples of hounds, selected from the drafts of the best kennels in England, are annually imported at a cost of 200 to 250 rupees (£20—£25) per couple ; the management is vested in a committee of three gentlemen, with the usual adjuncts of huntsman, a gentleman selected from the club, and secretary. The hunting season commences in November, and is considered to end in April ; but during the first month of the rainy season, June, the pack regularly meet. It would surprise the denizens of the chase in England, who proceed leisurely to the eleven o'clock meet, to hear that their brethren in the East conclude their day's sport ere theirs is begun. Such, however, is the fact : the chase-loving Anglo-Indian rises by candlelight, drives himself to cover, either at Dum Dum or Gowripore, a distance of eight or nine miles, where the hounds having also performed their journey on a spring van, throw off at sunrise, half-past five, and probably finish their second jackal by nine o'clock, returning home to breakfast by ten. The substitute for the English fox is the jackal—somewhat larger in size, and when fairly put to a stretch nowise inferior in speed; his nature too is similar, as he partakes of the love for poultry so strongly displayed in his English prototype. The country, technically so called, consists of plains or generally cultivated gardens, raised to avoid the inundation consequent on the rainy season; jungles of bamboos densely planted, on which the Indian village is situated, and which require no small skill on the part of the rider to hounds to thread when going the pace. The fences chiefly comprise bank, or rather mud-wall,—a kind of raised embankment usually from three to four feet high, with large ditches on either side,—being the boundaries of the respective gardens,—or bamboo-rails, about the height of an English sheep-hurdle; and almost the only drawback to Eastern hunting is the frequency of patches of jungle which occasion either a check or a change of jackal; and the difficulties of pushing the jackal through the villages, unless the hounds be close at his brush, frequently mar the best prospects of a run.

Horses of all descriptions make their appearance at the course side, from the little wiry Arab to the imported hunter; and it is frequently found that the former is the better adapted to a country where the ground is occasionally of the consistency of baked bricks, than the latter, whose feet were never meant to be battered; for this reason, the light weights usually have the best of it, and the pluck of the little Arab, which carries him over ditches large enough to engulf himself, rider and all, cannot be too much admired. The breeding of hounds, though attended with some success on the hills, has been found quite impracticable in Calcutta; and indeed there would appear something in the climate inimical to the very constitution of the English fox-hound, as it is with difficulty their lives are preserved through the hot and rainy season, and it seldom happens that out of the previous year's importation nine or ten couples remain to greet their new brethren on their arrival. That terrible scourge, the dil-i-baz, or palpitation of the heart, makes great havoc; diseased liver is also among the frequent curses of the kennel, insomuch that those hounds, who may, by dint of the apothecary's shop, bring their blue-pilled carcases to the cover side, after the second season in India, never manifest the dash and eagerness by which the English fox-hound is so pre-eminently distinguished.

The Calcutta hunt has numbered among its members many sportsmen of no mean reputation, among whom the gentleman who officiated as huntsman for several years previous to his departure for Europe, the Hon. J. E. Elliot, M.P. for Roxburghshire, stands pre-eminent; his reputation as a sportsman is known in three quarters of the globe, and it may be said to be owing to his popularity and *savoir-faire* that the Calcutta hunt was saved from the general downfal of every amusement, at the period of the great mercantile failures in 1832-33. Other sportsmen of lesser note from the East have distinguished themselves in the field in England, and it may be safely said, that a man, who can go well for half an hour over the Gowripore country, need not fear to make his appearance at any cover side in Europe; indeed, it is a well-authenticated fact, that no men ride harder, or in a more bruising style, than Indians when returned from exile; witness Capt. Lamb, the spirited owner of *Vivian*, Mr. T. B. Bayley, and some few others, who astonished the natives not a little at Leamington.

All field sports, with the exception, of course, of tiger-hunting, &c. may be attained easily at a short distance from Calcutta—hog-hunting parties frequently beset the jungles at Budge Budge, though since the days of the lamented Tent Club, great success has seldom attended the shikar parties, chiefly from the want of elephants to drive out the game; nevertheless, when a holiday, and *proh pudor!* a Sunday, come conveniently together, various adventurous youths take the field. Capital snipe-shooting may be had by crossing the Hooghly, at almost any time of the year; and by going a couple of days' journey into the country, the determined sportsman may meet with plenty of buffaloes, and taste the sweets of an encounter with a leopard. Fishing, save angling in the tanks preserved by wealthy natives, exists not in or about Calcutta:—no purling streams contain trout, and the best fish, the "rooe," is caught much in the same fashion as carp and tench in England. The cricket and racket clubs are both most popular in Calcutta; the former amusement is pursued regularly throughout the cold season, i. e. from October to April—and a very promising eleven can be mustered when the duties of office will permit; indeed, such as would do no discredit to Lord's and the Marylebone. The ground appropriated to cricket is also part of the esplanade, parallel with the river Hooghly, and is kept in excellent order. Every cold-weather evening, during the drive, may be seen the practice going on, i. e. master hitting and bowling, and blackey fagging. The native holidays afford time to the amateurs for playing matches, which constantly take place with the Dum-Dum and Chinsurah elevens: they are usually well contested, the rival eleven chiefly consisting of officers and private soldiers of the artillery or Queen's regiments, and it must be a poor regiment that cannot muster an eleven; failing these adversaries, the Civil Service or the Etonians *versus* the Calcutta Club furnish materials for a contest. The Racket Club, as may be supposed, consists but of a limited number of members, and the game is played the whole year round, during the hot season and rains (when dry enough) in the afternoon, and, during the cold season, early in the morning. The court is situated at the end of the Chowringhee Road, and is divided into two separate courts to the east and west, commodious and in good order. Among the votaries of the game, which, owing to the severity of the exercise, can be played constantly by those only who enjoy a state of health approximating as near as can be in an Indian climate to the robust, Mr. Oakes, a gentleman high in the civil service, stands pre-eminent; his eye and hand would be difficult to match in any quarter of the globe, and here he is unrivalled; tolerable players there are in abundance, but none able to compete even *longo intervallo* with him. Regattas or other rowing matches, between the boats' crews of the different vessels in the port, frequently take place during the cold weather, and the monotony of the evening drive is varied by the contest. The immense strength of the current in the Hooghly renders it unfitted for rowing parties, notwithstanding there have been crews formed both for pulling and sailing, though the amusement has never attained general popularity. Tandems and an occasional four-in-hand are seen now and then; and great was the astonishment of the aborigines, on first beholding Mr. Thomas Holroyd's drag: this gentleman, whose enthusiasm for the road was only equalled by his excellent driving, imported a real Brighton coach, and many an old withered Qui Hye screamed with delight on seeing the article, which was driven for a few days neat as imported, with the item " Brighton and London," in the pannel, bowling along the Strand. Mr. Holroyd also sported that most ticklish and rarely seen vehicle, a really well-put-together tandem, and right merrily his chesnuts stepped; others are occasionally seen, the produce of some ambitious writer, or a regular regimental turn-out from Fort William, betraying its aspirations to the name of tandem solely by the fact of having one horse before the other.

Hotels and Hotel Charges.—There are several hotels in Calcutta, the first of which are Spence's and The Auckland. The charges in all are pretty much alike, the difference in economy being generally attended by a material difference in comfort. Annexed are Spence's rates of charge, to which are appended those in force at popular private boarding establishments, of which there are several :—

SPENCE'S FAMILY HOTEL CHARGES.

	Co.'s Rs.	As.
A gentleman occupying a single room, per month	100	0
Per three weeks	90	0
Per fortnight	70	0
Per week	40	0
Per day	6	0
The above includes breakfast, cold tiffin, dinner, tea and coffee at the table d'hôte.		
Gentlemen ordering hot tiffin pay an additional charge of	2	0
Gentlemen inviting their friends to the table d'hôte pay as follows :		
Breakfast	1	8
Cold tiffin	1	0
Hot tiffin	2	0
Dinner	2	8
A lady and gentleman, or a single gentleman, occupying a private sitting and bed room, with separate table, per month	250	0
Per three weeks	225	0
Per fortnight	175	0
Per week	100	0
Per day	15	0
A gentleman occupying a private sitting and bed room, and dining, &c. at the table d'hôte, per month	200	0

	Co.'s Rs.	As.
Per three weeks	180	0
Per fortnight	140	0
Per week	80	0
Per day	12	0
For every additional room, per month	100	0
Families inviting their friends to dine, and giving previous notice, are charged for each guest	5	0
When no previous notice is given, the charge is the same as at the table d'hôte.		
Claret, 1st growth, per bot.	3	0
Ditto, 2nd ,, ,,	2	8
Vin de Grave, Barsac, and Sauterne ,,	2	8
Hock ,,	4	8
Champagne ,,	5	0
Burgundy ,,	5	0
Hermitage ,,	4	8
Sherry ,,	2	0
Sherry (superior) ,,	3	0
Port ,,	3	0
Madeira ,,	3	0
Brandy, Gin, and Whiskey ,,	2	8
Pale Ale and Porter ,,	1	0
Soda Water ,,	0	8

Four annas per bottle are charged for cooling wines of every description.

REGULATIONS.

Wines, beer, spirits, &c., are invariably furnished by the proprietors at the rates above mentioned, and no private supplies are admitted for consumption into the hotel. It is particularly requested that gentlemen will not smoke cigars, except in their own apartments, or at the table d'hôte after dinner. No servant is allowed to leave the premises, after meals, until the butler has counted his plate. No servant belonging to the establishment to be sent with letters or messages. Breakage of glass, crockery, furniture, &c., by servants, will be charged to their masters. Cards, games of chance, or gambling of any description, is prohibited. As the servants leave the premises at half-past ten, no suppers or refreshments of any description can be had after that hour; and it is expected that gentlemen at the table d'hôte will retire before eleven o'clock. It is requested that ladies and gentlemen, on leaving the hotel, will not give presents to the servants. Bills delivered at the end of the month, and to weekly and daily boarders every week.

PRIVATE BOARDING ESTABLISHMENT TERMS.

	Co.'s Rs.
Permanent residents per month	80
Temporary ditto ditto	90
Per fortnight	50
Per day	4
A lady and gentleman occupying a private sitting-room, with bed-room and separate table, per month	230
The same, per week	60
The same, per month, without separate table	180
The same, ,, with bed-room and use of drawing-room	150
Parties inviting their friends to pay as follows:—	
Breakfast	1
Tiffin	1
Dinner	2

Parties may find their own wines, &c., or be supplied from the house. Breakages of servants to be charged to the accounts of their respective employers; and no servants allowed to leave the premises until the plate, &c., be reported correct.

Bengal Club-House.—There is a handsome establishment under this denomination in the Chimghee-road. Gentlemen are elected by ballot; and the entrance and annual subscription entitle them to occupy rooms, to take their meals, play cards or billiards, read newspapers, &c. Of course, separate payments are made for the use of the apartments and for the different refections. The subscriptions, &c., cover house-rent, furniture, servants' wages, breakage, purchase of books, periodicals, newspapers, &c. The house is elegantly furnished, and the best male society is met within its walls.

PUBLIC CONVEYANCES.

PALANQUINS, &c.—The following are the rates and hire of Teeka palanquins and Teeka bearers, which have been fixed by the magistrates :—

PALANQUINS.

	As.
For a whole day, to be considered as consisting of fourteen hours	4
For half a day	2
Half a day to be considered any time exceeding one hour and not exceeding five.	

BEARERS.

For a whole day, to be considered as consisting of fourteen hours, allowing reasonable time for rest and refreshment	4
Half a day, to be considered any time exceeding one hour and not exceeding five	2

Palanquins or bearers employed for a less period than one hour, to be paid for at the rate of one anna per bearer and one anna per palanquin.

Any breach of the above rules will be, on conviction, punished as the law directs.

Carriages, buggies, horses, &c., obtainable at either of three livery-stables.

	Rs.
A buggy and horse, per month	150
Ditto, per day	8
A carriage and pair, per month	250
Ditto, per day	16
A landau or barouche, per month	300
Ditto, per day	20
A saddle or buggy horse, per month	100
Ditto, per day	5

Boats.—Wherries, or *dinghees*, manned by two rowers and a steersman, are to be found in numbers at all the wharfs; they are of a slight construction, spoon-bottomed, with a circular awning of bamboo-work, under which a person can sit; and though in general well managed, are by no means to be considered safe conveyances. They are used for going off to the shipping or across the river, and the usual fare for a European is an anna, equal to three-halfpence; but if to return or wait for the party, from two to four annas are considered reasonable; all depending on time. For trips up and down the river, within a day or two's journey of Calcutta, *baulcahs* and *budgerows* are to be had at all times. These have been elsewhere described.

Coolies.—In every street are to be found *coolies*, or porters, who carry burdens on their *heads*, however light or heavy the load may be, provided it do not exceed one *maund*, or eighty-two pounds weight avoirdupois. Their rates of remuneration would make one of the "fellowships" in London stare, being about one anna, or three-halfpence, per mile; for short distances, half that sum.

For the conveyance of heavy goods, *hackries*, or bullock-carts, are available. The rate of hire, for short trips within the town, is about four annas, or sixpence; for longer ones, from six to eight annas. These vehicles do not usually carry above half a ton, except of commercial produce, when they are limited to fifteen hundred, the utmost they can safely bear.

Bazaars.—There are two markets in Calcutta for the supply of butchers' meat, poultry, fish, vegetables, and fruits, chiefly for the consumption of Europeans and other Christians. The oldest is Tiretta's Bazaar (now the property of the Rajah of Burdwan), situated on the east side of Chitpore road, near the northern extremity of that part of the city occupied by Christians, and, consequently, in an inconvenient situation. It is kept in bad condition, and very dirty; so that few respectable persons seldom visit it, servants being deputed to make purchases; indeed, few people in Calcutta attend personally to such matters. The other bazaar is situated at the south-west corner of Dhurrumtollah-street, the northern extremity of the Chowringhee-road, an eligible site for the purpose. This bazaar has recently been remodelled and enlarged at considerable expense by the present proprietor. The stalls for meat, fish, and vegetables are well built, with square brick pillars, supporting lofty and substantial raftered and tiled roofs, the whole well drained and kept clean; the pathways with which it is intersected being somewhat convex, they are dry, so that people traverse this market with a degree of comfort not met with in other Calcutta bazaars; and, consequently, many respectable persons are seen there every morning. There are a great number of other bazaars in different parts of the city for edibles for the native population, and the streets abound with petty shops of a similar nature, to the great disfigurement of many of the, otherwise, best parts of the city.

Municipal Government—Police.—So far back as 1803, the Supreme Government declared itself sensible of the importance of paying strict attention to a system of watching, draining, warding, lighting, &c., the city of Calcutta. Arrangements were made for the formation of a proper conservancy committee, and the establishment of an improved police; and from that time to the present, changes, generally supposed to be for the better, have been introduced, but still the town is far from being well protected, or kept in a proper state of cleanliness. It has already been stated, that there are four magistrates and a superintendent of police, to detect, investigate, and punish such crimes as lay within their competency. Offences beyond their cognizance are sent up to the Supreme Court. For the suburbs there is a separate magistracy, whose power corresponds with that of the city officers. The *posse comitatus*, under the orders of these gentlemen, consists of a few European constables and some hundreds of native police, whose duties correspond with those of police officers in other parts of the world, but these duties are discharged in a manner peculiar to India. Serious crimes are fortunately not rife in Calcutta; about two thousand cases per annum are heard by the magistracy, and these are chiefly larcenies, burglaries, and petty assaults. To the chief magistrate, some native gentlemen, and the members of the military board, the conservancy of the town is intrusted; and this conservancy duty comprises the charge of every thing which relates to the cleanliness and health of the population, the watering and lighting of the town. The funds whence the means of the conservancy department are derived consist of the assessment on houses, the liquor licenses, &c. It is a mistake, therefore, to pretend that the inhabitants are exempt from taxation, for no one can occupy a house without feeling, in the rent he pays, that his landlord is a large contributor to the coffers of the state.

A VOYAGE FROM CALCUTTA TO ALLAHABAD.

THE hints offered in the section headed "RIVER TRAVELLING" having been taken, the traveller sets forth in a budgerow, or steamer, as the case may be.

A curious and interesting scene is that which the right bank of the Hooghly, between Calcutta and Cossipore, presents to the river traveller. It is well worth the passage against the tide, to mark the strange dioramic sights which are to be seen, instinct with life and motion, and telling a history of past Indian grandeur, as well as of present desolation. Embarking at Bankshall ghaut, you are instantly among the shipping, which crowds the river before Calcutta. Passing beneath the tall sides of the unladen vessels, the boat threads its way, now coming alongside of a British craft, now passing under the stern of an American, and now of an

Arab trader; whilst the curious eye will observe the various crews at work on board—the clean and healthy-looking British seamen, the uncouth-looking lascars, and here and there, sitting at the stern-windows of some empty vessel from Bombay, a little group of Parsees, high-turbaned and white-vested.

But the lofty masts of the shipping are soon left behind, and the boat passes the wide-ranging buildings of the Mint, with their tall chimneys, "grand against the sky." Steering through a forest of shapeless pariah brigs, and large, unwieldy salt-boats, we soon come to a spot suggestive of more painful thoughts, for there are the ghauts, where the dying are left to die—the Puttarah Ghaut, the Jora Bagan Ghaut—where the last ceremonies of the Gunga are performed, and then the Shussan, or place of cremation, where the bodies of the dead are burnt.

A strange, wild scene is this! Standing back at some distance from the river is a high blackened wall with flanks of masonry at either end, abutting upon the bank, which slopes, in a gentle descent, towards the river. In the centre of this wide black wall is an aperture, with a screen of masonry on the hither side, which shuts out the revolting scene from the road on the other side of the wall; and at each angle of the curtain which we have described, is built up a shapeless hut of mats to receive the poorer class of dying Hindoos, who cannot afford to pay the tax of the neighbouring ghauts. But turn you from the building, which is in itself, indeed, scarcely more than a great screen, erected to shut out the hideous scene of cremation from the road which passes it to the bank which slopes towards the river, black with the burnt ashes of the dead. Two or three fires are burning there, sending forth a dim red flame, whilst the spiral smoke ascends slowly, and one or two almost naked men crouch over the scanty pyres. There, too, are the charpoys, or rude native beds, on which the corpses have been brought forth; and hovering above are countless vultures, eager to glut themselves on the half-burnt corpses. Scores of these insatiate birds of prey are perched upon the abutting walls of the death-screen, waiting their opportunity to descend, whilst others, temporarily repulsed by the guardians of the funeral fires, fly heavily across the river, passing across the native boats, through the tattered sails of which you might mark their flight. Others again are feasting, a little way apart from the human death-place, upon the carcase of an animal there exposed, and contending eagerly with the huge adjutant-birds and ravenous pariah dogs. Altogether, it is a sickening sight, rendered infinitely more sickening by the abominable effluvia which issue from the bank of death.

But these are soon passed. The bank again is densely lined with native boats, their rude sterns arranged in thick serried lines, and their strange oar-rudders far projecting. These, you may see, are the homes of hundreds of human beings, who spend their lives there; in each boat some ten or more strong men may be seen lying lazily about, cooking or eating their dinners, whilst on the banks which these shapeless vessels skirt, are numberless natives, men and women, the inhabitants of the far-spreading suburbs of Calcutta. Motley and inconsistent rows of dwelling-houses stretch along the river bank, cottage and palace strangely commingled. Here a small group of miserable mat-huts, there a stately but somewhat dilapidated edifice, with lofty pillars and wide colonnades—remains of a former state of grandeur—towering above a line of salt-golahs, shapeless, matted structures, erected on scarp walls of masonry, which form, in some places, the embankment of the river. Then you see a crowded ghaut, perhaps of recent erection, or, far more probably, one fallen into decay, the lower steps of which have sunk into the bed of the river, whilst numberless chasms, as though made by an earthquake, are discernible in the upper flights. Here, again, is a large, rambling house, overhanging the stream, with a long verandah above, and beneath an arched passage, through which the inhabitants of these strange abodes communicate with the river, and there a Mahommedan mosque, with its domed cupolas, rising in a picturesque manner above a group of more humble edifices. Among these variform buildings, strangely interspersed, are here and there huge masses of heavy foliage, thick-leaved trees overhanging the water, with, in some places, their bare roots exposed to view, projecting beyond the bank. Everywhere the margin of the water is studded with human beings, some coming down to the river to bathe, others to fill their vessels with water, whilst many boys and men are sitting on the banks, fishing with the rude tackle of the country. It is altogether a strange and interesting scene.

At a distance of about twenty miles from Calcutta, after passing Cossipore, its villas, foundries, and factories, the village of Ishera, where there is a sugar and a rum manufactory, the Orphan Refuge and its pretty church, Tittaghur and its sylvan dwellings, we reach the park of Barrackpore on the right, and the town of Serampore on the left.

BARRACKPORE, called by the natives *Achánuck* (corrupted from *Charnock*, the founder of Calcutta, who abided here), consists of a large park and a military cantonment, in the former of which is the spacious country-house of the Governor-General, while the latter affords accommodation to six regiments of native infantry, and the full proportion of officers. There is nothing remarkable about the Government-House; it is a plain edifice of one story in height, with lofty rooms and very ordinary furniture. Its accessories are the best features it can boast of; an aviary and a menagerie, though neither are very thickly tenanted; a garden and a pleasant promenade, where the society of the station assemble, while one of the regimental bands plays upon the green sward, constitute the chief *agrémens* of the place. Lord Auckland established a native school at Barrackpore, and left funds for its support. The regiments here, with the artillery at Dum-Dum (seven miles from Calcutta), and the troops in Fort William, constitute the presidency division of the army, which is commanded by a general officer, who resides at Barrackpore. A brigadier immediately under him commands the station. The position of the troops is convenient for immediate service to the eastward of Bengal, and for the performance of military duties at Calcutta, where a large guard mounts, and is relieved once a month. There is a race-ground at Barrackpore, but races have not taken place there for some years. The sports of the place are confined to an occasional steeple-chase, a run with the Calcutta hounds, and a few balls and public dinners.

SERAMPORE.—This little settlement belongs to the Crown of Denmark. A governor, with a secretary, a judge, a magistrate, and a small detachment of troops, form the administrative and protective force of the place, which is now only remarkable as the residence of a body of missionaries, the site of the printing establishment of the best newspaper in India, and of an excellent paper manufactory, conducted by Mr. John Marshman. The college founded here by the celebrated missionary, Carey, has fallen to decay, though it still presents, as seen from the river, remains of architectural beauty. Many old gentlemen, pensioners of the East-India Company's government, reside at Serampore, as do several widows and poor families, from motives of economy. Serampore is the Alsatia of Calcutta and Barrackpore—the writs of the Supreme Court, for debts contracted at those places, do not run in Serampore, where the unfortunate debtor consequently resides in security, and is enabled there to make arrangements with his creditor for the indulgence refused him when within the operation of the law.

After passing Serampore, the banks of the river again present the varied scene described above, dotted here and there with small towns and factories, now in a partial state of decay. These latter occur in the following order :—

CHANDERNAGORE.—A small French settlement with a governor, staff, and a judicial administration.

CHINSURAH.—Formerly one of the Dutch settlements, and now a barrack for a single European regiment.

BANDEL.—Once a Portuguese settlement, and still famous for a Roman Catholic Church.

SANTIPORE.—Erst the site of one the East-India Company's factories, and now the situation of a rum distillery and sugar manufactory.

KULNA.—Remarkable for indigo and sugar factories. Numerous boats are here seen at the ghauts, ready to carry the produce to distant marts.

AUGERDEEP, DEWANGUNGE, KUTWA, RUNGAMATTEE.—Small villages exhibiting remains of commercial importance, but now only used as fuel depôts. In the neighbourhood of any of these places, the sportsman will find abundance of game to reward his pursuit, if he takes the trouble to step ashore with his gun.

BERHAMPORE AND MOORSHEDABAD.—In its outward aspect, there is no European station which can bear any comparison with Berhampore; it is situated on the left bank of the Hooghly, and is arrayed with the utmost splendour of foliage; the flowering trees attaining a gigantic size, and the more common offspring of the forest, the banian, tamarind, neem, peepul, and bamboo, occurring in great profusion, and seeming to riot in rich luxuriance.

The cantonments of Berhampore are well laid out and handsomely built; the quarters of the officers being of brick covered with cement, like the puckha palaces of Calcutta, and forming uniform ranges of considerable extent. The grand square, a spacious quadrangle, encloses an excellent parade-ground; and stately houses, belonging to civilians and other permanent residents, arise in convenient spots in the neighbourhood, giving to the whole station an air of importance not usually found in garrisons, where the pompous array of fortresses and bristling bulwarks is wanting. To contrast with all this beauty, and to shew the deceitfulness of outward appearances, a large arena, filled with monumental stones, gives mournful evidence of the unhealthiness of the atmosphere, and of the grim dominion of death in the midst of the most lavish productions of nature. Berhampore lies low, and has not been sufficiently drained before its occupation by European troops. Every breath of air which visits it comes over swamps and marshy lands; it abounds with ditches and stagnant pools, and its too redundant vegetation is rank and noisome. Commodious as the European quarters appear, they have not been constructed with a proper regard to the health of the inhabitants. It was formerly the custom in Bengal, and one which unfortunately has not been universally relinquished, to glaze the houses only upon what sailors would term the weather-side; close wooden shutters, or glass doors, not being supposed necessary except to keep off the storms of rain brought by the hurricanes from the north-west. Under this idea, the more sheltered parts of the house are merely furnished with venetians which never can be made to close so exactly as to keep out the damp air.

There are no fire-places in those summer residences; and persons compelled to dwell all the year round in them must undergo every change of atmosphere, without the possibility of preventing their exposure to diseases which are generated by sudden transitions from heat to cold.

There is a manufactory of silk at Berhampore, which furnishes the bandana handkerchiefs so much prized in England, together with taffetas and washing silks. Beautiful pieces of workmanship of various kinds in carved ivory are also brought for sale from the neighbouring city of Moorshedabad. Though the artisans of the native capital of the province of Bengal cannot support any comparison with the delicate performances of the Chinese, they exhibit considerable skill in the delineations of men and animals. The common kinds of chessmen, boards furnished with richly-cut pegs for the game of *solitaire*, paper-presses, and wafer-seals, are exceedingly well executed, and cheap, compared with the European prices for similar articles.

The amusements of Berhampore are considerably increased by its proximity to Moorshedabad, a city which was once the capital of Bengal, and which is still the residence of the pensioned descendant of its former rulers. The dominion which Jaffeer Khan, the founder of the family of the Nawab of Bengal, maintained against the will of the Moghul emperors, who vainly attempted to supersede him, faded away after the famous defeat at Plassy: not a single vestige of power now remains, and the princes of the present day are content to support an outward show of magnificence upon an income of sixteen lacs (£160,000) a year, allowed them by the East-India Company. The city of Moorshedabad is well situated, and forms a pleasing object from the river, but contains nothing worthy of notice, except the modern palace of the Nawab, which is a splendid building in the European style, of dazzling whiteness, and rising in glittering splendour amid stately groves of flowering trees.

During the life-time of the late Nawab, magnificent entertainments were given at his palace, in which the European residents were always invited to share. The great Mahomedan festivals, especially that of the *Bheurer*, were also celebrated with great pomp and splendour, more from a love of display on the part of the prince than from any particular devotion to the principles of his faith. But since his demise, matters have assumed a different aspect. The present Nawab is a minor, placed under the care and tutorship of a discreet officer, in the hope that when he is of an age to manage his own affairs, he will have learnt to make a rational use of the ample income at his command.

There is abundance of sport in the neighbourhood of Berhampore. The Rajmuhal hills upon the opposite side swarm with larger game, and the low lands around are alive with partridge, wild fowl, and hares, according to the season.

The scenery now resumes the aspect which it wore at the earlier part of the trip—ghauts, temples, villages, alternately decorate the banks. A late writer thus pleasantly and accurately describes the villages in Rajmuhal:—"I was greatly struck with the 'exceeding density,' with the 'boundless contiguity of shade,' in which the natives appeared to reside with such comfort. Place the rankest weeds—the most filthy, green, fat-scummed pools—the most umbrageous clumps of low, spreading bamboos, sprouting pollards, towering palms, tall feathery dates, and low dead or high living fences together—'mingle, mingle, all that mingle may'—and through them cast a stench the most villanous and nauseating, whether proceeding from decomposition of substances, animal or vegetable—put all these together in your imagination, and you will have a slight idea of the *agrémens* of the shady suburbs and village of Rajmuhal! But enter the village as an artist, and how massive, rich, and varied is the foliage! What exquisite foregrounds for Ruysdael or Hobima! What splendid lights and solemn murky shades for Rembrandt! What brutal, filthy clowns for Teniers! And what villanous, hairy faqueers, rugged stumps, mouldering ruins, and shocking old women, for Salvator! Large masses of the palace are now lying in the river. The Hindoo has not here left a vestige of his political power. The Mussulman is to be traced by his noble ruins."

SICKRIGULLEE.—Eighteen miles above Rajmuhal we come to Sickrigullee, a village at the base of a high rocky eminence, commanding a fine view of two ranges of hills. There is at this place the tomb of a celebrated Mahomedan saint, Peer Pointie, and a cave in a limestone rock, both of which are worthy inspection. Higher up is a place called Peer Pointie, now a mass of ruins, where another tomb of the saint is found.

COLGONG.—Three picturesque rocks covered with verdure. A few Hindoo devotees reside upon them, in wretched huts, surrounded by, and almost embedded in, vegetation as noxious as it is picturesque.

BHAUGULPORE.—The Ganges is here of great breadth. In the rainy season, when the waters have risen, the river is not less than eight miles across! The situation of Bhaugulpore is pretty and healthy. It commands a distant view of Mount Mandar, an insulated conical hill, renowned as a place of Hindoo pilgrimage. There are some silk manufactories here, which produce a coarse stuff, called baftah, and a lighter silk, termed tusser, much used, when stretched upon a frame, for room-punkahs, and also for gentlemen's blouses and ladies' morning-dresses. The station is a civil one; but a corps of Hill Rangers, composed of the Puharees, or hill men, is kept up in an excellent state of discipline, to protect the country from banditti, and otherwise to act as the magistrate may occasionally require. The Puharees, who inhabit the neighbouring hills, are not many degrees removed from the savage race. They live chiefly by the chase, and always go armed. They are hospitable and honest in their intercourse with one another, though accustomed to make predatory inroads upon their neighbours or hereditary foes. Their probity is remarkable, and they are faithful when employed as servants. They believe in a Supreme Being, to whom they offer up sacrifices, and have adopted the doctrine of metempsychosis.

JUNGHEERA.—Of the interesting places which lie between Rajmuhal and Monghyr, the most celebrated is the rock of Jungheera. It consists of several masses of grey granite, rising boldly from the river. It is supposed to have formerly been a point of land projecting from the shore, but it is now completely isolated by the violence of the current. Trees have imbedded their roots amid the crevices of this picturesque rock, and on its terraces several small temples are erected. It has been, during many ages, considered one of the most sacred places in the Ganges, and is a great resort of Hindoo devotees, who crowd to it, not only on account of its reputed sanctity, but to offer their homage at the shrine of Naragan, an idol of great celebrity at this place, whose figure is preserved in one of the pagodas, and sculptured upon several parts of the rock, together with those of Vishnu, Suree, and Sirooj. Jungheera is inhabited by Hindoo fakeers, who are not above asking charity of the European voyagers on the river.

Between the two rocks there is a ghaut, or landing-place, gently sloping into the water. From this ghaut the ascent to the summit is by flights of steps cut out of the solid rock. In the temple which crowns this height, the principal fakeer is usually to be seen sitting on a tiger-skin, by way of carpet, and having the skull of one of these animals by his side.

MONGHYR, when our possessions were more limited than they now are, formed one of the principal military stations of the British army. When it was selected for the depôt for ammunition, it enjoyed all the honours of a frontier fortress; but, in consequence of the immense portion of territory which now divides it from the boundaries of our possessions, it has been suffered to fall into decay. A few invalided soldiers garrison the dismantled citadel, and several invalid officers have selected it as a residence, on account of its cheapness and salubrity.

Monghyr is situated upon a rocky promontory abutting into the Ganges; and the walls of the fort, raised upon a sharp angle, have a fine effect, although they are rapidly wearing away. The point on which these walls stand, when the river is full and the current strong, renders the navigation difficult and dangerous to boats, which can only pass with a favourable wind, and run great risk of being driven against the rocks. The Ganges at this place is extremely wide, and vessels being often detained by contrary winds at the ghauts of Monghyr, when a change takes place, the whole surface of the water is covered with barks of every description. The remains of the fort are very striking; the plain is diversified by ridges of rock richly wooded; and upon some of the most favourable sites, the European residents have erected those palace-like houses, which give a regal air to the splendid landscapes of Bengal; some of the residences are painted a bright orange relieved with white. The native town is irregular, and in many parts extremely picturesque, several of the bazaars stretching in long lines beneath the umbrageous shelter of magnificent groves. The place of worship in most repute amongst the Mahomedans, is the monument of Peer Shah Lohouni, which is held in great reverence by all classes of the people; the Hindoos making frequent offerings at the shrine of this saint, so highly is his memory venerated throughout the district.

A considerable trade is carried on at Monghyr from the manufactories of the place; the workmen possess considerable skill, and construct palanquins, European carriages, and furniture, in a very creditable manner. Under the inspection of persons well acquainted with these arts, they can produce goods of a very good description, and at an astonishingly low price. The most famous of its manufactories is that of the blacksmith, who works up steel and iron into a great variety of forms; these goods are coarse, but they are useful, especially to the natives, and remarkably cheap. Double-barrelled guns are sold for thirty-two rupees each, rifles at thirty, and table-knives and forks at six rupees per dozen. Upon the arrival of a budgerow at Monghyr, the native venders of almost innumerable commodities repair to the water side in crowds, establishing a sort of fair upon the spot. Cages filled with specimens of rare birds from the hills, or with the more interesting of the reptiles, small deer, Seetakoond spring water, chairs, tables, work-boxes, baskets, and cutlery of all kinds, are brought down to tempt the new arrivals. It is perhaps safest to confine the purchases to iron goods of native construction; spears, which are necessary articles in the upper country, are of the best kind, and are sold at a rupee and a quarter each; and the *ungeetahs,* iron tripods in which charcoal is burned, are excellent. The guns and rifles constructed here are dangerous implements, from the worthlessness of the screws and brittleness of the barrels. Since the importation of European fashions, a vast number of new articles have been introduced into the shops of the natives; tea-kettles, tea-trays, toasting-forks, saucepans, and other culinary vessels, unknown in the kitchens of the Moslem or Hindoo, are exhibited for sale.

The fort of Monghyr occupies a large portion of ground, and, though no longer affording any idea of a place of defence, is both striking and ornamental. It has not, like Allahabad, been ever modernized, or adapted to the prevailing system of warfare, but retains all its Asiatic character. Within the walls there is a plain of considerable extent, sprinkled with some majestic trees, and having two large tanks of water.

The European society at Monghyr is rather limited; and in consequence of the major part being composed of persons belonging to the invalid establishment, who seek it as a place of retirement, the station is never a scene of gaiety; there are, however, appointments which are held by civil and military servants of the Company, who form a little circle amongst themselves, which is enlivened, occasionally, by the visits of strangers passing up and down, and officers upon military duties, surveys, &c., from Dinapore, which is situated at an easy distance. The attractions of Monghyr, as a residence, are confined to the scenery, which combines every beauty that the rich and fertile provinces on either side can produce. About five miles from Monghyr, there are some hot springs, which few people fail to visit who touch at the town. They are situated at Seeta-coond, "well of Seeta," and though not possessing any medicinal properties, the water is much sought after on account of its great purity. The springs are enclosed in a cistern of brick, eighteen feet square. The temperature is so hot (maximum, 163°), that the hand cannot be retained in it for many seconds. Large quantities of gas are continually disengaged from the basin. Rice, when thrown in, swells, and floats on the surface. The well is sacred, and several Brahmins are established in its neighbourhood, who are not above receiving a few copper coins for regenerating the pilgrims, who resort hither to bathe in a neighbouring pool.

The ground in the neighbourhood of these springs is exceedingly rocky, and furnishes many curious geological specimens; fluor and mica are plentiful, and *ubrue*, talc, or *lapis specularis*, also is very common. It is found in large masses, which divide easily into tough, thin laminæ, perfectly transparent. Formerly this substance was in much request with Europeans as a substitute for window-glass, but it is not now ever used for that purpose. It still forms the decorations at native festivals; and when painted with a variety of colours, and illuminated, it is often employed in the construction of mimic palaces, rivalling that of Aladdin in splendour. The hills in the distance are chiefly composed of lime-stone, far advanced in decomposition; they are exceedingly wild in their appearance, and inhabited by numerous tribes of savage animals.

In the cold season, Monghyr may be truly denominated a paradise, since there is nothing at other periods, save the heat of the climate, to detract from its enchantments. On the frontiers of Bengal and

Behar, and scarcely belonging to either, the district in which it stands, and which is known by the natives under the name of Jungleterry, partakes of the characteristics of the upper and lower provinces; the verdure of Bengal lingers on the borders of Hindostan Proper, while the low, flat plains of the former yield to the undulations which diversify the high table-land stretching to the Himalaya, and which is intersected by numerous valleys or ravines, presenting passes full of romantic beauty.

Agriculture, as well as manufactures, flourishes in the neighbourhood of Monghyr; grain of all kinds, sugar, and indigo, are in great abundance, and the country is celebrated for its opium. Immense fields of poppies, which, though they have been not unjustly described as all glare and starch, have a gay appearance—their flowers varying in colours, like the tulip or the anemone, and changing with every breeze that sweeps across them—render part of the cultivated district one wide parterre. Cotton plantations abound; the paths are strewed with pods full to bursting, which disclose the soft treasure within, appearing like a lump of wool intermixed with a few black seeds. There are also large tracts of indigo. Cocos are not supposed to grow luxuriantly except in the vicinity of the coast; but their cultivation in many inland situations in India shews that a little care alone is necessary for their introduction into the most remote parts of Hindostan.

The natives of Monghyr are a quiet, industrious race, rarely participating in the crimes which are so frequently perpetrated in the upper and lower country.

Like all other natives, however, they are exceedingly litigious, and the attention of the public courts is taken up by suits of the most frivolous nature.

Above Monghyr, on the opposite bank of the Ganges, a work has been constructed, which has excited the admiration of those who are capable of appreciating the importance of the benefit which it has conferred.

This is a bund (in its average dimensions forty-five feet wide at the base, ten in width at the top, and nine feet in height), forming an elevated road, on which carriages of any description may safely be driven. It was constructed to check the incursions of the river, which threatened to inundate the province. Another cross bund, supplied with sixteen sluices for the purpose of irrigation, is constructed in the same neighbourhood; and in the opinion of competent judges, the solidity of the construction is such, as to defy the utmost force of the river for many ages to come.

From Monghyr to Patna there is little of any interest upon the banks, in the shape of picturesque scenery or busy town. The places successively passed are Rassalpore, Soorajgurra, Decriapore, Bar, Phoolbarrea, and Futwa. Much grain grows upon and in the vicinity of the banks, but the major part of the country is meadow land, interspersed with villages and trees. Indeed, as Bishop Heber remarked, if the palm-trees were away, the prospect would pretty much resemble an English prospect. Fruit-trees are cultivated in the gardens of the village, especially the mango, the walnut, and the tarea palm. Numerous oxen (buffaloes) and cows—so sacred in the estimation of the Hindoo—are seen grazing near the river; and the lanky black pig of the country likewise contributes his presence to enliven the scene. At Bar there are a good many boats, and the appearance of an active trade. Beggars also swarm there, and are troublesomely importunate in their demands for alms. Futwa, a little beyond which the Pompon falls into the Ganges, is celebrated for the good quality and cheapness of the table-linen manufactured there. About ten miles higher up we come upon the suburbs of Patna, where remains of old walls, towers, and bastions, attest the original importance of this celebrated town,—celebrated for one of Clive's most gallant actions, and a law case, which occupies no trifling place in the early history of British occupation.

PATNA is the first native city of wealth and importance on the Ganges. It stands on the right bank of the river, and here the marshy soil of Bengal is exchanged for the arid sands of Hindostan: camels seldom penetrate farther, and from this point the hot winds cease to be felt.

Patna, though it does not contain any single building of great celebrity or peculiar beauty, is rich in the remains of Mussulman splendour, and its appearance from the river is highly picturesque. The houses of the wealthy classes are handsome buildings, flat-roofed, and surrounded by carved balustrades. The intermixture of these residences with perfect, broad ghauts, the remains of Gothic gateways of dark-red stone, and the numerous temples devoted to Hindoo and Mussulman worship, produces a striking effect.

Upon the first subjection of the upper country to

the Company, the city of Patna became the residence of the civilians employed by the government; but it has long been abandoned, in consequence of a treacherous attack made upon them by Cossim Ali, and they have now established themselves at Bankipore, a convenient spot by the river side, a short distance beyond the suburbs. The houses of the civil servants who belong to the Behar district are built in the style of those of Calcutta, and are chiefly *puckah;* many are very stately edifices, having broad terraces overlooking the Ganges, and being surrounded with luxuriant plantations.

The situation of Patna possesses many advantages. Being placed on the border of Bengal, it commands an easy communication with the upper and lower provinces; supplies are rapidly procured from Calcutta by the river, and the earliest choice of articles may be obtained from the cargoes.

The society in every part of India must always be susceptible of great fluctuation; but so extensive a district as Behar cannot, at any period, fail to possess a very fair proportion of the talent and intelligence of the country. It is not, therefore, surprising that the head-quarters, Bankipore, should generally be distinguished for the intellectuality of its principal residents.

The military cantonments of Dinapore are only a few miles distant, and at favourable periods contribute not a little to the gaiety of the district. The garrison of Dinapore is commanded by a brigadier-general, and, in addition to the native force, is usually the station of one royal regiment. The cantonments are handsome and well laid out; and the performances of the military bands in the evening, upon the parade-ground, attract the whole population to the spot.

Dinapore has the advantage of its neighbour in the beauty of the surrounding country; it is better wooded, and more picturesque; but it may be said with truth of almost every part of Hindostan, that the face of the country bears two aspects, being exceedingly ugly in the dry season, and very beautiful in the rains.

There are portions of the suburbs of Patna, particularly the view from a Mussulman cemetery of considerable extent, which are exceedingly interesting. No person should halt at Patna without paying a visit to this family burial-ground, which, excepting at one season of the year, is left to perfect solitude.

Patna is a stronghold of Mahomedanism, and the disciples of the prophet who dwell within its walls are far more fanatic and intolerant than their brethren of Bengal. The riches of the city enables it to celebrate the obsequies of the young martyrs, Hossein and Houssien, in a very splendid manner; and their noble square is selected for the final depository of the tazuhs, or tombs, which are carried about in commemoration of the funeral honours paid by the followers of Ali to his slaughtered sons.

Patna carries on an extensive trade, and is famous for its manufactories of table-linen, wax candles, lackered toys, and talc pictures. It also possesses very expert workmen in every department of mechanical art. Amongst the minor branches are bird-cages, constructed with great ingenuity and even elegance, the frames of some being delicately inlaid with ivory, while the wires of others are strung with coloured beads. The natives of India are fond of keeping birds as domestic pets. The beautiful little *avadavats*, or *lolls*, as they are commonly called by the natives, on account of their bright ruby colour, are in great request; these, together with many other kinds, are easily procurable at Patna. This city is a grand mart for opium. The soil is also favourable to the growth of potatoes, a vegetable which is much cultivated for native consumption in India.

The streets of Patna can only be traversed on horseback, or upon an elephant, being too narrow to admit of any wheel-carriage superior to the native *rhut*, a creaking vehicle, composed of wood and rope, in which the ladies of the country, concealed from public view by thick curtains, huddle themselves when they travel or pay visits; and the ecka, a light pony-gig, on two wheels, covered with cloth. The best houses face the river; many of these have a dismal appearance on the side of the street, shewing only a high blank wall, perforated with a few small windows in the upper story. Other mansions are enclosed in large walled courts; and in passing along the principal street, many porticoes are visible peeping out of recesses, or small quadrangles, which seem to be the entrances to buildings belonging to people of rank. The houses tenanted by the middling classes are exceedingly crazy, and have somewhat of a Chinese air, each story lessening in size, and standing in the verandah of the one below. They are removed a little from the public path, crowded during the day with men and animals, by being raised upon a platform about a foot high from the street. The houses occupy the centre of this platform, a margin being left all round, which sometimes stretches beyond the verandah, and forms a shelf, or counter, on which the goods of the inferior shopkeepers are displayed in baskets, none of the richer and more elegant articles being exposed to public view in India. The shop of the *hukeems,* or apothecaries, make the best appearance: they are furnished in the primitive style, with herbs of various kinds neatly arranged.

Amidst much that is unsightly, there is a something to admire in the long avenue which stretches from gate to gate of the city, every few yards bringing some picturesque object to view; lofty open cupolas, in the most elegant style of Mogul architecture, surmounting mosques, or contrasted with solid towers of the dark-red stone, which seems to have been the favourite material in former times. One of these latter is a singular building, somewhat resembling a glass-house; it was intended for a granary, but has never been used for that or any other public purpose, excepting as an occasional powder magazine.

On the opposite bank of the river, at Hadjeepore, or in its neighbourhood, at Sonepore, a fair is held annually, which attracts a vast concourse of people, both native and European, to its festivities. The period is regulated by the changes of the moon. The natives come in thousands to bathe at the confluence of the Ganges and the Gunduck, which of course possesses a *double* virtue. Duty carries some of the civil servants to the scene of action, and others proceed thither in order to recreate themselves, during a brief period, with the amusements which the assemblage of families from various parts of the country seldom fails to occasion. The fair takes place at a convenient season—the commencement of the cold weather. The visitors pitch their tents on the plain, and, when there is a full attendance, form extensive camps. Horse-races, balls, dinner-parties, concerts, and private theatricals, constitute the principal amusements of the Europeans.

The actual fair is, of course, a very secondary object; they, however, who have enough cash to make extensive purchases, may provide themselves with the richest productions of the East—shawls, pearls, gold ornaments, and precious stones. Elephants, horses, singing-birds, &c., are likewise obtainable in numbers. Many of the tents are extremely splendid, those of the wealthy natives, in particular, being bordered with scarlet cloth, cut into fanciful patterns. The double-poled tents of the civilians are scarcely, if at all, inferior in their external decoration, and the interiors are furnished with great elegance. Rich carpets are spread over the *settringees* which cover the floor, and small chandeliers are suspended from the roof. The walls are hung with some gay-patterned chintz, and the sideboards glitter with plate. No privations are felt by the dwellers under canvas: the repasts being equally well served in the midst of a sandy waste as in the kitchen attached to a magnificent mansion.

The city of Patna was formerly inhabited by natives of great rank and wealth, but there are now few of the former. Throughout the district there are men of every caste to be found. The lowest castes met with are the Chumar and Dome. These do not mingle with any other castes, and are considered so despicable that they are prohibited from enering the different villages. They make mats and baskets.

The Mahomedans, who consist of Syuds, Sheikhs, Moguls, and Patans, form a large part of the population of the city of Patna, which embraces about 300,000 souls. The Mohurrum festival is celebrated by them with great pomp, but the procession is joined by both Hindoos and Mussulmans. The principal Akhanas are the Ponjar Kutra and Chancroo Durriah, which take the lead in each year, alternately, and upwards of 3,000 Tazuhs are carried in procession at this festival before the Imaumbarah. The Syuds and Sheikhs intermarry, but no other castes do. All marriages are contracted through the parents, and they are usually celebrated in the months of January and February. There are many mosques or musjids in Patna, but the principal place of actual worship is the monument of Shah Arzani, about the middle of the western suburb. Adjacent to the tank is an Imaumbarah, where 100,000 people assemble, with the pageantry used in celebrating the Mohurrum, in commemoration of the grandsons of the prophet. The only places of worship at all remarkable among the followers of the Brahmins, are the temples of the great and little Patanadevi, Pataneswari, or the guardian of Patana, i. e. the city. The building is small, but avowedly recent, and has been erected at the expense of the priests.

Passing Dinapore and Deegah, once an extensive

farm, but now a provisioner's store, where every variety of cured pork and beef may be had in great abundance and of good quality, we pass the embouchure of the river Soane, or golden river, which rises in the distant mountainous country of Gundava. This river affords millions of beautiful pebbles and petrifactions, which are cut and sold for bracelets, &c. Above the mouth of this river are many Moslem and Hindoo ruins, but they are not visible unless the traveller lands.

Chuprah.—This is a civil station, the capital of Sarun. The town, which consists of one large and several small streets, contains a great many large native houses, and some mosques and pagodas. It extends for about a mile or more along the bank of the Ganges. The district of Sarun is one of the healthiest in India, but the roads are bad, and there is little or no game to reward the toil of the sportsman. The town of Chuprah contains 50,000 souls, which is about a twentieth part of the entire population of the district.

To the east of Chuprah lies the district of Tirhoot, where immense quantities of indigo are grown. The civil station of Tirhoot is Mozufferpore. This district is separated from the kingdom of Nepaul by a jungly swamp, called the Terai, which affords excellent cover for game, but is so unhealthy as to be impassable at certain seasons.

After passing Revelgunge, famous for the number of boats built there, and the villages of Boujpore and Bhulea, we reach Buxar, where the river runs rather narrow.

Buxar.—This place, celebrated in the history of British India as the scene of the battle which confirmed us in possession of Bengal and Behar, is a large Mussulman town. A few invalid soldiers reside in the fort, but the circumstance which chiefly imparts importance to the place, is the Company's stud which is kept up here and at Koruntadhee, on the opposite side of the river. These studs produce the finest horses for cavalry and artillery purposes in India. The country round about is rich in grain, wheat, oats, and barley. Here the thatched houses of the natives begin to disappear, and the tiled roofs, common to the upper provinces, to make their appearance.

Nothing further of interest presents itself on either bank beyond a ruined fort or two, and some indigo factories (where the river traveller always finds a welcome), until we get to

Ghazeepore.—A military cantonment where one royal regiment is generally quartered, a civil station, another stud depôt, and a celebrated place for the manufacture of rose-water. The appearance of the town, as seen from the river, is rather pleasing than otherwise. The houses are chiefly built of a flesh-coloured stone, procurable at the neighbouring station of Chunar, which gives them an imposing exterior. The most remarkable edifices are the palace of Cossim Ali Khan, a new fort, crumbling to decay, and the cenotaph to the memory of the Marquis of Cornwallis. This latter stands about 100 paces from the banks of the Ganges, in the rear of the barracks, and is built in imitation of the Sybil's temple. At the end of a grove is a circular enclosure, fenced by handsome iron railings eight feet high. In the centre of this is the tomb.

On passing through the gate, a noble flight of seventeen steps presents itself, for the purpose of ascending to the top of the casement, which may be reckoned as rising eight or nine feet above the ground. The periphery of the casement is eighty paces, and from its margin rise twelve Doric pillars, supporting an elegant entablature. These pillars are without pedestals, as was usual among the ancients, and each is composed of seven blocks of beautiful freestone:—the plinth, tori, cavetto, and cimbia, taking one piece, the shaft five pieces, and the upper cimbia and capital one piece. The girth of the column at the bottom is eleven feet! consequently the semi-diameter is about twenty-two inches. Between the base of the pillars and the wall of the central apartment, is a piazza fifteen feet in width, paved with large flags of freestone, of which material the building is composed. The walls, which are about four feet thick, are perforated in four places:—fronting the steps is a doorway eight feet wide by fourteen or fifteen high; on the opposite side is a corresponding opening, and to the right and left are apertures, perhaps five or six feet square, the tops of which are level with the summits of the portals. This room is about twenty-seven feet in diameter, and is paved with square slabs of dark grey or monumental marble. In the midst stands a marmorean monument almost of pearly whiteness, which has risen from beneath the masterly chisel of Flaxman. The body of the monument is about five feet square, and, arching gently at the top, is surmounted with the coronet of a marquis. On the face fronting the main entrance (or rather the only one, for the doorway farthest from the river opens only into the colonnade, there being no steps on that side for descending to the ground), between two natives, a Hindoo to the right and a Mahomedan to the left—in attitudes of lamentation, is a large medallion charged with a profile of Lord Cornwallis in bas relief. Beneath this, is the following legend:—

Sacred to the Memory of
CHARLES MARQUIS CORNWALLIS,
Knight of the Most Noble Order of the Garter,
General in His Majesty's army,
Governor-General and Commander-in-Chief in India,
&c. &c. &c.
His first Administration,
Commencing in September, 1786, and terminating in October, 1793,
Was not less distinguished, by the successful operations of war,
And by the forbearance and moderation with which he dictated the terms of peace,
Than by the just and liberal principle, which marked his internal government;
He regulated the remuneration of the servants of the State
On a scale calculated to ensure the purity of their conduct,
He laid the foundation of a system of revenue
Which, while it limited and defined the claims of government,
Was intended to confirm hereditary rights to the proprietors,
And to give security to the cultivators of the soil.
He framed a system of judicature
Which restrained within strict bounds the powers of public functionaries,
And extended to the population of India the effective protection of laws
Adapted to their usages, and promulgated in their own languages.
Invited, in December, 1804, to resume the same important station,
He did not hesitate, though in advanced age, to obey the call of his country.

During the short term of his last administration,
He was occupied in forming a plan for the pacification of India,
Which, having the sanction of his high authority, was carried into effect
By his successor.
He died near this spot, where his remains are deposited,
On the 5th day of October, 1805, in the 67th year of his age.
This monument, erected by the British Inhabitants of Calcutta,
Attests their sense of those virtues,
Which will live in the remembrance of grateful millions,
Long after it shall have mouldered in the dust.

The reverse side of the monument is occupied by a shield emblazoned with the Company's arms, on one side of which is a British grenadier, and on the other a native sepoy, both resting on their arms reversed. Below, is a long inscription in the Persian character, and on each side of the monument is a large wreath of laurel.

The roof of this apartment is a shallow dome, springing from the level of the cornice; but outside the building is carried up about ten feet, and then is rounded off, to the hemispherical form required. The apex of the dome rises about sixty feet above the ground level.

The palace of Cossim Ali Khan will, on inspection, repay the admirer of Saracenic architecture for the time he may bestow upon it. The English church is also a fine building, and the school and the jail are worth a brief visit. The celebrity of Ghazeepore for its rose-water justifies our giving some minute particulars of its manufacture, from a popular authoress who has spoken of it at large.

"The precious incense of the rose, the *atta-gool*, so celebrated throughout all the civilized parts of the world, is produced in considerable quantities in the gardens round Ghazeepore.

* * * * *

"The Indian rose, though its very name seems to imply distinction, can only sustain a comparison with its European sisters in the fragrance which it yields. It is beautiful, but, excepting at Agra, it does not attain to the magnificent size common in England, nor does it present the infinite varieties which adorn our gardens. The cultivators of India are content to take what the hand of nature has given them, and resort to few aids for the improvement of her lavish beauties; to a large majority, the rose appears to be too valuable a plant to be made the mere embellishment of a bouquet, and for commercial purposes, that which they have found indigenous to the soil proves quite sufficient. * * * The roses of Ghazeepore are planted formally in large fields, occupying many hundred acres of the adjacent country.

* * * * *

"The first process which the roses undergo, is that of distillation. They are put into the alembic with nearly double their weight of water. The *goolāābee pāūnee* (rose-water) thus obtained is poured into large shallow vessels, which are exposed uncovered to the open air during the night. The *navnes,* or jars, are skimmed occasionally; the essential oil floating on the surface, being the precious concentration of *aroma* so highly prized by the worshippers of the rose. It takes 200,000 flowers to produce the weight of a rupee in *atta.* This small quantity, when pure and unadulterated with sandal-oil, sells upon the spot at 100 rupees (£10), an enormous price, which, it is said, does not yield very large profits. A civilian having made the experiment, found that the rent of land producing the above-named quantity of *atta*, and the purchase of the utensils, alone, came to £5; to this sum the hire of labourers remained still to be added, to say nothing of the risk of an unproductive season. The Damascus, or rose of Sharon, is the flower in most esteem in some parts of India; in others, the common cabbage or hundred-leaved rose is the favourite. The oil produced by the above-mentioned process is not always of the same colour, being sometimes green, sometimes bright amber, and frequently of a reddish hue. When skimmed, the produce is carefully bottled, each vessel being hermetically sealed with wax, and the bottles are then exposed to the strongest heat of the sun during several days.

*   *   *   *   *

"Rose-water which has been skimmed is reckoned inferior to that which retains its essential oil, and is sold at Ghazeepore at a lower price; though, according to the opinion of many persons, there is scarcely, if any, perceptible difference in the quality. A *seer* (a full quart) of the best may be obtained for eight *annus* (about one shilling). Rose-water enters into almost every part of the domestic economy of natives of India: it is used for ablutions in medicine, and in cookery. Before the abolition of *nuzzurs* (presents), it made a part of the offering of persons who were not rich enough to load the trays with gifts of greater value. It is poured over the hands after meals; and at the festival of the *Hoolee*, all the guests are profusely sprinkled with it. Europeans, suffering under attacks of prickly heat, find the use of rose-water a great alleviation. Natives like it internally for all sorts of complaints; they consider it to be the sovereignest thing on earth for an inward bruise, and *eau-de-Cologne* cannot be more popular in France than the *goolāābee pāānee* in India. Rose-water, also, when bottled, is exposed to the sun for a fortnight at least."

The environs of Ghazeepore are planted with fine forest trees. Birds abound, the branches are loaded with the pendulous nests of the crested sparrow, and the blue jay sports in dangerous proximity to the Ganges, being selected at a barbarous Hindoo festival as a victim to the cruel Doorga. There are some fine old banian-trees in the neighbourhood of Ghazeepore; one in particular, which overshadows a *ghaut* in an adjacent village, may be styled the monarch of the Ganges. This tree, as well as the peepul, is sacred; and when a Brahmin takes up his abode under its boughs, it becomes an asylum for all sorts of animals: the fine old patriarch of the woods near Ghazeepore is the haunt of innumerable monkeys, which actually crowd the branches, and gambol along the steps of the *ghaut*, perch upon its balustrades, and play their antics with the bathers in perfect security, and in multitudes which remind the gazer of rabbits in a warren. Snakes are very numerous in this part of the country, and their deadly enemy, the mungoose, is frequently seen on the watch for his victims, which he pursues with unrelenting animosity.

Village and cultivated field, temple and factory, ghauts and stately trees, now greet the eye until the boat approaches the holy city of

BENARES. — Here Hindoo superstition has its chosen abode. Rank intolerance to this moment characterizes the bearing of its inhabitants towards people of all persuasions. In external appearance, Benares is a miniature Naples, being built upon a curve washed by the Ganges, which thus resembles a little bay. The city rises from the river; spires, temples, ghauts, with long flights of steps, balconies, lofty houses, intermixed with trees, walls, minarets, &c., all in close contiguity, giving it the air of a populous and densely-built town. The aspect within verifies the view from without. The streets are so narrow, that wheeled carriages cannot pass; an elephant will occupy the entire width, and make sad havoc with the wares placed a foot or two from the shop fronts. The most remarkable building is an observatory, originally erected for the use of the Hindoo astronomer, but now completely disused. The view from its summit is most striking. Oriental learning flourishes at Benares, and its wealth, considerable from the operations of commerce, is much enhanced by the frequent visits of pilgrims of the highest rank, who not only make propitiatory offerings, but spend considerable sums in their own pleasures. The trade of the town consists chiefly in shawls, precious stones, gold and silver brocades, called *Kincaubs*, gold and silver tissue, lace, and fringes. There are two military cantonments here, one at Secrole, four miles distant, where three infantry regiments and a proportion of artillery are quartered, and one at Sultanpore, a little higher up the river, where a regiment of light cavalry is stationed. At Secrole, there is a church, pretty theatre, and a racket-ground. The bungalows of the European officers are commodious buildings, and as the society of the station consists of some forty or fifty individuals, life glides away pleasantly enough; especially if the general officer who commands the division and the judge of the district are on harmonious terms, and set a good example of hospitality. The population of the district consists of nearly 520,000 souls, 174,000 of whom reside in the city.

The Hindoo population may be divided into the four great divisions of the Hindoo Shasters. The present Rajahs of Benares claim to be "Bhoomijas Brahmins," or Brahmins cultivating the soil. They represent themselves to be of the higher castes of pure descent.

Among the higher classes of the Hindoos, the strictest appearance of morality is maintained; and infidelity involves the penalty of loss of caste, ruin, and disgrace to the female—the husband being, likewise, an outcast, till he has performed certain religious atonements, and purchased restoration to his caste by feeding his brethren, or Brahmins. The lower classes wear the marriage tie lightly; but they are faithful, for the time, to the persons with whom they may be united, whether he be a husband or protector. Among these, the Dornes, Passees, and Bhurs, are apparently the aboriginal possessors of the country; but they now perform the lowest offices, being burners of the dead, watchmen, and scavengers. They are regarded as most impure by the higher classes of the Hindoos, and to touch or approach them is defilement. They are much given to theft and pilfering.

The Pagans may be considered as amounting to 457,417, and the Mahomedans to 62,486. In Benares and its vicinity there may be from 200 to 300 Christians, and the missionaries have many schools and chapels throughout the city. The Hindoo temples are extremely wealthy in endowments, and are in good repair, while the Mahomedan mosques are in many instances ruinous and deserted.

A few miles higher up the river stands CHUNAR, a fortress and a station, the latter composed of pretty villas within their separate compounds, and the former built in the native style, and kept up as a place of confinement for state prisoners. The garrison consists of some native invalids, a detachment of artillery and native infantry. Chunar is celebrated for its tobacco and its quarries of free-stone, which form an article of commerce throughout Bengal and Behar.

MIRZAPORE, a trading town of considerable consequence, is next reached. It is large and populous, not unlike Benares in its general aspect as well as in its position upon the river. The Mirzapore carpets are famous all over India; but the importance of the town is chiefly derived from its position as the emporium of all the cotton grown in the interior. Many hundred boats are employed to convey this staple, in its raw condition, to Calcutta, whence it is shipped to Europe and China, or worked up for consumption in the country. There is an establishment of civil officers here, and a regiment occupies the cantonment.

The river now winds considerably; the high lands, called the Bingic Hills, hitherto in view, are entirely lost sight of, and the banks become uninteresting as far up as the Dooab, where the junction of the waters of the rivers Jumna and Ganges takes place, and at the extremity of which stands Allahabad.

ALLAHABAD, or "the abode of God," acquired this name from the Mussulman conquerors of India, who have left memorials of their splendour in a fortress once unequalled in beauty, and now gaining in strength what it has lost in external appearance. The city itself does not display those remains of magnificence which might have been expected in a place once favoured by the presence of royalty. It now retains few vestiges of the Mogul conquest, save the appellation and the buildings before mentioned, its Mussulman inhabitants being limited in numbers, and of little importance as regards their wealth, rank, or talent. The city is almost wholly given up to idolatry, and has ever been celebrated for the pilgrimage of pious Hindoos, attracted to a spot blessed by the junction of two sacred rivers.

The principal object of curiosity and attraction at Allahabad is the fort, which is erected upon the point of land stretching into the waters of the Ganges and Jumna, whose broad currents are united beneath its walls. Though injured in its appearance by the alterations and additions necessary to transform an ancient Mogul castle into a place of strength, according to the modern art of fortification, it still retains somewhat of its oriental and feudal air, rising in majestic grandeur from the river, whence it may be espied at a very considerable distance.

There are low posterns leading to the glacis facing the river; but the principal entrance of the Fort of Allahabad is landward, and is not to be paralleled in magnificence by any building intended for a similar purpose. A noble arched hall, in the Gothic style, surmounted by a dome, and enriched with "arabesques of gold and flowers," appears beyond the ample portal, an entrance worthy of the finest citadel in the world. The interior, containing ranges of buildings not entirely divested of the beauty of their original architecture, affords, at least during two seasons of the year, some of the most delightful residences to be found in India. A suite of apartments, intended for the use of the Governor, but which is sometimes occupied by an inferior officer, commands a splendid view of the Jumna, with its craggy heights and wild sandy shores. From a balcony perched near the summit of a tower on which the windows of one of the chambers open, a prospect of singular beauty is obtained. The spectator looks down upon a grove of mango-trees, flanking a fine esplanade, and peopled with innumerable ring-necked paroquets. Above, upon pediment and pinnacle, other inhabitants of the air erect their nests, and plume their wings. Along the thickly-wooded shores of the Allahabad bank, buildings of various degrees of interest are interspersed on the small islands which rear their sandy platforms above the surface of the river; and the opposite shore of Bundelkund, rising in towering cliffs, crowned with pagodas or the remnants of hill forts, forms a noble back-ground.

The cantonments of Allahabad are beautifully picturesque, having a greater diversity of hill and dale than is usually seen upon the plains of India, and being finely wooded in every direction. Two or three regiments of Native Infantry and some artillery, commanded by an officer of rank, form the garrison of Allahabad.

The undulating surface of the country round Allahabad affords numerous advantageous sites for bungalows, many of which are erected in very excellent situations, commanding views of great beauty.

The station has never been remarkable for its festivities; yet its balls and parties sometimes attract visitors from the smaller and duller military posts of Chunar, Mirzapore, and Pertaubghur in Oude. There is a theatre at Allahabad, where amateurs occasionally perform: but the chief resource for the gentlemen appears to be the billiard-table. A tolerably well-supported book-club furnishes the floating literature of the day, to the many who seek for amusement only in the pages of a book. The rocky character of the bed of the Jumna affords to geologists a field for their pursuits, which they would seek in vain in the muddy alluvial soil watered by the Ganges. Amidst pebbles of little value, interesting and curious specimens of cornelians, and stones even more precious, are occasionally found. The opposite district of Bundelkund is famous for diamonds, equalling in value and splendour those of the Golconda mines, and in some particular spots they are found in considerable quantities. All below a certain weight are the property of the persons who may chance to gather them; the larger sort belong to a rajah, who is bound to give a certain price in the event of his claiming the privilege of purchase. The native method of gathering diamonds, which is the least expensive, and, perhaps, on that account, the best, is very simple. A few labourers clear a convenient space on a rocky surface, and when it is laid bare, they bring buckets of earth from the places supposed to be the most thickly sown with the gems, and sifting it through their hands, easily find the diamonds, which, even in their rough state, are extremely luminous. The hire of the workman comprises the whole of the outlay, and diligent seekers frequently gather a rich harvest.

The situation of Allahabad is said to be healthy; but either from its proximity to the two rivers, or the quantity of wood which gives the surrounding country so luxuriant an appearance, it is more humid than any other place in the Dooab, and is stated to possess a peculiar character of its own, the hot winds being considerably mitigated, and rain falling at seasons when other parts of the country are dry. The gardens are, in consequence, very productive; in those belonging to the British residents, artichokes in particular flourish, attaining a size unknown in less favourable soils in the neighbourhood. The rich tapestry of the jungles, those splendid creepers, which hang their fantastic wreaths upon every adjacent bough, are the great ornament of the pleasure-grounds of Allahabad. The native gardeners train them somewhat formally upon erect bamboos, whence they trail their magnificent gardens down to the ground, forming huge conical mounds.

Allahabad affords a mournful example of the want of public spirit in the Mussulman population of its neighbourhood. A noble caravanserai, built by Sultan

Khosroo, which forms a superb quadrangle, entered by four Gothic gateways, and surrounded by cloisters running along the four sides of a battlemented wall, the usual accommodation for travellers offered by an Indian hostel, has been permitted to fall into a state of deplorable decay. The garden adjoining, finely planted with mango-trees, is also in a neglected and deteriorated state. Three tombs, erected according to the fine taste displayed by the Mahomedans in the selection of the site of their mausoleums, in this garden, have, from the extraordinary solidity of their construction, escaped the destroying hand of time. Chaste, magnificent, and solemn, they are peculiarly adapted for the purpose to which they have been dedicated, and put to shame the diminutive monuments raised to kings and princes in the cathedrals of the western world. Splendid terraces, forming stately platforms, which are furnished with several apartments below, form the basement story. The central chamber in each contains a stone sarcophagus, in which the mortal remains of the dead are deposited. Above, and occupying the middle of each platform, a circular, dome-crowned hall, finely proportioned and profusely ornamented with rich sculpturing, delights the gazer's eye, who, in these palace-like tombs, sole survivors of the splendour of the Moguls, is impressed with one of the most amiable traits in the Moslem character—its reverence for the dead, and desire to perpetuate the memory of objects beloved in life.

Allahabad, or at least the confluence of the rivers which belong to it, is held in high estimation by the Hindoos, being a place of pilgrim-resort. When a pilgrim arrives here, he sits down on the brink of the river, and has his head and body shaved, so that each hair may fall into the water; the sacred writings promising him one million of years' residence in heaven for every hair thus deposited. After shaving, he bathes, and the same day, or the next, performs the obsequies, or *shraad,* of his deceased ancestors. Many persons renounce life at this holy confluence, by going in a boat, after performing certain solemnities, to the exact spot where the rivers unite, when the devotee plunges into the stream, with three pots of water tied to his body. Occasionally, also, some lose their lives by the eagerness of the devotees to rush in and bathe at the most sanctified spot, at a precise period of the moon, when the expiation possesses the highest efficacy. The Bengalees usually perform the pilgrimage of Gya, Benares, and Allahabad, in one journey, and thereby acquire great merit in the estimation of their countrymen. Allahabad is the permanent station of a court composed of a body of judges, whose office is the same, with regard to these provinces, as that of the Sudder Dewanny Adawlut, in Calcutta, is for the more eastern portions of the empire. This court makes circuits during the months which permit travelling, generally pitching their tents near towns, and holding their courts under trees; an arrangement extremely agreeable to native prejudices, especially those of the lower classes, who always feel afraid, and are under a constraint in a house, particularly if furnished after the European fashion, where they can neither tell their story well, nor attend to what is going on.

The steam-vessels which navigate the Ganges from Calcutta terminate their voyage at Allahabad, as there is not at all times sufficient water for a protracted trip. Since their establishment, the commerce of Allahabad has much increased, and establishments have sprung up which expressly provide for the comfort of the traveller about to proceed downward in the steamer, or higher up the country by boats (on the Jumna) or land conveyance. We close the river sketch here, as all other points may be reached by dawk, and it will be more convenient to trace land journeys, as distances can then be accurately given.

Calcutta to Ferozepore by Dawk (palanquin), including the trip to Cawnpore, Allyghur, Etawah, Agra, Delhi, Kurnaul, Umballa, Loodiana.

The distance from Calcutta to Ferozepore is about 1100 miles. It is divided into stages varying from ten to fifteen miles each.

CALCUTTA TO BURDWAN.

	Ms.	F.		Ms.	F.
Calcutta to Cox's Bungalow	10	0	Boindhee	10	4
Ghyretty Ghaut	9	0	Dular Bagar	13	0
Hooghly*	8	4	Burdwan	11	4
Terragoren	11	0		73	4

* It is not unusual to proceed thus far in a buggy—a hooded conveyance between a gig and a cabriolet.

After passing through the native part of the town of Calcutta, the palanquin proceeds along the Barrackpore road, an extensive avenue of trees skirted by villages, gardens, and rice-fields. Cox's Bungalow, the site of a building now used as stables for relays of horses, is on the right-hand side of the road, and here the first change of bearers takes place. This relay proceeds onwards through the cantonment of Barrackpore (already described), to Pultah Ghaut (or landing-place*), where the palanquin is placed in a boat and ferried across to Ghyretty. An excellent road then conducts the traveller to Hooghly, a civil station thickly inhabited, not far from which is the town of Chinsurah, once the property of the Dutch, but latterly ceded to the East-India Company. At Chinsurah, there is a barrack, where a single British regiment is generally quartered. The country between Hooghly and Burdwan is level and extensively cultivated. The roads are good, the small rivers are crossed at Satgaon and Muggra ghauts by suspension-bridges ; and there are bungalows at convenient intervals, and bazaars where supplies are plentiful. Burdwan is another civil station, where abide a revenue collector, a judge, and magistrate, with their assistants, a surgeon, two or three indigo planters, and a couple of missionaries. The town and surrounding zemindaree (or estate) was formerly governed by a Rajah, but the title only

* Ghauts are generally composed of broad flights of steps, to facilitate the landing or embarkation of river travellers. Here, too, the natives assemble in numbers early in the morning to bathe in the Ganges and offer up their prayers to Vishnu.

of the sovereignty has descended to his heirs, who for some years past have lived under the British Government as simple landholders. A letter of introduction will insure the traveller the hospitable attentions of any one of the residents, but failing this, or in case of the necessity or the inclination for a rapid journey, the dawk bungalow affords accommodation. A dawk, or staging bungalow, is a small house standing generally a few yards off the high road at intervals of about fifteen miles in those parts of the country most frequently traversed, and at greater intervals in less frequented districts. It usually consists of a thatched or tile-roofed house of one floor, raised a few feet from the ground, and divided into two small rooms, to each of which a bathing-room is attached. A verandah runs round three sides of the building, and there are out-offices for cooking, &c. Two servants constantly reside at each bungalow, one acting in the double capacity of khitmutgar, or table servant and cook, and the other as a bearer or mussalchee. While the former prepares such a repast as his farm-yard and private stores will allow, the latter procures jars of cold water, and assists the traveller to perform his toilette. These bungalows are under the control of some government officer at a neighbouring station, and a book is kept in which the visitor (who pays one rupee for the use of a bungalow for any time short of twenty-four hours) records any complaints he may have to make of the attendance of the domestics, the state of the building, &c.

BURDWAN TO BENARES.

	Ms.	F.
To Burdwan ..	73	4
Surool	11	4
Bood bood	11	4
Gopalpore	11	0
Undal	11	0
Bograh	12	0
Neamutpore	12	0
Neersa	12	0
Gobinpore	12	0
Rajafuta	12	0
Paopon	11	0
Doomree	11	0
Bagada	11	0
Uthka	10	0
Dhowrara	11	0
Burhee	13	0
Churparun*	12	0
Bulwar	9	0
Surwah	12	0
Sheerghattee	11	0
Mundunpore	16	0
Nowrunga	14	0
Baroon	14	0
Dharee	3	0
Sasseram	12	0
Jeparabad	16	0
Mohunca†	14	2
Nobulpore	14	4
Mogul Serai	15	4
Benares Cantonment ..	12	2
	420	4

From Burdwan to Benares, soon after entering the Bancoorah‡ district (Bograh), the road runs, for upwards of two hundred miles, though a jungle skirted by a chain of hills of no great altitude, which

* At this stage a road branches off in a northerly direction to the holy city of Gyah, which is likewise a civil station. The road is sandy and heavy. From Gyah the road runs north-easterly to Patna.

† At Acoree, in this neighbourhood, there is a branch road which leads to Ghazeepore, thence to Azinghur, and further on in a north-easterly direction to Goruckpore. Azinghur and Goruckpore are civil stations, but a regiment is generally stationed at the latter, to act in case of emergency against the people on the Nepaulese frontier.

‡ West of Burdwan, at a distance of 30 miles, is Bancoorah, a small military station. It is exactly 102 miles from Calcutta; and continuing the same road, parallel with the present route to Benares, we reach, at a distance of 240 miles, the salubrious hill-station of Huzareebagh, which has barracks for a European regiment.

constitute the country and the fastnesses of the Coles. Scarcely a building, beyond the occasional bungalow, is to be seen. The places whence the stages take their name are, for the most part, either invisible villages, solitary chowkies (post houses), or little temples. The bearers stand out upon the road or at its edge, awaiting the arrival of the palanquin at the appointed hour, and receive it upon their shoulders from the others, whom they relieve without depositing it upon the ground, unless desired to do so by the party within. The scenery along the road is more interesting than that which characterizes the dead level of Bengal and the provinces beyond Benares, but as there are no striking objects (excepting a mosque at Sasseram) to arrest attention, the traveller, if he does not admire scenery too wild to be very picturesque, and not lofty enough to be magnificent, and if he cannot read in the palanquin, will do well to go over his ground at night, halting at bungalows between nine A.M. and four P.M. to rest, bathe, dress, and take his meals. In fifty-eight hours' continual travelling, the Benares cantonment, already described, is reached, and, as at every place indeed where a European is to be found, the door of the resident is always open to the dawk traveller. Two or three days may be advantageously spent here in forming acquaintances and in visiting the Holy City and other remarkable places.

BENARES TO ALLAHABAD.

	Ms.	F.		Ms.	F.
To Benares	420	4	Sydabad	13	4
Mokun Serai	7	2	Jhoosee	13	6
Jamashabad	11	4	Allahabad	4	6
Goseah	10	4			
Ooji Chôwke	13	4		495	2

Leaving Benares, we proceed along an admirable road through a succession of villages, lagoons, and cultivated lands. In the months of October and November but little, however, is to be seen of the country, for the *bajra*, a grain much used in feeding cattle, is now at maturity, and as it grows to the height of six or seven feet, and is cultivated to the very edge of the made road, it necessarily veils the level land beyond it from the sight of a person in a palanquin. But from the month of December to the end of March the lands are sown with wheat, barley, vegetables, grass, &c., and the aspect is then green and pleasant to the eye, the horizon being generally terminated by groves of mango-trees, which are extremely numerous and abundantly fruitful. A little beyond Goseah, we pass through Gopeegunge, a large village and bazaar, which, if it happens to be market hours, is worthy inspection, as exhibiting the character of mofussil (provincial) commerce, and the products of the district. Further on, at Jhoosee, opposite Duragunge, the Ganges is crossed. The river is here one mile wide, but as the stream occupies during the dry season but one-third of the bed, the remaining space (sand) is traversed with difficulty. Soon after crossing the river we come to Allahabad, of which mention has already been made.

ALLAHABAD TO CAWNPORE.

	Ms.	F.		Ms.	F.
To Allahabad ..	495	2	Futtehpore	13	0
Moofti			Mulwa	10	0
Ka Poona	13	4	Avung	12	2
Kussea	15	4	Mahingpore	13	0
Lynée	10	0	Cawnpore	12	6
Katanghung	12	4			
Thurrias	11	4		619	2

The road from Allahabad to Cawnpore is as monotonous as that to Allahabad, which, in all that respects scenery, it much resembles, with probably somewhat less of picturesque effect. At the town of Futtehpore, however, the curious in old buildings, of no very great antiquity, will be interested by the numerous remains of mosques, houses, serais of the Mussulman era, and of the severest kind of Mahometan architecture. Futtehpore is a civil station, where two or three judicial and revenue functionaries reside, any one of whom will be glad to receive the passer-by if he prefers social intercourse to the solitude of the bungalow. Four stages from Futtehpore, one night's journey, lies Cawnpore, a large civil and military station.

The description given by the late Miss Emma Roberts of this station is so exact, and applies, with slight variation, to so great a number of military stations throughout India, that we cannot do better than quote a portion from her interesting work on Hindostan.* It will save the necessity for much

* Scenes and Characteristics of Hindostan. 2 vols.

repetition, inasmuch as the "bungalow," the "compound," and the "encampment," described by her, are nearly the same in every cantonment.

"Cawnpore is one of the principal stations of the mofussil, and is situated upon the right bank of the Ganges, about 600 miles from Calcutta.

"Nature has done little for Cawnpore; but the sandy plain, broken occasionally into ravines, which forms its site, has been so much embellished by the hand of man, that any one but a soldier, not subjected to the miseries of field days, will say that it possesses much picturesque beauty.

"The great objection to the station is its want of concentration; the lines of the various regiments straggle to the distance of five miles along the river's bank, and it is inconvenient to travel so far to visit a friend, but the scene is thereby agreeably diversified, and the compounds (a corruption of the Portuguese word *compania*), which surround the bungalows, are larger than could be the case if its limits were more circumscribed. Many of those compounds are beautifully planted, and have a very park-like appearance, particularly during the rainy season, when the cultivated parts of the plain have put on their green mantle. The prickly pear are greatly in request for fences; and the tall pagoda-like aloe, with a base resembling the crown of a gigantic pine-apple, frequently intervening, forms a magnificent embellishment to the plantations. The houses at Cawnpore are, with very few exceptions, *cutcha*, that is, built of unbaked mud, and either *chopperd* (thatched) or tiled; but they are, generally speaking, extremely large and commodious. The plans of bungalows are various, but the most common consist of three centre rooms; those opening on the front and back verandah being smaller than the one occupying the interior, which is called the hall: these rooms communicate with three others, much narrower, on each side, and at the four corners are bathing rooms, taken off the verandah, which stretches all round. The centre and largest room, has only the borrowed light permitted by eight, ten, or twelve doors, leading out of the surrounding apartments; these doors are always open, but some degree of privacy is obtained by a curtain attached to each, of a sort of gauze-work, formed of bamboo split very fine, coloured green, and called *chick;* these also serve to keep out the flies, while they admit air and all the light considered necessary by an Anglo-Indian, who excludes glare, on the principle that it communicates heat to the apartment. Many of the Cawnpore houses are handsomely furnished, the chairs, tables, and sofas, being of valuable wood, richly carved with cushions and coverings of damask, or of Bareilly manufacture, black, with gold flowers, resembling the japanned chairs, fashionable in England forty years ago. The floors, which are of *chunam* (finely tempered lime), are covered in the first instance with a matting, and in the second with a *settringee,* a peculiar manufacture of the country, of an exceeding thick texture, and usually worn in shaded blue stripes; or with calico printed in Brussels patterns, and so closely resembling a carpet, as to deceive all our practised eyes. This forms the general decoration of houses in the upper provinces. The exterior of a bungalow is usually very unpicturesque, bearing a strong resemblance to an overgrown barn; the roof slopes down from an immense height to the verandah, and whatever be the covering, whether of tiles or thatch, it is equally ugly; in many places the cantonments present to the eye a succession of large conical roofs resting upon low pillars; but in Cawnpore the addition of stone fronts to some of the houses, and of bowed ends to others, gives somewhat of architectural ornament to the station.

"The gardens rank amongst the finest in India. In consequence of there being so many settled residents, they are much cultivated and improved; all the European vegetables, with the exception of broad beans, come to great perfection during the cold season, and the grapes and peaches, which are not common to other stations, are particularly fine. The pine-apple does not grow in the upper provinces, but the mangos, plantains, melons, oranges, shaddocks, custard-apples, limes, and guavas, are of the finest quality. These gardens, intermixed with forest trees, give Cawnpore a very luxuriant appearance; it is an oasis reclaimed from the desert, for all around wastes of sand extend to a considerable distance.

"In the centre of the cantonments, and on the highest ground, are two stone buildings of a very imposing exterior—the assembly-rooms and the theatre; the latter a long oval, surrounded by a colonnade of pillars of the Roman Doric order, ornamental to the station, though not very well adapted to the purpose for which it was intended.

"Beyond the theatre, the road leads to the race-course, which is approached by an avenue well planted on either side, and watered during the dry season. This avenue forms the evening drive, and at sun-set it is thronged with the society of the station.

"The course, as it is termed, skirts a wide plain, bounded to the right by the native city, which, though possessing nothing worthy of a visit, forms a pretty object in the distance. The plain also affords a busy, and, to the stranger's eyes, an interesting scene. Groups of natives are to be seen seated round their fires, cooking, eating, or singing after a repast; and elephants and strings of home-bound camels, loaded with forage, likewise occupy the ground.

"Cawnpore, though usually a gay station, is, of course, subject to the vicissitudes produced by the fluctuating state of Indian society. It cannot, however, be so much affected by party spirit, or the indisposition of leading residents to enter into amusements, as smaller places; and amongst so many families, an agreeable circle must always be found. In its best days the entertainments were various, and suited to the different seasons.

"During the cold season all the infantry corps forming the garrison of Cawnpore usually encamp upon a wide plain in the vicinity, for the convenience of better ground for the performance of military évolutions than is to be found in the cantonments. An Indian camp affords a very striking and curious spectacle, and though the admixture of trees adds much to its beauty and heightens its effect, yet, when, as at Cawnpore, it arises in the midst of an uncultivated desert, the singularity of the scene it presents compensates for the loss of the more pleasing features of the landscape.

"Regular streets and squares of canvas stretch over an immense tract; each regiment is provided with its bazaar in the rear, and far beyond the lines, the almost innumerable camp-followers of every description form their bivouacs. The tents of the commanding officers are indicated by small red flags; but in no place is it so easy for strangers to lose their way, there is so much uniformity in the various avenues, and the natives make such strange havoc of English names, that an hour may be spent in wandering, before the abode of a friend can be found. All the mofussilites are accustomed to spend a large portion of their time under canvas, and in consequence of the necessity of providing a moveable habitation, there are tents which do not boast more comfort than can be easily imagined by those who are only acquainted with a European marquee. All are double, the interior and exterior covering being about a foot and a half apart; those which are double-poled contain several commodious apartments, and are furnished with glass doors to fit into the openings. They are usually lined with some gaily-coloured chintz; the floors are well covered with *settringes*, and they have a convenient space enclosed at the rear by *kanauts* (a wall of canvas), for out-offices and bathing-rooms. Moveable stoves are sometimes provided for the cold weather, but there is a better contrivance, inasmuch as smoke is thereby avoided, in an imitation of the Spanish *brassora*. A large brass or copper basin, in common use called a *chillumchee*, mounted on an iron tripod, is filled with red wood embers, and fuel thus prepared, without having the deleterious effect of charcoal, diffuses a general warmth throughout the tent, and is very necessary in the evening; for though, during the cold season, the sun is still too fierce at noon-day to confront without shelter, as soon as its rays are withdrawn, intense cold succeeds, a sharp piercing wind sweeps along the plains, and the thermometer sinks below the freezing point.

"Cawnpore is well supplied with every article of European manufacture necessary for comfort, or even luxury, though it must be confessed that things are frequently too high-priced to suit subalterns' allowances. The bazaars are second to none in India, beef, mutton, fish, and poultry being of the finest quality: vegetables of all kinds may be purchased by those who have not gardens of their own, there being a sufficient demand to induce the natives to cultivate exotics for the market. In addition to the shops kept by Europeans, there are many warehouses fitted with English and French goods, belonging to Hindoo and Mussulman merchants; and the jewellers are scarcely inferior to those of Delhi.

"Cawnpore is celebrated for the manufacture of saddlery, harness, and gloves; though less durable than those of English make, the cheapness and beauty of the two former articles recommend them to the purchaser; and the gloves offer a very respectable substitute for the importations from France. Prints of fashions supply the mantua-makers and tailors with ideas, and as there is no lack of materials, the ladies of Cawnpore are distinguished in the Mofussil for a more accurate imitation of the toilettes of London and Paris than can be achieved at more remote stations."

CAWNPORE TO MYNPOOREE.

	Ms.	F.		Ms.	F.
To Cawnpore ..	619	2	Goorsaigaye	14	0
Kullianpore	7	0	Chiberamore	15	0
Chobeepore	9	0	Buvur	13	2
Poorah	10	6	Bowgory	7	6
Urroul	13	4			
Meerun, Ke Serai ..	9	4		719	0

Quitting Cawnpore, we proceed through a level country, tolerably well cultivated, and dotted with jheels, which swarm with wild fowl and great varieties of the stork tribe. Turtle-doves are also seen in great numbers, and their natural enemy the kite, which in these parts is grey, with a whitish head, and a straight bill or beak. Many remains of magnificent serais (caravanserais) here attest the splendour of the Mahomedan dynasty. They are capacious, and chiefly of red brick, but have fallen into decay, the British Government having taken no pains to repair and preserve them for the uses of native travellers, who are obliged to resort to very small modern serais, constructed of earth and bamboos. A methranee, or female sweeper, generally has the custody of these serais; and a bunneeah, or grain-seller, within the building, or in close vicinity thereto, disposes of pulse, atta, tobacco, and firewood to the applicant. The well-water at these rude hostelries is sweet and good; and if the edifices themselves are not inviting, there are usually a few neem and peepul trees about them which afford an agreeable shade. At all the stages mentioned above there are small bazaars, well supplied, and good water. The road through the country is indifferent, owing to the sandy nature of the soil. Bowgory is close to Mynpooree, a station for a judge and a magistrate and half a regiment of sepoys.

MYNPOOREE TO ALLYGHUR.

	Ms.	F.		Ms.	F.
To Mynpooree ..	719	0	Secundrario	9	4
Korowlee	16	0	Akbarabad	10	4
Mullow	10	1	Coel	1	6
Etah	12	2	Allyghur Cantonment ..	12	6
Budwas	10	6		802	5

Etah is a large dirty village in a low dirty situation, surrounded by a mud wall, and, in the rains, nearly encompassed by a deep jheel. Supplies are plentiful.

The station of Coel is exceedingly like all other civil stations, but derives interest from its contiguity to the once famous fortress of Allyghur, which fell to Lord Lake's arms during the wars with Holkar, for whom the fort was held by a French officer, named Pedron. Our troops took it, by a vigorous assault, at day-break. Great numbers were killed in the attack, and the names of the officers of the 76th Foot, which bore the brunt of the action, are engraven on the entablature of a small monument erected to the memory of the slain.

As Allyghur lies in the direct road to Loodianah, we have gone on so far uninterruptedly; but to avoid going over much of the same ground, we may here retrace our steps to Cawnpore for a moment, and take the route thence to Agra by way of Etawah.

ALLYGHUR TO AGRA.

	Ms.	F.		Ms.	F.
To Cawnpore ..	619	2	Teewsabad	12	4
Secundra	50	0	Etimadpore	13	6
Etawah	50	0	Agra	14	0
Mooreedun Ke Serai ..	14	4			
Shekoabad	8	4		782	4

Going westerly from Cawnpore to Secundra, about forty miles, and then north-westerly for fifty more, Etawah is reached. This was once a flourishing place, the abode of omras and grandees of the Mogul empire, but it is now a mass of ruin and decay. Standing upon the banks of the Jumna, it possesses a splendid ghaut, which rather serves, by contrast with all else, to indicate the present poverty, than to illustrate the ancient importance of the place. A few bungalows scattered over a wide sandy plain, nearly destitute of trees, intermixed with other buildings of an inferior kind, announce the presence of civil and military residents. These are, however, few in number—the one being limited to a collector and magistrate, with their subordinate officers, and the other to the wing of a corps of Native Infantry; and as the civilians are only here occasionally, and the military detachment is frequently relieved, no one appears to have a motive for rendering the houses comfortable. Nothing can be imagined more dreary and desolate than this place as a residence; but for the naturalist it possesses attractions of no common order, the result, in a great measure, of the abundance of vegetation, arising from the absence of a large European population.

In no other part of India, with the exception of the hill-districts, are more brilliant and interesting specimens of birds and insects to be seen; extremely small brown doves, with pink breasts, appear amid every variety of the common colour; green pigeons, blue jays, crested woodpeckers, together with an infinite number of richly-plumed birds, glowing in purple, scarlet, and yellow, less familiar to unscientific persons, flock around. The tailor-bird and the fly-catcher are also inhabitants of the gardens, which are visited by miniature birds resembling those of Paradise. Nothing can be more beautiful than the effect produced by the brilliant colours of these birds, which congregate in large flocks; and by the flight of the ring-necked paroquets, and the byahs, or crested sparrows. Numbers of aquatic birds, too, feed upon the shores of the neighbouring Jumna.

The roads around Etawah are bad; they are the highways leading to the neighbouring stations, Mynpooree, Futtyghur, Agra, and Cawnpore, and afford no picturesque views within the range of a day's excursion. There is little temptation to drive out in the evening, the favourite method of taking air and exercise in India; a few mango-groves, skirting villages surrounded by high walls of mud, probably as a security against the incursions of wild beasts, alone diversify the bare and arid plains, while the ruts threaten dislocation, and the dust is nearly suffocating. The gardens afford a more agreeable method of passing the short period of daylight which the climate will permit to be spent in the open air. They are large and well planted; but the *mallees* (gardeners) are extremely ignorant of the European methods of cultivation, not having the same opportunity of acquiring knowledge as at larger stations. The pomegranate is of little value, except for its rich red flowers; for the fruit, when ripe, is crude and bitter. Sweet lemons, limes, oranges, and citrons, offer fruit of the finest quality; and grapes afford a grateful banquet, at a period of the year (the hot winds) in which they are most acceptable. The melons, which grow to a large size, and are abundant in the season, are chiefly procured from native gardens, on the banks of the Jumna, as they flourish on the sands which border that river. Mangoes and jacks occupy extensive plantations, exclusive of the gardens, and are left, as well as custard, apples, plantains, guavas, to the cultivation of the natives, the ground in the neighbourhood of a bungalow being chiefly appropriated to foreign productions. The seeds of European vegetables are sown after the rainy season, and come to perfection during the cold weather. Green peas, cauliflowers, and cos lettuce appear at Christmas, sustaining, without injury, night-frosts which would kill them in their native climes; but celery, beet-root, and carrots never attain to their proper size, and are frequently deficient in flavour. The oleanders, common all over India, are the pride of the jungles, spreading into large shrubs, and giving out their delicate perfume from clusters of pink and white flowers. The *baubool* also boast scent of the most exquisite nature. The sensitive plant grows in great abundance in the gardens of Etawah, spreading itself over whole borders.

Other flowers of great beauty and variety bespangle the plains and decorate the jungles. Butterflies of singular brilliancy, grasshoppers, beetles, with golden coats; insects, in short, of almost all the species known to the entomologist, swarm in the district. The jackal and the wolf prowl at night, and afford sport to the huntsman during the early part of day. Game of all kinds is likewise abundant. The river Jumna is well stocked with fish, and these, with excellent beef and mutton, leave the Etawah residents without excuse for an ill-furnished table.

At Shekoabad we get into the former route from Cawnpore, and twenty-five miles further on stands Agra.

The city of Agra, once the capital of the renowned Akbar, is situated on the left bank of the Jumna, in north latitude 27° 12′, and east longitude 78° 17′. The appearance of the city from the river is picturesque, without being imposing; the houses on the banks having a mean appearance, whilst their regularity is broken by trees and jutting banks. A fine strand road was constructed by the labour of the destitute poor during a famine that prevailed in 1838. It is eighty feet wide, and affords a noble promenade for crowds of pedestrians, who resort there in the evening, and is very convenient also for the landing of goods, &c. Several of the more opulent natives have adorned it with stone ghauts, which in the rainy season afford the inhabitants an easy access to the stream, and enable them to enjoy the luxury of bathing, offering libations, &c. &c. During the hot months, however, the bed of the river, next the town, is entirely dry; the channel being on the opposite bank, distant nearly half a mile. The city extends about four miles in length, and about three in depth; the houses are built chiefly of the red sandstone, which is procured in abundance from some neighbouring hills to the south. There is one fine broad street, which runs through the middle of the city, extending from the fort to the Padree tank: several of the houses in it are three and four stories high; most of the other streets are very narrow, but they are for the most part kept very clean. During the day the main street is thronged with passengers, and there is an appearance of much bustle and business, but, with the exception of a few merchants and bankers, the inhabitants are generally very poor. The shops contain very few articles; many of them are small cabins of about eight feet square, and contain goods in proportion. In the centre of the city is the *cutwallee*, police office, which is in a very efficient state, so that there are rarely any disturbances, whilst order, safety, and a cheerful tranquillity appear to prevail. From the fort there is a good road, though somewhat steep, leading to the cantonment, both considerably elevated above the level of the river. Here the military and the greater proportion of the Christian residents are located, whilst the civilians and writers in the public offices are in an opposite direction, with an intervening space of at least three miles, and in some instances five. Very few Europeans choose to live in the city on account of its closeness and insalubrity. The cantonments on the other hand are very open, and the bungalows are situated in the midst of extensive compounds, some of which are converted into beautiful gardens; these gardens, however, are rendered as useful as they are ornamental, for almost all the vegetables obtainable in the place are of our own produce. There is no regular market for the sale of these necessaries. A few greens (*turai*), melons, cucumbers, and occasionally cauliflowers, are produced, but there is no dependence upon regular supplies; and as for peas, asparagus, turnips, beans, and other table vegetables, they are scarcely ever cultivated by the native mallees (gardeners). The great obstacle, however, to the more general culture of gardens is the scarcity of good water. With but few exceptions the wells in Agra contain brackish water, and this proves fatal to all but a very few vegetable productions. But even when good water is procurable, the expense of watering and gardening is very considerable. A pair of bullocks and their keepers cost ten or twelve rupees a month; three or four mallees cost as much more; and as an individual family can seldom consume one-hundredth part of what it produces, there is much waste as well as much expense. The unsettled life, too, which many of the residents lead, precludes them from laying out so much money in a *fixture* like a garden; few tenants at will are so ultra generous as to make gardens for their landlords; the consequence is, their number is very few, and they belong chiefly to those who are likely to be more permanent settlers in the place. There is an equal want of farm produce, such as poultry, eggs, butter, butcher's meat; the latter article is generally so inferior that almost every individual kills his own mutton,—all these evils might, in a great measure, be obviated by a *joint stock farm.*

The *roads* of Agra have been much improved within the last few years—limestone, instead of pounded brick, being now used. It makes a hard and durable road, which resists the pressure of carriage wheels, and becomes more compact by rain. There are large beds of this material found in the neighbourhood; in fact, it is largely distributed over a considerable portion of the Dooab. Agra abounds in noble ruins. The old walls, which still remain, define the extent of the ancient city, which must have occupied at least ten times the space which it now does; portions, which are now productive fields, were formerly crowded with houses; remains of hammaums, or baths, and subterraneous rooms are often to be met with in the midst of ravines; the whole space opposite the river from the fort to the Taj was occupied by a series of noble palaces. Amidst these stupendous ruins a road has been cut to the Taj: the walls are sometimes eight and ten feet of solid masonry, and the cement by which they are held together is so firm that they resist the ordinary means of disintegration: another fine range of buildings including tombs, mosques, and Hindoo temples, extended from the present civil lines to Secundra. Two of the tombs being large and commodious, and not much decayed, have been appropriated as receptacles for orphan boys and girls—whilst a once beautiful villa adjacent to the girls' school is occupied by the superintendents of the female branch. It has two stories with balconies in the upper one, the whole of one side elaborately carved, and inlaid with slips of white marble and variegated stones. The cupolas surmounting the balustrades have still remains of that beautiful mazarin blue enamel which decks all the principal ruins, but the composition of which is now unknown. On the same road, a little to the right, is a spacious tank, now dry. It measures at least between three and four hundred feet square, and in the centre of each of the sides, a flight of steps leads to the bed; over these piazzas are constructed, and at each corner small towers of an octagonal form. The style of architecture of the generality of the Agra buildings is very heavy and destitute of grace. There is often exquisite beauty and elaboration in the details, but a sombre massiveness in the *tout ensemble* which would seem to insinuate that their design was less for comfort than durability,—less for enjoyment than for fame.

The trees, although not numerous are many of them truly venerable, and the cool shade which they offer to the passing traveller renders them objects of peculiar interest. The tamarind-tree is particularly admired, not only for its shade, but for the beauty and delicacy of its foliage; whilst under the broad covering of the peepul leaves, which, whilst they effectually screen the fiery rays of the King of Day, also produce, by their motion, a most refreshing coolness. The baubool is abundant, and is much used for hackery wheels, carts, and sometimes for rough furniture, as it is not liable to split. A species of wine is also made from its bark, which is much drank by Kaiths and some other castes. The sissoo is a highly valuable wood for doors and windows, but is very scarce, and yields to the more abundant saul. The climate of Agra, during the hot winds which prevail from April to July, is truly distressing; but the rains which fall, and which in regular seasons continue till October, cool the air most refreshingly. From the 1st of October, the misty mornings usher in, though by slow degrees, the cold season. In December, fires are lighted, and afford to cold subjects, not only comfortable warmth, but still more grateful reminiscences of home. Every one at this season of the year seems cheerful and revived. The scenery of nature is also irradiated with brightness and verdure. The holyoak, the balsam, and the refulgent marigold enliven the gardens, whilst beds of mignonnette and rows of the Indian myrtle perfume the atmosphere. Vegetables are now nearly fit for the table. Early peas, carrots, turnips, asparagus, artichokes, cauliflowers, French beans, are all in season, but in January they become more abundant. In February the air is most bland and balmy; it is the spring weather of England, and the lovely peach and apple blossoms unfold their delicate petals to the breeze. There are very few birds remarkable for the beauty of their plumage or the sweetness of their song. Parrots, minas, pigeons, doves, swallows, avadavats, piddis (a little bird similar to the last), kites, crows and sparrows, adjutants, vultures, and the petted peafowls, nearly make up the whole of the specimens of the winged tribe.

PUBLIC EDIFICES.—The desire of posthumous fame seems to be quite a passion among the inhabitants of the East. This feeling is chiefly gratified in the structure of magnificent tombs and temples. India abounds with them, and in the district of Agra there are some of the choicest specimens. Amongst these, surpassingly pre-eminent is the Taj Mehal, built by Shah Jehan, the King of the World, for his beautiful Queen, Noor Jehan, the Light of the World.

Every peer has his tomb, and they are numerous in and about Agra; they are often found in the compounds of our bungalows, and any attempt to remove them would be followed by a remonstrance from the Emaums.

The taj seems as fresh and almost as perfect as when it was just finished. The joinings of the marble slabs of which the exterior is composed are so close and compact, that not a fibre of vegetation is to be seen pressing from between them, nor does the rain or atmosphere have any effect in staining its polished surface. Another striking feature in this building is the admirable *finish* with which every thing about it is executed: every device is chaste and appropriate. The arches of the doors are neither pure Saxon nor Gothic, but allow of greater breadth than either, and are yet equally susceptible of strength. Under the central dome is a kind of octagonal palisade richly fretted, and within this are the tombs of the emperor and his empress; both exceedingly beautiful, and covered with a profusion of flowers—ornaments composed of various coloured stones let in—they are chiefly agates, cornelians, and blood-stone. Underneath these tombs is a vault where there are two other tombs of a plainer construction—on these garlands of flowers are constantly placed, and generally a light burning: on the panels or lower parts of the walls, flowers are carved in alto relievo. Nothing can be more graceful or perfect than the forms of these flowers; all is waving and natural, there is not the slightest degree of stiffness or bad drawing in them. The natives are, with good reason, proud of this unique specimen of the fine arts, but it is scarcely a matter of doubt that the entire design and superintendence were those of Italian artists. Bishop Heber immediately recognized, in the fretwork especially, pure Florentine art; and that there were Italians at Agra at the time, and even long before, is evident from their tombs being still extant in the Roman Catholic burying-ground: the dates of some still legible are within 1600 and 1650.

The beauty of this mausoleum has attracted the attention of many visitors, but none have done it such perfect justice as the author of the following sketch, published six years ago in the East-India United Service Journal:—

"I have been to visit the taj. I have returned, full of emotion. My mind enriched with visions of ideal beauty. When first I approached the taj, eleven years ago, I was disappointed. In after days, when my admiration for the loveliness of this building had grown into a passion, I have often inquired, why this should have been. And the only answer I can find is, that the symmetry is too perfect to strike at first. It meets you as the most natural of objects. It therefore does not startle, and you return from it disappointed that you have not been startled. But it grows upon you in all the harmony of its proportions, in all the exquisite delicacy of its adornment; and at each glance, some fresh beauty or grace is developed. And, besides, it stands so alone in the world of beauty. Imagination has never conceived a second taj, nor had any thing similar ever before occurred to it.

"View the taj at a distance! It is as the spirit of some happy dream, dwelling dim, but pure, upon the horizon of your hope, and reigning in virgin supremacy over the visible circle of the earth and sky. Approach it nearer, and its grandeur appears unlessened by the acuteness of its fabric, and swelling in all its fresh and fairy harmony, until you are at a loss for feelings worthy of its presence. Approach still nearer, and that which, as a whole, has proved so charming is found to be equally exquisite in the minutest detail. Here are no mere touches for distant effect. Here is no need to place the beholder in a particular spot to cast a partial light upon the performance,—the work which dazzles with its elegance at the *coup d'œil* will bear the scrutiny of the microscope. The sculpture of the panels, the fretwork and mosaic of the screen, the elegance of the marble pavement, the perfect finish of every jot and iota, as if the meanest architect had been one of those potent Genii, who were of yore compelled to adorn the palaces of necromancers and kings.

"We feel, as our eye wanders around this hallowed space, that we have hitherto lavished our admiration and our language in vain. We dread to think of it with feelings, which workmanship less exquisite has awakened, and we dare not use, in its praise, language hackneyed in the service of every-day minds. We seek for it a new train of associations, a fresher range of ideas, a greener and more sacred corner in the repository of our heart. And yet, wherefore should this be, since no terms applying to other works of beauty, excepting the most general, can be appropriated here? For those, there be phrases, established by usage, which their several classifications of style render intelligible to all acquainted with similar works of art. But in the taj, we fall upon a new and separate creation; which never *can* become a style, since it never can be imitated. It is like some bright and newly discovered winged thing, all beauteous, in a beauty peculiar to itself, and referable to no class or order on the roll of zoology, which the whole world flocks to gaze upon with silent delight — none presuming to designate the lovely stranger, nor to conjecture a kindred for it with the winged things of the earth. Suffice it—Love was its author,—Beauty its inspiration.

"Now take your seat upon the marble pavement, beside the upper tombs. Lie at full length upon your back, and send your companion to the vault underneath, to run slowly over the notes of his flute or guitar. Was ever melody like this? It haunts the air above and around. It distils in showers from the polished marble. It condenses into the mild shadows, and sublimes into the softened hallowed light of the dome. It rises, it falls; it swims mockingly, meltingly, around. It is the very element with which sweet dreams are builded. It is the melancholy echo of the past,—it is the bright delicate harping of the future. It is the atmosphere breathed by Ariel, and playing around the fountain of Chindara. It is the spirit of the taj, the voice of inspired love, which called into being this peerless wonder of the world, and elaborated its symmetry and composed its harmony, and eddying around its young minarets and domes, blended them without a line into the azure of immensity."

The garden of the taj is also an object of great attraction; it is intersected by wide paths, paved with flag-stones, and even those are arranged in fanciful devices. The avenue of cypress-trees, with a row of fountains between them, which still play on Sundays, is particularly fine; there is besides, in the centre of this avenue, a marble reservoir about forty feet square, in which there are five additional fountains, one in the centre and one at each corner. There are but few flowers in the garden, and but a scanty supply of fruit-trees, the vine being the principal; but there is a collection of noble trees of gigantic size which afford a delightful shade, and admit of a pleasant walk even in the middle of the day.

The Ram Bhag garden, which is across the water, is nearly of the same size as that of the taj, but it is not so regular nor elaborate. Many, however, prefer it on this account, and on account also of the greater variety of fruit and flowers, and particularly of groves of orange-trees, with which it abounds. At both these public gardens there are plain accommodations for invalids, and such as are in search of the picturesque. Parties often spend an agreeable week at these places.

The fort is one of the grandest in India. It occupies a large space of ground on the banks of the river, and within its lofty embattled walls are the palace, the Motee Musjid, the arsenal, and numerous compartments for all the paraphernalia of war. The fort, however, is far from being strong, and would soon fall under an assault from a few long sixteen-pounders.

The remains of the palace, with its gilded cupolas, and the rich tracery in gold and blue enamel on the walls and roofs of the principal rooms, shew what they must have been when occupied by royalty. The arsenal is very tastefully adorned with warlike instruments. An officer is daily on duty in the fort, with a company of sepoys. The depôt for medicines is also within the walls, and the treasure belonging to the collector's office is deposited here for safety. There is a broad wet ditch with drawbridges at convenient stations around the outer wall. There are also two terraces of considerable breadth, where a large body of troops might be paraded. The Motee Musjid, or Pearl Sanctuary, is one of the most unique things of the kind ever witnessed. It is made of pure marble, and has a dazzling white appearance: the floor of the musjid is paved with rows of slabs, each of which constitutes an altar on which the faithful sons of the prophet present their offerings of praise. Just outside of the fort, there is another immense pile called the *Jumma Musjid*, whither also the Moslems resort for prayer. The architecture of this building is described as possessing much merit. It has three domes of nearly the same size, and the terrace is surmounted with towers and minarets at the centres and corners; but the whole building is rapidly decaying, and immense pieces of stone appear ready to fall from their giddy heights.

Secundra is a part of the suburbs of Agra, and derives its name from the celebrated Alexander. In this spot is the mausoleum of the most celebrated of the Mahomedan kings, the great Akbar. This remarkable edifice is still in a high state of preservation; the foundation is supported on large massive arches twelve feet thick. The ground-floor rests on a plinth of immense area, and a piazza of prodigious strength runs all round the building: here in the cold season parties frequently resort to enjoy the salubrious air, and the pleasures of an English garden.

There are at Agra very few modern public buildings of any note; the only ones that have been built for public purposes are two extensive offices for the political and revenue departments, and two wings to the Government-House. To the above works of the executive officer may be added a handsome new steeple to the church, the conversion of the Nya Kee Mondee Hospital, an old native building, into a decent modern-looking house, and last, though not least, the Metcalfe Testimonial, which, although deficient in many architectural points, possesses considerable beauty of exterior.

The most striking of all the public buildings is the College, situated in the civil lines, and at a short distance from the town. It is a noble quadrangle, and in the Gothic style, with jutting corners, having four turrets at each of the corners, and two loftier ones flanking the two principal entrances. There are arched verandahs on each side, four handsome entrances, and four corner quadrangular rooms. A passage runs from north to south through the building, and on either side there are seven spacious rooms, including the centre hall, which is divided into two parts. The southern side of the building is appropriated to the vernacular department, and the northern to the English. The number of pupils attached to the former exclusively is about 120, to the latter 140. The Oriental languages taught are Sanscrit and Hindee, Arabic, Persian, Urdú; and arithmetic. The English instruction embraces history, poetry, morals, political economy, natural philosophy, mathematics, &c. The funds for the support of the college are derived from a number of villages bequeathed by a wealthy Zemindar, and yield about 2,000 rupees a month, or near 25,000 rupees a year; the monthly expenditure, independently of the principal's salary, is about 1,200 rupees.

The Government-House is about three miles and a half from the cantonments, but conveniently situated in the vicinity of the principal public offices. Sir Charles Metcalfe caused two handsome and commodious wings to be added; one is used for the officers, and the other for the accommodation of the private secretary.

Besides the offices of the Political and Revenue departments, there is the Civil Auditor's office, the Judge's Cutcherry, and that necessary appendage to social existence, the jail. The magistrate's Cutcherry is situated between the civil lines and cantonments. Nearly opposite is the Agra press. One of the most useful and most prosperous institutions in Agra is the bank. For a considerable time its operations were very limited, and confined chiefly to loans to the military; but its transactions have since been much extended, and it is now called the Agra and United Service Bank.

The Metcalfe Testimonial, in honour of Sir Charles Metcalfe, who was for some time Lieut.-Governor of Agra, is but one of the many tributes that have been paid to one of the most experienced and popular governors of India. There are two long and beautiful halls for dancing and supper, and a library intervening.

The Church is a spacious and handsome building, calculated to hold from 800 to 1,000 persons. The carpentry displayed in the structure of the pulpit, &c., is exceedingly coarse, owing to the absence of good workmen; but the masonry as well as the design are unexceptionable. A noble arch divides the altar from the court of the congregation. The larger part of the court is appropriated to the European soldiers, when a regiment is stationed in the place. The choir is usually composed of the band of the regiment. There are two Catholic chapels; divine service is performed in the morning at one, and in the evening at the other. There is also a Baptist chapel, which is generally well attended, but chiefly among the East-Indian community, and a chapel of ease is building.

Agra boasts of several charitable institutions. The Benevolent Institution supports and educates nearly three hundred native children, who are taught various arts, such as carpet-making, weaving, sewing, carpentry, smithery, shoemaking, gardening, &c. The Relief Society affords alms to the blind, lame, and indigent poor. The Government Dispensary supplies medical aid to the native sick. There is a Church Missionary Society at the station, supported by the Parent Society in England. It has originated several native schools, in and about the town, where instruction is given in the vernacular languages, the Bible being the principal class-book.

Agra is the seat of the government of the North-West Provinces. The district itself, by survey measurement, is only 1,862 square miles, containing 1,270 villages and hamlets, and a population of 509,700 souls; but the authority of the Governor extends much beyond the limits of the district itself. The climate of Agra is not unhealthy, as may be inferred from the fact of the mortality amongst the European troops having rarely exceeded, during the past fifteen years, *three per cent.* The seasons vary, as in other parts of India, excepting that the rains do not last so long here as elsewhere: they generally commence at the end of June and terminate in the middle of September.

In a direct line west of Agra lie the small native states of Bhurtpore, Jeypore, and Ajmeer, of whose dimensions and political status mention has already been made. Ajmeer is somewhat to the south of the Shekawrittee country, an extensive desert, divided into several chieftainships, which have sworn allegiance to the British Government, but which invariably exhibit a "moody frontier" when the time arrives for the payment of the usual tribute. The

Shekawrittee country extends to Bhutseer, which borders the protected Seikh states upon the left bank of the Sutlege.

There are political officers at Ajmeer, Jeypore, &c., and a brigade of irregular troops, to act against the Shekawrittee chieftains when occasion calls for the exercise of force; but we have no regular troops nearer to the country than at Nusserabad, a large cantonment south-east of Ajmeer, where a regiment of cavalry and three or four infantry corps are quartered.

AGRA TO DELHI.

	Ms.	F.		Ms.	F.
To Agra	782	4	Pulwal	0	0
Furrah	0	0	Boolundshur	0	0
Muttra	0	0	Goorgaon	134	0
Cosee	0	0		916	4

Proceeding from Agra to Delhi, the route runs parallel with the right or western bank of the river Jumna. The distance is 134 miles, through a flat, cultivated country, over which the *débris* of Mahomedan greatness are scattered. Muttra was once a military cantonment, but of late years it has been abandoned by the Government, to the infinite loss of the officers, who had built or purchased houses there, and were, consequently, obliged to sacrifice them (no successors appearing), the Government making them no compensation for the loss.

DELHI.—As the ancient seat of the Mogul empire, and the modern residence of the pensioner who still rejoices in the empty title of King, this is one of the most interesting towns in India. It stands in the middle of a plain, surrounded on every side with the ruins of the ancient metropolis, and the tasteful villas of the Europeans, who now exercise the business of local government. The site of these latter was once occupied by the famed gardens of Shalimar. Couched under a ridge of sand-stone rocks, called the *Mijnoon Pahar*, lie the military cantonments—an alternation of bungalows, huts, and groups of gaudy trees. The city of Delhi is enclosed by a wall, or rampart of red granite, battlemented and turreted, and wearing, in the distance, a more formidable appearance than is borne out by closer inspection. Mosques, minarets, and cupolas, enamelled and gilded, intermingle with clusters of cypresses, and present a pleasing and perfectly oriental aspect, when the town is contemplated from the distance. Within the city, the magnificence of the ancient edifices realizes the conception formed from the view without. The spacious regal palace—the marble hall of audience (now stripped of its former gilding and the peacock throne), bearing the inscription immortalized in Moore's "Lalla Rookh*—the Jumma Musjid, or principal mosque, &c.,—all vouch for the splendid conceptions and exquisite taste of the Emperors of the olden time. The principal street, or Chandney Choke, is a Regent-street in its way: it is broad and handsome; the architecture of the houses is varied, and fronted by trees, which form a beautiful avenue. As the King keeps up a certain degree of state, and maintains the royal privilege of conferring

* And, oh, if there be an Elysium on earth,
It is this—it is this!
Not quite an accurate translation, by the way.

khillauts, or dresses of honour, the wealthier natives affect the airs of an aristocracy, and attempt, by gaiety of costume and a swaggering indifference, to impress people with an idea of their importance. They are also active in their endeavours to imitate the chiefs and Omrah of old by the practice of petty political intrigues, in which they find active participators amongst the corrupt inhabitants of the imperial palace. His Majesty, the pensioner, sometimes emerges from his residence on his elephant, attended by a rabble of retainers; and on these occasions largesse is distributed to the crowd, and his name and titles are shouted by those who precede and surround him.

The works of the Europeans at Delhi are confined to a magnificent canal, an arsenal, where the implements and munitions of war are prepared, when occasion requires, on a grand scale; a church, a college, and a printing-press. The principal political officer is a sort of envoy or resident, ostensibly representing the British Government at the court of the Mogul; but, in point of fact, his business is rather to watch the straw sovereign, pay him his pension, and regulate his intercourse with strangers who may visit the city. There is a collector, a magistrate, and other lesser officers, at the station; and two or three regiments of infantry and a park of artillery compose the usual military force.

The manufactures of Delhi, for the most part, refer to the ornaments of life. Gay scarfs, embroidered shawls, pictures of buildings, jewellery, miniature paintings in ivory of the various Mahomedan emperors, swords, shields, ivory chess-men, horse and elephant trappings, &c., are obtainable in any quantity and at reasonable prices. Carriages of the European fashion are seen about the streets, and the contents of the shops, with their English placards and boards, indicate the introduction of articles of western manufacture.

The great objection to a residence at Delhi is the dust, which, from the exposed position of the town and the sand which covers the flat country for many miles around, renders the visitation of a gust of wind a most unpleasant affair. The accomplished tourist, to whom we are indebted for several passages in other parts of this volume, has felicitously described the effect of this and other climatic visitations; and as the same may be written of almost every other station in Upper or Lower India, similarly exposed to the hot winds and temporary dry storms, we may appropriately quote her sketch in this place:—

"The hot winds prevail between the middle of March and the whole of April and May. The wind usually rises about eight o'clock in the morning, and if coming from the right point (the west), and strong enough to cause sufficient evaporation, the *tatties* are put up—thick mats, made of the roots of a fragrant grass (*cuscus*), upon bamboo frames, fitting into the doors or windows; all the apertures in the contrary direction being closely shut. These *tatties* are kept constantly wet by men employed to throw water upon them on the outside, and the wind which comes through them is changed into a rush of cold air—so cold, sometimes, as to oblige the party within to put on additional clothing. While the wind continues steady, the only inconveniences to be borne are the darkness, common to Indian houses, and the confinement; for those who venture abroad pay dearly for their temerity. Exhaustion speedily follows, the breath and limbs fail, and, if long exposed to the scorching air, the skin will peel off. Yet this is the period chosen by the natives for their journeys and revelries; they cover their faces with a cloth, and with this simple precaution brave the fiercest blasts of the simoom. These winds usually subside at sunset, though they sometimes blow to a later hour, and are known to continue all night. If they should change to the eastward, the *tatties* are useless, producing only a hot damp steam. In this event, the only means of mitigating the heat is to exclude the wind by filling up the crevices, hanging thick curtains (*purdahs*) over the doors, and setting all the *punkahs* in motion: inefficient expedients, for, in despite of all, the atmosphere is scarcely bearable; excessive and continual thirst, languor of the most painful nature, and irritability produced by the prickly heat, render existence almost insupportable. Every article of furniture is burning to touch; the hardest wood, if not well covered with blankets, will split with a report like that of a pistol, and linen taken from the drawers appears as if just removed from a kitchen fire. The nights are terrible, every apartment being heated to excess. Gentlemen usually have their beds placed in the verandahs, or on the *chubootiar*, or terrace on the top of the house, as they incur little risk in sleeping in the open air at a season in which no dews fall, and there is scarcely any variation in the thermometer. Tornadoes are frequent during the hot winds; while they last, the skies, though cloudless, are darkened with dust, the sun is obscured, and a London fog cannot more effectually exclude the prospect. The birds are dreadful sufferers at this season; their wings droop, and their bills are open, as if gasping for breath; all animals are more or less affected. The breaking-up of the hot winds affords a magnificent spectacle; they depart in wrath, after a tremendous conflict with opposing elements. The approaching strife is made known by a cloud, or rather a wall of dust, which appears at the extremity of the horizon, becoming more lofty as it advances. The air is sultry and still, for the wind, which is tearing up the sand as it rushes along, is not felt in front of the billowy masses, whose mighty ramparts gather strength as they spread. At length the plain is surrounded, and the sky becomes as murk as midnight. Then the unchained thunder breaks forth, but its most awful peals are scarcely heard in the deep roar of the tempest; burst succeeds to burst, each more wild and furious than the former; the. forked lightnings flash in vain, for the dust, which is as thick as snow, flings an impenetrable veil around them. The wind having spent itself in a final effort, suddenly subsides, and the dust is as speedily dispersed by torrents of rain, which in a very short time flood the whole country. The *tatties* are immediately thrown down, and though they may have previously rendered shawls necessary, the relief experienced when breathing the fresh air of heaven, instead of that produced by artificial means, is indescribable. All the animal creation appear to be endued with fresh life and vigour, as they inhale the cooling breezes; the songs of the birds are heard again, and flocks and herds come forth rejoicing. Before the watery pools have penetrated into the parched earth, so rapid is the growth of vegetation, patches of green appear along the plain, and those who take up their posts in the verandah for an hour or two may literally see the grass grow. In the course of a single day the sandy hillocks will be covered with verdure, and in a very short time the grass becomes high and rank."

The chief buildings in the neighbourhood of Delhi, remnants of Moslem antiquity, are the Khotub Minar, a lofty column of red granite; the tomb of the Emperor Humayoon; the remains of a gigantic astronomical observatory; and the Path'an fortress, a place of resort for the amateurs of picnics, as well as for the curious in Saracenic architecture.

ALLYGHUR TO FEROZEPORE.

	Ms.	F.		Ms.	F.
To Allyghur ..	802	5	Kurnaul	50	0
Allyghur to Somnagunge	1	4	Thanesir	20	0
Khoonja	14	4	Umballa	40	0
Bolundshur	11	1	Sirhind	15	0
Golauttee	13	4	Loodiana	35	0
Haupper	9	4	Ferozepore	40	0
Kurkowda	8	2			
Meerut	11	2		1105	2
Sirdana	20	0			

MEERUT, KURNAUL, UMBALLA, LOODIANA, AND FEROZEPORE.—In bringing the travellers to Agra and Delhi from Allyghur, we have somewhat travelled out of the usual dawk route on the direct trip to Calcutta. We now go back to Allyghur to give the stages thence to Ferozepore, although there are no places on the route which call for any particular description. *Bolundshur* is a purely civil station. *Haupper* is the seat of a government stud, or establishmentfor the breed of horses. *Meerut* is a large military station, possessing all the characteristics of Cawnpore, but in a greater degree. *Sirdana*, formerly the residence of the famous Begum Sumroo, possesses a Catholic cathedral. *Kurnaul* was another Meerut, but the unhealthiness of the station has lately induced the government to abandon it as a large military cantonment, and to quarter the European regiments at Umballa, Loodiana, and Kowulsir, in the lower Himalaya range of mountains. Loodiana was, until the commencement of operations against the Affghans, the frontier station in the North-West of India, but Ferozepore is now the limit of our military occupation, though there seems good reason to suppose that even that will soon be crossed. The features of all the places named above, and the country which lies between them, correspond essentially with those of the cantonments and routes between Allahabad and Allyghur. Level land, mud villages, ruined serais, decayed mosques and temples, plots of cultivation, groves, &c., occur at frequent intervals; while strings of laden camels, howda-burdened elephants, gaily-caparisoned horses, detachments of troops, mark an activity of life peculiar to a military state, where the arts of peace have not been extensively cultivated.

To complete our information for the guidance of persons whose fate may carry them to the North-West of India, we subjoin an itinerary of the routes from the principal stations to places of lesser account.

Calcutta to Seharunpore, Dehra, Bareilly, Shahjehanpore, Pillibheet, Moradabad, Kumaon, &c.

To SEHARUNPORE, as far as Meerut, see above.

	Ms.	F.		Ms.	F.
Meerut to Douralla ..	8	2	Kujoorwalla	12	5
Kuffowlee	12	0	Seharunpore	8	5
Muzuffernuggur ..	15	0			
Deobund	15	4		72	0

The country is open, and pretty well cultivated; the roads good. A civilian or two will be found at Muzuffernuggur, and at Seharunpore several are stationed, together with a regiment of infantry. The chief object of interest at Seharunpore is the Botanic Garden, where the hardier plants, and the productions of Europe, are cultivated with much skill and good effect. At Deobund the Kolee Nuddee is crossed by a good bridge; but there is a nullah or small river at Muzuffernuggur, which a large detachment can only cross conveniently by a temporary bridge erected for the purpose.

Calcutta to Dehra.

	Ms.	F.		Ms.	F.
Seharunpore to Hurowrah	8	0	Shorepore	8	0
Kheree	8	2	Dehra	7	0
Mohun Chokee	10	4			
				41	6

Dehra is the principal place in the valley of the Dhoon. It is one of the most salubrious spots in India. Cultivation of the staples of India is here carried on upon an extensive scale; and many retired and invalid officers make it their place of residence, in preference to returning to England. The Sirmoor battalion of Goorka sepoys generally has its head-quarters here. Immediately above Dehra, on a ridge of the outer Himalaya, stands the cantonment, or depôt, of Landour. It was established in 1827, as a sanatarium for European troops, and the consequences have been most beneficial. Sick officers and soldiers sent there are speedily renovated, the climate in the winter and the hot months being remarkably salubrious. Near Landour is Mussooree, another elevated spot, studded with bungalows, and all appliances of comfort. Many of the officers stationed in the upper provinces resort to it in the warm weather.

Calcutta to Shahjehanpore.

(From Calcutta as far as Cawnpore already given.)

	Ms.	F.
Cawnpore to Meerun Ke Serai	9	4
Jellalabad	10	4
Khadagarge	9	2
Futtebghur	13	4
Husseinpore Ghaut, left bank of Ganges ..	2	4
Merutpore	10	2
Jellalabad	15	2
Kant	11	0
Shahjehanpore	10	3
	102	1

Four rivers are crossed in the course of this trip; supplies are abundant in the villages, and the road is generally good. One or two regiments are usually quartered at Shahjehanpore.

To Bareilly.

	Ms.	F.
Shajehanpore to Tillber..	13	4
Futtebgunge	11	1
Furreedpore	10	7
Bareilly	12	2
	47	6

The roads are tolerably good; the bazaars at each place well supplied, and the two rivers which intersect the route (the Bhagool and Nukter) are crossed by bridges of masonry. Bareilly is a military cantonment, and a place celebrated for the manufacture of elegant furniture.

Bareilly to Pillibheet.

	Ms.	F.
Bareilly to Rhentora	11	1
Nuwabgunge	10	2
Pillibheet	12	0
	33	3

Villages rich in supplies, good roads, and four small rivers, easily forded, or crossed by bridges.

Bareilly to Moradabad.

	Ms.	F.		Ms.	F.
Bareilly to Futtehgunge..	12	4	Guness Ghaut	11	5
Meergunge	9	1	Moradabad	14	4
Kumna Damora.. ..	11	4			
				59	2

Good water from wells or rivers, supplies in abundance at the village bazaars, and tolerably good roads, are the characteristics of this march.

Bareilly to Kumaon, Almorah.

	Ms.	F.		Ms.	F.
Bareilly to Sunka Nuddee	10	4	Bheem Tal	11	6
Shahee	8	6	Ramghur	11	7
Seesghur	14	2	Purah	10	5
Manpore	13	7	Almorah	8	6
Tundah	13	3			
Bhamaurie	15	3		119	1

A varied road, through cultivated plain, jungle,

and forest, intersected by streams, across which are fascine or suspension bridges. Supplies are plentiful in some places; in others they are not procurable at all. The plan is to obtain enough at the well-furnished bazaars to serve where scarcity prevails.

Almorah is the principal military station in this part of the Himalayan range. When we first took these hills, a considerable force was stationed at Almorah, with a permanent commandant and a major of brigade; but it is now diminished to one wing, and the head-quarters of a native regiment, and the magazine, artillery, &c., have been altogether abolished. There is not now even a brigade of six-pounders, with a detail of native artillery attached, they having been finally taken away in 1829.

There was also, formerly, a company of pioneers, all hill-men, stationed here, and good and numerous roads were made, one from the foot of the hills at Bhamaurie (four marches) to this place; another to Havil Bagh, the cantonment of the Kumaon (civil) local battalion, which is about six miles from Almorah; another to Lohooghat, four marches, and on, through that place, three more to Petora-Ghur; also one from Lohooghat to Birmdeo, the pass by which the hills are entered from Pillibheet, three marches, besides roads for taking air and exercise about Almorah.

The other wing of the native corps stationed at Almorah is divided in equal proportions, two companies at each, between the two out-posts of Lohooghat and Petora-Ghur, which were formerly garrisoned by a Goorka corps, the second Nusseree (military) local battalion.

There are forts at each of the military stations in these hills, one at Almorah, called "Fort Moira;" one at Lohooghat, "Fort Hastings;" and one at Petora-Ghur, denominated "Fort Loudon," as, likewise, at the latter place, a small fortified house, or tower, designated "Wilkie-Ghur," after Major James Wilkie, who had the building of the forts at Petora and Lohooghat. In a military point of view, however, these forts are all worthless, none of them containing water, or even commanding that near them.

There are stage-bungalows belonging to government all the way from Bhamaurie to Almorah, for the use of which travellers pay one rupee per diem. At each of them there is a bunniah; but, excepting such articles as he can supply, nothing, saving and excepting firewood, is procurable. The names of the stages are, first, Bhamaurie; second, Bheemtal; third, Ramghur; fourth, Pewra; fifth, Almorah. There are, likewise, similar bungalows on the road from Almorah to Lohooghat, and thence to Petora-Ghur, but these do not belong to government. One rupee per diem is paid for accommodation in these, the same as for the use of the government bungalows.

The names of the stages from Almorah to the outposts are, first, Dale; second, Dhee; third, Furka; fourth, Lohooghat; and, from Lohooghat to Petora, first, Durgurrah; second, Kunta-Gong; third, Petora-Ghur. At these bungalows there is no bunniah, and, consequently, nothing but firewood to be got. Travellers are, therefore, obliged to carry their own supplies of every sort, including grain.

The stages from Birmdeo to Lohooghat, on which road there are no bungalows, are as follows: first,

Birmdeo; second, Belkate; third, Malik Chaur, or Chaura Paunie; fourth, Lohooghat; and as no supplies are procurable at any of these places, travellers will do well to provide themselves accordingly. The wing of the regiment which is destined for Lohooghat and Petora-Ghur, and which should separate from the wing going to Almorah at Bareilly, goes by this route, it being much the nearest, and, consequently, least expensive in carriage, which, being entirely hill-coolies (no other kind of carriage is known in the hills), is very exorbitant. The usual quantum of carriage allowed to a regiment marching on the hills is four coolies to a subadar, three to a jemadar, one to non-commissioned officers, and one between every two sepoys; and this, as each man carries from twenty-five to thirty seers, pucka weight, should be sufficient.

The Kumaon local corps stationed at Havil-Bagh is, as well as all the other hill-corps, armed with fuzils, and dressed in green, with black facings.

At Almorah there are five bungalows, called sick bungalows, belonging to government; these are kept in good repair, and are exclusively for the use of such officers as may come up on sick leave, who are furnished with one to live in, free of all cost, on application, through the executive officer, in whose charge they are, to the officer commanding. It is only surprising, considering this, that more officers do not go there for their health, where they not only get a house (and that a good one) to live in, and medical attendance gratis, but also every thing else they can require very much cheaper than at Simla. These sick-houses are, of course, totally unfurnished.

As to climate, though not so cold as at Simla, Almorah is sufficiently cool and pleasant, and it is, unquestionably, a very healthy, renovating one. In regard to society, likewise, there is a sufficiency.

Those who visit Almorah on leave, merely for their own pleasure, can always procure bungalows for hire, to live in, there being more than are needed for the accommodation of the officers of the regiment, and others permanently residing at the place, and the rent charged is extremely reasonable.

The military cantonments are at the western extremity of, and close to, the city of Almorah, which is the capital of the province, and, in fact, the only place in the hills that can be called a city. Prior to our invasion and conquest of Kumaon, Almorah was the place of residence of the Goorka Viceroy, who was appointed from Katmandoo; and previous to the Goorka invasion, it was the seat of government of the Rajahs of Kumaon. It is situated in latitude 29° 24′, longitude 79° 39′, and is built on the top of a ridge, running east and west, at an elevation of 5,400 feet above the level of the sea. From the nature of its situation, the city of Almorah is principally composed of one long street, of nearly a mile in length, though there are suburbs which extend down a long way on both sides of the hill. It is paved with stone throughout, and the houses are generally very good, none being under two stories, and many three and four stories high; the houses, even of the poorest people, in this part of the hills, are all built of stone, and have slated roofs, so that they are remarkably substantial. Indeed, those in the town of Almorah, are unlike any thing one ever sees in the plains of India, and reminds one somewhat of England, to a small town in which country Almorah has altogether a greater resemblance than to one in Hindostan. The officer commanding at Almorah has, also, the general command of all the troops in the district.

Before proceeding further, it may be as well to give an outline description of the Himalaya chain, of which Almorah forms a link.

The range of the Himalaya embraces an area of 500,000 to 600,000 square miles. It consists of numerous ridges running parallel to the direction of the whole range from south-east to north-west, which are connected in many places by transverse ridges, and in others separated by deep and narrow ravines and glens, in which the different branches and tributary rivers of the Indus and Ganges run. The entire chain, from the Hindoo Koosh, near Cabul, to the easternmost valleys of Assam, is overtopped by an elevated range covered with eternal snow. The lowest chain of the mountains, immediately skirting the plains of India, is extremely picturesque and diversified. The sides of the mountains are covered with dwarf trees, or cultivation on small patches of table-land, formed by cutting the sloping earth into a series of terraces, resembling vast flights of steps. The valleys are extremely narrow, consisting of little else than the bed of a rivulet, or a rude road, and the habitations of the people, generally on elevated ground, few and far between. As we advance, by roads cut in the mountain sides, the hills assume a bolder and severer aspect. Steep sides, sometimes wooded by the pine and the oak, but more frequently composed only of vast faces of naked rock, dip down abruptly, forming huge chasms and ravines, through which the torrent forces itself over rude fragments, which have toppled from the summits to the deep abyss. The roads now become narrow paths, winding along the edges of precipices, and the rustic bridge is supplanted by rude *sangas*, or planks, or by *jhulas*, formed by ropes stretched across, constituting a species of loose parapet, and supporting a light ladder for the feet to rest upon. These mountains are seldom crossed by Europeans. The Tibetan traders visit Upper India by the northern passes, and intercourse takes place with the valley of Nepal, and the countries of Assam and Bhootan; but in all other respects, the mountains are regarded as the natural frontier of the British possessions, and are only penetrated as far, or as high, as may be requisite for purposes of health. Next to Mussoorie, spoken of above, the favourite places of resort are Simla, not many miles from Rampore, the chief town in the valley of the Upper Sutledge; and Darjeeling to the south-east, in the vicinity of the Nepalese territory. Almorah and Simla are about 7,000 feet above the level of the sea. We shall speak of Darjeeling hereafter. On the hills of Simla there are upwards of one hundred residences, built after the fashion of English cottages. As the chosen retreat of governors-general and commanders-in-chief, from the burning plains of India, the place has enjoyed for some years past many considerable advantages. The roads to the residences, and for some distance beyond them, are spacious and elegant. Shopkeepers have been induced to establish themselves and form emporiums of all the creature comforts. There is a reading-room and billiard-table, an amateur theatre, a church, a school, an observatory, and a pretty valley called Annandale, whose beauties owe something to the taste of a late resident; fancy fairs and races are held, and contribute to the embellishment of existence. As Simla and the neighbouring hills are the property of certain small chieftains, who reside in small townships, a political agent is stationed at the former place to regulate the respective responsibilities, and do the honours in behalf of the British government. The people of the hills are poor, simple, and tractable, subsisting entirely by the produce of their lands. They are Hindoos, and 400,000 in number. Though polygamy prevails in some parts, polyandry is a more common institution, for the insufficiency of the products of the soil renders it advisable to check the increase of the human race. It is by no means uncommon for one woman to reside in the same house with four or five men, and to fulfil the duties of a wife towards all. The women are good-looking and strong; they wear a slight cloth covering for the head, *not* concealing the face as in the plains, a chemise of coarse cloth, and trousers. The commercial products of these hills are iron, wax, honey, borax, musk, wool, ginger, and opium. The fruits are apricots, walnuts, strawberries, raspberries, quinces, greengages, red and black currants, rhubarb, wheat, grain, barley, rice, &c.; and in the kitchen gardens may be found peas, beans, potatoes, cabbages, lettuces, parsnips, &c.

The process of manufacturing iron by the hill people is rude and primitive—a description of it may interest the English reader.

The first step is to dig at random a hole, or shaft, about four feet wide and six feet deep, which, if no vein of ore is perceivable on its sides, they abandon or fill up, as the fancy strikes them, and go to another spot. If, on the contrary, they light upon a vein, they work it slanting downwards; but, from being so near the loose earth, and from want of regular supports, by the time they have got eight or ten feet horizontally into the earth, the mine falls in, and all further work there is relinquished. Two men are employed in each mine; the one, with a heavy pointed hammer, picks out the ore in small pieces, the largest being smaller than one's fist, whilst the other, with burning splints of pine-wood, chosen for the quantity of turpentine they contain, shews a light to the workman. The ore is next removed to large flat stones, where, being extremely friable, it is reduced to powder by repeated blows from smaller stones. The dust is then sifted in a sieve, which retains the larger particles of earth or rock, and yields a passage to the iron ore. When this has been performed, the ore is carried to a running stream in the neighbourhood, in which it is allowed to remain some time, that the water may wash away so much of the finer particles of impure earth that have escaped through the sieve, as will come away. This operation being concluded, the ore has the appearance of black-lead or steel-filings, and is very ponderous. The smelting furnace is the next stage. Each forge contains three or four furnaces, which are of sun-dried clay, about five feet high, by a foot wide, and are raised on a platform, three or four feet from the ground. At the bottom of the furnace is a plate made of charcoal, dust, and clay, dried in the sun, perforated with numerous holes to let off the dross. Just above this place, on each side, is a hole for the nozzle of a pair of bellows, made out of a goat-skin, tanned with the hair on, which are worked by women as well as by men. The fire is lighted early in the morning, and the bellows are set to work to ignite the charcoal properly; when this is accomplished, small quantities of the mineral are strewed on the surface of the fuel, more of which is added as required. Three people attend to each furnace; two at the bellows, and one to keep up the fire, and supply it with ore, and also to see that the grate at the bottom does not get choked; the holes being kept clear by continually thrusting an iron rod through them. The furnaces are kept burning for nine or ten hours at a time, when the plate at the bottom is broken by a sharp blow from beneath, and the iron falls out in a lump, at a white heat, accompanied by a stream of burning scoria, which gives, on a small scale, the idea of an irruption of lava from the crater of a volcano. In one day a single furnace will smelt from six to eight seers of iron, which, on coming out, is taken to a stone, no matter of what shape, ordained to do the duty of an anvil, and is cut into pieces of three or four seers each, which are left to cool. The following day these pieces are placed in a common forge, and submitted to a strong fire until they become red-hot, when each is hammered into something like a shape, and when again cold is in a fit condition for sale. Iron thus prepared is sold at the rate of about four rupees the maund; but the people generally, by preference, exchange it for cloth, grain, or any other article of which they may be in need. By means of a rude description of steel-yard, the weight and value of each mass is ascertained. The next thing being to apportion the produce of the forge then in hand amongst the proprietors, the iron is divided into four equal parts, of which the renter or owner of the ground, who is also the miner, receives one; the man who prepares the charcoal in the woods, and brings it to the forge, receives two; and the smelters and smiths, with their bellows-blowers, &c., receive the remaining share. The iron prepared in the hills is very good and soft. With a few Europeans, experienced in veining, the veins might be made much more profitable, for they are rich. The hills teem with ore; but the natives are not able to extract it so advantageously as they might, for by the time a vein is fairly opened the falling in of the mine claps an extinguisher on any further benefit.

The smelters are most wretched-looking objects, grimed, squalid, and miserable; they are of very low caste, a fact which is amply testified by their free use of swine's flesh. A breed of filthy, ugly, misshapen pigs, roam about the village, thrusting their un-ringed snouts into every place they can intrude themselves, in search of the wherewithal to assuage their hunger.

Access to Simla from the plains is very easy. A palanquin dawk from the stations of Kurnaul or Umballa brings the traveller to Bhar, at the foot of the hills, which is distant about thirty miles from

Simla; there are three stage bungalows situated at Chumbul, Hurreepore, and Syree, which lead to Simla. The ascent from Bhar to the first of these stages is considerable; the road winds up the face of an immense mountain, and brings the traveller to the summit, where he finds the first bungalow. From Chumbul to the Khutwar river, the descent is steep but not dangerous; the course of the traveller is for some miles along its banks through a well-cultivated valley, when by a sharp turn of the road he is suddenly brought to a chasm, flanked by perpendicular rocks about 800 or 1,000 feet in height, through which the river Gumber rolls. Passing through this gap along the banks of the Gumber, the traveller at length advances half a mile up a gentle ascent to the Hurreepore bungalow, and thence continuing gradually the ascent by a barren but good road, he reaches Syree, whence he proceeds to Simla. The roads are excellent and well fenced in.

Previous to ascending the hills, the traveller, as is usual, deposits his carriage, palanquin, or tent, &c.&c., in godowns belonging to a Simla firm at Bhar, and proceeds upwards with such indispensable articles of furniture only as are absolutely necessary. The usual mode of travelling is by "*jampauns*"—a conveyance not unlike a large clumsy chair, having a top from which curtains are suspended. They are carried by four men by means of poles fixed to the sides, and are supplied by the agents of the firm, together with bearers and porters. Every necessary advice and assistance is given at their Kurnaul establishment.

At about one-third the ascent we reach Subatoo,

a tolerably extensive piece of level land, where the head-quarters of the Nusseree battalion of Goorka sepoys are situated.

We now leave the Himalayas, and resume notice of the remarkable places on the plains. Due south of Deyra, on the western bank of the Ganges, and a little below the spot where, receiving tribute from another stream, it enters upon the level of Hindostan, lies Hurdwar, a place of great sanctity, whither Hindoo pilgrims resort in prodigious numbers. During the first fortnight in April of each year, a fair is held which attracts many thousands of people, who contrive to render their visit subservient, at one and the same time, to business and to devotion. Above Hurdwar is Khunkul, another sacred town. These two places have been recently described by Colonel Davidson, late of the Bengal Engineers, from whose graphic sketch we are tempted to borrow a few paragraphs :—

" Khunkhul is a teerut, or place of Hindoo pilgrimage, on the banks of the Ganges ; on the sides or banks of which, are many very handsome cut free-stone ghauts, or landing places, for the convenience of prayer and ablution. The town consists of a very handsome principal street, running north and south, parallel with the course of the river, and is composed of a number of magnificent houses (for Hindoos) belonging to rich Brahmins and merchants from all parts of India. To have a house at Khunkhul, is at once a mark of the proprietor's piety and wealth or importance. Most of them are built of brick and mortar, and the road front is generally painted in the pu re Hindostanee taste—that is, in the taste of English children, of from eight to twelve years of age. Many, if not all of the houses, rent out their lower apartments to dirty bunnias, or still filthier hulwaees, or confectioners, who project numerous grass roofs or choppers, which seem to have been attacked by the white ants, and to require, if not renewal, at least a fresh coating. Crowds of monkeys (who very soon find out a city where they are adored) crowd all parts of the houses, playing the most diverting tricks ; the females hopping about with their young ones clinging firmly to their backs, and occasionally descending with a pounce to snatch either grain or sweetmeats from the shops. The old fat males have a most ludicrous gravity of expression, until menaced, when their countenances are immediately distorted, and converted into the most hideous and amusing grins of rage and malice.

"To accommodate the immense number of pilgrims who visit Khunkhul, there are long, low, brick-and-mortar serais, built in a uniform manner, in which, in one promiscuous herd, are lodged wives, bullocks, husbands, cows, calves (come to be blessed), donkeys, boys, mules, camels, and tattoos (small ponies).

"Although the houses were tastily decorated, no Hindoo ever thought that the roads or streets should be made passable. They were broad enough, but so dreadfully heavy, from an accumulation of rich black mud, that it was a difficult matter to pass them in a buggy. The old road from Khunkhul to Hurdwar runs along the bank of the Ganges, and was lined with a parapet on each side of five feet high, with ornamented platforms at short distances, on which the Brahmins and their gulls used to sit; but these are now ruined and neglected, and covered over with weeds and rubbish.

"The new road, which has been recently made by our government, is in excellent order, and runs direct to Hurdwar. On each side of it, for a couple of miles, are pitched the large and comfortable tents belonging to the military and civil officers who visit the fair, either on duty, to purchase horses for the Honourable Company's Service, or to pass a week in the enjoyments of this celebrated fair. Rich natives, also, have their country-seats amongst the large mango groves, with their little jungly gardens filled with rare and fragrant exotics, such as marigolds, tulsu, cock's-combs, and sun-flowers.

"The view from Khunkhul, from any of the tops of the low hills on its west, is strikingly beautiful; the muddy streets and the filthy natives being out of sight.

"Hurdwar is built in a nearly similar manner, but is apparently older, and certainly even dirtier than Khunkhul. It lies close on the western bank of the Ganges, and many of the finest houses have their foundations in the bed of the sacred waters. They are generally of brick, but many have their lower stories of very fine white freestone. The bed of the river is here also intersected with low woody islands, and is a full mile broad in the rainy season. On the west bank are hills rising 600 feet high, covered with thick brushwood and low trees; now, after the winter, regaining a green and leafy appearance. There are but very few deciduous trees in Hindostan, and I suspect that they are nearly all exotics. The sides of these hills are divided with rugged ravines, which afford ample cover both to the leopards, or tigers, and wolves, who descend at night to inspect the gram-fed sheep or lambs of the English visitors. Lime-stone of a good quality is found in the bed of the river, both here and at Khunkhul, and is manufactured at a moderate price.

* * * * *

"This ghaut (the principal bathing ghaut) has been lately rebuilt in a most splendid manner by the government of Bengal, under the superintendence of an officer of engineers. It is now at once elegant and commodious; and the horrid waste of human life which had so often occurred by the sudden rush of the devotees through the old and narrow ghaut to reach the water at the propitious minute, often at midnight, is, it is to be hoped, for ever prevented.

* * * * *

"From Hurdwar towards Khunkhul, and thence to Hurdwar, for a mile on each side, with an average breadth of four hundred yards, is occupied with perhaps ten thousand horses, and nearly half a million of people. I am not aware that any census has ever been taken, and nothing is more difficult than to give a correct guess of a large widely-scattered mob. In every twelve years the number increases to nearly a million, and the fair is then called the *Coons*. It is even now a living swarm of cows, horses, bullocks, camels, elephants, tattoos or ponies, and mules from Osbeck Tartary to Benares, and pilgrims are found from Calcutta.

"The scene is in the highest degree interesting and diverting. The horse-merchants from Bokhara and Cabool occupy the stony central parts of the dry bed of the river, with their powerful and handsome, but generally old and blemished horses; while those from Toorkistan squat in the small compounds behind the houses of Hurdwar, separated from each other by dry stone walls. These men bring what are well known in India by their great power, and are chiefly galloways and ponies, called toorkies; their prices vary from 250 to as high as 800 rupees, according to their shapes, colours, and paces. They have all been previously taught to amble, a pace thoroughly unpleasant to most Englishmen, but delightful to all black men.

"The elephant-dealers incline to Khunkhul for the sake of fodder, but traverse the roads of the fair with their animals during the mornings and evenings, with large bells attached to their necks, to give warning to passengers, and for the better alarming of horses. The buneeas, hutwâus, cloth, toy, and shawl merchants, occupy the road-side close to the town, and have low cotton tents with two poles, and of a roof shape. Every here and there are large heaps of barley and wheat-straw, or bhoosa (troddur), surrounded by dead thorn hedges, on sale, for the bullocks of travellers.

"On the sides of the hill to the west are thousands of Seik families, with their huts, tents, camels, bullocks, mules, and horses, all pell-mell in the most astonishing confusion.

"The Seik women are awfully ugly, of dark-brown complexions, and wear their hair formed back into a conical shape, over which, when abroad, they throw their bhee, or white chaddurs, which give them a very picturesque and not ungraceful air. The men are hideous, and wear ear-rings. The Seiks bring only a few barren mares and mules.

"You will very often see two or three very snug and handsome huts, surrounded by bylees, with large well-fed, sleek, snowy bullocks, with gilt or brass-tipped horns; and generally lounging about the door either a shrivelled old hag, or lurcher-looking blackguard, with nicely curled and oiled locks hanging over his neck, who sufficiently indicate the naughty profession of its inhabitants.

"The pious rajah (who first of all bargains for his absolution from some holy Brahmin), with his large luskur of vagabonds, and their tag-rag and bob-tail assortment of animals, has generally a couple of tents, one for a dormitory, and the other for sitting under during the heat of the day; and also a sort of awning, supported by four poles, the fringes of both being tastefully ornamented with red khurwa, stars, crosses, and peacocks, enclosed within a compound of one hundred yards square. Amongst the horse-dealers some capitalists have a few select Persian horses, which they keep warmly clothed in a most handsome manner under spacious tents, which, on inquiry, will be found valued at from five to fifty thousand rupees; but which are, if sold at all, sold for eight hundred to one thousand rupees. The greatest attention is paid by a native horse-dealer in fattening his horse, till he resembles a stall-fed bullock, which is accomplished by cramming him with cordial stimulants, such as pounded ginger and sugar, or cardamums and treacle, with his boiled vetches; a man stands on each side of the horse stuffing large balls of the composition down his throat.

* * * * *

Hugh masses of assafœtida in bags, from the mountains beyond Cabool; tons of raisins of various sorts; almonds, pistachio-nuts; sheep, with four or five horns; Balkh cats, with long silken hair of singular beauty; faqueers begging, and abusing the uncharitable with the grossest and most filthy language; long strings of elderly ladies proceeding in a chant to the priests of the Lingum to bargain for bodily issue; ghaut priests presenting their books for the presents and signatures of the European visitors; groups of Hindoos surrounding a Brahmin, who gives each of them a certificate of his having performed the pilgrimage, fill up various spots, and infuse liveliness and spirit into the scene.

"The natives who supply the horse-dealers with grass (half of which is dried up, and half green), are a race of spurious hill people, who call themselves Brahmins and Chuttros. They are strikingly unlike the dwellers in the plains, being generally broad and lean, low and muscular. In their personal habits they are amazingly filthy. In summer and winter they wear a coarse blanket frock, which, however incredible it may appear, is never removed from their skins. But even out of this evil springs good, for this is the foundation of their personal chronology; they do not say, I am twenty or thirty years old, but, I have worn so many jackets! It is strictly true that the jackets are allowed to drop off from filth and rottenness."

Returning to Seharunpore, a few miles west of Hurdwar, and proceeding thence south-westerly, *viâ* Kurnaul, we come, at the distance of 120 miles, to

Hansi, once a place of some importance. It is not a very regularly built town; the principal street leading from the gate opposite the small lake to the esplanade of the fort is wide, and is intersected by another at right angles, which forms the Chouk. The by-lanes are crooked and numerous; dusty in dry weather, and ankle-deep after a heavy shower of rain. The population of the town is said to be 4,000 of all castes, Mahomedans and Hindoos, residing in houses of both brick and mud. It is surrounded by a brick wall, but of no stability, the ends of which terminate on the fort ditch. Hansi is of some antiquity; it was founded by Rajah Pethora of Delhi, and was captured by Mahomed of Ghizni, in the year 1035, 809 years ago. In recent days the celebrated adventurer George Thomas made it the capital of his short-lived independent state. The fort is an oblong, but slightly departing from the quadrangle, and is protected by a lower fort, or *fausse braye*, and a deep ditch, which can easily be filled by turning the canal into it. On the side next the town the glacis is short; but on other sides it is more prolonged. The entrance is from the town side, and is covered by bastions; at each corner of the *fausse braye*, also, there are bastions enfilading the ditch. The parapet of the upper fort is low, and the guns are fired *en barbette.* In the magazine-yard are many stone shells and balls, of the description used by native gunners, when iron projectiles are not forthcoming. Besides the magazine, the fort contains a couple of houses for the conductor in charge of the ordnance, and one formerly devoted to the officer on fort duty; a small powder-magazine, bomb-proof, a sunk store-room, and the remains of some Mahomedan erections. Amongst the latter is the tomb of one of the defenders of the fort on a former occasion, who, it is said, fought from the gate of the fort up to the place where he was interred, *without his head!* Great numbers assemble here every Thursday evening to pray, who firmly believe the legend, and would stigmatize as heterodox any one who ventured to doubt its authenticity. Supposing the fort in a state of siege, or blockade, the garrison would have had one well to depend on for water; this is situated within the *fausse braye*, near the gate, and is about 120 feet deep. There are two wells in the upper fort, but one of them is dry, and the other turned out bad, the water being brackish. In the centre of the fort is a cistern for receiving rain-water that could be filled from below; it is tiled over, and is about forty feet long by thirty feet broad, and is more than twenty-five deep, so that it would contain a pretty good supply, about one hundred and eighty-four thousand gallons; there is now six feet of water in the cistern, or about forty-four thousand gallons. The cantonment is to the south of the fort, and contains lines for the Hurriana Light Infantry, and the 1st Local Horse. Through most of the streets run channels from the canal for supplying water to the bungalows, as it is too expensive to sink wells, from the depth of soil to be cut through ere the springs rise. Hansi used to be an extremely healthy station.

After leaving Hansi, no places of any consequence occur north of Agra that have not been described above. Due south of Agra, distant seventy-four miles, stands Gwalior, the seat of the ancient sovereignty of Scindia. The recent death of the Maharajah, and the serious disruption which has resulted therefrom, has rendered it necessary for the Governor-General of India to march a large force to the frontier of the state; and while we pen these pages, it is quite impossible to say whether the self-appointed regent, who has seized the reins of power, has been confirmed in his authority, or whether the British Government has intervened, and placed the country on the footing of other states enjoying our protection. By the latest accounts, all was anarchy and confusion. We must, therefore, in this place, content ourselves with a brief description of the town and fortress. The city is approached by a footpath, over some trifling clay and sand-stone heights, from which it is seen to advantage, lying under the wing of the giant stronghold, which rises in a complete precipice from its very bosom; and interspersed with trees and minarets, after the usual fashion of native cities. The suburbs are somewhat scanty, and there is no wall of defence to the town; which, however, by means of strong portals connecting the parallel streets, and opening or closing the communication at the pleasure of the inhabitants, as well as by the aid of the external gates, is capable of making a brief defence against any irregular attack. These gateways are singularly elegant, although a jumble of modern and Hindoo architecture. They are built of sand-stone. The gateway itself is an architrave of stone, supported upon ornamented columns of the same. Above this rises the pointed Saracenic arch, and above that are elegant arabesque bas-reliefs, the roof of the structure being flat.

The Jumma Musjid is a handsome building, in the style of those at Lucknow. On turning the flank of the defences, we come upon the grandest and most imposing exhibition of military architecture ever beheld. We doubt if the world contains any thing so magnificent as this long line of Gothic towers, scarped by an overhanging precipice; poised in mid-air, dignified by the impress of the ages that have passed over their heads, yet unimpaired in strength and beauty, and presenting, not the blind aspect of mere holds of power, in which a garrison is pent up and excluded from the outer world, but that of the fittest possible residence for a mighty sovereign, the object of all regards, raised above the world by his grandeur, and gazing down, from its unapproachable eminence, upon the kingdom submitted to his rule. It is impossible to imagine this noble mass of architecture designed for the vile purposes for which its isolated position afterwards rendered it convenient. But in exact proportion to our admiration of the structure is our indignation at the tyranny, the cruelty, the barbarous and murderous policy, for which no language has epithets sufficiently severe, of which Gwalior was the theatre, and continues the memorial; and as we gaze upon its lofty battlements, and recal to memory the hundreds of unhappy captives, condemned to waste away in perpetual imprisonment, or to escape this prolongation of misery, only by the slow operation of a poison, that destroys by sapping all the fountains of life, and poisoning all the springs of enjoyment, and breaking down the firmness of a heart that would have defied, in its health, the extremity of torture; thus reducing the noblest to the quality of the vilest, and making him, previous to his end,* the scorn even of himself;—when, we say, we reflect, how many victims to royal jealousy, have here rotted away into oblivion, their only crime that of having hung at the same breast with their murderer, or, perchance, of having a better claim than his to the throne, or of having excelled him in virtue, or, being beloved by their fellow-men, we turn shuddering from the grandeur which had so greatly excited our admiration, and mourn that infamy should have been permitted so unsuitable a shrine. Had those towers been clad in some of the gloomy horrors which their interior has witnessed, they would have been a beacon of terror to the world. To the thoughtful they yet hold out an humbling lesson of the vanity of outward appearance, and the madness of any ambition that has not virtue for its aim.

It is not possible to give any thing like an adequate idea of this surpassing fortress without the aid of the pencil and colours. The cliff upon which it stands is perfectly perpendicular, formed, apparently, of sand-stone, and it extends round the entire circuit of the fortified height. The defences, which, on the other sides, though adequate to their object, are dwindled into comparative insignificance by immediate contrast with the massive hill on which they

* The gallant, accomplished Suleiman, nephew to Aurungzebe, when delivered up to his murderous uncle by the treachery of the Rajah of Sininagurh, entreated the tyrant, in the most solemn manner, to award him any death rather than this slow and fearful consumption of life and spirit; to which his uncle answered, in the same solemn terms, that no evil was intended him. His apprehensions were too well founded; and if he ever believed the assurance of the monster, it must have added an additional pang to his lingering tortures.

stand, are here of the noblest dimensions and the most graceful form, being a long series of circular towers, closely connected by curtains of nearly similar height, and roofed-in with small domes of masonry; the whole having, in addition to shot-holes, embrasures, &c., an abundance of glazed windows, betokening the dwelling of rational creatures; while the masonry itself is adorned with glazed tiles, which, whatever their effect when recent, retain, at present, only those tints which become a venerable fabric, and that fabric of the Gothic style. The entire circuit of these defences appeared to me about three miles, their form an oblong rectangle. The summit of the height, as is usual in the sand formation, is nearly flat. The height of the precipice is about 200 feet, and the height from the foot of the precipice to the level of the town about 200 feet more, making a total height of about 400 feet.

In the steepest face of the cliff, at the north aspect and north-east angle, are several caves, probably communicating by subterranean galleries with the interior. One, in particular, contains a gigantic image of Pars Nath, distinctly visible from beneath. These caves may be convenient to the garrison during siege, but are extremely dangerous to the safety of the place, as a single ten-inch shell, would, by exploding within the cavity, in all probability, bring down the whole of the north-east angle, which is, even now, overhanging the perpendicular. They appear, however, to be intended as temples, rather than posts of observation.

The great facility of breaching, by means of mines, a fort thus constructed, renders it, in the hands of most native states, a mere bugbear in the face of an enterprising enemy. The Jats, however, would make a gallant defence in the breach of such a lofty eminence; and, in the hands of the English, famine alone, or failure in military supplies, could render it untenable; for the extent is too great to afford much fear from shells, and any imaginable breach in that cliff, with a crowd of armed Britons at the summit, would be an awful ladder to renown. These are considerations too much neglected by us in the present day. We find these forts yield to our arms almost without a struggle, and we attribute to defect of construction what is really due to the cowardice of the besieged. It is true that the plunging fire from their walls is not much to be dreaded, and that, without trenches, the operation of mining may at once be commenced beneath the cliff; but, on the other hand, the garrison are exempt from all molestation by the fire of the besiegers, excepting in the instance of their shells, and would thus be enabled to preserve their strength unbroken for the breach. Upon that breach not a gun could be brought to bear from below; and the neighbouring heights, all considerably depressed beneath the level of the works, and at no inconsiderable distance from them, would afford no position from which an effectual fire could be maintained, or from which a shot could be ventured during the assault; while the breach itself would, in all probability, be a steep hill-side, encumbered with massive fragments, sufficiently difficult to surmount in the absence of danger, and almost hopeless in the face of a determined enemy, who could not be molested in entrenching it. A sap carried up such a height would be a most arduous and desperate un-undertaking, and, unless some means of nightly escalade could be devised, the efforts of the besiegers would be sufficiently hopeless. We have seen and felt what it is to surmount a lofty wall of soft sand in the case of Bhurtpore, which is a mere mole-hill in comparison. So that, if the Government is desirous of preserving a few strongholds in the country, which were no unwise policy, it could scarcely do better than retain such hill forts as Gwalior, when they chance to fall into its hands. Of the city of Gwalior little need be said. With every facility for building at hand, it possesses few edifices that can attract the attention, and, for the capital of a large state, is very far below mediocrity in every respect, whether we regard the narrowness of its limits, the poverty of its streets and buildings, or the almost entire want of that appearance of busy traffic, which characterizes all important towns under the British Government. Indeed, there is little temptation to the import of merchandize into a country so infested with open robbers, and with every species of extortion, under the plea of customs.

The residency at Gwalior is a mean building, and scarcely, any sort of state has been kept up by the British representative. It has only been on the occasion of a visit of ceremony from the Governor-General to the Maharajah that the place has presented any scenes of pomp. Scindia kept up an army of semi-disciplined troops, 30,000 strong, officered by Portuguese and Eurasian gentlemen; but how this will stand after the present chaos has been reduced to order it is difficult to say.

Two hundred and sixteen miles to the north-east of Gwalior, and fifty-three miles from Cawnpore, is Lucknow, the capital of the decayed kingdom of Oude. It is a fine old Mahomedan town, where some vestiges of ancient pomp may still be traced, and when the king sits in state, a scene is presented not unlike that already described as occurring at Delhi. A resident, or ambassador, here represents British interests, and a force is kept up, officered from the line of the Bengal Army, which is charged upon the revenues of the Oude territory. There are very few made roads in the country, excepting a military road which connects Cawnpore with Lucknow. The cantonment of Oude is called Sultanpore, and is most easily accessible by the river Ghoomtee from Lucknow, on the north-west of Ghazepore; Benares and Juanpore on the south-east. The manners and customs accord with those of other parts of Hindostan. Wealthy Zemindars present small rent-free lands to Brahmins, sufficient to insure them the necessaries of life, which cost them little expense. These grantees do not cultivate the ground, but employ field labourers, being restricted by their caste from so doing. They are kind and indulgent masters, and usually assist their dependents with small pecuniary advances, especially at the celebration of marriages, which are conducted in the following manner:—The procession consists of the bridegroom's friends, the officiating pundit, and a set of dancing women, and on the third day accompanies the bridegroom to the bride's house, where the party remains three days. The bridegroom is carried in a palkee, either bought or borrowed; the whole ceremony occupies seven or eight days, and the expenses are divided equally between the fathers of the couple, who are about thirteen years of age, and sometimes older, but never below nine. The population of the towns and principal villages of Oude may be estimated at 650,000 souls, consisting of Hindoos and Mussulmans; the former of whom are in the proportion of three to two of the latter. The natives are naturally humane, and exhibit a love for justice and forbearance; but the principle of government, both in its protective and judicial functions, gives scope for cupidity, personal dislike, envy, vindictiveness, and all the worst passions of human nature.

Having now disposed of the whole of the places of any importance lying north-west of Calcutta, we bring back the reader to the British-Indian metropolis, and proceed thence to stations lying to the north, the south, the east, and the direct west, whither duty, business, or pleasure may carry him. It seems needless, however, to mention the names of *all* the intermediate stages, which consist of merely a village, or often of a single hut, the distances and the remarkable objects being the utmost that can possibly interest or serve the traveller.

Calcutta to Mulda (180 *miles*), *through Dum Dum, Barraset, Kishnaghur, Berhampore.*

Dum Dum, eight miles from Calcutta, is the head-quarters of the Bengal Artillery. It is a spacious cantonment, with an extensive *maidaun*, or esplanade, for purposes of parade, artillery practice, and review. Two thousand men can here be accommodated. There is an arsenal and laboratory, where the gunners are taught their duty, and where the ammunition, stores, implements, &c., required by the service, are prepared. The church is an elegant building, and contains the monuments of some officers who have distinguished themselves. The mess-house, to which is attached a spacious library and ball-room, is the finest building of the kind in India. The officers frequently entertain their Calcutta and Barrackpore friends here in unexampled good style. All artillery cadets, on their arrival in Bengal, proceed to Dum Dum, and undergo a certain amount of drill before they are detached to the Mofussil. Barraset was once a depôt for infantry cadets, but has long been abandoned, and is now a salt manufactory. Kishnaghur is a civil station. Many indigo factories are established here and in the neighbourhood; and missionary labour has found among the native population a fruitful soil. Printed muslins of a superior kind are manufactured here, though of a uniform colour, and these artisans have likewise acquired a reputation for their excellent models of figures illustrative of the great variety of castes and classes of the population of Hindostan. The figures are composed of rags and straw, covered with a coating of cement. Malda is a civil station; there are few residents, excepting the government officers and some planters. A few miles to the south of Malda, the antiquary will find matter of interest in the ruins of Gour, once the capital of Bengal. Its decline and abandonment were caused by the desertion of the Ganges, which formerly flowed beside its walls. About two hundred years ago, the course of the river took a new direction, turning off to a considerable distance from the place to which it had brought wealth and sanctity. To no part of the city, occupying a space of twenty square miles, does the Ganges now approach nearer than four miles and a half, and places formerly navigable are now twelve miles from the stream, which so unaccountably and capriciously forsook its ancient bed. The wild luxuriance of vegetation which characterizes Bengal has nearly choked up the magnificent remains of Gour; and the splendours of the city can only be estimated by a few majestic remains of mosques, towers, and gateways, which still exist to shew how deeply it was indebted to architectural taste and skill. The buildings of Gour were very solidly constructed of brick and stone. Vast quantities of the materials have been carried away and sold for building in the neighbouring towns and villages; but there are still masses of strong masonry scattered over the surface of the ground, which have been so completely covered with brushwood, and so intermixed with the gigantic roots of trees, forcing themselves through the rifts made by time and the elements, as more to resemble huge mounds of earth than the remains of human habitations.

Calcutta to Purneah (271 *miles*).

The usual route is to Malda in the first instance, whence the road is west for a few miles, then abruptly proceeding to the north. There is nothing remarkable in the scenery or places passed. Purneah is a civil station, and much indigo is manufactured in its vicinage. Much sport is afforded to the hog and tiger hunter of the station, and, in fact, the whole district swarms with game.

Calcutta to Dinagepore (356 *miles*).

To Purneah in the first instance, whence, eight stages across roads only moderately good. Small rivers occur at every stage, and are crossed by ferries or temporary bridges.

Calcutta to Darjeeling.

The dawk traveller may go as far as Dinagepore in the first instance, whence he may proceed due north, *viâ* Jarbarry and Titalya. But as Darjeeling is more a sanatarium for sick people from Calcutta who resort to it for a change of air, than a station, it is better to proceed by water up the Hooghly and Jellinghee, *viâ* Kishnaghur, to Beuleah, and thence to Berhampore. From Berhampore to Titalyah there is a carriage-road, and at the latter place a person in the employ of the Darjeeling Association supplies a palanquin, carriage, and ponies, which take the traveller to the foot of the hills. Here chairs borne by the Lepchas, a hill people, or ponies, are procurable for conveyance all the way to Darjeeling. It is advisable, however, to stop at Kursiong, to rest for a day or two. There is a hotel at Kursiong, and the scenery is sufficiently beautiful to tempt the visitor to linger for a time. Darjeeling is upwards of 7,000 feet above the level of the sea. The mean temperature is 24° below that of Calcutta. During the hot season of the plains it is a delightful place of resort, independently of its invigorating effects upon the sick. The scenery is superb; vegetation is so luxuriant, that the whole of the country, from the base of the hills to their summit, forms a forest, and the snowy range of the Himalayas is visible at no great apparent distance. There are a good many private residences built at Darjeeling, and an excellent hotel; but the comforts of life are necessarily expensive, as most of the supplies are obtained from Calcutta and the adjacent plains.

Calcutta to Rungpore.

Vide the route to Dinagepore, whence, in an easterly direction, the route runs for forty-three miles. Rungpore is one of the most northerly stations under the Bengal Presidency. The revenue and judicial duties are administered by three European covenanted and half a dozen native uncovenanted officers, of the extent of whose duties some idea may be formed when we mention that the district is 118 miles long, and 60 broad, containing 6,526 villages, and a population of 1,214,300 Mussulmans and Hindoos, chiefly the former. The manufactures are numerous, consisting chiefly of carpets, silk, indigo, and sugar. There are not less than fifty large and 400 small indigo factories.

East and east-north-east of Rungpore, a post and banghy road leads to Assam, where a commissioner with an adequate number of assistants, a large police force, and a small body of troops, maintains the integrity of the British frontier in that direction. The usual mode, however, of proceeding to Assam from Bengal, is by water, as there is a free communication between the Berhampooter and the Ganges, and boats of the largest burthen easily pass from one into the other. The valley of Assam consists of a rich soil covered with verdure and abundantly watered. Too much of the country, however, is still covered with jungle; and it will probably be many years before European capital and skill have cleared away the noxious vegetation and developed the wealth of the land. At present, European enterprise confines itself to the search for coal and caoutchouc, which are found in great abundance, and to the cultivation of the tea tree. The exports of the Assam Tea Company to England have already been considerable, and the quality of the tea has been well spoken of by the London tea-brokers.

Calcutta to Dacca (186 *miles.*)

The post and banghy road is in a straight line to the north-east of Calcutta, *viâ* Dum Dum, skirting the district of Kishnaghur, then passing through that of Jessore, crossing the Ganges at a place called Hurryranpore. There are nineteen stages on the route. The road is good, excepting from the ninth to the twelfth stages, and supplies are procurable the whole way in abundance. But land travelling is only practicable between the months of November and June; the inundations and the rise of the various rivers which intersect the road, rendering it impassable during the rains.

The trip from Calcutta is effected by means of

boats of large burthen at all periods of the year. Dacca is both a civil and a military station, and many indigo-planters likewise reside there, or in the neighbourhood. The following is the best description of the place that we have fallen in with :—

"The city of Dacca, with its minarets and spacious buildings, appears, during the season of inundation, like that of Venice in the West, to rise from the surface of the water, and, like the generality of native towns, presents an irregular appearance.

"The works and places of public utility, public buildings, institutions, and establishments, in the city and suburbs, are, ten thannahs or police stations, ten bridges across the Dallye creek, and its branch, which intersects the town; thirteen ghauts or landing places; seven ferry stations; twelve bazaars, in which the common articles of food are sold daily; three endaras or wells; the Magistrate's Cutcherry; the Judge's ditto; Collector's ditto; Revenue Commissioner's ditto; Moonsiff's ditto; Post-office (hence five branch mails are sent to Calcutta, also mails to Chittagong and Arracan; to Mymunsing, Jumalpore and Assam; to Sylhet, Cherra Poonjee, and to Burrisaul); the Cotwallee; the Jail; Jail Hospital; Lunatic Asylum; Native Hospital; Vaccine Establishment; Charitable Fund; St. Thomas's Church; Baptist Mission Meeting House; Roman Catholic Church; Armenian Church; Greek Church; one hundred and nineteen Hindoo places of worship; Government School; eleven Baptist Mission Schools; fourteen Hindoo and Mahomedan Schools; one hundred and eighty Mahomedan places of worship; Commissariat department; English, Armenian, and

Greek Cemeteries; Executive officer's Establishment; Commissariat office; Military Orphan Station Committee; Cantonment; Elephant depôt.

"Within an enclosure 200 yards square, and called the Chowra, are congregated the majority of the trades of Dacca; and innumerable petty shopkeepers here dispose of their caps, cotton and chintz dresses, hardware, fish-hooks, betel-nut-crackers, looking-glasses, seetul pattee, or cool mats for sleeping on, cane petarrahs for travellers, shoes of an infinite variety of patterns, cocoa-nuts prepared for hookahs, and the usual &c., &c.

* * * * *

"The principal part of the commerce of the city is confined to this square, which is perfectly surrounded by shops, and to the roads leading from it towards the southern part of the town, occupied by the military and civilians; a comparatively small space, running from the river backwards, not more than 350 yards.

"Such is the extreme unhealthiness of the cantonments, that fever is now an almost certain consequence of a residence within its boundaries; and hence officers attached to the corps on duty at Dacca, are permitted to live within the city. The houses of the Europeans were principally, if not wholly, built while Dacca contained the celebrated muslin factory; and although large, commodious, and upper-roomed, can only command a rent of from 60 to 135 rupees per mansion. Pretty little gardens are attached to most of them, and such as face the river Booree are certainly most desirable and pleasant residences.

"There is an Armenian church at Dacca. The floor of the interior of the building is divided into three parts: one enclosed by a railing, for the altar; a central portion, into which two folding-doors open; and another railed off, which is exclusively occupied by the women and children, has a gallery over it. The walls are disfigured by wretched prints of the Virgin Mary, &c. The altar stands in a semicircle, about four feet distant from the wall: it appears to be made of wood, and is raised, to the height of about ten feet, by steps. These steps sustain twenty-four wax-candles, each three feet long, and also a number of small crosses, of some gilt or shining metal.

"The floor of the verandah contains many tomb-stones, in memory of departed Armenian Christians, who formerly abounded in the city of Dacca, where they are still an influential and wealthy body. Within fifteen feet of the church, but quite separated, stands a coarse square tower, having four spiracles at its summit. At the base, within the square of the four walls, a few feet from the ground, a marble tablet has been placed in the wall, with an inscription, both in the Armenian and English languages, signifying that this *superb* and *magnificent steeple* was dedicated to the honour and glory of God, &c.

"Within the military cantonments are several very handsome upper and lower-roomed spacious houses, for which no tenants can be found. A large marsh diffuses deadly malaria close to the very edge, if not actually within the lines; and there are several tanks, which, no doubt, contribute their portion of the poison. During the rains, there is a quantity of stagnant water to the north of the cantonments, which dries up slowly during the cold weather.

"But the chief cause of the destruction of the city of Dacca is to be traced to the loss of the muslin trade, which has almost entirely disappeared. It is true that, by giving a commission, an extremely delicate article may be still procured, at the rate of 150 rupees, or £15 for ten yards; but at that rate, as may be readily imagined, little can be sold, as the demand must be necessarily very small.

"The working of shawl-scarfs with flossed silk is carried to great perfection, and many are despatched by banghy to Calcutta. Beautiful ear-rings and other ornaments, made of the purest silver, and of an infinite variety of patterns, can be supplied at a very short notice, and at reasonable prices.

"The suburbs of Dacca were formerly inhabited by thousands of families of muslin-weavers, who, from the extreme delicacy of their manufacture, were obliged to work in pits, sheltered from the heat of the sun and changes of the weather; and even after that precaution, only while the dew lay on the ground, as the increasing heat destroyed the extremely delicate thread. When the manufacture ceased, these pits were wholly deserted, and they are now filled with rain after every shower, which speedily becomes putrid, and favours the production of the rankest vegetation.

"The majority of the weavers have long since deserted Dacca, to seek employment in agriculture. The vacant ground has been in vain offered at the lowest rates to capitalists, who assert that the expense of bringing it into cultivation is so great, that they cannot secure any chance of profit. The consequence is, that within half a mile of the city there exists one of the most pestilential jungles in India; nay, the skirts of the city itself are beginning to bear the same appearance, from the scantiness of its rapidly diminishing population.

"The city contains a few rich and respectable indigo-planters, who, in addition to that manufacture, speculate in government lands, which they rent out to zemindars and ryots. A considerable time has elapsed since they introduced the coffee-plant; but they meet with innumerable difficulties and unforeseen obstacles in its culture, finding it almost impossible, by any arts of persuasion, to induce the natives to pay it the requisite attention in weeding, so as to make it a paying crop. There is no fault in the soil or climate, for the plant bears very abundantly, and the berry is of fair quality.

"The betel-nut trees produce very heavy crops, and they form one of the staples of the country. Many of the areas attached to native houses near the city may be seen almost choked with them. Its slender elegance commands admiration.

"Dacca has now but three manufactures worthy of the name, but they are very curious ones. The most important is that of violins. Great numbers are made and sold at the low rate of two rupees, or four shillings sterling! Few manjees, or steersmen of boats, leave the city without purchasing some, either on speculation or for their own private enjoyment during their tedious voyages. The sounds of the violin may be heard at all hours of the day and night. The Bengalees are, in fact, a highly musical people, as any one may discover by frequenting the streets of Dacca during the night; when, if you peep into a shop where an industrious mechanic is following his trade, you will most probably find another recreating himself, after his daily labour, either with a violin or a sarwegee, and occasionally singing to his own music, but never English airs. Groups may be also seen walking along, and singing to the utmost pitch of their voices.

"The second manufacture consists in the formation of bracelets, of different diameters, both for children and women; being sections of a sea-shell, called 'sunk,' evidently because they are found under water! Necklaces, called krantas, are also formed of the thick part of the same shell, enough to furnish almost the whole of the Bengal army. The former are cut by a half-moon-shaped saw, about three feet long, worked by the right hand, having a moveable edge, which is replaced when destroyed by long use. The shells are a species of univalve, strongly resembling, if not the *murax tulipa*, procured from Calcutta, where they are purchased at the cheap rate of two and a half annas per hundred. They are from four to seven inches long, vary in diameter, from two inches to two inches and a half thick, are very heavy, and in whiteness far exceed ivory. More than three hundred mechanics are constantly employed in this curious manufacture. The tribe occupy a whole street of the most picturesque and ancient houses in Dacca, running behind the Kotwallee, towards the area formerly the site of the Honourable Company's Presidency. The single houses in this street vary from ten to fifteen feet in breadth, and are from two to three stories. The narrow ones appear as if built of cards, and all are curiously decorated with Ionic, Doric, and Corinthian pilasters, supporting nothing, and such-like heathenish devices.

"The third manufacture, in a mercantile point of view, is hardly worthy of record; it is merely that of idols! They are made of a certain black stone, not quite three feet long, and very nicely polished. After receiving consecration from some priestly Brahmin, they are set up for public worship, as a rival to the living God. So accustomed are Englishmen to see such objects of worship, that they hardly ever elicit a remark."

From Dacca there is a post road to Sylhet, on the borders of Assam, where a political officer, supported by a couple of regiments, resides, for the conduct of the relations with the Munniporeans and other neighbouring chiefs. Due east of Sylhet are Cachar and Munnipore, states taken under British protection during the Burmese war, the former now constituting part of our possessions, and the latter in close and friendly alliance with our government. Above Sylhet rise the Cossya hills, the chief station in which, Cherrapoonjee, has become a sanatarium for sick people from Calcutta. Cherra, the station, is 4,200, and Cherrapoonjee, the village, 4,500 feet above the level of the sea. The climate is as salubrious and invigorating as that of Great Britain. Proceeding by dawk from Calcutta, the sanatarium may be reached in five or six days, but the voyage by water through the Soonderbunds occupies upwards of three weeks. The natives of the hills are a very savage race, but no molestation is ever offered by them to the European residents. The chief products of the country are fir-trees and limestone; but there are groves of orange-trees, the fruit of which is so abundant that two hundred may be obtained for a rupee.

Calcutta to Chittagong, Arracan, &c.

The results of the war with the Burmese placed the coast on the upper eastern side of the Bay of Bengal entirely in our possession; but it has not been deemed necessary to occupy more than four stations with troops. Communication with these stations is generally effected by sea, as the land route is circuitous. The latter runs *viâ* Dacca, whence the traveller proceeds southerly and westerly, crossing the Megna, at Bhowanygunge, and reaching Chittagong after a journey of 144 miles and four furlongs. The road is excellent, supplies profuse, and only two nullahs intersect the way. A commissioner resides at Chittagong, and one or two regiments are generally stationed there.

The possession of the province of Arracan has been of the utmost importance to the British Government, in a commercial and political point of view. The exports of rice and salt to Bengal, the Coromandel Coast, and the Tenasserim provinces, give employment to seven or eight hundred small vessels annually; while the position of the troops at Akyub and Khyonk Phoo enables us to watch and check the operations of the Burmese, when the caprice or bad faith of the sovereign of Ava threatens a descent, or other disturbances of existing relations. The manner in which Arracan is reached by sea is described in another part of this work, treating of sea travelling in India generally.

The population of Arracan, which includes two millions and a half of souls, may be divided into three classes: the Mughs, or proper Arracanese, and Burmahs; the Mussulmans and the hill tribes, the chief of which are the Koonrees; the Tong Moos, the Keangs, and Karains. There are also a considerable number of recent settlers from Bengal, both Hindoos and Mussulmans, but chiefly the latter. The kings of the country before the Burmese invaded it, about the year 1783, were Mughs, but in 1784 the royal family were carried off to Ava, from which time the country remained subject to the Burmese, until 1825, when they were expelled by the British forces sent from Bengal.

In disposition the Mughs and Burmese are frank, manly, and straightforward; they are also kind and hospitable, with much more of independence and good-nature than sycophancy or meanness in their bearing, and they are of an obliging and forgiving nature, but improvident and averse to labour, much given to gambling and drinking, and extremely passionate; the Burmese are particularly so, and very sanguinary; perhaps the greatest blemish in the character of both races is the unmerciful manner in which, when excited, they beat their wives, not unfrequently endangering their lives; nevertheless, they are not without affection, and both sexes are very fond of their children. The women are reckoned faithful, and are allowed to go about without any restraint—they are as industrious as the men are idle. The whole labour of the house falls upon them: they go to market, fetch the food, the water, and every necessary; they beat out the rice, cook the meals, make cloth for the whole family, and even assist their husbands in the field and in looking after the cattle.

The marriage tie is, however, held in but slight respect amongst the Mughs, and divorces for trifling causes are common. The Burmese regularly court their wives, and after the consent of the parents has been obtained, a day is fixed for the wedding, and all the friends and relatives of the parties are invited to a feast at the house of the bride's father; after the dowry has been settled, they all sit down to the feast, the bride and bridegroom eat out of the same dish, which binds the contract, and they are declared to be man and wife; the son-in-law often remains a member of the family till his wife desires a house of her own and he can afford one. The Mughs go through the same ceremony, with this difference, that when young, the match is made for them by their parents, and they never see each other till the marriage day; but widowers or grown-up lads do not attend to this, but generally choose for themselves.

When a divorce is sought for by both parties, nothing more is requisite than that they should go before a village assembly, and make a declaration of their wishes. Their property is then equally divided, and they separate, probably to rejoin as soon as some little feeling of anger subsides. When the husband wishes to separate from his wife against her will, he must give up all the property, and take upon him all her debts, and leave the house with nothing on but his gombong and dhootie; but should a woman seek a divorce from her husband, she has only to tender to him, before a competent judicial authority, the sum of twenty-five rupees, which by law he is in ordinary cases bound to accept, or at the utmost she returns her husband the ornaments he may have given her, also repays the sum of money he gave her parents on the wedding, which is usually all the cost to him of the marriage, and then the release is effected by the wife breaking a paun-leaf in two, eating one half herself, and giving the other to her husband.

Should there be any children, they are in all cases divided according to their sexes, the boys being given to the father, the girls to the mother. They are considered far from a burthen in a country where food is abundant, and a livelihood so easily obtained.

The Mughs have no fixed method of disposing of their dead; the more orthodox plan is to burn; the poor, however, usually bury them. The coffins, which are used alike in burning and burying, of persons of any substance, are in the shape of a sarcophagus, and if the family can afford it they are often richly ornamented with tinsel and so forth: in this the corpse, dressed in a new suit of clothes, is laid face downwards, a piece of gold or silver coin, or a jewel, being put in the mouth, the great toes and the thumbs are tied together, and if a female, six pieces of wood are laid on the back, if a male, only three.

When a female dies pregnant, she is not burnt, but buried, the child being first cut out of the womb and interred alongside of the mother; lepers, temple-slaves, suicides, victims of cholera, criminals, and all those considered unclean, ought to be buried, not burnt. The chief priests and men in power are generally embalmed, and their bodies preserved for some years, after which they are burnt with great ceremony; quicksilver is the principal ingredient used in cleaning the intestines; music and dancing take place at the funerals of those who can afford to pay for it, and a feast is given to the neighbours seven days afterwards, at which, although Bhuddists are prohibited the use of liquor on any occasion, it often happens that a scene of much dissipation and riot takes place. The day after the funeral, the family repair to the spot where the body has been burnt or buried, and spread food for the deceased.

The children are usually named three or four months after their birth. The astrologers fix the name and the day, and the parents give a feast, at which there is music, dancing, and great revelry.

At boring the child's ears, which takes place when ten or twelve years of age, the whole family and relatives also assemble, and there is great carousing and festivity; and when the boy goes to school with the priests, the whole family, and the majority of the villagers accompany him in procession, gaily dressed out in their very best, and attended with music. On the following day a feast is given to the priests and neighbours; but this is almost the only occasion on which intoxicating liquors are not introduced. On all these occasions those who can afford it give theatrical entertainments, which consist of an exhibition of puppets, who go through all the action of a play in the most natural and correct manner, whilst persons concealed behind the scenes deliver the dialogue, the action being admirably adapted to the same; a band of native music attends, and a stage, with foot-lights, is erected for the performance.

The people of Arracan, of whatever class or denomination, all live in houses, built of posts and bamboo mat walls, the flooring being raised four or five feet from the ground, and the roof made of bamboos and leaves.

Young men who are bachelors do not sleep in their fathers' houses, but each village has a separate building for the young men, where they sleep by themselves. They are fond of wrestling, dancing, and various games, especially of a kind of foot-ball, played with a spherical rattan wicker-basket, which they kick from one to another, or hit with any part of the body except the hands. Four or five good players will keep it in the air without its falling to the ground for several minutes.

Although forbidden to take the life of any animal, the Mughs and Burmahs pay as little attention to this commandment as to that against drinking. They are luxurious, but at the same time dirty in their eating, and there is scarcely any species of animal, from the elephant to the frog and snake, that the poorer classes will not eat, except dogs, cats, and rats, and even these the hill tribes eat readily, and it matters not whether the animal has died a natural death or been killed. Fish and the flesh of the superior animals, such as bullocks, deer, goats, &c., are much sought after; rice is the staple article of food with all classes, and the mess is rendered savoury by the addition of salt, agapee, or bala-choung (which is a compound of decayed shrimps and other small fish), chillies, ginger, turmeric, and numerous kinds of vegetables. These are arranged around the large dish of rice, in small China cups, and give to the repast a rather refined appearance; milk, oil, or ghee, are rarely partaken of. The favourite drink of the Mughs and Burmese is tarry, or the juice of a species of the palm, which also furnishes the leaves used in thatching their houses. It is sweet, slightly intoxicating, but harmless; strong spirits are also distilled from rice; all classes chew the paun and betel-nut mixed up with khut, tobacco, and lime; and so universal is the habit of smoking tobacco, that even children of four years old may constantly be seen with a cigar in their mouths.

Both men and women are robust in form, but they are not a handsome race; they are, however, fond of finery. The men usually wear a head-dress, or gombong, composed of book muslin twisted round, but not over the head, and it is often gracefully entwined with their long hair, which they prize so much that it is not uncommon for them to wear false hair; a jacket which is tied at the throat and closed over the chest and reaches half-way down the thigh, and a dhootie, often of brilliant-coloured silk, complete their costume. The women go with the head bare, but the hair is neatly braided off and tied in a knot behind; a red cloth is wrapt tightly round the bosom, from which descends a petticoat, which, in the case of Burmese, is generally very gaudily coloured, and open up one side, so that in walking, much of the leg and even thigh is often exposed. The petticoat of the Mugh women is usually less gaudy and more decent in its dimensions. They also wear a loose muslin jacket reaching to the middle, with tight sleeves and a gay cotton handkerchief thrown carelessly over the head or shoulder. The young girls are sometimes very pretty and always merry-looking.

The Mussulmans of Arracan are supposed to be the descendants of slaves imported from Bengal by the great people in early times, and one portion of them, called Kumuuchees, chiefly resident in Ramree, were formerly the body-guard archers of the Rajahs of Arracan; these have no knowledge of the use of the bow, and have become dyers in indigo, merchants, &c. The Mahomedans have retained the language and customs of their forefathers, but have adopted the dress of the country, particularly the becoming gambon, or head-dress, and wear their hair long, tied in a knot on the top of the head, like the Mughs and Burmese. They resolutely resist all attempts to make them shave their heads, but wear very goat-like beards, which the Mughs do not. They are respectable and industrious, and much more provident than the Mughs. All the regular fishermen are Mahomedans, and are generally wealthy.

The Koonrees, Taugmros, Kyengs, and Karains, are mountaineers living in a state of barbarism; they build their houses entirely of bamboos, and very high from the ground, and live in communities of from fifteen or twenty to forty or fifty families. They change the site of their village every second or third year as the soil on the hill sides in their neighbourhood becomes exhausted. They are frequently at war with each other, but such as have descended into the low country, and there occupy the isolated ranges of small hills, are very quiet and inoffensive people, though much addicted to drunkenness, for the gratification of which vice they distil a very potent liquor from rice. They are of a very roving disposition, and on the occurrence of any unusual sickness or misfortune, immediately remove the whole village to a new site. Their attachment to their native mountains is, however, very strong; and those who have been driven by the oppression of other tribes to seek a residence in the islands or the plains, even collect the ashes of their dead, and on the first opportunity, be it years afterwards, convey them back to their native country. Nothing will induce them to intermarry with any other people, or inhabit a Mugh village. In language, and indeed in every respect, they are a distinct people: they wear scarcely any clothing beyond a rag round the loins, and another round the head, and in cold weather the rich have a cotton wrapper or chudder over the shoulders; they have no religion, but worship nature and perform various ceremonies to propitiate the Nats or demons; they are not litigious, but very revengeful; and although in some instances a compromise may be effected for any injury, yet in general the loss of life can only be satisfied by taking the life of the offender. The women appear to have formerly set a high value on chastity, for they still adhere to a singular custom of making their faces quite blue by tattooing them in a frightful manner, which is supposed to have originated in a desire to disfigure their beauty, for which they are said to have been so celebrated, that they were eagerly sought after, and seized, as slaves and concubines, by their more powerful neighbours, who greatly esteemed them. The custom is said to have much declined since the introduction of British rule, and may certainly be very safely abandoned, for the mountain population are extremely ugly and abominably dirty: they eat and drink every thing that comes in their way, and are most perfect savages.

Amongst the Mughs and Burmese, slavery and bondage were tolerated in all shapes, but a few years ago every thing of the kind was abolished in Arracan; now all persons are free, or may be so on applying for release.

The established religion of Arracan, under the native sovereigns, was Bhuddism, and of Mughs and Burmese Bhuddists there are now about 206,000 in the province. They reject the immortality of the soul and the existence of a living God. They believe in the influence of superhuman powers, both of good and of evil, and expect after death repeated transmigrations, either for better or for worse, according to their conduct in this life, and ultimately entire absorption and cessation from all future troubles. They have no castes, and are free from bigotry; still, were a Bhuddist to eat with some of the lower castes of Hindoos, such as Dooms, sweepers, washermen, barbers, bearers, and some particular classes of their own creed, lepers, temple slaves, and unclean persons, they would be expelled from all society. All persons except the unclean are eligible to the priesthood, which is entered voluntarily and for indefinite periods; it is only necessary that votaries should renounce the world, assume the sacred garb, present the priests with fruits, &c., and obtain their permission to take up their abode in the Keoung or monastery; after which, they must lead the life of strict ascetics, eschewing all female connection and interference with secular affairs. The priests, or phoongees, trust entirely to charity for their daily subsistence: they cook no food for themselves, lest in so doing they should take the life of any animal, but they will eat food dressed by others. They do not actually beg, but they go forth daily into the streets and thoroughfares, which they traverse generally without stopping; and if food is given to them as they expect it will be, it is put into a basket usually carried by one of their pupils, and they pass on, counting their beads, without returning thanks or inquiring what caste person gave it. They are precluded taking money or any thing not purely essential to their support, or the ornament of the Keoung; they are usually followed by a string of youths, their disciples or scholars, some of whom carry the lacquered baskets for the reception of alms. They are clothed in a large yellow mantle, sometimes of silk or satin, folded loosely around them, passing over the left shoulder, and leaving the right arm and breast uncovered. They shave their heads and beards, wear no ornaments, and go barefooted. They are usually clean, remarkably civil, and well conducted, kind and hospitable to strangers, and are reputed to have more learning than any other class. They are, in fact, the gratuitous teachers of the land; all the boys being placed under them for the purpose of being taught to read and write. The priests generally act well up to their tenets in all their austerity; and as they may at any time leave the convent and marry, which is frequently done, it rarely happens that any scandal befalls them, for should a brother prove frail, he is quietly dismissed, and returns to the world without notice being attracted.

The Keoungs are usually most substantially and often beautifully built, and as a mark of distinction they have two or three roofs raised one above the other. Any person may visit the interior; they are generally well stocked with numerous images of Gautama of all sizes and materials, white and black marble, alabaster, wood, stone-clay, or copper, most of which are, either wholly or partially, gilt with gold or silver. Glass and metal vessels, with real and artificial flowers, and various other simple articles of ornament, are also seen arranged in front of the images: immediately over them there is usually a canopy of fine cloth ornamented with gold leaf and tinsel: and black wooden cases, the panelling of which is inlaid with little squares of glass of all colours surmounted by images of Gautama, and in which the priests keep their books and sacred records, occupy the back ground, and other parts of the hall. Hanging lamps, wall shades, crystal decanters, and such things, are also much sought after for the ornament of the Keoung.

In all the mountains and forests of Arracan, the elephant, tiger, leopard, tiger-cat, bear, deer of various kinds, and the wild hog, are to be found. The elephant is, however, scarce on the islands, and neither it nor the tiger is to be found on Cheedooba. The bos-gaurus, the wild buffalo, the sha, an animal something like the chamois, and a kind of wild dog or wolf, also a species of racoon, the wild cat, the balla soor, and a kind of civet, are found in the hills. There are no jackals, hares, or foxes, but asses and monkeys of numerous kinds inhabit the jungles. Of birds, there are nearly all that are common to Bengal, with some beautiful kinds of pheasants, including the argus species. The snakes and other reptiles seem, also, to be much the same as in other parts of India, but are not particularly numerous or troublesome; and of fish there is an abundance of all the kinds usually found in tropical seas and rivers—the shark, crocodile, alligator, saw-fish, turtle, sole, pomfert, mullet, rock-cod, skate, sword-fish, bumaloe, cockup, crabs, lobsters, shrimps, oysters, cockles, periwinkles, and various others, are in great perfection. The Mughs enumerate more than 200 kinds of fish.

The botanical productions of Arracan are but little known. The bamboo everywhere covers the hills and the lower ranges of mountains; teak and a species of oak are also found amongst the hills, but both are rendered valueless, as are many other magnificent timbers, the names of which are unknown, from the distance at which they grow from good water-carriage; the red and white jarrool, praing (a kind of iron wood), the toon, sissoo, telsur (which yields dammer), gurjun (from which oil is extracted), the semel or cotton (silk) tree, peepul, and all the common trees of India, abound; likewise several kinds of palms, from one of which (the nippah) the liquor called tarree is extracted; sugar, also, may be made from it, and the leaves are universally used as covering to the houses. The mangrove, which is valuable as fuel, especially for steam purposes, is most abundant, and long grass covers the waste plains. Iron is found on the island of Ramree, and so are coal and lime.

Calcutta to Cuttack (247 *miles*).

Cuttack is the southernmost station under the Bengal Presidency. The road, which is a continuation of the great Benares line, leads to Pooree, the seat of the Temple of Juggernauth, and a delightful place of resort for sea-bathers from Calcutta. Cuttack, from its vicinity to the sea, and the total absence of all vegetation, is one of the most agreeable and healthful stations in India. The society is small, consisting, as it does, of a few civilians and a small proportion of military; but the contiguity of Cuttack to other small stations renders a considerable re-union of visitors a matter of no great difficulty. The finest salt in India is manufactured on the coast of Cuttack, yielding the Government a revenue little short of eighteen lacs of rupees. The produce, distinguished for its whiteness and purity, before it has passed into the hands of the merchant, is of the species called pangah, procured by boiling. The process observed by the molunghees, or manufacturers, is rude and simple to the last degree. The sea-water, which is brought up by various small channels to the neighbourhood of the manufacturing stations, or khalaries, is first mixed up and saturated with a quantity of the salt earth, or efflorescence, which forms on the surface of the low ground all around, after it has been overflowed by the high tides, and which, being scraped off by the molunghees, is thrown into cylindrical receptacles of earth, having a vent underneath, and a false bottom made of twigs and straw. The strongly impregnated brine filtering through the grass, &c., is carried, by a channel dug underground, to a spot at hand, surrounded with an enclosure of mats, in the centre of which a number of oblong earthen pots, generally about two hundred, are cemented together by mud in the form of a dome, under which is a fire-place, or oven. The brine is poured into this collection of pots, or choolas, and boiled until a sufficient degree of evaporation has taken place, when the salt is taken out, as it forms, with iron ladles, and collected in heaps in the open air. The heaps are afterwards thatched with reeds, and remain in this state until sold or removed by the officers of the agency.

There is little trade carried on from Cuttack; but in seasons of great scarcity, and on the occurrence of the furious gales and inundations to which the coast is peculiarly exposed, large importations of grain, rice, &c., take place.

The great Temple of Juggernauth, at Pooree, presents, from the sea-view, an imposing appearance; it is, on a close inspection, neither remarkable for its architecture nor the materials of which it is composed, the latter being rough stone, overlaid with a coating of coarse chunam. The Khek, chief tower, and other minor buildings connected with it, are comprised within a wall surrounding a platform, raised high above the ground, and no less than 650 feet in length: the height of the tower is 200 feet. According to ancient Brahminical records preserved in the building, the Temple of Sri Jeo, or Juggernauth (some writers spell the word without the h), existed many centuries before Christ; was destroyed and rebuilt sundry times, and was lastly restored A.D. 1198, by Rajah Bhim Deo of Orissa, who is said to have expended nearly £500,000 on the work! Within its holy precincts many inferior deities are provided with lodgings and attendants; but the most revered of the divine occupants are Juggernauth (the Lord of the World), an *alias* of the many-named Vishnu, Buldeo (his brother), and their sister, the saffron-coloured Subhadra.

The average number of pilgrims who annually resort to Pooree is said to be 120,000; many of whom are destined never to return. Thousands of these poor wretches die from famine or over-fatigue during the journey. Many of these fanatics actually *crawl* from great distances to this, the Mecca of their hopes.

Immense numbers are also destroyed by the pernicious climate of the rainy season; and their corpses, which are thrown on the sands, near the English station, are either burnt or left to be devoured by the troops of Pariah dogs, jackals, and vultures, with which this place, so rich in food for them, swarms. It is said, that in the space of half an acre of ground, as many as 150 bodies have been seen, with twice as many of the before-mentioned scavengers fighting over their horrid feast. The grand ceremony of the installation of the idol on his triumphal car (which is called Rath Jatra) takes place in June. The usual influx of pilgrims at this epoch is enormous; but their numbers decrease yearly, and the sanctity of Juggernauth wanes in proportion to the progress of civilization in India. The mad fanaticism which formerly led hundreds of voluntary victims to immolate themselves beneath the wheels of the idol's car is now much sobered down.

The temple is enclosed by a high stone wall, square, about 250 yards each way; gates are in the middle of each face, which look to the cardinal points. The eastern, or lion door, is the principal entrance, and is guarded by two stone animals, which the most depraved imagination has denominated lions. The gateways all rise in a pyramidal shape, with rude sculpture and the portraiture of hideous figures. On looking through the eastern gate, the entrance for pilgrims, the only thing to be seen is a broad flight of steps, which leads to the temple. A handsome black stone pillar, the shaft of one piece and twenty-five feet long, stands immediately before the entrance. It is one of the most chaste and elegant pieces of art ever seen, and is said to be equal in design and proportion to any pillar of the Corinthian order.

The grand temple in which the idols are lodged is a very high tower in the middle of the square, and, as before observed, from its great elevation, it forms a conspicuous landmark to sailors coming from different parts of the world. Its form is square for the distance of two-thirds, from whence it decreases by a slight curve to the top; thus it follows the usual configuration of Hindoo temples; it is also fluted in this part. On the top of this is a large circular, flat, black stone, cut like a melon. On the summit of this stone is the *chucker*, or wheel—the distinguishing symbol of Vishnu, and precisely resembling the wheel of a ship's rudder. The whole is surmounted by flags and pennons of the appropriate colours of the god in whose honour they are displayed.

The modes are various by which the devotees conceive they render their piety more striking and propitiatory.

The great ceremony is that of the *Rath Jatra;* but a minor and prefatory ceremony is that of bathing the idols. Their godships are formed up in line, on an elevated terrace within the enclosure, and protected from the night dews by an extensive and gaudy canopy of many-coloured cloths. They consist of three frightful wooden faces, of the respective colours of black, brown, and yellow; the lower portions of the figures being closely swathed in cloth wrappers.

The following day the idols are consigned to their respective niches in the temple. Upon this occasion it is the annual custom for Juggernauth to declare himself to be *en petite santé,* from the effects of a severe cold, consequent, probably, upon his bath, which continues to afflict him until the day of the grand ceremony, when, by the wise treatment of his physicians, he is restored to his usual good health!

To such a length as this is carried the blind superstition of this simple people; and it is carefully nourished and fostered by the crafty Brahmins, who doubtless secure to themselves a large share of the offerings paid at the shrine of the idolized but helpless King Log. At the festival of the Rath Jatra, the idols are conducted in state to visit their country-seat, one mile and a half from Pooree; a journey of three days. By all accounts, the matter of inducting their worships from the temple to their raths or cars is not remarkably ceremonious. Ropes being fastened round their throats, they are dragged "neck and heels" down the grand steps through the mud, and are finally hauled by the same gallows-like process into their respective vehicles, where they are decorated by the priests, and welcomed by shouts of admiration and triumph from the fanatical multitude. The raths on which the monster-deities are drawn are of lofty and massive dimensions and clumsy architecture; that of Sri Jeo is nearly forty-five feet in height, has a platform of thirty-five feet square, and moves upon sixteen wheels of solid timber.

The *Black Pagoda* is situate sixteen miles north of Pooree, near the village of Kauarac. It was built by Narsing Deo Langora, Rajah of Orissa, in A.D. 1241; but other writers attribute its erection to a much earlier date. In its ancient days of celebrity it was designated the Temple of the Sun, and was dedicated to his worship, under the title of Suriga, in consequence of that deity having cured the son of Vishnu of leprosy, with which he was infected as a punishment for having seen (accidentally) some young ladies of the palace (but whose palace the record saith not) during the operation of bathing. What remains of the building is the pagoda, or square building, the sides to the cardinal points; the walls are fifty feet high, and of amazing thickness. From thence upward the roof is an exact pyramid, on the apex of which are the remains of some symbol of the god. The pyramidal part is divided into compartments, each overhanging the other, like the roof of a Chinese temple, flat and decreasing to the top. The part still most perfect is the inferior tower, and is called the Jug Mohun.

The sanctuary in which the idol was lodged is almost destroyed; what does remain marks a freak in the operations of time, or whatever is the destroying power. The sanctuary was in the shape of a tall tower, exceeding in height the other part of the temple. From half-way down it had a slight curvature and terminated in a point. Only one quarter of this building is still erect; the other three are prostrate in indistinguishable ruin; it seems as if the tower had divided in half and then cross-wise, cutting it into four pieces. When the three parts fell it was difficult to account for the fourth retaining its perpendicular; but the time is not far distant when it will soon follow the others, now at its feet. From the altitude of the Black Pagoda, and its contiguity to the sea, it is a conspicuous landmark for seamen.

The temple is chiefly formed of a stone easily affected by time and the elements; though about the doorways there is a remarkably hard greenish stone used. The eastern, or principal, entrance has had the greatest share of ornamental labour. There is an entablature over this gateway, sculptured in the most excellent manner, both in design and execution.

Foliage is springing up in its crevices, and will soon lay its glories in the dust. A complete shrubbery has grown upon the summit of the temple, which was once graced with the Leer Chucker, or blue wheel of Vishnu. An absurd notion prevailed among the Hindoos of the temple having a load-stone on its top, which attracting the ships passing, drew them to destruction. Some desperate foreigners, having suffered a like catastrophe, stormed the pagoda and carried away the magnet. The sanctuary being thus defiled, the shrine was deserted by the Brahmins, and many of its ornaments removed to the temple of Juggernauth.

In the north-west of Cuttack lie certain districts inhabited by hill tribes, who were in a state of revolt against the authority of the British Government so far back as 1832-33, but who are now obedient subjects. The country is termed the Colehan—the people the Coles. A political commissioner resides in the territory, and a corps of local infantry is placed at his disposal. The upper boundary of this tract of country forms the south-west frontier of the possessions subordinate to the Supreme Government.

BOMBAY.

Although secondary to Madras in respect to the extent of territory subordinate to the local government, and consequently inferior in the magnitude of its public establishments, army, revenue, &c., Bombay has become, since the establishment of a regular monthly communication with England *viâ* the Red

Sea, a more important presidency than its neighbour. We therefore assign precedence to it in our order of description.

Externally, Bombay is particularly attractive. As the bay is entered, the passenger beholds on either side mountains rising apparently at no great distance marking the western boundaries of the vast continent of India. To the left, and within half a mile of the ordinary anchorage, is the island of Bombay, fronted by a fortress bristling with guns, and forming the enclosure to the town. The steeples of two churches, a Protestant cathedral and a Scotch chapel, are the only architectural objects that rise above the mass of buildings, but sufficient is seen of the private houses running landward to indicate the wealth and populousness of the place. Large and commodious boats resembling the famous Deal boats, and here called *bunder* (or pier) boats, quickly come off for the conveyance of passengers ashore, and if the new arrival has been expected, and his or her reception arranged, it does not unfrequently occur that a head servant, or purvoe, is the bearer of a note containing a special invitation to the house of some respectable resident. As yet, Bombay has made but little progress towards the establishment of good hotels or boarding-houses. The hospitality for which British India was at one time proverbial, therefore continues in full force on this picturesque island. It does, however, happen that a party arrives at the presidency without the introductions that will ensure him a reception within a private domicile, or, having them, he may find the spare rooms of his friend pre-occupied, or the host himself absent from town. Under such circumstances, he has only the choice of an indifferent hotel (even while we write it may, such is the progress of improvement, have become a comfortable establishment), or of a tent upon the esplanade. Between the south-westernmost point of the Fort and the seashore, a corner of the esplanade, or plain, which stretches across the entire land-face of the fortifications, is appropriated to an encampment for the accommodation of strangers, or residents who prefer the sea breezes and a canvas habitation to the stifling heat of the close and dusty town. A word to one of the dubashes, a superior sort of *valet de place* and cicerone, who presents himself on board most newly arrived vessels, will ensure to the passenger, within twenty-four hours, a comfortably furnished tent and a small retinue of servants, at an expense not greater than will be incurred at the hotel, and with the advantage of perfect seclusion and independence. The cadet or the Queen's officer, however, whether introduced or not, is relieved of these cares for his personal comfort, as the superintending officer who has charge of the former provides immediate quarters for the newly arrived, and the latter invariably receives an invitation from the regiment quartered in the town, or Fort George Barracks, to accept the hospitalities of the mess, and is put into appropriate apartments by the barrack-master. Once landed, the stranger commences *life in India*, and as we have spoken of this very fully at pages 202 to 227, little need be said upon that score in this place. Still, as every town in India has its peculiarities and distinctive features, it may not be amiss, in view to the completeness at which a guide-book should aim, to give a portion of the latest description that has been published of a city which is now resorted to each month by scores of persons from England, who either proceed thither to take up their residence, or to join the services to which they may have been appointed. A writer in the *Asiatic Journal*, speaking of "Bombay in 1843," gives a sketch of manners and customs which does not essentially vary from the usages of Europeans at Calcutta; but the article proceeds to depict the shops, &c., in a style so graphic that it is worth transplantation here:—

"There is neither a theatre nor a concert-room in Bombay; this, perhaps, is fortunate, as late hours are destructive to health in a tropical climate. Still, much time might be agreeably passed, if music, as an accomplishment, were more cultivated—for it would increase sociability, and win many from less graceful pastimes; but, unfortunately, all the machinery of the fine arts is procured with difficulty, and it is therefore only among persons of extraordinary energy that their practice is continued. Bombay, indeed, possesses shops, and they deserve notice as a portion of its physiognomy; but the high charges and paucity of supplies, confined also to what is most commonly on demand, render them ill calculated to give a stimulus to the arts. In proof of this, let us imagine ourselves to have entered one of the principal shops, and the scene will afford a fair sample of their contents, and will also shew how inefficient they are to gratify taste, or to satisfy the numerous wants of civilized life.

"The Parsee master, attired in a white cotton garment, and pointed head-dress of glazed chintz, meets the visitor at the door, and with something more grave than a nod, yet scarcely graceful enough to be called a bow, ushers him along between a double row of glass cases; less, certainly, but of the same form as those which English gardeners use for raising cucumbers. These are locked; but as soon as the article sought for is supposed to be seen, the Parsee produces from a large pocket in the side of his dress a small bunch of keys, when something remembered to be in fashion or invented ten years ago is laid before the purchaser. Nothing of the kind can carry disappointment farther than a Parsee shop, where, in lieu of the improvements of modern times, where the highest degree of convenience is the object desired by the manufacturer, are to be found articles only of the most cumbrous kind; the mechanism, where any exists, totally deranged, and the intrinsic value consequently lost. The poor Parsee, however, knows little of all this, and prices his various goods with amusing inconsistency, making all pay for his bad debts and damaged wares.

"A very excellent chemist's shop is established in the fort, which disseminates the blessing of soda-water over the whole presidency. But the most important want is that of a boot and shoe maker, notwithstanding that there are two well-meaning but very incapable persons, father and son, natives of the Celestial empire, who wander from house to house, with white coats, red slippers, straw-hats, flat features, and long plaited hair, holding in their hands little bundles, containing silk and satin shoes intended to fit everybody, and consequently fitting nobody. These worthy Crispins receive orders, and with bad leather, coarse linen, and paste in abundance, essay their execution, the result being, that the public pay for their want of skill, in the penalty of uneasy or distorted feet.

"Two or three Portuguese have libraries in the fort —dark, dismal places, containing a few standard and elementary works that no one ever reads, and which certainly cannot rank with either cheap or entertaining literature; but then, for reference, there is the splendid library of the Town Hall; and for purchase, the scattered volumes of a Borah's basket, purchased at the sale of an officer's effects, or perhaps bartered by a new arrival for a packet of Windsor soap, or a new bridle for his cream-coloured tattoo. The Borah, like the reader of a circulating library, values books according to the lateness of their date of publication; he learns the title-pages by rote, and sets a store upon illustrations, quite indifferent whether they are of John Gilpin or the Book of Beauty.

"In olden times, before steamers brought out crowds of ladies attired in Parisian fashions, and before it was considered necessary to send to England for regular supplies of tasteful attire, the Borahs, who purchased vast quantities of goods strangely thrown together in the lots of a hurried auction, arranged at the instigation of the master of a Liverpool brig, were looked to for all that was required, from a paper of pins to a ball dress. But things have changed, and Borahs are daily becoming of less repute; their taste is questioned, their fashions laughed at, and their self-importance shaken; still, one or two retain their *entrée* to the morning room, and many beautiful women in Bombay still owe much of their attire to a 'Borah's basket.'

"One Borah was accustomed almost daily to make his appearance in a bullock-garee (cart), well covered-in, and containing three or four parcels of rich merchandize. In one was displayed a rich pile of Cashmere shawls and Delhie scarfs; in another, fine muslins and pretty China silks; in a third, chintzes, calicoes, crapes, and woollens. Very probably you care not for any of these things: the fat Borah wipes his brow and beckons to a cooley, whispering a word in his ear; the man disappears, but soon returns; in his hand is a small mahogany box, which he hands to his master; the Borah seeks a key, it opens, and a blaze of jewels, some of great value, glitters before the eyes of the sorely-tempted; rubies, emeralds, sapphires, and diamonds, some well set, others in their native state. Sometimes, with humbler aim and smaller capital, laces and bobbins form the stock in trade of a simple-minded Borah; but sometimes, again, the itinerant trader deals largely in pearls, bringing with him a capacious box, containing thousands, loose and undrilled, large and small together, selling them by weight; you take up a handful, and the owner looks calmly on, as if they were grains of corn.

"Next appears the vender of coral, jasper, and cornelian; of ivory boxes and inlaid watch-stands; but only the newly-arrived or the speedily-departing patronise them much. It is otherwise, however, with the general or "chow chow" Borah, as he is called, for his soap, pickles, whips, vinegar, cotton socks, eau-de-cologne, essence of ginger, and orange marmalade, find ready purchasers everywhere.

"As I have said, the time is at hand when the trade of the Borahs will cease. They are a distinct feature in the physiognomy of Bombay, however, and as such their loss will be regretted; for though their eau-de-cologne is little better than spirits of wine, their calico too often rotten, and their Scotch marmalade the production of Surat, yet the Borah is a character, and one often possessing a great fund of drollery and good-nature. This is particularly displayed at times when the Borah is required to exchange, as well as to sell goods; this arrangement being also part of his calling, and commonly conducted in a way that is replete with amusement to the looker-on. The Borah will purchase any thing, animate or inanimate—blankets, mathematical instruments, goats, or horses. Occasionally, an old pony is exchanged for a pair of pistols, or a much-worn copy of Chaucer for a new tandem whip, when a great deal of raillery is frequently carried on between the buyer and seller; for public indulgence allows much latitude to the Borah among those to whom his character and calling afford constant amusement during the leisure hours of a hot day in India.

"The horse-dealers are also among the characteristics of Bombay. In the centre nearly of the great bazaar, the stranger observes a long row of thatched buildings, surrounded by a mud wall; these are the Arab stables, and here is centred a considerable portion of the happiness of the male community.

Lounging on benches outside the wall, are to be seen the dealers, chatting with their Persian friends, who are usually moonshees, in the employ of the European officers, or merchants in the town; the costume of the horse-dealers consists of under-garments of white cotton, over which are robes with hanging sleeves, in colour either pale, blue, or orange, with handsome waist-shawls and crimson slippers; their turbans are commonly of striped silk and cotton, tasselled like the handkerchiefs of the Bedouins, and beneath these, gleam eyes radiant with the cunning which accompanies an intimate knowledge of their peculiar calling.

"When a boat-load of horses arrives fresh from the Persian Gulf, nothing can exceed the excitement produced amongst the racing members of the Bombay Society, with that of the hunting portion of the world generally who may chance to be for the time at the presidency. The horses, from having been stowed closely together, much as the poor Africans are described to be on board a slaver, with little food, less water, and no exercise, lose all their beauty of appearance, and are commonly reduced to mere bone and muscle; the experienced eye, however, judges better of them in this state, roundness of form being quite unnecessary for shewing the real power or symmetry of a high caste Arab; therefore, as soon as the 'dow' discharges its cargo, the sporting men hurry to the stables, and make an immediate selection, frequently paying three or four hundred pounds for what, to an unskilled eye, might seem but the diseased frame-work of a horse. After this, the Arab dealers exert all their skill to pass off at the best prices the nags that are considered unworthy to contest the glories of either the turf or the 'jungle-side,' and this they effect with admirable jockeyship. Being all excellent riders (for clinging to a horse seems not a matter of acquirement, but of nature, with an Arab, like a sixth sense), a servant of the stables will fling himself on the bare back of the most vicious animal in his master's possession, perhaps, and with tangled locks, and garments wildly flowing, gallop him backwards and forwards, while the uninitiated and hoped-for purchaser wonderingly looks on, convinced that the heavy-shouldered, hatchet-headed, zebra-striped brute before him must be the perfection of high caste and fine temper, to be so managed with a single rope-bridle and the spur of a bare heel; and in this spirit the dealer persuades his victim to give a large sum for a horse that runs away with him the first day he mounts him, and kicks him off the second. The deluded purchaser seldom likes to acknowledge this, and the dealer, therefore, hears no more of him: the dupe of his skill hastens to barter the ill-conditioned animal with a friend, and, as 'doing business,' as it is called, is a great amusement among the young men in India, the matter is soon arranged, and the original purchaser gets rid of the horse for, perhaps, a clever pony, a 'Macintosh,' and a dozen or two of pale ale, and, after all, when in experienced hands, the horse often turns out a valuable hunter, and earns great reputation.

"The sportsman ever dislikes Bombay; for, beautiful as the island is, with its rocky mountain scenery, and dense jungles along the coast, studded with the cave temples of an ancient superstition, it is not a country that can be ridden over; and although some species of game are to be found in abundance about the underwood of Salsette, and the back of the island itself, yet the marshy character of the ground, and its ill reputation for malaria, cause shooting to be avoided, even by the most zealous sportsman. Bombay itself, before our occupation of it, was a mere swamp, covered with jungle, abounding with wild beasts, and studded with magnificent temples, carved, like those of Petra, in the living rock, while it was inhabited by a class of Hindoos of whom little is now known; in the present day it is well drained, and rice is abundantly grown in its low grounds; yet Nature will sometimes prove herself the stronger, and so in Bombay, about the woods of Mahim, the jungles of Salsette, and even nearer still, around the very bazaar itself, in the outskirts of the native town, the same original character exists. In healthy situations, in Bombay, Europeans appear to retain their health better than at out-stations, which may, perhaps, be attributed to good water, and the refreshing influence of the sea-breeze; but it is remarked, that they soon lose the healthy look which those have been able to retain who remain at the out-stations, while they have a more generally delicate and pallid appearance.

"The damp, relaxing climate, and the comparatively luxurious habits of living at the presidency, may have something to do with producing this effect; for although part of the green, near the Esplanade, forms a cricket-ground, and there is a good racket-court at the entrance of the bazaar, few of the old residents avail themselves of such means of exercise, being content with that afforded by an easy palanquin or well-appointed carriage; while, at an out-station, horse-exercise and hunting form the chief recreation of life, and tend to balance the evils of hot winds, sand-storms, and other miseries to which people are there subject.

"Few things can afford more interesting or picturesque effects than the great bazaar, beginning with the gay, open Esplanade, its pretty bungalows and animated groups, with the fort and bay in advance, and ending with the dark cocoa-nut woods, speckled with the handsome villas of the European gentry.

"The beautiful Parsee women, with their gay green and orange-coloured sarees, chatting at the wells to the graceful, handsome sepoys, whose high caste compels them to draw water for themselves; the crowded ways, peopled with professors of almost every known creed, and natives of almost every land; the open shops, filled with goods to suit all tastes, 'corn, and wine, and oil,' in their literal sense, with women's bracelets (a trade in itself), culinary utensils, and fair ivory work; the gorgeous temples, beneath whose porticoes young girls weave blossoms of fresh flowers; the quaint, though barbarous, paintings that deck many of the exteriors of the houses;* the streets devoted to the cunning

* Colonel Davidson has given a most amusing and just description of these paintings :—

"The fashion of this painting is something as follows, though I fear I shall not be able to give a good idea :—An Englishman, of immense bulk ('for that,' as Dousterswivel says, 'is essential') is impaled on the edge of an English-built chair, in a grotesque military caricature dress of black, red, and brown, with a round hat, and smart black cockade, holding a stick in both hands, in the most resolute and determined manner; or, work of gold and silver; the richly-carved decorations: the variety of costumes that meet the eye, and the languages that fall upon the ear; the native procession that stops the way; the devotee, performing his unnatural penance; the harmonies of light and colour; the rich dresses; the contrasts of life and character—such as the stately yet half-nude Brahmin, the intoxicated English sailor, the dancing-girl, and the devotee, with the intermediate shades—each, and all, to the reflecting mind, are full of interest; and although, towards twilight, the bazaar is deeply shadowed, and the fresh breeze reaches it not,—although the dust rises in clouds, the air is stagnant,

he has a stick in one hand, and a wine-glass half-full of red wine in the other; with a row of three or four servants, all gradually ascending into the air, with yak (or Tartarian cow) tail in their hands, and one of them insinuating a hooka snake through the arm-chair elbows; or, a band of nautch-girls, of terrific beauty, with large black eyes, each three inches long, surrounding a well-dressed and mustachioed rajah, over whose head are flying tremendous nondescript animals, half-carp and half-scorpion! The rajah is seated on a large square charpoy, or bed, the fore-feet of which are on the ground and the hind in the sky, and is evidently smitten, not only with the nautch-girls, but also with the music of a gentle swain, who discharges a torrent of sound through a fife with two holes, which he holds in his hands from right to left. The huzoor's countenance, however, is as immovably tranquil as that of Boodh; and he appears to enjoy the most serene complacency of mind, while two of his faithful sepoys in the rear are killing an enormous tiger, with a full mouth of teeth, in the most masterly and ingenious manner; one kneeling, and covering his head with a shield, while the other, seeing the brute's attention thus happily diverted, leaps on his back, and coolly cuts him up to kabobs! Meanwhile, peacocks, monkeys, alligators, and carps, are hovering in mid-air, with the most wasteful profusion! The lower-story windows and gateways are painted in flowers, and compartments to resemble mosaic, and have a very lively and pretty effect. The favourite colours are bright yellow, crimson, pea-green, and blue."

and the native drivers care nothing for the right of road, pressing to either side as suits them best, causing irritation, suspense, and danger to all whom they encounter; still, the Bombay bazaar outbalances, in interest, all its worst annoyances, and is, in its peculiarities, *unique.*

"The number and variety of persons who now arrive monthly at the Bombay presidency lessen most materially the interest of new arrivals. Bachelors, weary of their state, no longer hurry down to catch the first glimpse of a new belle; nor does the solitary officer, on outpost duty, pen an elaborate proposal of marriage to a lady he has never seen, lest some happier man anticipate his hopes. A ship may arrive from London, and some individual, who has a box of millinery or of saddlery on board, is charmed at the news, and by the same day's post writes to his agents about her; but here it ends; there is no general interest felt. A Liverpool brig comes into port, and no kind husband hurries on board to secure the prettiest bonnet in the captain's cargo for his wife; nor do ladies' hearts beat more quickly at the prospect of seeing London fashions of only six months' date; all this is changed, or changing: steam is exerting its influence on the whole character of India, and of its European society. There is now no longer a want of interest on literary or other subjects. English periodicals and newspapers arrive in Bombay almost damp from the press.

"Such is some portion of the good which rapid communication is effecting for the European society of India, and of Bombay particularly; but the greatest and most valuable is that which we may expect it to produce on the opinions of the native population.

"The Parsees are the most progressive and also the most positively enlightened people among the natives of Western India, owing to their freedom from the shackles of caste, and the commercial zeal which brings them more acquainted with foreign habits and society; and the effect is, that several of the Parsee gentlemen, with the exception of their costume, and some strict ideas about the seclusion of their women, differ little from Europeans in the liberality of their views and their anxiety for public good."

Of the government of Bombay, the army at its disposal, &c., we have already (pages 67 and 99) given a full account. Its police establishment, municipal laws and regulations, &c., differ in scarcely any respect from those of the metropolis of Eastern India. We have likewise spoken of its press, ecclesiastical establishment, &c. A few words upon the subject of the state of native education may be added.

The advantages of rapid communication between Europe and Asia do not end by merely affording with readiness the means and appliances for gratifying private tastes, or presenting materials for agreeable converse. They awaken that powerful, necessary, and mutual interest between the countries, which the enormous distance which separated them by the olden track, seemed to render hopeless. Our men of science in the East may now be speedily assisted and encouraged in their labours from home; and the *savans* of Europe be instructed and delighted with discoveries, the necessary energies required for which being excited and strengthened by a ready correspondence with the learned communities of Europe. Our Indian branch societies are thus nourished and protected by the parent roots; without whose support they must long have languished in their original weakling condition. The native society is elevating itself, by means of newly-acquired intelligence, to a point which must soon lead to the desirable object of mutual appreciation between European and native talent, and a desire on the part of the most intelligent among the people, that their sons should obtain, by means of an English education, similar information to that which, through the medium of unreserved intercourse with us, they discover we possess.*

The groundwork for so desirable a superstructure as the perfect civilization of the native gentry, is already laid by the college and schools which have lately been so warmly protected by the general society of Bombay.

These institutions (the Elphinstone College and Native Education Society's Schools) are at present the great fountains from which it may be expected that the blessings of education will flow for the people of Western India. Both are yet in an infant state, more particularly so the college, as its progress and objects have been impeded by an internal schism tending materially to interrupt the circulation of its benefits.

The Native Education Society's Schools are situated near the great bazaars, at the extreme end

* This and several of the following pages are derived from Mrs. Postans' "Western India."

of the esplanade. Committees and examinations are held in the library, a splendid apartment fitted with a good collection of useful works, with globes, maps, and papers, and adorned at either end with full-length portraits of the great benefactor of the institution, Sir John Malcolm, and the Hon. Mountstuart Elphinstone.

The number of boys admitted to the society's schools is about four hundred; with fifteen hundred in branch and infant schools connected with the institution; the only qualification for admission being a knowledge by the applicant of the vernacular dialect. Eighteen scholarships, endowed by Lord Clare and Sir Edward West, are in the gift of the society; the lads who enjoy these distinctions are allowed a grant of ten rupees a month; but at the expiration of three years it ceases, although clever boys are frequently retained as monitors after that period, and their services rewarded with good salaries. The regulations require that four endowed scholars should leave the school annually, when two fresh candidates are admitted. Pupils from the schools of Dharwar and Poona are eligible for scholarships, but applications for them are not frequently made.

After public examinations, prizes are annually adjudged to the best scholars; these consist of two gold medals, with handsome chains attached; and six, bearing a similar device, in silver. The gold medals, which are intrinsically valuable, are usually awarded to proficients in the mathematical classes. Modern times having rendered the elements of knowledge, comparatively speaking, very easy of acquirement, it is still with unmixed surprise that one first witnesses the kind and degree of information possessed by the students of the school.

There can remain but little doubt that, in the early epochs of Indian history, seminaries and colleges existed for the education of youth. The Viharas of the Buddhists were probably connected with such objects; and the Brahmins of Central India were doubtless the supporters of such preparatory measures as were required to train the younger members of the priestly caste in the paths of learning, at that period untrodden but by the exclusive few. The lads who now form classes in the society's schools are many of them Brahmins by caste; the descendants of men, whose tenets, religious and moral, formed the very acme of intolerance, and who would have been considered polluted for days, had the mere shadow of an European fallen across their path. Yet now, a Brahmin youth, still wearing the triple cord, his garments of a fashion similar to those worn by his forefathers some centuries since, stands with folded arms, and eyes sparkling with all the eagerness of newly awakened curiosity, to receive instruction from his European master, and become initiated into those mysteries of science of which his fathers dreamt not.

Such changes in human feeling, all working to a particular end, as inevitable as the progress of time itself, are curious and attractive to the intelligent observer, and few places can afford higher gratification to such, than the examination rooms of the society's schools. English history, mental arithmetic, mathematics, and English literature, are the favourite objects of study, and in which, consequently, the greatest proficiency is achieved.

This energetic desire for improvement is highly encouraging to the masters, and affords proof that the natives of India cannot be by nature a mentally indolent race, however condemned by circumstances to leave unexercised their higher faculties, and seek recreations of a merely sensual order. Mathematics is undoubtedly the most valuable science to which the native youth could be attracted, inasmuch as it is that most eminently calculated to prepare and educate the judgment, for weighing and appreciating the facts with which physiology and physic will assay to bear down the ramparts of prejudice, which have stood the attacks of time, and rendered null every attempt to innovate or change.

A medical college has been established in Bombay, and proves a magnificent and well-chosen monument to the memory of the amiable man, the late Sir Robert Grant, whose anxiety to advance the best interests of the natives of India it is designed to commemorate.

Objections are frequently made to the description of studies pursued in the schools; general opinion seeming to support the idea, that abstract learning might be well exchanged for information of a more practical and useful kind. These objections would seem more important, but for the existence of the infant branches of the institution, where reading, writing, and the common rules of arithmetic are taught, together with the vernacular dialects, and the rudiments of the English language.

The aim of education must be to civilize, and,

through the medium of civilization, to *christianize* the natives of India. If so, the first object would seem to be, to prepare the mental faculties of the students to judge and reason of such facts as a knowledge of the various branches of natural science will place under their consideration. The pupils of the society's schools are members of the native aristocracy; were they tradesmen or artizans, the features of the case would alter; but these are the lads who, endowed with wealth and influence, in after years may effect much by example and opinion over all the classes who form the general native community of Western India.

Many amiable and excellent persons also desire that the Scriptures should be made a considerable study in the schools, with a view of introducing a knowledge of their truths and a conviction of their value. To this the natives object with a very mild and rational argument: "We," say they, "make no effort to introduce our bedas and puranas; why, therefore, do you urge the study of your holy books?—let this matter alone, make us as learned as yourselves, but do not seek to instruct our youth to despise the religion of their ancestors."

There is little doubt but that the present generation of these educated natives will become deists; but having taken one step away from the altars of Paganism, we may hope that their posterity, having no prejudices of priestcraft to combat, may arrive, assisted by a higher influence, at the fair truths of our Christian faith.

The principal public buildings within the town of Bombay are, the Town Hall, the Docks, the Government-House, now used as the office of the Secretaries to Government, the two churches before-named, the Mint, the Barracks, and the Castle, which contains the Arsenal. All these are upon a large and handsome scale. The rest of the edifices devoted to public purposes were formerly private dwellings, but, like the residences at present in use, they are capacious buildings, wanting only the flat roofs, terraces, and balustrades peculiar to Calcutta, to render them ornamental. The Governor of Bombay resides either at Parell, a mansion prettily situated in the midst of gardens four miles from the Fort, or at Malabar Point, a bungalow erected upon a rock projecting into the sea at the extreme westerly point of the island.

The scenery in and about the island of Bombay is extremely beautiful, because of the admixture of rice plains, gardens, handsome bungalows, and wooded hills, with occasional peeps of the seashore, and the open main or land-locked bays. The climate is, perhaps, superior in point of salubrity to that of Bengal; but the cold season scarcely merits the name, for there is nothing like the bracing weather experienced at the same period of the year in the neighbouring presidency. One peculiarity of Bombay consists in the wind blowing hot and cold at the same time, an alternation attended with the inconvenience of afflicting with temporary rheumatism those persons who being lightly clad to resist the one are suddenly assailed by the other.

The population of Bombay is computed at 400,000 souls, not more than 450 of whom are European and East-Indian residents, not in the civil or military service of the East-India Company. The European society of Bombay, which includes all persons, whether in or out of the service, eligible for reception at the Government-House, amounts probably to about 600 persons, 150 of whom are ladies. The natives of the place are Mussulmans, Parsees, and Hindoos.

Of merchants, traders, shopkeepers, &c., there are 31 English merchants and agents; 1 Portuguese mercantile firm; 1 Armenian ditto; 2 Jew, 1 Arab, 2 Mogul, 52 Hindoo, and 14 Parsee merchants; 13 brokers; 4 auctioneers and wine merchants; 25 shopkeepers and wine dealers; 4 booksellers; 4 bakers; 4 horse-brokers; and 4 apothecaries and druggists. The rest of the trades are distributed amongst an infinite number of very small establishments.

The European and Parsee community of the Western Presidency have done much for the civilization of the place, and the advancement of great objects, independently of the formation of the educational institutions alluded to above. There is an excellent club, corresponding in character with that of Calcutta; a branch of the Asiatic Society, with a capital library and museum; two banks, several Insurance Societies, a Chamber of Commerce, a Medical and Physical Society, an Agricultural and Horticultural Association, an Exchange Room, a Benevolent Society, several Bible Auxiliary and other Religious Institutions, a Sailors' Home, &c.

The manufactures of Bombay, which, as we have elsewhere said, is rather an emporium for the products of other countries than fruitful in itself, are very few in number. Perhaps the most remarkable offspring of the ingenuity of its inhabitants are the inlaid or Mosaic work-boxes, card-cases, writing-desks, &c.

The Mosaic is sometimes used as a sort of veneer over the whole surface of an article, and at others, simply as an inlaid bordering on cedar or ivory, being frequently enriched by the addition of silver to the varied and beautiful colours which compose the Mosaic. This art is of Sindhian origin, now, however, exercised to a very considerable extent in Bombay, the ivory-cutters pursuing their labours in the open shops of the bazaars. Two planes of ivory, silver, or whatever it is desired should form the extreme edges of the bordering, are placed, by means of a frame constructed for this purpose, one above the other, at a given distance. Small rods of variously-stained ivory are first dipped in strong colourless glue, and then placed horizontally between the planes, with such arrangements as shall hereafter form the desired pattern. The whole is submitted to heavy pressure until perfectly dry. Bordering being required, the ivory-cutter severs from either end of the prepared planes a portion of about half a quarter of an inch thick, when the most perfect pattern of Mosaic bordering is obtained. By this ingenious method, two six-inch planes of ivory will afford patterns for a considerable number of pretty articles, which are sold at a third of the price which would be required, were each strip of the Mosaic bordering arranged expressly for the purpose. The value of a handsome desk or work-box of the Bombay work is about six guineas, but an ornamented watch-stand or card-case may be obtained for a few shillings.

At page 225, mention has been made of the holiday *agrémens* of Bombay, the chief of which are a trip to the island of Elephanta and to Gora Bunder. Of the remarkable features of the former, its cavern temples, particular mention is made in Moor's Pantheon. They are curious works of art, but are now falling rapidly to decay.

The Gora Bunder river flows between lofty hills, beautifully wooded, and studded here and there with antique ruins, and huge masses of dark rock, which, fringed with luxuriant creepers, start from amid the rich and glossy underwood, while the graceful bamboo, crowned with tasselled creepers, form vegetating arches of brilliant blossoms, decorating the river's banks. Above the landing-place, embedded among the summits of luxuriant and lofty trees, is an age-stained and many-turretted monastery, at the foot of which, reached by a narrow, wooded, and rocky pass, it is customary for the picnic visitor to pitch a tent. A double-poled tent forms a commodious dining-room; the marching cots are placed in a smaller one beyond it, while the humble bechober is laid out with Bath and toilette table; and the attendant servants, in a routie apart, make the necessary preparations for the approaching meal. The doors of the large tents open into each other; carpets spread over the well-swept ground give an air of comfort to the whole; and green checks, suspended to the outer door, shade from the eye the glare of the neighbouring soil.

The Portuguese monastery of Gora Bunder has been fitted with a Mahomedan dome. It contains several excellent apartments, lighted by large windows, barred with wood, and commanding magnificent views of the surrounding scenery. On one side may be observed the picturesque windings of the beautiful and placid river, its rocks, and trees, and mountain scenery; while on the other, a wide plain, covered with fine plantations of rice and sugar-cane, stretches away to a considerable distance, where the river, forming a natural boundary on the one side, on the other washes the extensive walls of the city of Bassein.

A Parsee tower, and trifling ruins of cloistered avenues, are scattered about the uneven ground on which the monastery stands: while the rich and tangled underwood, flourishing in wild luxuriance among the massy rocks, affords shelter to innumerable sojourners of the tiger and serpent class, who find abundant lairs in the fastnesses of such a home.

The city of Bassein has been long forsaken; a few fishermen and shikarries alone occupy a spot once replete with luxury and power, and still containing magnificent evidences of taste, in the application of great and national wealth. The market-place, cloisters, and churches, are in a state of ruin and desolation, embedded in rich verdure, and garlanded with parasitical plants, hastening their decay.

The city contains about eight churches, of considerable size and great architectural beauty; their square towers and ruined galleries surmount the dense masses of foliage which shade the lower portions of the buildings, and from every point of view which the traveller can select, present exquisite studies for graphic delineation.

But thirty-five years have elapsed since the city of Bassein was inhabited; and still in one church, the human sympathies of the observer may be excited by the whitened remnants of mortality exposed in an open grave, doubtless desecrated, from the opinion commonly received among the natives, that individuals blessed with the goods of fortune often, with selfish anxiety, desire that their treasure should, rather than pass to other hands, be deposited with themselves, where corruption hastens unto dust.

The most perfect and handsome churches now remaining at Bassein are those of St. Paulo and St. Francis: both have square towers, with cloisters and priestly residences attached; but the most exquisite remnants of the past are to be found in the interiors of beautiful chapels, where, through a vista of ruined arches, the eye dwells on the richly wooded scene beyond, and nature, in her sunniest dress, contrasts with the dark and mouldering stone, which she, like a laughing child, decking its gray and aged sire with summer blossoms, hangs with bright lichens and many-coloured weeds. In one of these picturesque and beautiful buildings, a lofty arch remains, supporting the roofless walls, worn in unequal turrets by the season's change: a single and slender stem of the graceful banyan, springing from the fertile soil, has shot upwards to the centre of the roof, like a graceful column, whose capital of sunny leaves crowns the high arch with its umbrageous shade.

In strolling among the ruins of Bassein, the foot

of the traveller will occasionally strike against a flat and humble block, or his eye rest on a richly chiselled tomb, whose inscriptions afford abundant matter for philosophic meditation, on the decline of the eastern power of Portugal and the changed and humbled character of her chivalrous and daring sons. Tradition and romance have shed a charm of enchanting interest around the ancient history of that singular people, which is here touchingly recalled, as the traveller's eye traces many names which he at once must recognize as claiming ancestry with the noble blood of the first among those who fought for and established their country's power on the Indian soil. The names of Don Lorenço,* of Alfonso Albuquerque,† of many of the greatest and noblest heroes whom the policy of Portugal selected to fix her empire in the East, cannot be read without emotion; the more so when, surrounded by ruin and desolation, the relics of a power itself tottering in decay. Of the immense oriental empire of Portugal, little now remains but *Goa*, its ancient capital; still, indeed, a fine and curious city, but inhabited by a class far different from those, the early delegates of their sovereign's power. Hondura and Severndroog, with the important chain of forts once guarding the shores of the Southern Concan, look desolate and bleak, amid the dash and roar of old Ocean's surges; while the great fortress of Diu, which the chivalrous Nuno de Cunha first gained for an ungrateful

* Don Lorenço encountered first the Turkish armada near Diu.

† In 1515 Albuquerque took the important seaport of Goa, and established it as the seat of the Portuguese government.

master,* has become a comparatively small and unimportant spot: and the churches of St. Paulo and St. Francis, with the lovely chapels of Bassein, in whose aisles, perhaps, the descendants of the great Apostle of India† lifted up their voice in prayer for the idolatrous nation among whom they dwelt, will soon be noted but as a heap of rubbish, resounding with the unearthly yell of the hyena, delighting in its wild shelter of desolation.

Besides Gora Bunda and Bassein, the caves of Karlee, on the island of Salsette, the villas at Ambolee, on the same island—which, by the way, is connected with Bombay by a superb causeway—afford subjects of interest and pleasant places of resort to holiday-people and strangers.

Connected with Bombay by another causeway, at the south-westerly corner of the island, is the smaller island of Colaba, where there is a gun-carriage manufactory, an observatory, a lighthouse, and barracks for a regiment of infantry.

We have mentioned, in connection with our sketch of Calcutta, the Sanataria at Darjeeling and the Cassyah Hills, places to which sick people retire for the benefit of a healthful and invigorating climate. Bombay, too, has its Sanatarium—the Mahabaleshwur Hills, which are situated in 17° 56′ north latitude, and in longitude 73° 30′ east, and are distant twenty-five miles due east from the sea, and sixty-nine miles from Bombay, which bears north 29° west. They form a portion of the extensive chain of mountains

* John the Third of Portugal, 1546.

† Francis Xavier.

known under the name of the Western Ghats, or Syhadree mountains. On their western side they rise with an abrupt and precipitous ascent from the Concan, which separates them from the sea, while their eastern face presents a somewhat less rapid and steep descent into the table-land of the Deccan.

The general elevation of the station is 4,500 feet above the level of the sea, while its highest summit attains an altitude of 4,700 feet. It is elevated upwards of 4,000 feet above the subjacent country on the Concan side, and about 2,300 feet above the general level of the Deccan at its eastern base. Its greatest breadth at the northern extremity is about fifteen miles, and about eight at its southern boundary. The average direct length north and south does not exceed five miles, though from north-east to south-west it extends diagonally seventeen miles.

Excellent roads have been made in almost every direction. These already extend over a space of upwards of forty miles, more than one-half of which are carriage-roads, and the remainder bridle-paths, and have been so laid-out as to open up to the visitor a varied succession of mountain scenery, which, for grandeur and beauty, it is believed, can be equalled in few parts of the world.

The soil consists principally of a red clay (formed by the disintegration of cellular ferruginous clay-stone, which constitutes the surface rock), intermixed with the débris of trap-rock, and in many places with a considerable portion of decayed vegetable matter, forming a brown mould, which is found to be very productive. An abundant supply of excellent water is at all seasons procurable, either from wells, which vary from twenty to forty feet in depth, or from the small streamlets which traverse the hills, some of which retain their water during the whole of the hot season. An extensive artificial lake, which is now being constructed, will add materially to the supply of water already available, whether for cultivation or for domestic use.

The most striking feature in the vegetation of these hills is the profusion of the common brake (pterio aquilina), which serves to recall the association of a more northern clime. A species of curcuma, the root of which yields an excellent description of arrowroot, grows everywhere in the greatest abundance. There is a considerable variety of parasitic orchidave, some of which possess great beauty; and the trunks and branches of many of the trees are covered with a variety of lichens and musei.

Potatoes of excellent quality are cultivated very extensively, both for the consumption of the station and for the supply of the Bombay and Poona markets. A plentiful supply of all the common culinary vegetables of the best description can be procured at reasonable rates. The excessive heaviness of the rains prevents the successful cultivation of European fruits.

The village of Malcolm Peth (so named by the Rajah of Sattara in honour of the late Sir John Malcolm, the distinguished founder of the station) contains several European shops, where European supplies of almost every description are procurable at the same rates as at Poona, and very little higher than at Bombay. The station is also visited by numerous itinerant hawkers (Borahs) from Bombay, whose baskets are usually filled with a varied assortment both of European and Indian goods. The Malcolm Peth Bazaar is a tolerably large one, and is well supplied with all articles of consumption, which are the produce of the country, and generally at moderate rates. The mutton, which is small, but of excellent quality, is sold at one and a half annas per pound; beef at one anna per pound; fowls at three or four annas each. Grain is principally imported from Wye (a distance of twenty miles), and is usually about eight or ten per cent. higher than in the Deccan. Firewood is abundant and cheap; grass is of rather inferior quality. A monthly nerrik, or price current, is circulated for the information of visitors; but, under existing regulations, its observance cannot be enforced on the dealers, though they almost invariably conform to it.

Mahabaleshwur is easily accessible both from Bombay and from the principal stations of the Deccan and Concan. The visitor from Bombay, by sailing down the coast to Bancoote, and thence up the Sawitree river to Mhar (a distance of seventy miles by sea and thirty by river), is brought within twenty-seven miles land journey from the hills; or, should he object to even this short sea-trip, he can cross the harbour to Nagotna (which is effected in one tide), from which the distance by land is only seventy miles, along an excellent road, with a public bungalow at each stage. The distance from Poona, by an indifferent hilly route, is seventy miles, and from Sattara only thirty miles, by a very good carriage-road. The approach, both from the Concan and from the Deccan side, is at all times safe, as there is no intervening jungle, and no danger to be apprehended from attacks of fever or other diseases of malarious origin.

This station was ceded to the British Government, by the Rajah of Sattara, in exchange for another village, and was subsequently annexed to the Zillah of the Concan. Its European establishment consists only of a chaplain and a medical officer. The former visits Dapoolee once a month, and Rutnagherry once in two months, during the fair season; and during the rains he performs the duties of chaplain at Malligaum. The medical officer is also superintendent of the station and a first assistant to the magistrate, and has charge of a treasure-chest for the payment of sick officers and their families. A detachment of fifty sepoys, under the command of a jemadar, is kept up to supply the usual guards.

The public buildings consist of a sanatarium, containing eight sets of quarters, and five detached bungalows, for the accommodation of sick officers and their families; a church, which was built by private subscription, and accommodates 180 people; a small subsidiary gaol, containing sixty Chinese convicts, who are employed in the construction and repair of roads, a chowrie, and a Dhurumsallah for native travellers. There is a subscription library, containing many hundred volumes, and a hotel, on a very small scale, has recently been completed.

The private dwelling-houses are seventy in number; of which fifty-three are substantially built of hewn stone and lime, and the remainder of rough stone and mortar, sun-dried bricks, or wattle-work. The greater number of them are thatched, tiles having been found not to resist the monsoon rain. Allotments of ground, for building, are granted by Government, on a twenty-one years' lease, the principal provisions of which are, that the lessee shall pay an annual rent, at the rate of a rupee an acre; that he shall build a substantial bungalow, and erect suitable landmarks on the boundaries of his allotment; that he shall not be permitted to cut down trees which are close to the public road; and that he shall obey all regulations existing in the Mofussil, so far as they are not of a personal nature, but are incidental to the possession of immovable property, and so far, also, as they affect the health, safety, and convenience of the other inhabitants of the station. The average size of individual allotments, granted during the last three years, is six acres.

The agency of the climate of the hills, in the preservation of health and the prevention of disease, is probably greater and more beneficial than its direct therapeutic efficacy, more particularly in relation to females and children. The practice, which is now so prevalent in the Bombay presidency, of withdrawing children from the pernicious influence of the excessive heat of the low country during the hot season, and of transferring them, during these months, to this temperate and equable climate, has the incalculably beneficial effect of warding off many of the acute attacks incident to childhood, and more especially to the period of dentition; of supporting the energies of their constitution on a nearer level with the European standard during the first years of their growth, when such constitutional invigoration is of vital importance; and of lessening the liability to future disease and future delicacy of constitution, to which children, born and reared for some years in this country, are more or less liable.

Bombay to Calcutta, viâ *Poona, Hyderabad, &c.*

At page 73, the limits of the territories subordinate to the Bombay Government are indicated. Within these, the most important places are Poona, Sattara, Baroda, Surat, Ahmedabad, Mhow, Booj (in Cutch), Hyderabad in Lower, and Sukkur in Upper, Scinde. The methods of reaching them are various, and often depending upon the will of the traveller. Those stations which lie to the east, north-east, or south-east of Bombay, are connected with the presidency by good roads; in proceeding thither, therefore, the traveller has the choice of marching or going by dawk. With the north and south stations the communication is generally by water, in steamers, pattamars, or occasional ships. But we will take each station separately hereafter, referring the reader to the instructions given in a foregoing page for setting forth and accomplishing each journey with ease. Meanwhile, for the convenience of those who, arriving at Bombay, have their ultimate destination on the other side of India, we will sketch the routes to Calcutta.

Dawk from Bombay to Hyderabad.

Sending over the palanquin, &c., to Panwell, the nearest station on the continent, where the first set of bearers is posted, the traveller proceeds thither in a small steamer, and thence commences his journey to Poona, four stages.*

The first stage to Khalapoor over a lovely country is only interesting to the stranger from its contrast with the crowded city aspect of Bombay. The alternation of jungle with paddy (rice) fields and poor but picturesque villages constitutes the main features of the scenery for the first eighteen miles; but when at Khalapoor, the foot of the ghaut, or mountain, is reached, the sublime begins to take precedence of the beautiful. It is advisable, if travelling in the cool season, from October to March, to leave Panwell at about three in the morning, for the first stage is then accomplished by eight A. M., and the ascent of the ghaut can be commenced at an hour when the magnificence of the scenery can be contemplated to advantage. The varied foliage which covers the mountains' sides; the deep, rocky ravines; the lofty ascent by a well-constructed road; the occasional rencontre of the laden elephant and burthened camel; the song of birds; the costumes of the native pedestrian traveller, or the equipment of the wealthier merchant, squatted in his singularly constructed car; the pensioned or tributary Mahratta chieftain, with his little band of retainers, bristling with arms, constitute a varied picture which pleasantly beguiles the wayfarer of his fatigue. At Karlee, at the top of the ghaut, one-half of the journey to Poona has been accomplished, and here it may be as well to halt and take

* If the trip is to be limited to Poona, there will be no occasion to go to the trouble of providing palanquin, &c., as there is a mail curricle running between Panwell and Poona.

breakfast. The bungalow, or resting-house, at Karlee is advantageously situated, commanding a superb view of a part of the western ghauts on the one side, and of the table-land to the eastward. At the bungalow are two servants, one of whom will immediately kill a fowl, and cook a curry or a grill, and set the kettle on the fire, while the other prepares a refreshing cold water bath, and attends to the unpacking of the pettarahs (if necessary), or the arrangement of the toilette of the stranger. Paying a gratuity of one rupee, and inscribing, in a book kept for that purpose, his contentment, or otherwise, with his treatment, he resumes his journey in the evening. Tulligaon, and the country on either side, are thus passed during the night; but it may be as well to mention, for the guidance of those who may prefer travelling in the day-time, that excepting an occasional temple, a tank constructed by devotees, there is not a single object worthy of particular inspection. The road lies through a gently undulating country, extensively cultivated, and the atmosphere is wonderfully clear and pure, by reason of the elevation of the land. At Tulligaon there is a bungalow corresponding in all respects with the one at Karlee. We reach Poona at the end of a nine hours' journey, and proceed at once to the dawk bungalow, or to the residence of any one to whom letters of introduction may have been previously sent.

Poona, once the capital of the dominions of the Peishwa (now a prisoner at Benares), is one of the largest and healthiest military stations in India. There are seldom less than six or seven infantry regiments cantoned there, with a brigade of horse artillery. At the distance of five or six miles from Poona is Kirkee, where are barracks for a regiment of British dragoons. The governor of Bombay frequently resides at Poona during the summer season, at a place in the neighbourhood, called Dapooree, where there is a botanic garden. The description given of the Cawnpore cantonment, in a former part of this work, applies, with little variation, to that of Poona, the only difference being that the climate of the Deccan is more salubrious than that of Cawnpore, the scenery more attractive, the dust of the station less offensive, and the buildings less scattered.

Poona was, at the early period of the British possession of the country, most famous for field-sports. The wild boar, familiarly called the hog, was then so common, that whole sounders have been known to dash through the camp in mid-day. The clearing away of jungle, the occupation of a large extent of land, and the great industry of our Nimrods, have now thinned the vicinage of the station of its ancient wild inhabitants; but the Deccan is still very celebrated as a sporting country, and affords the resident many an opportunity of whiling away leisure in an exciting and noble pastime. The hog is pursued in India in a much more manly way than in any other country in the world. Disdaining the aid of dogs and the use of fire-arms, the Indian hog-hunter saddles his little Arab, and, vaulting into his seat, spear in hand, rides to the cover with a few companions, all equally eager for the honour of inflicting the first wound. Sometimes native rustics are employed to beat the jungle, the sugar-cane plantations, or other haunt of the grizzly boar, and drive him into the plain; but in some places this process is unnecessary, as "the pigs" come out of their own accord, to take the air or wallow in some neighbouring jheel. The moment they are seen, the hunters make for them at a killing pace. Away goes the boar, over rocky ground, swamps, nullahs, and jungles. The chase is prolonged, over a wide extent of country, for half an hour or more: sometimes the boar gets away; sometimes, driven to his last shifts, he turns about and gallantly charges his foes. Then comes the critical moment. If the Arab swerves, or the spear is untrue, a fearful gash in the belly or a leg of the horse assures the boar escape, at least from one opponent; if otherwise—if the horse obeys the bridle, maintains his stand, and enables the huntsman to deliver his spear just above the shoulder of the boar, the grey monster dies, and while his tusks adorn the tent or bungalow of the victor, his fat sides furnish forth a repast with which domestic pork-chops will bear no kind of comparison. In some parts of India our sportsmen *throw* the spear—in others they thrust or *job* it. Controversies upon the relative merits of these systems were rife in the *Bombay* and *Bengal Sporting Magazines;* but it is difficult to say which plan is admitted to be the most efficacious.

Leaving Poona, whence a new dawk must be laid by the Poona post-master, the road runs south-easterly to Sholapore, nine stages, averaging sixteen miles each, through a fertile, well-governed country. Sholapore is another military station, at the eastern boundary of the dominions of the Rajah of Sattara.

A very small military force is kept up here, as the country is in a settled state, and large military cantonments are within a few days' march of the place.

Two stages from Sholapore we get to Nuldroog, beyond the territories of the East-India Company. Here it will be necessary to wait for eight days, unless the dawk traveller took the precaution, when at Bombay or Poona, to give that number of days' notice to the Resident at Hyderabad, whence the bearers will have to be sent. If he has been sufficiently provident, he will find the bearers awaiting him, and can proceed on his journey. The distance from Nuldroog to Secunderabad, the military cantonment of Hyderabad, is about 160 miles, through a fertile but ill-governed country, belonging to the Nizam. The distance is divided into eight stages, of about twenty miles each in length.

In the centre of a valley surrounded by hills of moderate height, diversified by the bold, rugged aspect of some, and the picturesque and romantic appearance of others, stands Hyderabad, the Mahomedan capital of the Deccan. The view of the city from the hill through which the road, from the military cantonment of Secunderabad leads to the British residency, is commanding and extensive. Due south, and immediately in front, is seen the city, expanded over a considerable space and gradually losing itself in the perspective distance. From this hill appears a rich variety of mosques, palaces, houses, and other edifices, interspersed with trees, which give to the whole the character of a city built in the midst of an immense garden. The most prominent objects which engage the attention are

Char Minar, or four minarets; the *Musjid Juma*, or great mosque; and the *Barra Darí*, or palace, with twelve gates, of the late prime minister of the Nizam. To the west, at the distance of about eight miles, stands the strong fortress of Golconda, on a rock of some eminence, in the adjacent plain of which are six or seven noble mausolea, built in the Saracenic order of architecture, the sepulchres of the Kutb Shahi dynasty of the kings of Golconda. Descending the hill and proceeding towards the city, the view becomes gradually less extensive until the traveller arrives at the suburbs, a great part of which is called, *par eminence*, "the Residency," as containing the establishment of the Company's Resident at the court of his Highness the Nizam. Between this part of the suburbs and the city runs a small stream, which, in the rainy season, however, swells to a river of considerable width and rapidity of course. Here is seen the massive stone wall which surrounds Hyderabad, supposed to have been built by Kooli Kootb Shah, the fourth monarch of that dynasty. This wall, in some places, owing to the unevenness of ground, reaches the height of forty feet; but its average altitude on the outside is about twenty feet, and its thickness ten feet. The height of the side within the city is much less. There is a rampart sufficiently broad for four persons to walk abreast, and a parapet, about five feet high, through which loop-holes are pierced for musquetry. This, if properly defended, must have been a strong protection to the city from the attacks of a native army. The stream just mentioned is called Músí, by the natives, and winds its course about half round the city. From the rampart is a fine view of this river and the surrounding country, particularly on that part of the wall to the right of the *Dehlí* gate in entering the city, when an interesting and picturesque sight presents itself, of elephants, with their variegated howdahs, rich caparisons, and gorgeously painted trunks; native, Persian, Patan, Turkoman, Affghan, and Arab horsemen, together with camels and their riders, palanquins, and foot-passengers continually passing to and from the city, and crossing the ford, as there is no bridge over this part of the river.

Within the city of Hyderabad are some extensive edifices and gardens, laid out in a tasteful and elegant manner. Of these, the most remarkable are the *burra daree,* a word applied to the palaces and mansions of the newábs and rajahs, as they were originally erected with twelve gates to them. They consist of a range of buildings of stone and wood, generally detached from each other and separated by quadrangular areas, some of which are flower-gardens; in some are reservoirs of water, containing rare fishes, and in others a variety of playing fountains and jets-d'eau. At one end of others, again, are artificial cascades, constructed in such a manner as to be capable of having their falling waters either accelerated or retarded according to pleasure. Most of the edifices are two or three stories high, and have verandahs round the compartments of the ground-floor, with slight pillars, painted green and occasionally gilt.

The administration of the civil affairs of Hyderabad rests exclusively with the Nizam himself, and it is, therefore, needless to say that it is characterized by all the vices which distinguished native rule in the olden time. Some British troops, forming a portion of the Madras army, garrison Secunderabad; but the Nizam has a separate force of his own, chiefly officered from the British army. This service (the Nizam's) is composed of five regiments of cavalry, four companies of artillery, one company of sappers and miners, or engineers, as they are sometimes called, eight regiments of infantry, one garrison, and one invalid battalion.

The horse, or, as it is termed, the reformed horse, are a fine body of men (Moors, of course, in the greatest ratio), four corps of which are similar in most respects of duties, discipline, and interior economy, to the Bengal local horse corps. The remaining, or fifth, regiment is disciplined and conducted on the plan of *regular* native cavalry corps, and on this account is not held in very high esteem by their "brethren of the jack-boot." The men also are, we are told, by no means such exclusives in caste and Bahaduri (pompousness of manner) as in the irregular corps.

The arms and accoutrements of the cavalry are similar, in most respects, to the Bengal and Bombay local corps. They consist of sword, spear, and pistols; black leathern belts and jack-boots; dress uniform, in the native fashion, of dark green;* a

* The uniform of the four *first* corps is green, and white facings with gold lace. The style of embroidery on the officers' jackets corresponds with that of the Madras horse artillery. The *fifth* regiment, which, as has been said, is a *regular* cavalry corps, is clothed like the Hon. Company's regular cavalry, their jackets, however, being green and their facings yellow. The officers and men wear helmets.

red turban generally; but on these points the general orders are not very strict, as amongst some of the men, and in one or two of the regiments, *variety is considered pleasing.* The *regular* regiment of horse is accoutred similarly to troopers of native cavalry. The Silladari and Bargheer system prevails in all the regiments. There are eight troops, and about sixty men per troop, giving a complement of four hundred and eighty per corps, besides non-commissioned officers, native jemadars, the great man in each corps—the rissaldar—and European captain-commandant, adjutant, and now and then a captain and subaltern officer attached.* It is understood that there ought to be three officers to each regiment; but staff appointments, absence, and other duties, do not always allow this number to be complete.

Two complete regiments of this branch are always kept at Mominabad, the head-quarters of the cavalry division, for scientific instruction in a part of the cavalry movements. The other corps are stationed at the remaining division head-quarter posts of his highness's army.

The reliefs occur every second year, all visiting in turn the "Alma Mater" (Mominabad), where they have the benefit of the immediate superintendence of the brigadier, to whom alone, next to the commander-in-chief, the resident, are they responsible

* The rissaldar gets 500 rupees per month pay. The horses are chiefly Deccan and Arab, valued at the rate of from 300 to 450 and 500 rupees per horse. The rissaldars are generally rich, and having considerable landed property, and other sources of wealth, are incited by the glory of arms to service.

for their interior economy, orders, &c., and through whom alone are all duties, &c., transacted.

The two corps not at divisional head-quarters are visited by the cavalry brigadier annually, for the purposes of review, inspection, &c.

The artillery consists of several companies, distributed over the country. Their strength and equipment differ according to the quantum of ordnance belonging to each. It is understood, however, that the zeal and *shoukh* (fancy) of the commandants have much to do with these departments. Every company has, nevertheless, four six-pounders and a brace of eighteens, to which are occasionally added a mortar and one or two howitzers; and when this is the case, the ordinary strength of each company is enlarged. The usual complement of a company is about sixty-five or seventy men. Two conductors and a quarter-master's serjeant assist the artillery captain-commandant, besides the soobadar and jemadar of the company. The clothing, accoutrements, and discipline are exactly similar to those adopted in the Company's service, and his Highness the Nizam allows plenty of powder and a few rounds of ammunition balled to practise. The commandants of the artillery, at stations where there is no engineer officer (and of whom there are only two, always, at Bolarum), are generally called upon to shew their agility in managing the duties of commissary of stores, and executive officer also. At Bolarum, the commandant of artillery does the duty of commissary of stores, and the commandant of the small company of sappers and miners officiates as executive engineer. There is a very extensive store-house and magazine, under the superintendence of the former officer, at this station, which is furnished by the arsenal of Fort St. George (Madras) with all military stores, and for which it is understood his highness makes acknowledgment by no small per-centage on the articles in proportion to value.

The small company of sappers and miners is a most useful and efficient body, stationary at Bolarum, under a commandant and an adjutant. The companies of artillery are also stationary, and never relieve each other.

Come we next to the infantry, which are all regular, and assimilate closely in respect to duties, dress, &c., to the Madras native infantry. Each regiment has its captain-commandant, and the usual complement of officers, four in number, including the adjutant, who is allowed to hold charge of companies in turn, and according to seniority. There is also a serjeant-major and quarter-master-serjeant attached to each regiment, upon the same footing as in the Madras native infantry corps; the former being generally considered an assistant to the adjutant in his office and not at parade duties; the latter attending chiefly to the internal economy of the regimental magazine or store-room. There is also a surgeon to each corps, assisted by three dressers, two of whom are generally Indo-Britons, and the third a native. Like the system in the Madras army, the chief aid to the adjutant in parade duties is afforded by a "native adjutant," selected from the jemadars. The corps are efficient and well disciplined, recruited from all quarters, but chiefly from the south. There are, however, many Hindoostan men in the ranks, and these are much prized, especially if of a good height for a grenadier. The general run of the corps in height is much the same as through the Madras army, and of comparatively small stature after looking at Bengal corps. They are not the less smart and active for this though, and are certainly not inferior to any Company's troops. The regiments relieve each other occasionally, and remain three years, or sometimes a shorter period, at a station. The dress of the infantry is according to the Madras regiments, and differs little from the other presidency soldiery. The collars of the coatees are deeper, and there is much more tape on the breast than in Bengal. The havresack (made of strong white cloth, bleached and washed) is also worn as an article of accoutrement, in light and heavy marching order. The pattern of the turban is any thing but becoming, especially to those accustomed to the neat ones of the Bengal presidency, but it much resembles the Madras pattern. The hot weather costume (of the Nizamites) looks any thing but cool and pleasant. The white jacket is an ungreka, or native cut of that garment, which does not look military when united with buff belts, knapsacks, and "linen pantaloons, dyed black," which latter are worn throughout the year (except on occasions of dress or full dress, when white is substituted), hot weather and cold; for the Nizam's government do not think proper to issue woollen trowsers to the poor fellows. Coats are issued once in two years.

Musters are taken once in two months, by the major of brigade at each division head-quarters, and the intervening months have a regimental muster on the first of each. The system on this point is quite different from that of the Bengal presidency, and would appear to be of minor importance as a military duty.

Each division station has a capital mess-house and store-room attached to it, for the use of the officers. Supplies are chiefly procured from Bombay. Donations and subscriptions to this establishment are reasonable enough; fifty rupees donation (which is returned to the subscriber when leaving the station with his regiment), and a monthly subscription of three or four rupees, or *ad libitum*, for keeping up the papers, periodicals, &c., of the different presidencies. It is quite optional with an officer to become a member or not. The government (Nizam's) also grant an allowance *per mensem* of 150 or 160 rupees in support of the establishment.

Misdemeanours are tried in the regimental house by Punchayet, and the other branches by courts-martial—division, line, and regimental. Furloughs (annual) are granted to the troops; and a pension establishment for soldiers wounded in the service, and meritorious servants after twenty years' service, is provided. The business of the army is conducted through the resident's military secretary, through whom are issued general orders on the part of the Nizam's government from time to time. All officers, after twelve years' service in India, are promoted to the rank of captain, and medical officers (if only assistant-surgeon) to that of surgeon after ten years' service. King and Company's officers are entitled to draw the "pay proper" of their grade in their own service, independent of Nizam's allowances.

Officers must pass an examination in Hindostanee before they are eligible for an adjutancy or interpretership. The allowance, however, for the latter is no great incentive to work a little harder for the latter examination, which is somewhat stricter than that required for the former. But, thrown so much more, as is an officer in the Nizam's service, amongst the natives, we suspect there are very few who, as far as this qualification is considered, are not fully competent for either situation. Pure Hindostanee is, however, not generally spoken in the Hyderabad service, from the great mixture of men from both coasts and other southern districts, and the consequent jumble of Tellinghoo, Tamul, Canarese, Mahratta, and Guzrattee, with the pure northern dialect, or Oordoo. The Hindostanee of southern India is often a strange jargon, a compound of many tongues, well worthy of Babel. All patronage in the Nizam's service is in the hands of the Governor-General, and we believe the situation of captains-commandant, and brigade-major or paymaster, cannot now be directly conferred by the Resident, without the form of a recommendation to the Supreme Government. Local officers cannot now enter the service, their admission having been put a stop to by Lord William Bentinck.

The regular portion of the service—i. e. engineers, artillery, and infantry—are directed to be guided by the regulations, standing orders, &c., for the Madras army. The pay and allowances are higher than those in the Company's service, but they are not issued with the same regularity.

The purely Oriental character of the state kept up

at Hyderabad, and the hospitality of the British officers, will amply repay the traveller for a few days' stay at the cantonment.

Seven stages, of about twelve miles each in length, carry the traveller to Soonipet, the limits of the Nizam's territories, and eighteen miles further on he gets to Monegalah, in the Company's territory. From this place to Masulipatam, bearers are provided by the collector of the latter station, on due notice being given to him. From Masulipatam, on the Coromandel coast, the trip to Calcutta may be made by boat, or any ship touching there, or by dawk through Rajamundry, Vizagapatam, Berhampore (Gangam) to Cuttack, of which we have already spoken, and whence the journey to Calcutta is brief.

If a traveller leaves Cuttack at five o'clock in the afternoon, he will arrive at Bhareepore, half-way to Balasore, about eight or nine o'clock the next morning, where there is a bungalow for the accommodation of travellers. He can remain at Bhareepore during the heat of the day, start again in the evening, and reach Balasore to breakfast; proceed again in the cool of the evening, and arrive at Dantoon, halfway to Midnapore, early next morning; where there is a comfortable house for the accommodation of travellers. In like manner, if he goes on again in the evening to Midnapore, another night will take him to Tumlook, where he gets into a boat and proceeds up the Hooghly to Calcutta.

A traveller with one set, consisting of 8 bearers, 2 bangy burdars, and 2 mausals, pays 8 annas per mile, agreeably to regulation, and pays 2 annas per man *per diem* for detaining the bearers on the road; or he may pay 3 annas per man for each stage from Tanghee to Khutnaghur.

During the monsoon it is recommended to travellers from Midnapore to run to Tumlook, which is 51 miles—viz. *viâ* Debrah and Purtabpoor—and embark there on the Roopnarain river, a branch of the Hooghly. The passage is about 15 hours to Calcutta. The expense from Jellasore to Tumlook, 12 stages, is 26¼ rupees for bearers, and 1¾ rupees for oil, being for 12 bearers, 2 bangy burdars, and 1 mussaljee.

The following is an abstract of the expenses of the trip.

	Rs.	A.	P.
Poona range, 259 miles, costs for 12 hamals and 1 massal at each stage	326	2	50
Oil and Muckadums, fees perhaps additional	20	0	0
Nizam's Territory, 257m. 4f. for 12 hamals, 1 massal, would cost	700	0	0
Masulipatam collectorship, 105m. 4f. costs	33	0	0
Rajamundry ditto 100m. 4f. suppose ½r. a mile ..	55	0	0
Vizagapatam ditto 122m. 1f. costs	24	0	0
Chicacole ditto 125m. 1f.	31	0	0
Cuttack ditto 112m. 0f.	34	2	0
Jellasore ditto 126m. 0f.	42	1	0
Jellasore, through Midnapore to Tumlook, 95 miles, cost	26	1	0
Total 1,320m. 6f. Expense, Rs.	1,292	2	50

The distance by sea from Bombay to Panwell, about 20 miles, and from Tumlook to Calcutta, about 90 miles, should be added to make the whole distance from Bombay to Calcutta. The distance by land, however, from Tumlook to Calcutta, is only 50 miles.

Good hammals will go four miles an hour, sometimes more, but the time occupied in the journey depends principally on the traveller himself. From twenty to twenty-two days is a reasonable allowance for the journey to a stout man.

There is another and more direct route from Bombay to Calcutta, but it lies for the most part through an almost uninhabited, and in many parts unhealthy, country, and is therefore seldom selected by dawk travellers, although it is the regular route for the public post. This road branches off at Poona in a north-easterly direction, and passing through Seroor and Ahmednuggur, stations for Bombay troops, enters the Nizam's territory a little to the south of Aurungabad. Thence, traversing the territory at its entire northern breadth, we enter upon the Nagpore state, where a British resident and an auxiliary force ensure to the people the blessings of tolerably good government, peace and security. The road there takes a direction *due east*, across an insalubrious, jungly country, governed by different petty rajahs, and successively passing the unnoticeable stages of Raepore, Jumbulpore, and Jotepore, the traveller reaches Midnapore eighty miles from Calcutta.

The third route from Bombay to Calcutta, or rather to the north-west stations subordinate to the Supreme Government, is through the Northern Concan, Deccan, various native states, Central India, Bundlecund, &c. The advantage of a knowledge of this route to Bombay, Madras, and Bengal officers, arriving in the first instance at Bombay, consists in the circumstance of its embracing many stations belonging to the different presidencies which may be the more readily reached from Bombay.

The traveller proceeds in the first instance from

Bombay in a north-easterly direction to Nassuck, 174 miles along a good-made road, with plenty of supplies accessible. Nine miles further on he reaches the cantonment of Malligaum, occupied by Bombay troops. Here he enters the district of Kandeish, under the Bombay Government, and proceeds without interruption for 105 miles to Mundlaisir, a town on the right bank of the river Nerbudda, where an assistant political agent resides. The scenery along this road is particularly interesting. The undulating nature of the ground lends variety to the landscape, and the eye is pleasantly relieved by an agreeable alternation of rock and jungle, ruined towns and pagodas, old fortresses, &c., which we do not see in any other part of Hindostan. Still, the country is not easily traversed by troops or by officers marching with their own baggage. The road is in many places rocky and bad, the jungle thick and infested with wild animals; the fords and ferries over small rivers indifferent. Leaving Mundlaisir behind us, we make for Mhow, due north, the principal station in Central India, where a considerable body of troops is always to be found, commanded by a general officer. To compress within the narrow compass of this work even a faint outline of Central India were impossible. We refer the reader, therefore, to Sir John Malcolm's interesting work upon a country so rich in resources, the scene of so much strife and political intrigue, and the theatre of British triumphs over its most gallant foe. Indore, the seat of the political agency, lies a few miles north of Mhow. This country is the property of Holkar, a native chief. The route now takes an easterly direction through the territories of the Dewas chief, Scindia and the Bhopal Nawaub, until we reach Ashta (a large town and fort on the right bank of the Parbuttee river, distant from Mundlaisir 87 miles), whence we incline northerly, passing across the territories of the Bhopal Nuwaub, and arrive at Sehore. Between this place and Saugor, where a British commissioner resides, supported by some Madras troops and a strong police force, recently organized to check freebooters and enforce the payment of revenue and tribute by the petty and turbulent chiefs, the distance is 135 miles. The face of the country is essentially the same as that spoken of above; an alternation of rocky hill, deep jungle, nullah and cultivated country.

From Saugor to the cantonment of Mirzapore, north-east, is 285 miles, through the various native territories of Dummow, Punnah, the rich valley of Bundlecund, Ooncheria, Sohawul, and Rewah—territories which have, until very recently, been the scenes of much discord, calling for the armed interference of the British Government, and an alteration in some of our political relations with the chieftains. Dawk travelling is not difficult in times of peace and during the prevalence of good order; but marching is rendered disagreeable by the character of the roads, of which no native governments take sufficient care, and by the occasional scarcity of water and the necessaries of (sepoy) life. Saugor is a desirable station for military men and young civilians, as, indeed, are most of the places in our occupation in the neighbourhood of the Nerbudda. The sports of tiger-hunting and fishing are enjoyed in great perfection there, and the number of persons congregated at Saugor afford opportunities for the various pastimes and pleasant social reunions common to civilized life.

To return to Bombay. The stations garrisoned by the forces of this presidency are few, though the tract of country under the direction of its civil officers is extensive. The places of the greatest consequence are (to the south as far as Goa, the last remnant of the Portuguese territories), Dapoolee, Severndroog, Rutnagherry, Malwan, Vingorla (all reduced fortresses in the Southern Concan), to Belgaum in the east; and to the north, Surat, Broach, Baroda, Kaira, and Ahmedabad, in Guzerat, as far as Palunpore, on the southern border of the Shekawuttee territory. Baroda is under the Guicowar, a native prince, long on a friendly footing with the British Government, at whose court we have a resident and a subsidiary force. East of Palunpore, distant about one hundred miles, lies Neemuch, the most westerly cantonment belonging to the Supreme Government, and occupied by Bengal troops. West of Baroda is the peninsula of Kattewar, where a political agent resides, with a small body of troops at his bidding, in the central cantonment of Rajcote. The treaty with the chieftain of Kattewar is offensive and defensive. He has the right to claim protection, internal and external, from the British, and we do not interfere in the management of his own affairs, though bound to assist him in realizing his claims from his own subjects. A similar treaty exists with the Guicowar of Baroda.

Separated from Kattewar by a gulf is the Runn

and territory of Cutch, bordering upon Scinde. Cutch, governed by a Rao, who is supreme in his own territory, has long been tributary to the British authority, which has retained a resident and a proportion of troops at Bhooj. Its chief importance, as a friendly state, has arisen from the circumstance of its having formed a species of barrier between our possessions in Western India and the territory of Scinde. Of the condition of this latter country it were difficult to speak at the present moment, and in a book aspiring to a *permanent* utility, for a few months may produce some changes in its political condition. It exists now as a portion of the British empire, won by the sword, and maintained at a terrible cost of life, through sickness among the troops who occupy the principal stations of Hyderabad, Sukkur, Shikarpore, &c.; but the sympathies which have been excited in favour of the dethroned Ameers may lead to the country's being placed upon the same footing with other native states; a small subsidiary or other force, detached from the Bombay army, occupying a part of the country, as a guarantee for our preservation of the free navigation of the Indus, and certain political objects in reference to our North-Western neighbours.

MADRAS.

This presidency, the most important in the early part of British Indian history, from the brilliant campaigns of which it was the theatre, now ranks low in the scale, for the very satisfactory reason, that the country which forms its limits is in a settled state, abundantly fertile, and making a pleasant progress towards civilization. The town of Madras, which is a place of great resort, owing to its position as the port of arrival for all those persons who are nominated to the civil and military service of the Government, and to its commercial importance, is in every respect most uninviting. The land is low, and no range of mountains fills up the background and relieves the landscape. A heavy swell rolls on to the shore, and this, as rendering the navigation of boats a matter of some difficulty and hazard, lends to the scene the only excitement of which it is susceptible. Large boats, called *mussoolahs,* and diminutive rafters, formed of two logs of wood and termed *catamarrans,* are the only objects that float upon the billows and dare the hazard of a landing. The latter, paddled by two men, stripped to the skin, usually come off to vessels arriving in the roads. The boatmen bear *chits* (or notes) in their little conical caps, and are thus the emissaries from the hospitable residents, whose doors are open to the introduced stranger. We land in the broad mussoolah boat, ingeniously rowed by a gaily-attired native crew, whose song, like that of the gondolier, keeps time to the plash of oars. As the shore is approached, they watch the action of the waves, and seizing the happy moment when a lofty billow rolls towards the stern, they pull a vigorous stroke, and the boat is borne on the bosom of the surf to the appointed landing-place, whence it is dragged high and dry before another wave can swamp or even wet the passengers.

The beach at Madras is lined with houses, many of them places of business. They are lofty and well ventilated, better looking than the generality of the town residences at Bombay, but far inferior in elegance of exterior to those of Calcutta. The hotels, to which the touters, who go off to the ships or line the shore, invite the stranger, are wretched places, affording but little accomodation, and abounding with dirt, bad viands, and worse wines. If, therefore, the newly arrived visitor is destitute of personal friends, or those credentials which ordinarily ensure an invitation to a private dwelling, he will do well to present himself at the Madras Club, and seek his election as a member. This club is an admirable institution. Without insisting upon an aristocratic exclusiveness, it is nevertheless strictly an asylum for gentlemen. It is well and liberally conducted, and the charges come within the means of most persons in the upper circle of society. If the stranger is not likely to be a permanent resident at Madras, a good word from his fellow-passengers to influential members on shore will procure him reception as an honorary member. Living at the club costs about a guinea (ten rupees) *per diem*, or something more. The accounts of honorary members are settled weekly.

The Fort and the Black Town are the most striking objects on the shore. In the former is an arsenal and several of the Government offices; the latter, as its title imports, contains the residences of the natives, and the shops of Europeans and natives. The choice place of residence for the more respectable orders of Europeans is the Mount Road, a magnificent road, six miles in length, bordered by trees and villas. This and the South Beach are the fashionable places of resort during the evening drive. At St. Thomas's Mount, at the end of the Mount Road, the artillery are quartered, and near this place is the race-course, where two race meetings are annually held.

We have been so precise in our descriptions of the governments of India, the Courts of Law, the usages of English society, and the manners and characters of the natives of India, that the task of describing the features of the third presidency is essentially narrowed. There is nothing to add to what has been said of the army, the civil service, the clergy, &c. It only remains to mention the chief institutions and establishments.

The Government-House claims precedence, rather from the importance of its purpose than from its magnificence. It is comparatively a poor building, not better than those occupied by many private gentlemen; but it contains some good suites of rooms; and a banqueting-room, some eighty yards or so from the building, is the scene of many a brilliant ball. The College Hall consists of a library, a hall where concerts and public meetings are held, a museum, &c., but the rooms are all in a dilapidated condition. There are barracks, hospitals, and a handsome church, within the fort, which is called Fort St. George, and a monument to the Marquis Cornwallis. On the Mount Road is another cenotaph to the memory of that nobleman, and between the fort and the Government-House, a beautiful equestrian statue of Sir Thomas Munro, for several years the enlightened governor of Madras. These, with an ice-house and a light-house, constitute all the public edifices of any note.

CHURCHES, &c.—St. George's Church, Mount Road; St. Mary's Church, in the Fort; the Vepery Church; the Black Town District Church; the Church Mission Chapel; the Trinity Chapel; St Andrew's Church (Scotch); the Armenian Church of St. Mary; the Church of St. Thomé (Roman Catholic); the London Missionary Society's Chapels; the Wesleyan Missionary Chapels; the Unitarian Chapels.

RELIGIOUS SOCIETIES.—The Society for Promoting Christian Knowledge; the Incorporated Society for the Propagation of the Gospel in foreign parts; the Church Missionary Society; the Wesleyan Missionary Society; the London Missionary Society; the Indian Missionary Society; the Armenian Board of Missions; the Armenian Baptist Missions; the British and Foreign Bible Society; the Madras Religious Tract Society; the Hindoo Christians' Religious Book Society.

The titles of most of the above bespeak their uses. By some of them native schools are maintained, and there is no concealing the fact that the course of preparation therein pursued is more calculated to produce Christian converts than the most zealous efforts of missionaries bestowed upon the adult, "wedded fast to some dear falsehood."

CHARITABLE INSTITUTIONS, SCHOOLS, &c.—The Military Male Orphan Asylum; the Military Female Orphan Asylum; the Vepery Mission Institutions; the Protestant Charity School; the Vepery

Free School; the Church Endowment and Building Society; the General Assembly's School; the Armenian Orphans' Fund; the Armenian School; the Infants' Schools; the London Missionary Society's Free Schools; the Native Education Society; the Garrison Girls' Day School; Bishop Corrie's Grammar School; the Union Free School; the Roman Catholic Seminaries; the Ladies' Institution for the Education of the Daughters of Europeans and their descendants; the Madras School-Book Society; the Madras Philanthropic Association; the Moneygar Choultry; the Madras Friend in Need Society; the Madras Temperance Society; the Home and Temperance Rooms; the South Indian Temperance Rooms.

We conceive it to be impossible for any Englishman to behold the above array of admirable institutions without strong emotions of pride and pleasure. They furnish magnificent evidence of the noble purposes to which various classes of our countrymen appropriate a portion of their wealth in India, and give the lie to the insinuation that they resort to the country to pluck the golden fruit from its trees, and leave it bare and miserable. The orphan, the native female, the outcast, the illiterate, the destitute, all are cared for, provided with asylums, clothed, fed, and taught. Were we to be driven out of India to-morrow, we should have left behind us, in the results of instruction and in the moral example set to successors, more enduring monuments of worthy rule than the finest productions of the sculptor's chisel or the architect's ingenuity.

Of other societies existing at Madras for useful purposes, we have only to mention the Literary, and the Agricultural and Horticultural Societies; and of commercial institutions there are but the Madras Bank, chartered two years ago, the Savings Bank, and the Chamber of Commerce.

The European and Eurasian population of Madras is considerable. Independently of those who are in the Government service, there are about 400, whose avocations are various. There are of commercial houses, 13; of architects and sculptors, 1; of auctioneers and commission salesmen, 8; of cabinet makers, 9; of chemists and druggists, 4; of jewellers, 6; of wine merchants, 5; of watch and clock makers, 6; of tailors, 6; of tanners and boot makers, 7; of undertakers, 4; besides a number of milliners, musical instrument repairers, 5 coach makers, 3 saddlers, numerous missionaries, merchants' clerks, booksellers, gentlemen of the press, &c.

There are four masonic lodges at Madras, to which the most distinguished men at the presidency belong.

The cost of living at Madras, the manner in which police and municipal affairs are conducted, &c., correspond so materially with the charges and usages at the other presidencies, that a separate detail of them need not occupy space here. We will, therefore, merely add in this place some particulars respecting rates of wages that may be useful to the future resident.

The following is the rate of cart and cooly hire from the Fort to the new custom-house:—

	A.	P.
A bandy drawn by four bullocks	9	11
Ditto two ditto	4	11
A cooly load	1	2

A cooly load is to consist of 18 quart bottles of wine, or any other liquor, or 72 lbs. weight of any other article.

A carriage bullock load is three dozen of quart bottles, or 144 lbs. weight of any other article.

A cart load is to consist of 12 dozen quart bottles of wine, or any other liquor, and 125 lbs. weight of any other article, or altogether 720 lbs. weight of any article.

One driver is to attend each cart, and one driver is to attend from one to three carriage bullocks, and so on in proportion to an increase in the number.

Batta.—If a person in the course of a journey remains at a place, he must for the first three days pay each cooly one anna and three pice batta; each carriage bullock one anna and ten pice for the first five days. If he remains more than the days before specified, he shall pay each cooly three annas and nine pice; each carriage bullock three annas and three pice; each cart seven annas a day. If a person hire a cooly, carriage bullock, or cart, and afterwards not employ either, he shall pay the cooly and carriage bullock at the rate of three annas and nine pice, and the cart fourteen annas each day for the time he may have detained either. Half the hire to coolies and carriage bullocks, and three-quarters to a cart, to be paid in advance, and the remainder when arrived at the place of destination.

Field Pay.—A cooly seven rupees; a carriage

bullock with a driver twenty-six rupees and four annas per month, no batta. A day's journey for a cooly and carriage bullock is twenty English miles, a cart fifteen miles. The hire of a double cart is one-half more than the hire of a single one.

Rates of hire of Artificers, Coolies, &c.

	Monthly Pay.			Daily Pay.		
	R.	A.	P.	R.	A.	P.
BRICKLAYERS.						
Maistry	17	8	0	0	9	4
Good workman	14	0	0	0	7	6
Medium	12	4	0	0	6	6
Common	10	8	0	0	5	7
CARPENTERS.						
Maistry	17	8	0	0	9	4
Good workman	14	0	0	0	7	6
Medium	12	13	4	0	6	10
Common	10	8	0	0	5	7
Hand Sawer, common	11	10	8	0	6	3
Great ditto, exclusive of tools ..	11	10	8	0	6	3
SMITHS.						
Maistry	17	8	0	0	9	4
Good workman	14	0	0	0	7	6
Medium	12	13	4	0	6	10
Common	10	8	0	0	5	7
Hammer-man	8	12	0	0	4	8
Bellows-boys	3	8	0	0	1	3
BRAZIERS.						
Maistry	17	8	0	0	9	4
Good workman	14	0	0	0	7	6
Medium	12	4	0	0	6	10
Common	10	8	0	0	5	7
Hammer-man, &c.	8	2	8	0	4	4

	Monthly Pay.			Daily Pay.		
	R.	A.	P.	R.	A.	P.
PAINTERS.						
Maistry	14	0	0	0	7	6
Good workman	12	4	0	0	6	6
Medium	10	8	0	0	5	7
Common	9	5	4	0	5	0
STONE CUTTERS.						
Maistry	17	8	0	0	9	4
Good workman, exclusive of tools ..	14	0	0	0	7	6
Medium	12	4	0	0	6	6
Common	10	8	0	0	5	7
TANK DIGGERS.						
Maistry	9	5	4	0	5	1
Cooly man	7	0	0	0	3	3
Ditto woman	4	1	4	0	2	3
COOLIES.						
Maistry	9	5	4	0	5	0
Man	7	0	0	0	3	1
Woman	4	1	4	0	2	2
Boy and girl	3	8	0	0	1	10
CHUCKLERS.						
Good workman	11	10	8	0	6	3
Medium	9	5	0	0	5	1
Common	7	0	0	0	3	9
CHINA CARPENTERS.						
Good workman	44	15	7	1	7	9
Medium	29	15	9	0	15	11
TAILORS.						
Good workman, tent workman ..	14	0	0	0	7	6
Medium	10	8	0	0	5	7
Common	7	0	0	0	3	9

For shoeing a horse, 14 annas and 11 pice.

Artificers go to work in the Black Town and Fort St. George at seven o'clock in the morning, rest from twelve to two o'clock in the middle of the day, and then leave off work at six o'clock in the evening. Working at the gardens, they commence at half-past seven, rest until half-past two in the middle of the day, and leave off work at six o'clock in the evening.

The wages of maistries and superior workmen, who may be entitled to higher rates than the above, will be settled by the superintendent of police on application.

We have said, in a previous page, that each presidency has its sanatarium, or neighbouring hills, where health and invigoration may be sought. Calcutta has its Darjeeling, Bombay its Mahabuleshwar; to Madras belong the beautiful Neilgherry hills.

The Neilgherries, situated in the south of India, on the confines of Coimbatoor and Malabar, extend from 11° 10′ to 11° 32′ north latitude, and from 76° 59′ to 77° 31′ east longitude. Their greatest oblique extent from south-west to north-east is from thirty-eight to forty miles, and their extreme breadth fifteen. Their superficial area may be computed equal to 700 square miles. Four stations are at present occupied, viz. Ootacamund, Kotagherry, Dimhutty, and Coonoor.

Ootacamund is the principal station, and is situated nearly in the centre of the table-land of Mysore, about ten miles from the southern edge of the range, and seven from the northern, immediately at the base, and on the western side of Dodabetta, and is open only towards the W.N.W., the other three sides being completely sheltered by this mountain. Its elevation is 7,400 feet above the level of the sea, and it is the best locality amongst the other stations.

It has decidedly the most perfectly European climate of any in these hills, and is less affected by the changes of monsoons, rains, &c., than any other, which arises from its forming the line of separation between the north-east Madras monsoon and the south-west Malabar monsoon.

Kotagherry is situated sixteen miles distant from Ootacamund, on the eastern division, and is inferior in elevation, being 6,571 feet above the level of the sea. The climate is much milder, and the extreme and daily range less. The minimum is 43°, and the maximum 76°, a range of 5° less than the extreme of Ootacamund. The air is moister and the nights less cold. In June, July, and August, the weather is clear, bright, and fair at this station, whilst at Ootacamund there is pretty constant fog, drizzle, or rain during this time. This difference arises from the former place being less subject to the influence of the south-west monsoon. It is also reckoned a more eligible residence during the monsoons for delicate people, whereas Ootacamund is decidedly preferred for those in tolerably confirmed health.

Less rain falls at this place, and it is generally dry here when it rains at Ootacamund, from being affected by a different monsoon.

Dimhutty is situated on a plateau between Kotagherry and the Orange Valley, the latter of which rises at the north-east angle of Dodabetta, and is so named from the number of wild orange and lime trees found in it. The elevation of Dimhutty above the sea is 4,500 feet, and its temperature is much higher than that of the two former stations.

Coonoor, which is ten miles distant from Ootacamund and the head-quarters of the pioneer corps, is situated south of the range, close to the edge of the hills, and rises 5,806 feet above the sea. Its mean temperature is probably 6° warmer than that of Ootacamund; and from its proximity to the ghaut it is subject, at particular seasons, to fogs; on the other hand, it has the advantage of being on the direct road to Ootacamund, and is well adapted for sick travellers.

Over the whole extent of the table-land, and on the summit of the hills, the soil is exceedingly rich and of considerable depth, caused by swamps of various extent; but situation, exposure, command of water, and other less obvious circumstances, confine the cultivation to the extremity of the hills and to the south and east of the range.

The different natural products are coarse barley, keeree-mow, poppies, garlic, and onions. The following have been introduced by European visitants; viz. wheat, oats, potatoes, cabbage, cauliflower, savoys, French beans, spinage, peas, lettuces, beet-root, radishes, celery, turnips, carrots, &c. &c., sea-kale, asparagus, tomatas, plums, peaches, nectarines, apples, citrons, loquats. Oranges and limes grow wild. Brazil cherry, commonly known as the topara, gooseberry, capers, strawberry, raspberry, blackberries. The *Orchis mascula*, from the root of which the salpi misree is obtained, is in abundance, and several other plants, resembling the genus *Orchis Lucerne*. Tobacco is also found.

From the elevated position of the hills, the curative and restorative powers of the climate on Indian diseases must be apparent to all. An important consideration, also, connected with them, is the preventive powers of their climate, which has not yet met with the attention it deserves. A transfer at once to the climate of the hills of those suffering from various diseases and ailments is highly recommended.

The bazaar at Ootacamund is exceedingly well supplied, and the prices are a little higher than those of the low country. There are two excellent Parsee shops, containing every thing in the way of liquors, Europe supplies, cheese, pickles, preserves, &c. &c., which are good and at reasonable prices; but those who are particular in the choice of their port wine and beer are recommended to take a small stock with them. Salt provisions of very good quality, cured on the hills, are to be had in considerable quantities in the bazaar. Cattle and swine might be procured to any extent in the low country round the hills, and fruits and vegetables of every description have advantageously been cultivated.

In Kotagherry there is a deficiency of supplies, owing to the want of a regular bazaar, a market being held only once a week. There are only twelve or thirteen houses, besides the quarters at Dimhutty, at the disposal of the public, whilst at Ootacamund there are upwards of seventy habitable houses. At Coonoor there is no accommodation for travellers, except the public bungalow, which is forbid to them for upwards of three days.

Good men-servants of every description (except, perhaps, head-servants and dressing-boys) are available at Ootacamund. Female servants are seldom found, and should be brought up.

Beds, chairs, tables, carpets, may be easily had on the hills. Crockery may be arranged for with the Parsee shopkeepers. The essential requisites to be taken are plate, bed and table linen, and warm clothing.

The following distances shew the convenience of these mountains from the principal points on the south side of India, and the dawk expenses incident to a visit to them :—

	Miles.	Expenses.
From Madras *viâ* Trichinopoly	393	200 Rs.
Ditto ditto *viâ* Salem	332	150
Ditto ditto *viâ* Bangalore	385	150-70
From Trichinopoly	153	60
Ditto Bangalore	176	80
Ditto Calicut	156	60
Ditto Tellichery (Cannanore)	130	50

In marching or travelling by stages, the expense is, of course, much less.

We may conclude this notice of these hills with some hints to invalids.

Warm clothing is of vital importance on the hills, and even in the low country, a light flannel banian (jacket or shirt) is of service; every invalid, as he values life, should be provided with a good stock of flannel banians, flannel cummerbunds (belts, made so as to have strings to be firmly tied round the middle and double over), drawers, and worsted stockings, and a stock of stout shoes and boots. Avoid exposure to the night air, and never be out after sunset. Early rising is neither necessary nor prudent; the invalid should wait till the sun has attained sufficient height to drive away the cold and moisture of the night; care should be taken to return home before nine A.M., so as to avoid the powerful effects of the sun. Diet must, of course, be regulated by circumstances. In general, however, adhere to light animal food, with bread or biscuit, and vegetables, pastry, cheese, &c. Port or sherry is preferable to the lighter wines; beer unnecessary. Invalids should diminish their usual quantity of these stimulants until acclimatized, and observe early hours for diet. Exercise should be taken so as to produce a gentle action on the skin, and not fatigue, but avoid exposure to the sun. Riding is to be preferred to walking, it being less exciting. When acclimatized, exercise should be gradually increased, and when fairly recovered, as much daylight in the open air as strength will permit should be passed. Those who have suffered from fever should be cautious to avoid the jungle at the foot of the hills, and if unfortunately detained there, a course of purgatives, followed by small doses of quinine, should be pursued. Cold feet (a general complaint with new comers, especially females) are remedied by adopting lambs'-wool or worsted stockings, which should form the stock of people in good or indifferent health.

The climate of Madras is considered to be less sultry than that of Bengal; those stations which are situated on the highest ground of the table-land enjoy a very agreeable temperature. The large cantonment of Bangalore is three thousand feet above the level of the sea, and the thermometer rarely rises above eighty degrees; but the duties of the civil and military servants of the presidency often call them to less favoured places, and those who have suffered under the prostrating effects of a Mysore fever have no reason to rejoice that their destinies did not lead them to Bengal.

In spite, however, of its pestilential climate, there are few places in the peninsula more attractive to a visitor than the scene of the splendid victory gained by the British arms in 1799. The island of Seringapatam, which is surrounded on every side by the Cavery, a wide and rapid river, to which the Carnatic owes its agricultural wealth, is a place of great beauty and fertility; but the reminiscences connected with it are of a nature too overpowering to permit the mind to dwell upon minor circumstances.

The goodar-houses and pavilions of Tippoo Saib are now frequently occupied by European officers, whom military duty or curiosity leads to Seringapatam, and who, of course, receive the most courteous attentions from the heads of the reigning family. A large mansion in the Dowlut Baugh, amongst other decorations, is ornamented with a painting representing the defeat of Colonel Baillie; in which the artist, more intent upon pleasing his patron than in giving a faithful delineation of the scene, has taken care not only to depict the conquering Hyder after the most triumphant fashion, but to exaggerate the disasters and distresses of the enemy.

Few persons can now indulge in a sojourn in the Dowlut Baugh without experiencing some injurious attack of disease; the whole island retains its fatal power over European constitutions, and from time immemorial it has only been the natives of the soil who could successfully resist the deleterious effects of the climate. We are told that out of many thousand natives, compulsorily brought by Hyder and his son from the Malabar coast, and forced to settle in the new territory, only five hundred survived at the end of ten years to relate the story of their tragic expulsion from their own homes; and five years sufficed to reduce the number of European officers and artificers in the sultan's service, imported from the Isle of France, from five hundred to twenty-five.

Bangalore, though not equalling in aspect the luxuriant, though deleterious beauty of the adjacent territories, is prettily situated in a moderately-wooded and well-watered country; there are barracks for two Royal regiments, one of cavalry and one of infantry; and, in addition, the garrison consists of three native infantry and one cavalry regiment, with a proportionate number of battalions of artillery, the requisite staff, &c.

Bangalore has always been distinguished throughout the Madras presidency for its festivities. It possesses very handsome assembly-rooms, and a theatre, in which the amateur performances are often above par.

The fancy balls are upon a grand scale; and when the society happens to be composed of choice spirits, amusements of this nature go off with great *éclat*. The superior size and loftiness of reception-rooms in India render them much better adapted for large assemblages than those belonging to the same class of society in England; and even in the most sultry seasons, less inconvenience is sustained from the heat, the nights being always comparatively cool, and a free circulation of air secured by the multitude of open doors. During the cold season, the European residents of Bangalore amuse themselves with pic-nic parties, as there are numerous objects of curiosity in the vicinity to attract the visitant. There is nothing throughout Hindostan to equal the remains of Southern India; the pagodas of Benares, and even those of Bunderabund and Muttra, are mean in comparison to the splendid temples which are spread along the plains of Mysore and the Carnatic. Those in the neighbourhood of Bangalore do not yield in magnificence to the most celebrated pagodas of the peninsula, and they are the favourite resort of all who possess any taste for architectural beauty; while, to the less intellectual portion of the community, the music, dancing, the banquet, and perhaps above all, the feats of jugglers, offer high gratification.

The Madras jugglers are famous all over the world; and though the exhibition of similar acts of dexterity is often more extraordinary than pleasing, the display of legerdemain in India would almost induce the belief that the age of necromancy had not passed away. A man who, in 1828, seated himself in the air without any apparent support, excited as much interest and curiosity as the automaton chess-player, who astonished all Europe a few years ago; drawings were exhibited in all the Indian papers, and various conjectures formed respecting the secret of his art, but no very satisfactory discovery was made of the means by which he effected an apparent impossibility. The bodies of the Madras jugglers are so lithe and supple, as to resemble those of serpents, rather than men.

Swallowing the sword is a common operation even by those who are not considered to be the most expert; and they have various other exploits with naked weapons of a most frightful nature. A more agreeable display of the lightness and activity which would enable the performers to tread over flowers without bending them, is shewn upon a piece of thin linen cloth stretched out slightly in the hands of four persons, which is traversed without ruffling it, or forcing it from the grasp of the holders. The lifting of heavy weights with the eyelids is another very disgusting exhibition. Some of the optical deceptions are exceedingly curious, and inquirers are to this day puzzled to guess how plants and flowers can be instantaneously produced from seeds.

The Madras jugglers travel to all parts of India, but it is not often that the most celebrated are to be found at a distance from the theatre of their education. Snake-charmers are common everywhere; they belong to a peculiar cast of Hindoos, and though their reputation is upon the wane, they still excite considerable curiosity in Southern India.

The *cobra capella* is the dancing-snake of the East, and the production of the snake-stone is exclusively confined to this species. There is not, it is said, much difficulty in extracting the poison of a serpent, which is contained in a very small reservoir, running along the palate of the mouth and passing out at each fang. The natives are supposed to be very dexterous in forcing their captives to eject this venom, and are then enabled to handle them without the least danger. Some persons, however, well acquainted with the habits of snake-charmers, deny that they extract the poison, and attribute the impunity with which they handle these dangerous reptiles to their accurate knowledge of the temper and disposition of the animal, and their ready method of soothing down irritation. The natives boast the possession of various antidotes to the bite of a snake, and often pretend to have imbibed the venom and effected a cure. There is a plant which goes by the name *choudraca*, in which considerable confidence is placed; and arsenic, which enters very largely into the composition of the celebrated Tanjore pill, is often employed as a counteracting power. Volatile alkalies are most generally tried by European practitioners, and very often prove successful; but the different degrees of strength in the venom of snakes render it doubtful whether, in the worst cases, they would have any beneficial effect. Some medical men aver, that the bite of a *cobra capella* in full vigour, and in possession of all its poisonous qualities, is as surely fatal as a pistol-ball; and that it is only when this poison is weakened by expenditure that medicine can be of any avail.

For the distances of the various stations under the Madras Presidency, from Madras itself, we refer the reader to the Appendix, where they are stated minutely. The method of reaching them is by dawk or pattamar, of which we have already spoken very fully in former pages, which may be traced on reference to the Index.

Beyond the continent of India there is the station of Moulmein, on the Tenasserim coast, and the islands of Penang and Malacca, which are supplied with troops from Madras. Moulmein is kept up for the double purpose of protecting the trade between British India and Burmah, and furnishing a point of rendezvous in the event of hostile measures against the Burmese government being at any time necessary. The Tenasserim provinces extend about from 17° 30′ to 10° 10′ north latitude, between the parallels 97° 30′ and 99° 20′ east longitude. Their length is about five hundred miles, varying in breadth from eighty to forty; bounded on the north by the Thoungyeen river, on the south by the Pak-Chan, on the east by the Siamese mountains, and on the west by the sea. The superficial area is about thirty thousand square miles, of which, probably, not more than one-tenth is under cultivation. The territory is divided into four provinces, viz. Amherst, Ye, Tavoy, and Mergui; these again are divided into districts, under the superintendence of Goung-Gyaups. The only towns are those known by the same names as the provinces, and Moulmein, the chief civil and military station on the coast.

The appearance of the country is extremely bold and mountainous, numerous ranges of hills running through it, chiefly in a direction from north to south, except in the northern part of Amherst province, where successive ranges, rising one above the other, may be seen stretching from west to east. Extensive plains intervene usually between the rivers and the bases of the hills, and, from an elevated position, present the appearance of a dead flat, broken only by very remarkable isolated rocks of limestone formation, rising perpendicularly from the plains, in some instances to a great height. The soil in the plains is admirably adapted to paddy cultivation, to which it is almost exclusively applied; whilst the banks of the rivers and the islands above the influence of the tide, which are annually inundated and thus receive periodical deposits of rich alluvium, present a soil suited to the growth of cotton, tobacco, indigo, and a variety of vegetables. The islands within the influence of the tides are chiefly occupied by cocoanut and areka trees; and the banks of the nullahs with nepah trees.

Many of the woods in the teak-forests of Tenasserim are admirably adapted for ship and house-building, but from their never having been employed, there is a prejudice against them. Of this description is the *thengan*, which might be had in any quantity, especially in the Tavoy province, and which is little, if at all, inferior to teak itself: there are also the *pema*, the *padouk*, and numerous others. The teak, however, is the only timber which attracts speculators, or is at all exported.

This timber is found only in Amherst province. The forests are chiefly situated on the banks of the Attaran, commencing about fifty miles from Moulmein, and extending perhaps 100 miles along both banks of the river: never having been surveyed, their actual extent is not known. By order of Government, these forests were thrown open to the public in 1829; since which, Europeans and natives have been vieing with each other who should fell the largest quantity; every patch of forest has long since been occupied, and many of the smaller patches have been exhausted. The only qualification required to obtain a permit to cut, has been the expression of the wish to do so, and the subscribing to a few regulations restricting the felling of trees to such as were four and a half feet in circumference, and to such as were duly seasoned; and engaging to pay a duty of 15 per cent. to Government on the arrival of the timber at Moulmein.

The trees are usually killed by barking them all round in the months of February and March, when the sap is down. After standing in this state from one and a half to two years, they are felled and floated down during the rains: without being thus seasoned, the timber will not float.

There are also some forests on the northern frontier river; but there were obstacles just below the junction of that river with the Salween, which have until lately deterred wood-cutters from engaging in them. There also, however, they are now hard at work.

We have now endeavoured to convey to our readers a tolerably correct notion of those parts of the continent of British India which are the principal places of resort of Englishmen proceeding from this country to enter the service of the Government, or embark in commercial, agricultural, or other pursuits. Much has been left unsaid that we should have been glad to have included, especially as regards the islands of Penang and Singapore, and the new acquisitions in Scinde, but the indulgence of our inclination to enter into fuller details would have swollen this volume to a size totally inconsistent with the title which it bears. The reader who would desire to know more than we have told him must consult some of the manifold works from which we have derived some portion of our *matériel,* and to which we have made special and thankful reference in our preface.

APPENDIX.

TABLE OF DISTANCES FROM CALCUTTA TO SOME OF THE PRINCIPAL PLACES IN INDIA.

Place	British Miles.
Adoni, S.W.	1030
Ajmere, W.N.W.	1030
Agra, W.N.W.	839
Allahabad, W.N.W.	544
Amedabad, W.	1234
Amednughur, W.	1119
Anjengo, S.W.	1577
Arracan, S.E.	475
Arcot, S.W.	1070
Assam (Ghergong, capital of), N.E.	660
Attock, N.W.	1700
Ava, E.	1150
Aurungabad, W.	1022
Bahar, N.W.	297
Balasore, S.W.	141
Bareilly, W.N.W.	910
Broach, W.	1220
Basseen, W.	1317
Beder, W.N.W.	980
Bednore, N.W.	1290
Benares, W.N.W.	460
Bilsah, W.	867
Beerbhoom, N.W.	131
Bisnagur, S.W.	1120
Boglipore, N.N.W.	255
Bombay, W.	1301
Bopaltol, W.	892
Berhampore, W.	978
Buxar, N.W.	408
Cabul, N.W.	1815
Calberga, W.S.W.	1018
Calingapatam, S.W.	480
Calpee, W.N.W.	699
Cambay, W.	1253
Candahar, N.W.	2047
Canoge, W.N.W.	824
Cashmere (capital of), N.W.	1564
Cuttack, S.W.	251
Cawnpore, W.N.W.	700
Chatterpour, W.N.W.	698
Cheitore, W.N.W.	1063
Chittagong, E.	317
Chunargur, W.N.W.	469
Chicacole, S.W.	490
Comorin Cape, S.W.	1770
Condavir, or Guntoor, S.W.	491
Corah, W.N.W.	655
Dacca, N.E.	177
Delhi, N.W.	976
Dellamcotta, N.	344
Dinagepore, N.	233
Dinapore, N.W.	350
Dowlatabad, W.S.W.	1020
Ellichpour, W.	844
Ellore, S.W.	719
Etawah, W.N.W.	768
Furruckabad, N.W.	755
Futtyghur, N.W.	730
Gangpour, W.	393
Ganjam, S.W.	369
Gazypour, N.W.	450
Goa, W.S.W.	1300
Gohud, W.N.W.	783
Golconda, S.W.	907
Guntoor, see Condavir	491
Gwalior, W.N.W.	805
Hurdwar, N.W.	975
Hussingabad Ghaut, W.	909
Hydrabad, W.S.W.	902
Indore, W.	1030

	British Miles.
Jagarnaut, S.W.	311
Joinagur, or Jaépour, W. N.W.	975
Lahore, N.W.	1356
Lassa, N.N.E.	850
Lucknow, N.W.	649
Madras, S.W.	1030
Madura, S.W.	1336
Masulipatam, S.W. ..	764
Meerta, W.N.W.	1092
Midnapore, W.	72
Mindygaut, N.W. ..	713
Mirzapore, N.W. ..	493
Monghyr, N.W. ..	275
Moorshedabad, N. ..	118
Moultan, W.N.W. ..	1470
Mundilla, W.	634
Muttra, W.N.W. ..	875
Mysore, S.W.	1178
Nagpour, W.	722
Napaul, N.N.W... ..	591
Narwah, W.N.W. ..	817
Ongole, S.W.	829
Oude, N.W.	562
Ougein, W.	997
Patna, N.W.	340
Pondicherry, S.W. ..	1130
Poona, W.S.W.	1208
Purneah, N.	263
Rajahmundry, S.W. ..	665
Ramghaut, N.W. ..	879
Ruttumpour, W. ..	493
Sagur, W.	806
Sattarah, S.S.W. ..	1232
Seringapatam, S.W. ..	1170
Sindy, or Tatta, W. ..	1602
Sirong, W.	849
Sumbulpour, W.S.W. ..	438
Surat, W.	1238
Sylhet, N.E.	325
Tanjore, S.W.	1235
Trichinopoly, S.W. ..	1238
Vizagapatam, S.W. ..	557
Viziapour, W.S.W. ..	1183

TABLE OF DISTANCES FROM MADRAS TO SOME OF THE PRINCIPAL PLACES IN INDIA.

	British Miles.
Adoni, N.W.	310
Ajmere, N.N.W. ..	1152
Agra, N.	1158
Allahabad, N.	1055
Amedabad, N.W. ..	1049
Anjengo, S.W	476
Arcot, W.S.W.	73
Arnee	81
Aurungabad, N.W. ..	689
Balasore, N.E. ..	689
Bancapore, W.N.W. ..	416
Bandamalanka, N.N.E. ..	358
Bangalore, W.	208
Broach, N.W.	947
Beder, N.N.W.	470
Bednore, W.	445
Belgaum	515
Bellary, N.W.	317
Benares, W.	1103
Bisnagur, N.N.W. ..	386
Bombay, N.W.	774
Berhampour, N.N.W. ..	675
Cabul, N.N.W.	2134
Calicut, W.S.W. ..	423
Calberga, N.W. ..	422
Cambay, N.W. ..	998
Cannanore, W.S.W. ..	418
Canoge, N.	1141
Canoul, N.W.	279
Carangooly, S.W. ..	49
Cashmere, N.N.W. ..	1882
Cuttack, N.E.	812
Chandegherry, W.N.W. ..	991
Chatterpur, N.	75

	British Miles.
Cheitore, N.N.W. ..	1065
Chicacole, N.N.W. ..	566
Chingleput, S.W. ..	36
Chittledroog, W.N.W. ..	345
Chittoor	99
Coimbatore, S.W. ..	332
Combam, or Commum, N.N.W.	228
Combacanum, S.S.W. ..	179
Comorin Cape, W.S.W. ..	440
Condapilly, N.	278
Condavir, or Guntoor, N.	255
Conjaveram, W.S.W. ..	45
Corah, N.	1080
Cuddalore, S.S.W. ..	104
Cuddapah, N.W.	165
Calmacherry, W.N.W. ..	115
Delhi, N.	1295
Dindigul, S.W.	271
Dowlatabad, N.W. ..	655
Ellichpour, N.N.W. ..	751
Ellore, N.	314
Ganjam, N.N.E.	697
Goa, S.S.W.	589
Golconda, N.N.W. ..	358
Gooty, N.W.	264
Guntoor, see Condavir ..	255
Gurramconda, W.N.W. ..	149
Gwalior, N.	1078
Hurryhur, W.N.W. ..	400
Hyderabad, N.N.W. ..	388
Jargarnaut, N.E. ..	719
Jaulnah	668
Indore, N.N.W.	902
Ingeram, N.N.E. ..	390
Innacondah, N.	237
Lahore, N.N.W.	1675
Maddepollam, N. ..	233
Madura, S.S.W.	289
Mangalore, W.	446
Masulipatam, N.N.E. ..	265
Mirzapore, N.	1074
Moorshedabad, N.E. ..	1148
Mysore, W.	294
Naggery, W.N.W. ..	57
Nagore, S.	174
Nagpore, N.	704
Narsingapatam, N.E. ..	716
Negapatam, S.	178
Nellore, N.N.W. ..	111
Nundydroog, W.	199
Ongole, N.	19
Oude, N.	1163
Ougein, N.N.W.	1024
Palamcottah, S.S.W. ..	388
Palaveram	12
Patna, N.N.E.	1266
Paulghautcherry, S.W. ..	364
Pondicherry, S.S.W. ..	88
Poona, N.W.	672
Poonamalée, W.S.W. ..	13
Pulicat	27
Quilon	448
Rachore, N.W.	349
Rajahmundry, N. ..	370
Ramnad	321
Raolcondah, N.W. ..	382
Ruttumpore, N.N.E. ..	903
Ryacottah, W.S.W. ..	183
Salem, S.W.	219
Sankerrydroog, S.W. ..	245
Sattara, N.W.	616
Secunderabad	394
Seringapatam, W. ..	284
Siccacollam, N. ..	267
Sindy, or Tatta, N.W. ..	1467
Sirong, N.N.W.	905
St. Thomas's Mount ..	8
Surat, N.W.	903
Tanjore, W.S.W. ..	206
Tellicherry, W.S.W. ..	405
Timerycottah, S. ..	291
Tinnevelly, S.S.W. ..	401
Tranquebar, S.	160
Travancore, S.W. ..	515
Trichinopoly, S.S.W. ..	207
Tripassore, W.	31
Tutacorin, S.S.W. ..	421
Vellore, W.	87
Visiapore, N.W.	534
Vizagapatam, N.N.E. ..	498
Wallajahbad, S.W. ..	40
Warangole, N.	414

TABLE OF DISTANCES FROM BOMBAY TO SOME OF THE PRINCIPAL PLACES IN INDIA.

	British Miles.
Ajmere, N.N.E.	650
Agra, N.E.	848
Allahabad, N.E.	977
Amedabad, N.	321
Amednugur, E.	181
Anjengo, S.S.E.	900
Arcot, S.E.	722
Aurungabad, E.	260
Broach, N.	221
Baroda, N.	260
Basseen, N.	27
Beder, E.S.E.	426
Bednore, S.S.E.	452
Benares, N.E.	950
Bisnagur, S.E.	398
Berhampour, N.E. ..	340
Calberga, E.S.E.	386
Calcutta, E.	1301
Callian, N.E.	32
Calpee, N.E.	821
Cambay, N.	281
Canoge, N.E.	889
Cashmere, N.	1277
Cuttack, E.	1034
Chatterpour, N.E. ..	747
Cheitore, E.N.E. ..	547
Cochin, S.S.E.	780
Corah, N.E.	853
Delhi, N.N.E.	880
Dowlatabad, E.	258
Goa, S.	292
Golconda, E.S.E. ..	475
Gwalior, N.E.	768
Hussingabad Ghaut, E.N.E.	500
Hyderabad, E.S.E. ..	480
Jansi, N.E.	728
Jargarnaut, E.	1052
Jesselmere, N.	680
Indore, N.E.	456
Joinagur, or Jaepour, N..	740
Lahore, N.	1070
Lucknow, N.E.	923
Madras, S.E.	758
Mangalore, S.S.E. ..	518
Masulipatam, E.S.E. ..	686
Mirzapour, E.N.E. ..	952
Moorshedabad, E.N.E. ..	1259
Moultan, N.	950
Mysore, S.S.E.	630
Nagpour, E.N.E. ..	552
Narwah, N.E.	721
Onore, S.S.E.	398
Oude, N.E.	1013
Ougein, N.E.	480
Patna, E.N.E.	1145
Pawangur, N.	286
Pondicherry, S.E. ..	805
Poona, S.E.	98
Ruttumpour, E.N.E. ..	772
Saler Mouler, N.E. ..	182
Sattara, S.E.	146
Seringapatam, S.S.E. ..	622
Sindy, or Tatta, W.N.W.	741
Sirong, N.E.	595
Sumbulpour, E.N.E. ..	826
Surat, N.	177
Tellicherry, S.S.E. ..	615
Viziapour, S.E.	234
Vizrabuy, N.N.E. ..	48

[The foregoing three Tables are extracted from the East-India Register.]

LENGTH OF SOME INDIAN RIVERS.

	Miles.		Miles.
Indus (to the Sea) ..	1700	Nerbudda	700
Brahmapootra	1650	Mahanuddy	550
Ganges	1500	Taptee	460
Godavery	850	Cauvery	470
Kistna	700	Sutledge (to Indus) ..	900
Jumna (to Ganges) ..	780	Thylum	750
Gunduk (ditto)	450		

General Abstract Statement of the Population of the Provinces under the Madras Government, with the exception of Madras, estimated at about 600,000.

Districts.	Population.	Districts.	Population.
Arcot, N.D... ..	506,831	Masulipatam ..	332,039
Arcot, S.D.	530,239	Mysore	2,271,754
Bellary	1,112,839	Nellore	846,572
Canara	759,776	Rajahmundry ..	578,529
Chingleput	336,219	Salem	905,190
Coimbatore	807,964	Tanjore	1,128,730
Coorg	20,000	Tinnevelly	850,891
Cuddapah	1,063,164	Travancore and Cochin	1,128,000
Ganjam	588,079	Trichinopoly ..	554,730
Guntoor	519,318	Vizigapatam ..	1,047,414
Madura	1,135,411		
Malabar	1,140,916	Total ..	18,184,605

PRECEDENCE IN THE EAST INDIES.

The Governor-General.

The Vice-President, or Governor for the time being.

The Governor of Madras for the time being.

The Governor of Bombay for the time being.

The Governor of Prince of Wales' Island, Singapore, and Malacca.

The Chief Justices of Bengal, Madras, and Bombay.

The Bishops of Calcutta, Madras, and Bombay.

Members of Council, according to their situations in the Council of their respective Presidencies.

The Puisne Judge of the Supreme Court of Judicature.

The Recorder of Prince of Wales' Island, &c.

The Commander-in-Chief of her Majesty's Naval Forces, and the Commander-in-Chief of the Army, at the several Presidencies, according to relative ranks in their respective services.

Military and Naval Officers above the rank of Major-General.

All other persons to take place according to general usage.

The Archdeacon to be considered as next in rank to the Senior Merchants.

All Ladies to take place according to the rank assigned to their respective husbands, with the exception of Ladies having precedence in England, who are to take place according to their several ranks, with reference to such precedence, after the Wives of the Members of Council, at the Presidencies in India.

INDEX.

PAGE
Addiscombe College (rules) . 108
Agra described 426
Agricultural Society of India 321
Ajmere 441
Allahabad 402
Allyghur 422
Almorah 453
Army, the Indian 99
Arracan 493
Arsenal of Calcutta ... 339
Assam 484
Assistant Surgeons ... 108

Bandel 371
Bangalore 584
Bareilly 451
Barrackpore 369
Bassein 537
Bazaars, Boats, &c. (Calcutta) 362
Benares 399
Ditto to Allahabad ... 413
Berhampore 371
Bhaugulpore 376
Bolundshur 449
Bombay 514
Ditto Territories ... 566
Ditto to Hyderabad ... 546
Ditto to Calcutta ... 562
Botanical Garden, Calcutta . 327
Borahs 518
Bungalows (stage) 410
Burdwan 409
Ditto to Benares ... 408
Burmese, their manners and customs 494
Buxar 392

Cairo 172
Calcutta described 242
Cantonments 414
Cawnpore ... ... *ib.*
Ditto to Mynpooree ... 421
Chandernagore 371

PAGE
Charitable Institutions (Calcutta) 315
Cherrapoonjee 492
Chaplains 136
Chinsurah 371
Chittagong 493
Chronology, Indian ... 1
Chuprah 391
Civil Service 88
Climate 27
Coel 423
Colleges, Schools, &c. (Calcutta) 315
Commerce 52
Currency 62
Cuttack 506
Ditto to Calcutta ... 561

Dacca 486
Darjeeling 483
Dawk Travelling 187
Ditto 412
Dehra, route to 450
Delhi 442
Dinagepore, route to ... 483
Division of the Day (Mahomedan) 9
Ditto (Hindoo) 10
Dock-yards, Calcutta ... 342
Domestic Expenditure ... 227

East Indians 47
Etawah 423
Europeans 50

Ferozepore, journey to ... 408
Foreign Relations 85
Foundry of Cossipore ... 341
Furlough Rules 123

Ghazeepore 392
Gour, ruins of 481
Government of India ... 67
Gwalior 472

Haileybury College ... 89
Hansi 471

PAGE

Hauper 449
Himalayan Rauge 457
Hindoo Castes 35
Hindoo College (Calcutta) . 269
History of British India ... 11
Hooghly, scene on the river 365
Horse-dealers of Bombay ... 520
Hotels,Boarding-Houses,&c. 359
Hot Winds... 445
Hurdwar 466
Hyderabad, Nizam's territories) 551

Indian Navy 128
Indian Jugglers 585
Indus, voyage on 199
Institutions in Calcutta ... 315
Insurance Offices in Calcutta 316
Iron, manufacture of ... 415

Juggernauth, temple of ... 507

Khunkul 464
Kishnaghur... 481
Kulna 371
Kumaon 452
Kurnaul 449

Land Travelling 187
Laws 138
Lucknow 479

Mahabuleshwar 540
Madras 567
Malda 481
Manners and Customs ... 34
Masulipatam 561
Medical College (Calcutta)... 290
Meerutt 449
Mirzapore 401
Monetary System 62
Monghyr 377
Moorshedabad 371
Moradabad, route to ... 452
Mosaic Work 535
Mugs (manners and customs) 494

Native Education 527
Native States 82
Navy, Indian 128
Neilgherries 577
Nizam's Army 554

Overland Passage to India... 167

PAGE

Painting in India ... 524
Patna 384
Pension Regulations ... 119
Police (Calcutta) 138
Poona 548
Population, character of Indian 34
Population of Calcutta ... 259
Portuguese of India ... 44
Press, the Indian 144
Productions... 30
Public Buildings in Calcutta 266
Public Conveyances in Calcutta 361
Purneah, route to 482

Rajmahal 374
Religious Institutions (Calcutta) 214
River travelling 191
Do. steamers 193
Do. equipments 196
Rungpore 484

Salt, manufacture of ... 506
Santipore 371
Scharunpore, route to ... 450
Serais 412
Scrampore 370
Seringapatam 583
Servants, Indian 229
Shahjehanpore, route to ... 451
Simla 458
Sirdana 449
Social habits in India ... 202
Society ... ... *ib.*
Sports of Calcutta 348
Sylhet 492

Taj Mahal, Agra 433
Tenasserim Provinces ... 589
Topography of Calcutta ... 246
Travelling in India by land 187
Do. by sea ... 201

Voyage outward to India, preparations 156
Do. described ... 164
Do. overland ... 167
Do. from Calcutta to Allahabad 365

Weights and Measures ... 67